ROUTLEDGE LIBRARY EDITIONS:
BRITISH IN INDIA

Volume 23

THE STATE, INDUSTRIALIZATION
AND CLASS FORMATIONS
IN INDIA

THE STATE, INDUSTRIALIZATION AND CLASS FORMATIONS IN INDIA

A neo-Marxist perspective on colonialism, underdevelopment and development

ANUPAM SEN

Routledge
Taylor & Francis Group

LONDON AND NEW YORK

First published in 1982 by Routledge & Kegan Paul Ltd

This edition first published in 2017
by Routledge
2 Park Square, Milton Park, Abingdon, Oxon OX14 4RN

and by Routledge
711 Third Avenue, New York, NY 10017

Routledge is an imprint of the Taylor & Francis Group, an informa business

British Library Cataloguing in Publication Data
A catalogue record for this book is available from the British Library

ISBN: 978-1-138-22929-7 (Set)
ISBN: 978-1-315-20179-5 (Set) (ebk)
ISBN: 978-0-415-39760-5 (Volume 23) (hbk)
ISBN: 978-0-415-31539-5 (Volume 23) (pbk)
ISBN: 978-1-315-22988-1 (Volume 23) (ebk)

Publisher's Note
The publisher has gone to great lengths to ensure the quality of this reprint but points out that some imperfections in the original copies may be apparent.

Disclaimer
The publisher has made every effort to trace copyright holders and would welcome correspondence from those they have been unable to trace.

The state, industrialization and class formations in India

A neo-Marxist perspective on colonialism, underdevelopment and development

Anupam Sen

Routledge & Kegan Paul

London, Boston and Henley

First published in 1982
by Routledge & Kegan Paul Ltd
39 Store Street, London WC1E 7DD,
9 Park Street, Boston, Mass, 02108, USA and
Broadway House, Newtown Road,
Henley-on-Thames, Oxon RG9 1EN
Set in Times, 10 on 12 pt by
Aurophotosetters, India
and printed in Great Britain by
T.J. Press (Padstow) Ltd
© Anupam Sen 1982

Library of Congress Cataloging in Publication Data

Sen, Anupam, 1940–

The state, industrialization, and class formations in India.
Originally presented as the author's thesis
(Ph. D. —McMaster University, 1979)
Bibliography
Includes Index.
1. Industry and state—India. 2. India—
Economic policy. 3. Social classes—India.
4. Socialism—India. I. Title.
HD3616.I42S35 1981   338.954   81–5142

ISBN 0-7100-0888-0   AACR2

Contents

Tables

Acknowledgments

This work springs from a PhD dissertation which I wrote in the second half of 1978 at McMaster University, Canada. In the course of this work I have accumulated many debts of gratitude. First of all, I must thank Dr Peta Sheriff, Dr Carl Cuneo and Professor S. Ahmed of McMaster University, who spent a great deal of time and effort in going through the entire manuscript. They offered many useful criticisms in various stages of the study. Most gratefully I acknowledge my immense debt to Dr Ivar Oxaal of Hull University, England, who had been a constant source of encouragement to me during his sojourn at McMaster University in 1978–9. His valuable suggestions and generous assistance are deeply appreciated.

I am particularly grateful to Dr A.K. Nazmul Karim of Dacca University who first roused my interest in the study of social structure of the Indian subcontinent when I was an undergraduate student at that University in 1960–2.

This study was made possible by a McMaster University scholarship. A research and travel grant from the University in the winter of 1977 enabled me to go to India and Bangladesh to collect the necessary data for the study. I am indebted to McMaster University for its generous financial assistance.

I wish to express my deep gratitude to the management of Routledge & Kegan Paul and particularly to its editorial director, Mr Peter Hopkins, without whose help this book might not have been published so soon. My appreciative thanks are also extended to the staff of the editorial and production departments for their selfless co-operation.

Finally, I am grateful to my mother, Mrs Snehalata Sen and my wife, Mrs Uma Sen who gave me much encouragement and support from afar, without which it would have been impossible for me to complete the study.

Foreword

Once the most prized jewel of the British Empire and later the centre of a dramatic and successful anti-colonial struggle which gave promise of a democratic socialist path to economic and social development, the dominant image of India in the West has long since dissolved into a picture of monumental persistent poverty combined with social and political stagnation.

The causes of this debacle have been variously ascribed, by scholars and media reports alike, to the unrelieved population explosion, the inherent limitations of even revolutionary technical advances in agriculture, the continued operation of the caste system, nepotism and oligarchy in the highest reaches of government, the traditional and ingrained preference of Indians for irrational remedies through reliance on astrological forecasts, their mass escape into the banal outpourings of the Bombay film industry and their fatalistic immersion in a culture permeated by mystical nostalgia. 'It is well that Indians are unable to look at their country directly,' V.S. Naipaul wrote in *An Area of Darkness* in the 1960s, 'for the distress they would see would drive them mad. And it is well that they have no sense of history, for how then would they be able to continue to squat amid their ruins . . . ?'

Dr Sen's study by contrast, it may be anticipated, has little in common with that vein of writing on India which has accounted for its failure to achieve material prosperity by reference to the stranglehold of autonomous cultural values. It stands apart, as well, from that genre of writings on economic development in which autonomy is ascribed, if only implicitly, to economic variables and determinants narrowly conceived. Instead, the author has attempted, by means of a bold historical essay, to situate the post-independence immobilism of Indian society in relation to the perpetuation of a macro-structural stalemate of antagonistic social classes, each potentially creative but frustrated in its aims, above which the

Indian state—its transformative role crippled by the need to defend its own interests and by the legacies of the Asiatic mode of production—retains a high degree of autonomy and decisional authority. Thus the country has so far been the recipient of neither a classic bourgeois transformation on the European model, with the commercialization of agriculture and the reduction of the rural population as the accompaniment to industrialization, nor yet has it reaped the dynamic consequences of a full-scale revolution based on the urban proletariat and its potential allies in the countryside.

Why and how this stalemate emerged is explained with clarity and insights which owe so much to the original writings of Marx and Engels—and, indeed, to their admirer Max Weber—as to render the designation 'neo-' in the subtitle to this work superfluous except in so far as it addresses itself critically to the theoretical writings of several recent European theorists sometimes grouped under this label.

Refreshingly open and direct in its statement of basic philosophical and methodological assumptions, this is far from being a narrowly polemical study of interest to students of India or underdevelopment alone. I believe that, in a sense, the real subject of this investigation is not India but Europe—or, better put, it is both at the same time. This is particularly clear in the conclusion to the book where the reader is invited to juxtapose the historical role of Bismarck's Prussian bureaucracy in the industrialization of Germany with the position of Nehru and the Congress party after independence with reference to the prospects of Indian industrialization. As the author persuasively contends here and elsewhere, such arresting juxtapositions flow from the universal, comparative character of the Marxist approach to the study of societal evolution within which the problem of economic development, as conceived at the present historical moment, is not to be understood in isolation from the appearance and actions of the major protagonists in history: social classes operating within the historically conditioned structure of constraints or opportunities provided by the pre-existing modes of production. It is this model of the dynamics of history which enables this gifted sociologist to explain why Bismarck succeeded while Nehru failed, and why India continues to be the way it is.

Ivar Oxaal
University of Hull

1 Introduction

Purpose and method of the study and relevant literature

The purpose of this book is to probe the nature of the state in India and the role played by it in the evolution of the social economy, particularly in the growth of industry. In fact, the problematic of the state and its relationship with socio-economic progression or regression is a dialectic process. What we will attempt here is to unravel this dialectic – by following the theory and method of Marxism. The Marxian dialectic views the state not as an embodiment of some abstract idea of political will or sovereignty but as a reflection of the social dynamics resulting from either the constant change or relative stability of a mode or modes of production and the resultant class configurations. How far the development of a mode or modes of production contributes towards social formations and classes depends on the level of development of the forces and relations of production. As these vary from society to society, depending on various natural (as well as human) factors – such as aridity of land, which is an object of production – the character and form of the state and its role also vary from society to society. The singularity and uniqueness of the Marxian analysis of the state thus rest on the fact that it is not only a political but also a social analysis – and includes a concrete study of social formations. Henri Lefebvre says:

> the critical analysis of the state in any Marxian sense must be based on specific studies of every known mode of production, every historical phase, every country. And this in terms of both the structural aspect (classes) and the conjunctural aspect (conquests, domination, characteristics of the conquerors and their armies, etc.). Governments reveal the particularities of the

society they administer and set themselves above; they sum up
... its struggles and conflicts. Conversely, specific sociological
and historical studies help us understand governments by taking
into account the multiple conditions under which one or another
state was formed. For Marx, just as for Hegel, truth is always
concrete, specific, particular (and yet has its place within the
whole or totality). However, in this connection as in other, Marx
put the Hegelian formulations 'back on their feet.' The concrete
is social, not political.[1]

Our analysis of the state in India will, therefore, deal with the
nature of the modes of production and their transformation, which
have historically provided the base for the state in India. In this
process, as we will endeavour to show, the classes had and have
been playing either an active or a relatively passive role, depending
on the conjuncture of the social formation and its constituent mode
or modes of production. The state, in Marxian analysis, is an object
of class conflict. But what form the state would take in the process,
reflecting the class formations and their struggles, depends on the
mode of production. However, the process is not always one-way.
Once the state takes a definite form, it reacts on the evolution of a
mode of production and, in turn, is determined by its changing
nature. Engels comes to grips with the interaction between the state
and the economy thus:

> Society gives rise to certain functions which it cannot dispense
> with. The persons selected for these functions form a new branch
> of the division of labour within society. This gives them
> particular interests, distinct too from the interests of those who
> gave them their office; they make themselves independent of the
> latter and – the state is in being. And now the development as it
> was with commodity trade and later with money trade; the new
> independent power, while having in the main to follow the
> movement of production, also, owing to its inward independence
> (the relative independence originally transferred to it and
> gradually further developed) reacts in its turn upon the
> conditions and course of production. It is the interaction of two
> unequal forces: on one hand the economic movement, on the
> other the new political power, *which strives for as much
> independence* [emphasis added] as possible, and which, having

once been established, is also endowed with a movement of its own.... The reaction of the state power upon economic development can be one of three kinds: it can run in the same direction, and then development is more rapid; it can oppose the line of development in which case nowadays state power in every great nation will go to pieces in the long run; or it can cut off the economic development from certain paths, and impose on it certain others. This case ultimately reduces itself to one of the two previous ones. But it is obvious that in cases two and three the political power can do great damage to the economic development and result in the squandering of great masses of energy and material.[2]

Thus, according to Engels, because of the division of labour within society, the functionaries of the state[3] develop distinct interests which do not always and necessarily correspond to the interests of those who entrust them with state power. Their particular interests are distinct from the general interests of society or the class they represent. One of these interests is the state's autonomous power that comes into being in the very moment of its formation. It is, therefore, in their own particular interests that the state functionaries strive for as much independence as possible for the state power, because it reflects their own power.

Normally, economic movement determines the course of action of the political power of the state. That is, if state power does not operate in the interests of the gradual unfolding of the dominant forces and relations of production, state power jeopardizes its own existence. For example – as Marx pointed out – the Tories or the party of aristocrats in England were compelled to rule in the interests of the bourgeoisie because they could not, or dared not, go against the tide of capitalism. Marx says, 'In a word, the whole artistocracy is convinced of the need to govern in the interests of the bourgeoisie; but at the same time it is determined not to allow the latter to take charge of the matter itself.'[4] Thus, although there is a disjunction between political and economic powers, political power follows economic movement. By going against the rising tide of the forces and relations of production of capitalism, the state functionaries – in this case the aristocrats – would have endangered their own future as well as possibly damaging the normal process of growth of the economy.

Two things are to be noted in Engels's formulation of the relationship between the state and the social economy. First, the state (i.e. its functionaries) always endeavours to acquire as much independence as possible. The source of this striving is the relative independence with which the state is first endowed at its inception. But this relative independence or autonomy may result in more independence or autonomy from society or the social classes, depending on the development of the latter and the mode or modes of production – in short, depending on the conjuncture of the social formation. Marx and Engels have repeatedly pointed out in their concrete political studies such as 'The Eighteenth Brumaire', *The Peasants' War in Germany*, *The Class Struggle in France*, *The Constitutional Question in Germany*, *The Prussian Constitution*, etc., as well as in their writings on the countries of Asia, how the apparatus of the state could acquire 'complete independence'[5] from the control of the social classes. The state attains this superior position over the social classes under certain favourable circumstances, such as when contending classes balance one another's power in a particular social formation; or when the generation of social classes is weak as a result of the characteristic development of a particular mode of production; or even because of military conquest. Second, the resulting independence of the state may lead the state functionaries to pursue economic policies that are not in consonance with the economic movement, which may be a gradually unfolding mode of production attempting to regulate other modes in the social formation for its own reproduction. A good example, as we will explain below, is the endeavour of the merchant capitalists in India in the seventeenth and early eighteenth centuries – a section of whom metamorphosed themselves into industrial capitalists – to transform urban artisan industries in the service of the court into manufacturing industries that could cater to the world market. This attempt was accompanied by a simultaneous attempt to weaken the central power of the state. But even in decline, as we will see, the autonomous state power in India operated as a fetter on the growth of the capitalist class, thus resisting the unfolding of the incipient capitalist mode of production which – deriving impetus from the demand of Indian goods in the world market – was gradually undermining the existing Asiatic mode of production. This failure of the state in India to follow the economic movement not only obstructed the growth of the capitalist mode of production but also ushered in its own disintegration and defeat at the hands of the colonizing countries.

These two instances indicate how the state can facilitate or obstruct economic movement or the growth of a mode of production. In England, the state facilitated the growth of the capitalist mode of production; in India, it was a positive hindrance to such development.

It is noteworthy, in this connection, that the state's ability to obstruct the development of an unfolding mode depends largely on the relative strength of the pre-existing mode which is being superseded, and on the power of the classes that come into being with the emerging mode. The relations of production are shattered and a revolution occurs which replaces the existing state structure, as Marx and Engels have observed, only after the forces of production of the new mode mature to such an extent that the new class configuration makes it impossible to let the existing state structure continue. However, a situation can occur when no mode of production is in a position to establish its sway in the social formation, and, as a result, the class conflict may lead to 'the common ruin of the contending classes' and society.[6] This was the case – as Marx has argued in *Capital*, vol. III – when the slave mode of production began to dissolve in Roman society, but no new mode replaced it and, as a consequence, the class struggle between the patricians and plebeians, and also among the various factions of the patricians, brought in the 'common ruin of the contending classes' and the Roman state.[7] Whether the class conflict would lead to the victory of a particular class and the reconstitution of society at large – i.e. the victory of a particular mode of production in the social formation – is, to a considerable extent, dependent upon the nature of the dissolution of the old mode and its succession by a new one which, in turn, is determined by the character of the class struggle.

Thus, in Marxian analysis, what form the state will take – its autonomy or independence, and its interrelationship with the economy – does not follow a unilinear or monocausal path, as is commonly believed. The Marxian analysis of the state and its relationship with the economy is multidimensional and dialectical. It can only be based on a concrete study of a social formation, and the social classes that emerge within it, their strengths and weaknesses, and the nature of the struggle they wage to take control of the state to use it in their own interests.

It should also to be noted that, in Marxian analysis, political power is not just an appendage to economic power, as is popularly believed. How the economy will evolve depends, to a great extent, on political power. That is why in Marxism political power or the state is the object of class conflict. As it is necessary for the bourgeoisie to capture state power to maintain its economic domination, so it is necessary for the proletariat to conquer this power to mould the economy in its own interests. The state, moreover, as we have already noted, endeavours to obtain as much independence as possible, so that it does not have to be subservient to any class. This point was repeatedly emphasised by Marx and Engels in their political studies. To preserve its independence – the particular interest of the functionaries of the state as distinct from the general interests of the society or its dominant or contending classes – the state would often pursue policies that would make it difficult for any class to become dominant enough to subordinate the state under its own hegemony. These policies in a historical conjuncture, depending on the forces of production and class formation, may foster or undermine economic development in many ways.

Our study of the state in India and its relationship with the social economy has shown that the state which emerged on the basis of the Asiatic mode of production later became an obstacle in the path of the bourgeoisie – which grew rapidly in the seventeenth and early eighteenth centuries – towards gaining hegemony. The weakness of the social classes *vis-à-vis* the state resulted not only in the colonization of India, to which we have already referred, but also had (and still has) other far-reaching effects on India's economy: these we will examine later.

Briefly our thesis is this: the state in India, conditioned by the nature of its social formation, was and still is autonomous, and this autonomy has had and still has a positive impact on the character of the economic development or underdevelopment of India during the pre-British, British and post-Independence periods.

On the basis of our study of the social conjunctures of these three periods of Indian history, an analysis can be presented in the form of three theses. First, the autonomy of the state which resulted from the Asiatic mode of production obstructed India's transition to capitalism and thus undermined her economic development and led to her colonization. Second, the continuation of the state's autonomy *vis-à-vis* the indigenous social classes during the colonial period – due to a social formation which was partly Asiatic, partly feudal, and partly capitalist, and to the colonial state's subservience to the metropolitan bourgeoisie – enabled the state to transfer colossal resource from India to the metropolitan centres, and led to India's underdevelopment and low productivity of labour. Third – and the major concern of this study – the attempt by the post-independent state in India to maintain its autonomy, which is derived more or less from the same social formation inherited from the colonial period, has resulted in extensive state control of the private corporate sector, the concentration of basic industries in the state sector, the support and encouragement of the artisan and petty industries as a counterpoise to the private corporate industries, and the failure of the bourgeoisie to transform agriculture into a capitalist undertaking. These measures, in turn, have led to a lop-sided development of the economy in which the condition of the masses and the direct producers has gradually deteriorated and an uncertain future threatens.

It may not be out of place to mention here that to the author's knowledge there has been no work, since the classical studies of Marx, Engels and Lenin, in which a systematic analysis of the state and its relationship with the social economy – in particular, the process of industrialization – has been attempted: moreover one which specifically relates to the social formation (composed of a mode or modes of production) and class configurations. In fact there have been very few works, since those of Marx, Engels and Lenin, which have attempted to analyse the problematic of the state with reference to a concrete social formation. James O'Connor has tried to underline the nature of the state's participation in the capital accumulation of the capitalist class in the U.S.A.[8], but his study does not analyse the historically determined relationship between the state and the social formation.

Ralph Miliband and Nicos Poulantzas have explained at a general level the state's role in economic development as the guardian of the interests of the capitalist class.[9] For Miliband, the modern state is primarily a coercive/ideological instrument of class rule. The state is embodied in its various 'apparatuses' – the bureaucracy, the police, the judiciary, the military, etc. – and all these organs of government in this instrumentalist view are recruited from, and subordinate to (hence, have no autonomy from) private capital. In contrast, Poulantzas thinks that the main function of the state is to preserve and strengthen the capitalist mode of production and in so doing the state secures the rule of the economically dominant classes. Paradoxically, to perform this function adequately the state, Poulantzas contends, needs a relative autonomy from the dominant classes. The argument runs like this: the capitalist class is not a homogeneous class; it is divided into various factions and sectors (finance capital, industrial capital, commercial capital, etc.) whose economic, political, and ideological interests are not always identical. To preserve the unity and cohesion of the capitalist class, in a word, to safeguard the general interests of the bourgeoisie as a whole, it becomes necessary for the state to acquire freedom of action or functional autonomy with regard to the fractions of capital, so that it does not endanger the common interests of the capitalist class by promoting particular interests. The common affairs of the whole bourgeoisie, according to Poulantzas, can only be managed by advancing the unity of the capitalist social formation. To do so it sometimes becomes necessary for the state to make some political and economic concessions to the dominated classes at the cost of the immediate interests of the ruling classes. Thus, the rule of the internally fragmented capitalist class does not depend on the condition of its direct governing, nor even on its physical presence in the government, but on the capability of the state to maintain its autonomy *vis-à-vis* particular interests so that it can secure the general interests of the capitalist class and its hegemony over the dominated classes.

The hegemony of the dominant classes over the dominated classes, Poulantzas maintains, is effected through a power block of all dominant classes which is itself under the hegemony of a class or a fraction of the ruling class. The autonomy of the state enables it to maintain the unity of the power block by effecting a compromise between the conflicting interests of the various fractions of the power block and to represent the interests of the hegemonic class or fraction as those of all classes. The independence of the state, Poulantzas argues, enables it to gloss over the primary contradiction between dominant and dominated classes as well as the secondary contradiction among the dominant classes, and also makes it possible for the state to appear as the political representative of all sections of society without really being so.

Poulantzas's criticism of Miliband for viewing the bourgeoisie as a homogeneous entity is essentially correct. Moreover, it need not be necessary for the state elite to be recruited from the capitalist class, as Miliband argues, to serve the capitalist interests; nor does the state always act in support of the interests of the dominant classes. Miliband's great contribution, however, lies in his repudiation of the liberal and pluralist views of the state. The capitalist state, he argues, cannot be a state of the whole people; it is always the state of the capitalist class.

Poulantzas's structuralist view of the state, however, suffers from a few shortcomings.[10] For example, why should the state functionaries, when they do come from a different class background, espouse the cause of capitalist reproduction? Poulantzas's answer is: it is their objective situation which compels them to do so. The answer is substantially true, but his rigorous structuralist exposition obfuscates the role of the classes in the state formation. In fact, as Marx has shown in the case of Britain – the instance we cited above – the state functionaries would support an economic movement or a production system only on the basis of how they perceive it to be in their own interests.[11] Engels demonstrated in his study of Germany (see Conclusion, chapter 8) how the state functionaries attempted with all their means to obstruct the growth of the capitalist class in the early nineteenth century, since they considered its rising power as a threat to their own independence. Similarly, we have tried to show how the state in India, in the historical conjuncture of the seventeenth and eighteenth centuries, failed to identify its interests with those of the slowly evolving incipient capitalist class.

If we analyse these examples we observe that, in the case of England, the relatively autonomous state, manned by the nobility, functioned in the interests of the bourgeoisie; and the hegemony of the bourgeoisie in the state was here clearly established. In the transitional social formation of Germany, we find, the rule of the bourgeoisie was yet to be established; the primarily bureaucratic autonomous state was engaged in a losing battle to preserve its independence. In India, the state was the major obstacle on which the bourgeoisie floundered, leading to the colonization of the country. In all these instances, the state functionaries have been motivated to pursue goals in accordance with their perception of their objective situation. This is the point which Poulantzas misses but which Marx and Engels have referred to repeatedly in their studies. It is not the objective position itself, but its perception by the state functionaries that determines the role of a state in a particular conjuncture. The state structure is the result of this interaction between the state and the classes – not the classes in themselves but the classes *for* themselves (i.e. the classes which seek to establish their hegemony in the social formation). In this respect, Poulantzas's discourse on the state in *Political Power and Social Classes* – where he also discusses pre-capitalist social formations – is inadequate because he fails to point out that in certain social formations the autonomy of the state does not result in the hegemony of the dominant class.

Thomas Bamat, in his study of the relative autonomy of the state in Brazil and Peru, has highlighted this weakness of the Poulantzian conceptualization of the autonomy of the state, and in particular the difficulty of applying it in the case of third world countries.

> [An] obstacle in the utilization of the concept of relative autonomy remains, and is particularly vexing when analysing the dependent countries of Latin America and the Third World. The absence of dominant class hegemony in such formation is not exceptional or conjunctural. It tends to be a chronic condition of class relations, and it implies distinct roles and a peculiar relative autonomy for the state. The functional correlation between relative State autonomy and the achievement of hegemony in the Poulantzian formulation is broken. The State is relatively autonomous, but it does not assure dominant class hegemony.[12]

Bamat tries to show that the autonomous state in Peru and Brazil is not founded on the dominant class hegemony, and to demonstrate this he concentrates on only two aspects of the state's relative autonomy.

> I will discuss its autonomy from local dominant classes; and I will discuss the State's essentially economic interventions, that is, its relation to production and accumulation.[13]

In terms of purpose, Bamat's study closely resembles mine. He has shown with deep insight how the weak development of the social classes, particularly the bourgeoisie, has resulted in the failure of the capitalist class to bring the state under its own hegemony. But as he himself admits, his is not a study of how the state emanates from a social formation and how, in turn, it influences the evolution of social formation.

This article is meant to contribute to an understanding of the important concept of relative state autonomy, particularly its utility and limitations as formulated by Poulantzas. It is not a political analysis of 'cases' or concrete social formations, and should not be understood as such.[14]

Apart from Bamat's work, the most important contribution on independence or autonomy of the state in the third world is Hamza Alavi's study of 'The state in post-colonial societies'. The study mainly focuses on Pakistan and Bangladesh but occasionally refers to India. His main argument is as follows: in the colonial period the bureaucratic military state apparatus was overdeveloped because it had to exercise dominion over the native social classes. In the post-colonial period too, Alavi argues, the state has remained autonomous, because no single class has succeeded in establishing its rule over the over-developed state. In the exposition of his thesis he has made some shrewd observations about the relationship between the post-colonial state and the indigenous social classes that are highly relevant to our study.

At the moment of independence weak indigenous bourgeoisies have found themselves enmeshed in bureaucratic controls by which those at the top of the hierarchy of the bureaucratic military apparatus of the state are able to control their activities and their prospects. The classical Marxist theory conceives of the development of the superstructures of the state in keeping with the development of the economic foundations of society, namely the capitalist relations of production and the ascendant bourgeoisie. But in post colonial societies we find the contrary, namely that the development of the superstructure of the state, has taken place in advance of the development of the indigenous infrastructure, or the economic foundations of society, and the rise of the indigenous bourgeoisie. The superstructure of the state, in the post colonial state is, therefore, relatively overdeveloped, i.e., in relation to the underdeveloped economic infrastructure and the domestic bourgeoisie.[15]

He adds that the state is

autonomous because, once the controlling hand of the

metropolitan bourgeoisie is lifted at the moment of independence, no single class has exclusive command over it. But their [the state functionaries'] autonomy is predicated not only on this negative condition but also on the positive conditions which stem from the new economic role of the state in the process of 'planned' development. The state not only regulates economic activity but also disposes of a large proportion of the economic surplus generated in the post colonial societies which it 'mobilizes' for development.[16]

Alavi's assertions, particularly those regarding weakness of the bourgeoisie and the state's role in the economy – though he does not advance any evidence in their support – are true, as we have demonstrated below in our study of India.[17] Alavi's merit lies in his intuitive grasp of the fact that the state in Bangladesh, Pakistan and India is autonomous *vis-à-vis* the social classes. But the reason he puts forward is not wholly satisfactory. It is true that, as he asserts, the classes in most Third World countries are underdeveloped. But it is not true, as he claims, that the state apparatus was over-developed in the colonial period. In fact, in many independent but semi-colonized countries – such as most Latin American countries and Nepal, Thailand, Afghanistan and Iran for example – the state apparatus, the bureaucracy, the judiciary, etc., remained under-developed. Yet in most Third World nations, including the ones referred to, the state is autonomous *vis-à-vis* the social classes. And these weak domestic social classes of post-colonial society, as Alavi maintains, have the impossible task of subordinating, without undergoing a social revolution, the state apparatus which has institutionalized their own subordinate relationship in the past.

The social classes in most post-colonial Third World societies have failed to establish their hegemony over the state not because the state apparatus was overdeveloped by the colonial rulers, as Alavi argues, but because the state was stronger than the social classes long before these societies were colonized. The state apparatus in most pre-colonial societies was patriarchal but superior *vis-à-vis* the indigenous social classes. The colonial state apparatus, at least in the case of India (as well as Pakistan and Bangladesh), evolved from the patriarchal Moghul state which the colonizing power inherited. The shortcomings in Alavi's study stem from his failure to analyse historically the social formation of the Indian sub-continent which still bears its pre-colonial roots, and to relate these changing societies to the state. Moreover, his contention that the presence of the metropolitan bourgeoisie in post-colonial societies has balanced and neutralized the power of the two indigenous dominant classes, the landlords and the capitalists, thus enabling the state to retain its independence, though ingenious, is not supported by facts.

Both Alavi and Bamat have rightly reasoned that the autonomy or independence of the state in the majority of Third World countries is based on the weakness of the social classes. They have traced the source of this weakness to the underdevelopment caused by colonial economic control. In this respect their views are similar to those of Samir Amin, Arghiri Emmanuel, etc., who find the cause of the Third World's economic backwardness in its integration into the world capitalist system. These arguments are substantially correct in designating the cause, but the analyses are partial in the sense that their major emphasis is on external capitalist relations. They fail to explain that the success of external capital, to a great extent, was determined by the pre-capitalist relations of production that it encountered in Third World societies. The present study attempts to integrate an analysis of the impact of external capital with that of the internal forces and relations of production in a social formation (i.e., its mode of production, classes, and relationship with the state), on the basis of a concrete study of a Third World country, namely India. This study thus claims originality, and presents a perspective which, with some modifications, may be used in the study of other Third World societies.

2 The mode of production and social formation in pre-British India

Prolegomena

The process of industrialization in India, as in any other country, is closely associated with the character and form of development of social classes and the state. It must be remembered in the study of industrialization that this process was not an organic growth in India as it was in Europe. The industrial revolution in Europe was preceded by the growth of a commercial capitalist class which succeeded in establishing its control over the state. Furthermore, the development of the capitalist class, as the bearer of commerce and industry, was facilitated by the existence of feudalism in Europe. The arena for the growth of merchants' capital was provided by feudal relations. Thus, in spite of differences based on their past social structure, economy and cultural history, the industrialization process in European countries had a certain uniformity in that it was part of an economic system which was generated by internal economic forces. Born in the womb of feudalism, these forces developed through merchant capitalism into industrial capitalism.

In the East in general, as well as in India, capitalism did not grow from the soil; it was transplanted by colonial rule. One of the reasons for this differential growth was that, in Asia, the nature of social evolution was different from that in the West. In Asia, the dissolution of the primitive society or clan organization was not followed by a slave system and feudalism, but by the Asiatic mode of production. The Asiatic mode of production led to the emergence of the 'Oriental Despotic State' which acted as a fetter on the growth of the social classes. The subservience of the social classes to the state, i.e., the hegemony and independence of the state, made it very difficult for the bourgeoisie to overcome its weakness *vis-à-vis* the state.

In Europe in the twelfth and thirteenth centuries, the opening of long-distance trade undermined the 'natural economy' of feudalism.[1] The spread of commerce created a demand for luxuries among the aristocrats, which, in its turn, led to the replacement of 'labour rent' by 'money rent'.[2] The development of a market exchange encouraged the feudal estates to produce a surplus for sale outside the locality, and the lords themselves became dependent on money income and trade.[3] The establishment of trading towns, encouraged by the feudal lords within their own jurisdiction for raising revenue, led to the development and consolidation of power by the bourgeoisie.[4]

The expansion of trade not only increased the volume of the merchants' capital, it also increased the exploitation of the peasants by the feudal lords whose needs for surplus grew with an expanding commerce and its corollary consumption.[5] The intensification of exploitation of peasants and serfs, the flow of merchants' capital into land purchase and the subsequent commercialization of agriculture, created a surplus in the agricultural sector and transformed an important segment of the peasantry into landless wage-labourers.[6] It must be borne in mind that the relations of production, i.e., the recognition of the proprietary rights of the lord over land and serfs, was fundamental in Europe in separating the producers from the land and creating a relationship of antagonism between lords and peasants.[7] In India, the fact that the nobility had no ownership rights over land made it impossible for them to separate the producers from their means of labour. Their function was restricted merely to the collection of revenue.

In Europe primitive capital accumulation was made possible through enclosures and other methods whereby the peasants, serfs, craftsmen, etc., were alienated from their means of work.[8] However, before capital could organize production in Europe, it appeared in the specific form of merchants' capital.[9] The role of merchants' capital was to exchange commodities, no matter what their basis of production might be. The merchants' wealth always existed in the form of money and their money always served as capital.[10] This commerce had a corrosive effect on the countries between which commodities were exchanged.

> It [commerce] will subject production more and more to
> exchange value, by making enjoyment and subsistence more

dependent on the sale than on the immediate use of the products. Thereby it dissolves all old conditions. It increases the circulation of money. It seizes no longer upon the surplus of production, but corrodes production itself more and more, making entire lines of production dependent upon it.[11]

But what form this dissolution will lead to does not depend upon commerce but upon the old mode of production of the producing country. The extent of dissolution also depends upon the solidity of the old mode of production.[12] In India international trade with Europe created merchants' capital, which perhaps in size was not inferior to that in Europe (see below).

This merchants' capital also took the significant step of bringing in workers under a common roof.[13] However, before it could make the transition to the new mode of production of industrial capitalism, the country was colonized.

The weakness of capital in India stemmed from three factors. Firstly, the unity of agriculture and industry in village communities and the absence of legal rights of ownership of the lord over land made it almost impossible for the bourgeoisie to alienate the labourer (peasant) from his means of labour (land). Secondly, the absence of decentralization of political power (in the form of feudalism) made it difficult for the bourgeoisie to overcome the restraints imposed by the state, which remained powerful, even when it was disintegrating. In Europe, capitalist production arose within feudal relations that were partly destroyed by the commodity economy which, in turn, had grown out of the development of the market exchanges. The merchants' capital was necessarily a preliminary stage of capitalist production. It developed not on the basis of capitalist production, but on that of cottage industry and handicrafts.[14] In Europe, however, before capital could organize production, i.e., before the introduction of the capitalist mode of production, merchants' capital was able to consolidate its influence over the state through the establishment of absolutism in politics.[15] Absolute states in Europe, in the seventeenth century, were the result of the alignment of the bourgeoisie and the king. This alignment was helpful in curtailing the power of feudal lords and removing restraints on the further growth of capital.[16] Bourgeois revolutions against absolutism marked the final victory of capital in establishing its own state.[17]

The merchant capital in India, as we will see below, despite its dissolving effect on the centralized state, could not attain political power in the absence of a countervailing feudal power (against the state). The internal social structure, resulting from the solidity of the Asiatic mode of production, although showing signs of weakening, could not be totally subordinated by the emergent forms before the country was colonized. Time thus became a crucial factor in the destiny of nations. Long-distance trade gave rise to the development of merchant capital in both Asia and Europe. In Europe the new form (capitalism) could establish its predominance over the older form (feudalism) at an early date, and was successful in establishing its own state. In Asia the resistant forces of the older form (Asiatic mode) were more stubborn, and the Asiatic state, even in disintegration, maintained its hegemony over the rising merchant class.

Herein lies the secret of how a small country like England could conquer a vast country like India. In the analysis of 'the development of the underdevelopment of the colonized countries', this social weakness of the underdeveloped countries has seldom been pointed out.

In the following pages, we will show why the Asiatic mode of production (as in India) was more stubborn than feudalism and why it resisted the attempt of capitalism to evolve out of it and eventually overcome it. The reasons can be found in the characteristics that distinguish the Asiatic from the feudal mode of production.

(i) In the Asiatic mode of production, the collectors of revenue, i.e., the nobility, did not enjoy the same proprietary rights in land as did the feudal lords in Europe. Their claim to the surplus from the soil depended on, and was limited by, imperial regulation or the state. Thus, in the Asiatic mode of production in India, the *jagirdars*, *zamindars*, etc., i.e. the nobility, could not emerge as an independent class outside of the state as the feudal lords in Europe did.

(ii) Since the collectors of revenue in the Asiatic mode of production were not owners of the soil as the feudal lords in Europe were, they could not treat the direct producers as tenants-at-will and alienate them from the land. Thus one of the preconditions for the emergence of capitalism, i.e., wage labour, was hardly present in the Asiatic mode of production. On the other hand, feudalism, in the form of feudal lords' rights in the soil, provided the mechanism for separating workers from the land. In other words the feudal lords, as owners of the land, could alienate the direct producers, serfs, peasants, etc., from the land and transform them into wage labourers.

(iii) Under the Asiatic mode of production, as the revenue collectors had no independent claim outside that of the state to the surplus from the soil, they were not co-sharers in the sovereignty of the state. In other words, unlike the landlords in feudalism, the collectors of revenue in the Asiatic mode of production were not engaged in a struggle with the king or emperor to establish their hegemony over the state. Thus, there was no decentralization of sovereignty, and the state's hegemony in the absence of a feudal class (in the proper sense of the term) remained unchallenged. This, in turn, affected the bourgeoisie's stake in gaining power. In the absence of a conflict between the feudal lords and the king, the bourgeoisie in the Asiatic mode could not support the king and exact in return concessions from him in the form of functional sovereignty in towns, in guild regulations, etc. That is to say, the bourgeoisie in the Asiatic mode of production could not at first try to balance the power of the emperor with that of the revenue collectors and emerge as an independent class, challenging the hegemony of the state. Even when in decline, the state remained superior to the incipient bourgeoisie in the Asiatic social formation.

(iv) Finally, the nature of interdependence between agriculture and industry in the Asiatic mode of production is different from that in feudalism. In the former all artisan industries, such as blacksmiths, carpenters, potters, weavers, etc., are employees of the village. They provide all tools and other manufactured products necessary for the peasants and villagers, and in return get a share in the produce of the peasants, and sometimes also some agricultural land for their own use. Thus the self-sustaining unity of manufacture and agriculture, as Marx points out, contains all the conditions for reproduction and surplus production within the village itself.[18] This provides great stability to the Asiatic mode of production. In feudalism, on the other hand, the serf or peasant himself produces the implements and other commodities he needs in most cases. Only among the lord's domestic serfs was there some kind of division of labour: some made implements and commodities and others farmed. But here, unlike the Asiatic mode of production, there were no village artisan employees on whom the cultivators could depend for tools. The cultivators' dependence on external sources for manufactured products and implements, therefore, was not totally closed. The village communities under feudalism were not totally independent self-sustaining entities which contained all the conditions for reproduction and surplus production. Thus the feudal mode was not as stable as the Asiatic mode of production. Moreover, the conflict between the king, the feudal lords and the bourgeoisie provided a chance for the serfs to flee to the growing towns (which had acquired functional sovereignty) and become craftsmen there. There were, therefore, greater tensions in the feudal than in the Asiatic mode of production.

All studies of the Asiatic mode of production, including those of Krader, Hindess and Hirst, Lichtheim and Thorner have failed to single out its above-mentioned characteristics[19] (as implied in Marx's writing), i.e. that it is more difficult for capitalism to evolve from it than from feudalism. Almost all of them have failed to understand the significance of the Indian artisan industry – although Marx repeatedly referred to its unity with agriculture – its role in providing stability to the Asiatic mode of production, and its differences from the artisan industry of European feudalism.

In this chapter these characteristics of the Asiatic mode of production and their differences with feudalism will be discussed in detail, showing how they impeded the growth of the bourgeoisie in India and its attempt to gain hegemony over the state.

The social economy of pre-British India

The nature of the social classes in any society depends on the nature of the economy in that society. The fact that, in the Indian subcontinent, the professional classes and state employees play such an important role has been determined by various historical factors. Unlike the West, the Indian economy has not undergone the following stages of development: the ancient or the slave, the feudal, and the capitalist. The Indian social system was conditioned by what Marx has termed the 'Asiatic mode of production'.

The distinctive feature of the Asiatic mode of production was the absence of private ownership in land.

> A closer study of the Asiatic, especially of Indian forms of communal ownership, would show how from the different forms

of primitive communism different forms of its dissolution have developed.[20]

What was the different form of dissolution that gave birth to the 'Asiatic economy'? The answer can be found in a famous letter written by Engels to Marx on 6 June 1853:

> How comes it that the orientals did not reach to landed property or feudalism? I think the reason lies principally in the climate, combined with conditions of the soil, especially the great desert stretches which reach from the Sahara right through Arabia, Persia, India and Tartary to the highest Asiatic uplands. Artificial irrigation is here the first condition of cultivation and this is the concern either for the communes, the provinces or the central government.[21]

This, in the opinion of Marx and Engels, necessitated the dependence of the individual on the state and village commune, and prevented the mobilization of power by classes and estates.[22]

In India, unlike feudal Europe, land did not belong to any private landlord.[23] The king simply delegated to some persons the specific and individual rights of *zamin*, i.e., the revenue collecting power. These *zamindars* and *jagirdars* (revenue collectors) were created by the state and could be removed by the state at any moment. According to Azizul Huque:

> In the Moghul revenue administration, the zamindar was ... an agent of the Emperor for making due collections on behalf of the Emperor and was remunerated with a percentage out of his collections for his labour. The term 'zamindar' was a later development in the land system of the country. In the Ayeen-i-Akbari, he was the Amul-Guzar or collector of the revenues and he was directed to annually assist the husbandmen with loans of money and to receive payment at distant and convenient periods. ... Certain allotments of land were usually given to him rent free for his maintenance known as nankar.[24]

Irfan Habib describes the *jagirdars* in his monumental work, *The Agrarian System of Mughal India*, as follows:

Over the large portion of the Empire, he [Emperor]
transferred his right to the land revenue and other taxes to
certain of his subjects. The areas whose revenues were thus
assigned were known as jagirs. The assignees were known as
jagirdars [holders of jagirs]. . . . The jagirdars were usually
mansabdars, holding ranks (mansabs) bestowed upon them by
the Emperor [e.g. how many soldiers could be commanded].
These ranks were generally dual, viz., zat and sarwar, the former
chiefly means to indicate personal pay, while the latter
determined the contingents which the officer was obliged to
maintain. The pay scales for both ranks were minutely laid down
and the mansabdars received their emoluments either in cash
(nagd) from the treasury or, as was more common, were assigned
particular areas as jagirs. The assignee was entitled to collect the
entire revenue due to the state, and though this consisted
principally of land revenue, it also embraced the various cesses
and petty taxes which were probably exacted even in the
remotest rural areas . . . . The jagirs were constantly transferred
after short periods so that a particular assignment was seldom
held by the same person for more than three or four years.[25]

This unique nature of tax-farming was noted by François Bernier,
the great sociological-minded traveller who came to India in the
seventeenth century:

The king as the proprietor of the land, makes over a certain
quantity to military men, as an equivalent for their pay; and this
grant is called jah-ghir, or as in Turkey, timar; the word jah-ghir
signifies the spot from which to draw, or the place of salary.
Similar grants are made to governors, also for the support of
their troops, on condition that they pay certain sums annually to
the king out of any surplus revenue that the land may yield.[26]

These *jagirdars* and *zamindars* were not feudal lords in the western sense of the term. In the words of Max Weber, they were the
holders of 'office prebend'. The distinctive characteristic of land
relationship in the East was that it was 'prebendalization', not
'feudalization'.

In India, as in the Orient generally, a characteristic seigniory developed rather out of tax farming and the military and tax prebends of a far more bureaucratic state. The oriental seigniory therefore remained in essence a 'prebend' and did not become a 'fief'; not feudalization but prebendalization of the patrimonial state occurred.[27]

In contrast, feudalism in Europe was based on the proprietary right of the lord over the land:

Feudal landed property gives its name to its lords, as does a kingdom give its name to its king. His family history, the history of his house, etc. – all this makes the landed property individual to him, makes it formally belong to a house, to a person.[28]

This proprietary right gives the landlord a legal basis to alienate the peasants and the serfs from their means of labour (land). Moreover, the feudal mode of production creates dependency:

Here, instead of the independent man, we find everyone dependent, serfs and lords, vassals land suzerains, laymen and clergy. Personal dependence here characterizes the social relations of production just as much as it does other spheres of life organized on the basis of that production.[29]

In feudal Europe the ownership of land confronted the producers as an alien power. It created a relationship of antagonism in social relations. The rule of private property, which served as the basis for the growth of capitalist relations as well as accumulation, began with the appropriation of land by the feudal lords:

The domination of the land as an alien power over men is already inherent in feudal landed property. The serf is the adjunct of the land. Likewise, the lord of an entailed estate, the first born son, belongs to the land. It inherits him. Indeed, the domination of private property begins with property in land – that is its basis. But in feudal landed property the lord at least appears as the king of the estate. Similarly there still exists the semblance of a more intimate connection between the proprietor and the land than that of mere material wealth. The estate is individualized with its lord: it has his rank, is baronial or ducal with him, has his privileges, his jurisdiction, his political position, etc. It appears as the inorganic body of its lord. Hence the proverb: *nulle terre sans maître* (there is no land without its master), which expresses the fusion of nobility and landed property.[30]

The intimate relationship between the lord and his dependents began to dissolve with the growth of international trade and commerce.[31] For the emergence of capital, it became necessary that the landed property be shorn of its feudal romantic glory and be transformed into a commodity. It took various forms in different countries of Europe, the classical example was the enclosure movement in England.[32] Through this movement, not only was the personal relationship between the lord and his dependents destroyed, and not only were the peasants ejected from the soil, but for the first time the soil was brought under the domain of capitalist production.[33] The noteworthy point here is that the commercialization of agriculture was made possible by the feudal mode of production which provided the mechanism of alienation – the private ownership of land.[34] While feudalism had been characterized by personal relationships, with the introduction of the capitalist mode of production, the rule of private property began to appear as the rule of mere capital.[35]

In India, on the other hand, the landlords, i.e., the collectors of revenue, were not the owners of the land. Land belonged communally (as usufruct) to the village, although ultimate ownership remained vested in the state.[36] In fact, the state's ownership of land was not in the nature of private but of collective ownership. That is why Shelvankar maintains that in India the king could not create subordinate owners of land, because he himself was not the supreme owner of the land. He had only the right of revenue collection.[37] The right of collective ownership of the state determined why the king could transfer the right of revenue collection from one person to another but could not create vassals.[38] On the other hand, the responsibility for the payment of the state's revenue was not an individual responsibility but the collective responsibility of the community. As Radhakamal Mukerjee says:

> The fiscal system of the Muhammadan conquerors encouraged the original joint administration developed from undeveloped clan or the joint family by emphasising collective fiscal responsibility.[39]

In the Occident, the rise and fall of the value of feudal rent, as distinct from the state's revenue in the Orient, played an important role in leading the feudal lords to expropriate land.[40] The decline of seigniorial revenue also encouraged the feudal lords to rent their land to the better-off peasants, thus paving the way for the introduction of the capitalist mode of production in agriculture.[41] This could not occur in the Orient. There the *de facto* control of land remained vested in the village communities, and the supreme landlord was the state. This does not, however, mean that there was no individual possession of land.

> To what extent the laborer, the self-sustaining serf [under European feudalism], can here secure for himself a surplus above his indispensable necessities of life, a surplus above the thing which we would call wages under the capitalist mode of production, depends, other circumstances remaining unchanged, upon the proportion, in which his labor time is divided into labor time for himself and forced labor time for his feudal lord. This surplus above the indispensable requirements of life, the germ of that which appears as profit under the capitalist mode of production, is therefore wholly determined by the size of the ground-rent, which in this case not only is unpaid surplus labor, but also appears as such. It is unpaid surplus labor for the 'owner' of the means of production, which here coincide with the land, and so far as they differ from it, are mere accessories to it. That the product of the laboring serf must suffice to reproduce both his subsistence and his requirements of production, is a fact which remains the same under all modes of production. For it is not a result of its specific form, but a natural requisite of all continuous and reproductive labor, of any continued production, which is always a reproduction, including the reproduction of its own labor conditions. It is furthermore evident that in all forms, in which the direct laborer remains the 'possessor' of the means of production and labor conditions of his own means of subsistence, the property relation must at the same time assert itself as a direct relation between rulers and servants, so that the direct producer is not free. This is a lack of freedom which may be modified from serfdom with forced labor [in feudalism in the Occident] to the point of a mere tributary relation [in the Asiatic mode of production in the Orient]. The

direct producer, according to our assumption, is here in possession of his own means of production, of the material labor conditions required for the realization of his labor and the production of his means of subsistence. He carries on his agriculture and the rural house industries connected with it as an independent producer. This independence is not abolished by the fact that these small farmers may form among themselves a more or less natural commune in production, as they do in India, since it is here merely a question of independence from the nominal lord of the soil. Under such conditions the surplus labor for the nominal owner of the land cannot be filched from them by any economic measures, but must be forced from them by other measures, whatever may be the form assumed by them.

This is different from slave or plantation economy, in that the the slave works with conditions of labor belonging to another. He does not work as an independent producer. This requires conditions of personal dependence, a lack of personal freedom, no matter to what extent, a bondage to the soil as its accessory, a serfdom in the strict meaning of the word. If the direct producers are not under the sovereignty of a private landlord, but rather under that of a state which stands over them as their direct landlord and sovereign, then rent and taxes coincide, or rather, there is no tax which differs from this form of ground-rent. Under these circumstances the subject need not be politically or economically under any harder pressure than that common to all subjection to that state. The state is then supreme landlord. The sovereignty consists here in the ownership of land concentrated on a national scale. But, on the other hand, no private ownership of land exists, although there is both private and common possession and use of land.[42]

In the above statement we find the following characteristics which distinguish the feudal from the Indian (or Asiatic, – Marx also sometimes denotes it as tributary) mode of production.

(i) The direct producer in the feudal mode of production – the serf – does not own the means of production or labour conditions of his own means of subsistence, i.e. land; so he has to provide to the owner of the land unpaid surplus labour which is the ground rent extracted from him by the private landlord by virtue of his owner-ship of the soil, this being the main form of wealth or means of production in feudalism. In India, on the other hand, the direct producer, the peasant, possesses the means of production and labour conditions of his own means of subsistence, i.e., land. His surplus labour is extracted from him in the form of tax not by any private landlord but by the state.

(ii) In the feudal mode, private ownership of land exists, the predominant pattern being the private landlord's ownership. In the Asiatic mode there is no private ownership of land, although there is both private and common possession and use of land. It is important to note here that although the direct labourer remains the 'possessor' of the means of production, i.e. land, he is not absolutely free because *the property relation asserts itself as a direct relation between ruler and servant*. Thus, the actual possessors of land in India, whether as private occupants (which later under the British rule came to be known as *ryotwari* areas) or as collective occupants (*mahalwari* areas) remain subservient to the supreme landlord or real owner of the soil – the state.[43]

(iii) In the feudal mode, the landlord is the sovereign over the serf. In the Asiatic mode, the state is the sovereign, because it is the supreme landlord. By using the term 'supreme landlord', Marx implies that there might be revenue farmers (known as landlords) in India but they were not co-sharers of sovereignty with the state. Under the feudal system, the sovereignty or political power of the state is decentralized because the private landlords are regarded as the owners of the soil.[44] Under the Asiatic system the sovereignty of the state is undivided and concentrated because of the state's monopolization of landownership.

Again, Marx adds:

The specific economic form, in which unpaid surplus labour is pumped out of the direct producers, determines the relations of rulers and ruled, as it grows immediately out of production itself and reacts upon it as a determining element. Upon this is founded the entire formation of the economic community which grows up out of the conditions of production itself, and this also determines its specific political shape. It is always the direct relation of the owners of the conditions of production to the direct producers, which reveals the innermost secret, the hidden foundation of the *entire social construction, and with it of the political form of the relations between sovereignty and*

dependence, in short, of the corresponding form of the state.
This does not prevent the same economic basis from showing
infinite variations and gradations in its appearance, even though
its principal conditions are everywhere the same. This is due to
innumerable outside circumstances, natural environment, race
peculiarities, outside historical influences, and so forth, all of
which must be ascertained by careful analysis[45] (emphasis
added).

In India, as well as in the Asiatic mode, the 'owners of the
conditions of production' was the state. Therefore, the claim on the
surplus labour of the producers here lies with the state. The state
extracted the surplus labour in the form of surplus commodity (both
in kind and cash):

> It is the surplus alone that becomes a commodity, and a portion
> of even that not until it has reached the hands of the State, into
> whose hands from time immemorial a certain quantity of these
> products has found its way in the shape of rent in kind.[46]

Thus, the claim of the state as the supreme owner of the soil, on the
surplus labour of the direct producers determined the nature of
social formation and the state structure in India. In short, the state's
domination over, and independence from, the social classes was
ensured by its supreme landownership. The classes that grew were
naturally subservient to the state either as direct producers or as
hangers-on (as nobility or revenue collectors, literati and even
merchants). Indian and foreign scholars have argued incessantly
about whether the *zamindars* and *jagirdars*, i.e. the revenue collectors, had the right to sell or alienate their rights of revenue
collection. But this is not important. The crucial question (for the
development of capitalism) is whether the *zamindars* or *jagirdars*
had proprietary rights over disposal of the soil, i.e. whether they
could create a class of wage labourers by evicting peasants from the
soil.
  Irfan Habib maintains that since the reign of Akbar (late sixteenth century), the *zamindars* attained the right to sell their *zamindari* with the approval of the state but they failed to acquire the
proprietary rights over the land[47] which was the hallmark of the
landed aristocracy in Europe.

The zamindar's right to a part of the produce of the soil was
limited both by custom and by imperial or official regulation.
The zamindar might formally be known as malik and his right
termed milkiyat, but nothing will be more inaccurate than to
imagine him to be like a landed proprietor of the colonial era,
paying the land tax and collecting rents fixed by himself from his
tenants-at-will. Zamindari, therefore, did not signify a
proprietary right over the land.[48]

Irfan Habib adds that

the share of the zamindar in the surplus produce of the peasant,
wherever the land happened to be within a zamindari, was still
a subordinate one compared with the land-revenue demand
levied on the same land by the authorities [i.e., the state].[49]

It is this proprietary right which the revenue collectors in India
failed to achieve that distinguished the Indian pre-capitalist mode of
production from that of the West. In India, unlike feudal Europe,
the revenue collectors could neither raise the revenue (or rent) nor
evict the peasants because they were not the owners of the soil.
Thus, one of the prime factors – the separation of the peasants from
their land – for the emergence of wage labour was virtually non-
existent in India. The revenue collector's share in the surplus was
dependent on the state's surplus (which varied from one tenth to
one fourth of the state revenue, depending on various factors), and
the state's approval was required to impose a separate rate on the
peasants (only in cases where the *zamindars* were not allowed to
take a share from the state revenue). This mode of surplus extraction made the nobility in India, a class dependent on the state.

However, as Marx points out, the economic form of surplus
extraction not only determines the relations between the rulers and
the ruled and acts on the development of forces of production – it
also depends on the nature of production itself.

The nature of production in India was conditioned by the existence of the village communities, characterized by an organic unity
between agriculture and industry.[50] To quote, in brief, the classic
description of the village system given by Marx:

The constitution of these communities varies in different parts of

India. In those of the simplest form, the land is tilled in common, and the produce divided among the members. At the same time, spinning and weaving are carried on in each family as subsidiary industries. Side by side with the masses thus occupied with one and the same work we find the chief inhabitant, who is judge, police and tax-gatherer in one; the bookkeeper who keeps the accounts of the village ... the overseer who distributes the water from the common tanks for irrigation ... the schoolmaster who on the sand teaches the children reading and writing ... a smith and a carpenter, who make and repair all the agricultural implements; the potter who makes all the pottery of the village; the barber, the washerman;... the silversmith, here and there the poet. This dozen of individuals is maintained at the expense of the whole community.... The simplicity of the organisation for production in these self-sufficing communities that constantly reproduce themselves in the same form, and when accidentally destroyed, spring up again on the same spot and with the same name – this simplicity supplies the key to the secret of the unchangeableness in such striking contrast with the constant dissolution and refounding of Asiatic states, and the never ceasing changes of dynasty. The superstructure of the economic element of society remains untouched by the storm clouds of the political sky.[51]

Probably commenting on this description of the village community, Weber says:

Karl Marx has characterised the peculiar position of the artisan in the Indian village – his dependence upon fixed payment in kind instead of upon production for the market – as the reason for the specific stability of the Asiatic peoples. In this Marx was correct.[52]

Evidently, production relations in these small communities were not based on exchange but on use value. In fact, the artisans in a sense were the employees of the village; craft production could function only as a subsidiary to agriculture. The artisans and other professionals were maintained at the expense of the whole community. They used to receive a fixed share of the produce from each cultivator for the services they rendered.[53]

There is no doubt that this kind of payment stood in the way of the emergence of wage labour in the East.

> One of the prerequisites of wage labour and one of the historic conditions for capital is free labour and the exchange of free labour against money, in order to reproduce and to convert it into values, in order to be consumed by money, not as use value for enjoyment, but as use value for money.[54]

But why could wage labour not emerge in the East? Here Weber missed the real point, which is, as Marx emphasized, the natural unity of labour with its material prerequisites:

> Another pre-requisite is the separation of free labour from the objective conditions of its realisation – from the means and material of labour. This means above all that the worker must be separated from the land, which functions as his natural laboratory. This means the dissolution both of free petty landownership and of communal landed property, based on the oriental commune.[55]

In the evolution of western society, the transition to capitalism was facilitated by the existence of feudalism. One of the significant factors in the development of western society was the emergence of serfdom and the appropriation of land by the feudal lords. This led to a sharp polarization of interests between the lords and the direct producers, the serfs and peasants. In the Orient, because of communal ownership by the village community, and the absence of legal ownership, the tax collector was, as in the West, not a co-sharer of sovereignty with the king. Therefore there was no conflict between the peasantry and the landlord over the physical possession of land and of labour services which was the bone of contention between the feudal lords and the serfs in Europe.[56]

The conflicts, of course, were there between the village and the state but these were confined to the size of the revenue or the surplus of the soil.[57] The basis of agriculture remained unchanged. Hence, Marx says, in spite of incessant changes of the dynasties, the structure of the economic element of society, i.e., the village community, remained untouched by the political sky. This is also the reason why there was no fundamental change in the nature of the state structure.

The absence of a conflict of interests between the peasants and the revenue collectors over the question of disposal of the land did not lead to the workers' separation from the land.[58] Furthermore, the self-sustaining unity of agriculture and manufacturing 'contained all the conditions for reproduction and surplus production within itself.[59] Where such small self-sufficient units exist as part of a larger unity, it is very natural that they would provide a part of their surplus products to the large unity for maintaining communication, irrigation, etc.[60] A part of the surplus is also spent by the larger unity for such items as war, religious worship, etc.[61]

So herein lies the secret – the unity of manufacturing and agriculture – of how the Asiatic society resisted disintegration and economic evolution. As Marx says:

> The Asiatic form necessarily survives longest and most stubbornly. This is due to the fundamental principle on which it is based, that is, that the individual does not become independent of the community; that the circle of production is self-sustaining, unity of agriculture and craft manufacture, etc.[62]

To quote D.R. Gadgil:

> The office of the village artisan being hereditary, it stereotyped the whole life of the village. It was no doubt a very good device for insuring that the services required for the village would be regularly provided for, especially during troublous times, but, at the same time, it insured against progress in the methods of the artisans. To begin with, the artisan, who did all the miscellaneous duties connected with his occupation in the village did not specialize, and the division of labour was extremely limited. The proficiency therefore, of the artisan in his craft could not be expected to be great. It also effectively protected the artisan from the pressure of external competition. For a cultivator was not likely to buy his pots from an outside potter – even though his wares were superior – if he had been paying the village potter to supply them to him.[63]

The difference in the development of Asiatic artisan industry and feudal artisan industry can be gleaned from the following description of the feudal industry by Leo Huberman:

Whatever industry existed formerly had been carried on in the peasant's own house. Did his family need furniture? Then there was no calling in the carpenter to make it or no purchasing it at the furniture store on Main Street. Not at all. The peasant's own family chopped and cut and carved until it had whatever furniture it needed. Did the members of the family need clothing? Then the members of the family spun, and wove, and stitched, and sewed – their own. Industry was carried on in the home, and the purpose of production was simply to satisfy the needs of the household. Among the lord's domestic serfs there were some who did only this sort of work while the others farmed. In the ecclesiastical houses, also, there were some craftsmen who specialized in one craft and so became quite skilled at their jobs of weaving or working in wood or iron. But this, too, was not commercial industry supplying a market – it was simply serving the requirements of the household. The market had to grow before craftsmen as such could exist in their separate professions. The rise of towns and the use of money gave craftsmen a chance to give up farming and make a living by their craft.[64]

The feudal craftsmen, therefore, did not enjoy the same security as the craftsmen in Indian villages. Moreover, their subservience to the noblemen and clergy made them desirous of seeking independence which the rising free towns could provide. The conflicts between lords and serfs, and also between the bourgeoisie and the lords, were, thus, a source of change in the forces of production in feudal industry.

Indian towns: a source of weakness of the Indian bourgeoisie

Another reason for the stagnation of the Indian economy was that the state stood in the way of the development of cities on the western model, a necessary precondition for the emergence of the bourgeoisie. On the development of cities in history, Marx says:

Ancient classical history is the history of cities, but cities based on land ownership and agriculture; Asian history is a kind of undifferentiated unity of town and country (the large city properly speaking, must be regarded merely as a princely camp, superimposed on the real economic structure); the Middle Ages (Germanic period) starts with the countryside as the locus of history, whose further development then proceeds through the opposition of town and country; modern (history) is the urbanisation of the countryside, not, as among the ancients, the ruralisation of the city.[65]

The cities in India, and also those of other Asiatic countries were mostly centres of pilgrimage and administration. According to D.R. Gadgil:

Most of the towns in India owed their existence to one of the three following reasons: (i) they were places of pilgrimage or sacred places of some sort; (ii) they were the seat of a court or the capital of a province; or (iii) they were commercial depots, owing their importance to their peculiar position along trade routes. Of these reasons, the first two were by far the most important.[66]

This does not mean that Indian or Asian towns at this time had no industries, but rather that the industries were not the cause of their importance. Industries grew in these towns to satisfy the needs of the courts, the nobility, the *fauzdars, subadars* (Governors), etc., who were the agents of the despotic state.[67] So, when the court moved (on campaign, etc.), the industries also moved. To quote Sir Henry Maine, one of the ablest authorities on the village community in the East and West:

Nearly all the movable capital of the empire or kingdom was at once swept away to its temporary centre, which became the exclusive seat of skilled manufacture or decorative art.
Every man who claimed to belong to the higher class of artificers took his loom or tools and followed in the train of the king.[68]

Marx also noted this dependency of the merchants and artisans on the nobility:

this will not appear so very astonishing to one who understands the particular condition and the government of the country, namely that the king is the one and only proprietor of all the land in the kingdom, from which it follows as a necessary consequence, that a whole capital city, like Delhi or Agra, lives almost entirely on the army and is therefore obliged to follow the king if he takes to the field for any length of time. For these towns neither are, nor can be, anything like a Paris, being virtually nothing but military camps.... Moreover, the same merchants who keep the bazaars in Delhi are forced to maintain them during a campaign.[69]

In the development of the cities in the West, the significant factor was the opposition between the town and the country. The feudal lords in the tenth, eleventh and twelfth centuries encouraged town development within their areas because it brought them increased revenue.[70] In these towns the bourgeoisie soon became powerful enough to challenge the power of the feudal lords.[71] In the West a threefold conflict between the crown, the feudal lords and the bourgeoisie paved the way for the bourgeoisie to consolidate its power, by aligning itself first with the crown against the feudal lords, and then by curtailing the power of the crown itself. A.L. Morton has given a graphic description of how the English bourgeoisie consolidated its power in the battle against the Spanish Armada:

Up to 1588, the English bourgeoisie were fighting for existence: after that they fought for power. For this reason, the defeat of the Armada is a turning point in the internal history of England as well as in foreign affairs. It was the merchants with their own ships and their own money, who had won the victory and they had won it almost in spite of the half-heartedness and ineptitude of the crown and council, whose enthusiasm diminished as the war assumed a more revolutionary character. The victory transformed the whole character of the class relations that had existed for a century. The bourgeoisie became aware of their strength and with the coming of this awareness the long alliance between them and the monarchy began to dissolve. It might still need their support but they no longer needed its protection. Even before the death of Elizabeth, Parliament began to show an independence previously unknown.[72]

Thus we find, in the western situation, there were three forces which facilitated the capture of political power by the bourgeoisie: the king, the feudal lords, and the serfs. In the struggle against the feudal lords, the king had to surrender to his ally, the bourgeoisie, the legal and functional sovereignty of the city.[73] The attainment of charters, in particular for the states in Southern Europe, ensured to the bourgeoisie its victory against feudal fetters.[74]

A critical analysis of the social factors which formed the basis of occidental cities will show what enabled them to acquire freedom through charters. As mentioned earlier, there was an antagonism between town and country in medieval Europe which emanated from the feudal order of society. The solution to this problem was sought in containing the mercantile activities within the towns where it could be regulated and controlled. The feudal order and its ethic was apprehensive of the corrosive influence of commerce:

> It was not that trade in itself was despised, but that the institutions, the activities and the rather obvious commercial instincts of professional merchants were clearly not consistent with the ideological precepts of the feudal order. Attempts to organize trade on a non-professional basis were insufficient, however, and the rank society was forced to rely on a professional merchant class which appeared, in some respects, to threaten its moral bases.[75]

No such danger was present in India, and therefore no such development occurred. India's development was similar to China's, as described by Weber in the following words:

> In contrast to the Occident, the cities in China and throughout the Orient lacked political autonomy. The Oriental city was not a polis, in the sense of antiquity, and it knew nothing of the 'city law' of the Middle Ages, for it was not a 'commune' with political privileges of its own. Nor was there a citizenry in the sense of self-equipped military estates such as existed in Occidental antiquity. No military oath-bound communities like the Campagna communes of Genoa or other coniurationes ever sprang up to fight or ally themselves with the feudal lords of the city in order to attain autonomy. No forces emerged like the consuls, councils, or political associations of merchant and craft guilds such as Mercanza which were based upon the military

independence of the city district. Revolts of the urban populace which forced the officials to flee into the citadels had always been the order of the day. But they always aimed at removing a concrete official or a concrete decree, especially a new tax, never at gaining a charter which might at least in the relative way, guarantee the freedom of the city.[76]

In the absence of feudalism in the East, the merchants and artisans in the city could not play the feudal forces against the king in their attempt at consolidation of power.[77] The cities in India, as in other parts of Asia, could not win the 'political autonomy' or 'political privileges' that the medieval cities in the occident did. The nobles, however powerful in their own area of jurisdiction, were nothing but mere tax collectors and public functionaries. The dependence of the Moghul bureaucracy or the nobility on the state is clearly brought out by Irfan Habib:

> The principal obligation of the mansabdars was the maintenance of cavalry contingents with horses of standard breeds. There was, therefore, an intimate connection between the military power of the Mughals and the jagirdari or assignment system. It was the great merit of the latter that it made the mansabdars completely dependent upon the will of the Emperor, so that the imperial government was able to assemble and despatch them with their contingents to any point at any time where and when the need arose.... There was one great struggle in protest from the nobility and the theocracy – the revolt of 1580 – but once it had been quelled, the Empire never really faced a serious revolt from within the ranks of its own bureaucracy.[78]

Habib adds:

> The jagirdar as an individual member of the governing class had no rights or privileges apart from those received from the Emperor. He could not manage his jagir just as he pleased, and had to conform to imperial regulations. The rate of the land-revenue demand and the methods by which it was to be assessed and collected were all prescribed by the imperial administration. The Emperor also decreed what other taxes were to be collected. The conduct of the jagirdar and his agents

was watched over and checked by officials such as qanungos and chaudhuris, and fauzdars and newswriters.[79]

Hence the merchants and artisans in the oriental cities could not acquire power by balancing the feudal lords against the emperor. They had to remain satisfied with playing a role subordinate to the courts, noblemen, priests and soldiers. In the East, the city could not become a centre of bourgeoisie power to struggle first against feudal restraints[80] and then against the state itself, as was the case in feudalism. The bourgeoisie failed to overcome the hegemony of the state.

This weakness of the Asian merchants and artisan classes *vis-à-vis* state power was one of the reasons why these countries were defeated by the rising bourgeoisie of the West. It is interesting to note that most of the countries in Asia were colonized by various companies, by the bourgeoisie itself. The Western bourgeoisie was victorious not only in its home ocuntry, but also in its bid for power on foreign soil.

The rise and decline of a nascent bourgeoisie

In the preceding pages the factors which stood in the way of the development of an indigenous capitalism in India have been described. Now we will see how, despite these impediments, a prosperous merchant class came into existence in the seventeenth and eighteenth centuries as a result of the opening of trade with the West. The question is, how could this merchant class emerge as a social force when the Asiatic mode of production was a stagnant system based on a more or less inalienable interdependence between agriculture and the village artisan industry.

The point to be emphasized is this: it would be wrong to conclude from the above discussion that the Indian social economy was totally immobile. No mode of production can be absolutely static. In fact, under the impact of international trade, the Indian economy was undergoing a formidable change. It has already been mentioned that in the urban centres of India (see note 18) there were merchants and artisans who catered to the needs of the court. With the expansion of sea trade, the demand for their products in foreign markets outstripped the demands of the court and its hangers-on.

Consequently, these merchants and urban artisans became less dependent on the court and emerged slowly as an incipient capitalist class which began to erode the autonomy of the village economy.

When the Europeans came to India, trade with the British East India Company, the Dutch East India Company, the French East India Company and others, led to an efflorescence of commercial activities in India. Indian industrial commodities were very much sought after all over Europe.[81] Since the beginning of the sixteenth century, Indian goods began to enter Europe directly via sea routes. This gave a tremendous boost to production in India, particularly to urban crafts. In 1601 the various East India Companies exported 22,000 pounds sterling worth of bullion to India to import Indian commodities into Europe; at the end of the century, the bullion export totalled about 800,000 pounds annually.[82] From the beginning of the seventeenth century to the end of the eighteenth, India's export to England increased consistently:

At the beginning of English trade in calicoes,
13,000 pieces of calico were exported in 1618–19. The figure rose
sharply to 200,000 pieces in 1629. Between 1680–83 about
two million pieces of cotton goods and silk stuffs were imported
per annum on an average by the English India Company for the
English and European markets. In 1720, the year of the
imposition of fresh restriction of the import of calicoes to
England, the aggregate import was 1,502,498 pieces, including
calicoes, wrought silk and sooseys. The value of such cotton
goods has not been accurately estimated. Between 1677–1680
the aggregate value of the cloth goods was roughly estimated in
the English Parliament between £200,000 and £300,000 of which
the calicoes alone accounted for £150,000 to £160,000. In 1796–
97 the value of piecegoods from India imported into England was
£2,776,082 or one-third of the whole volume of the imports from
India. In the sixteen years between 1793–94 and 1809–10 the
imports of Indian piece goods amounted to
£26,171,125.[83]

Other East India companies were also actively engaged in importing huge amounts of Indian textiles to Europe:

The total annual export of Indian hand loom products by sea in the seventeenth century has been estimated by Moreland at 50,000 million square yards, 15,000 bales of cotton goods being exported by the English merchants and 10,000 bales by the Dutch to Europe, making a total of 25,000 bales or 32 million sq. yds. for Europe excluding the trades of the French, the Portuguese and the Danes. Markets in the Far East, the Red Sea and Persian Gulf supplied by the Europeans as well as by Indian, Javan and Siamese merchants absorbed, it is roughly computed, another 18 million sq. yds. of cloth. 1½ to 3 million sq. yds. more represented the cloth export to Persia and Central Asia up to the borders of the Caspian Sea by land routes.... Tavernier estimates that the Dutch took from Bengal 6,000 to 7,000 bales of silk annually, and the merchants of Tartary took another 6,000 to 7,000 bales. Reckoning a bale at about 1,400 sq. yds. the Bengal silk trade alone may be taken as somewhere about 19.6 millions of square yards at this period.[84]

In 1791 the import of Indian cotton piece goods by France amounted to £1.2 million, while a considerable quantity of these was also exported in American vessels (valued at Rs 5,600,000).[85]

Due to this huge trade the Indian merchant class of various urban centres was gradually becoming stronger and bolder. The principal dynamic in the formation of this class was international trade. The capital (in money form) accumulation of this class became so large that merchants began making loans to European trading companies:

> Before the Dutch financiers came to the rescue of the English trading corporation, the English merchants trading in India had on many occasions to resort to borrowing of capital from the native bankers.[86]

They even started to give loans to revenue farmers. Radhakamal Mukerjee has given a graphic description of how this class was becoming stronger despite various restrictions imposed on it by the agents of the state.

> In spite of the variety of imposts, fines and exactions, a class of rich shop keepers, traders and financiers developed in the large towns of India. In the imperial capital, Delhi, Mandelso records

there were 80 caravanserais for foreign merchants, most of them three stories high, with very noble lodgings, store houses, vaults and stables belonging to them. It was estimated by Manrique that at the town of Patna there were as many as 600 brokers and middlemen most of whom were wealthy.... Similarly in Bengal there were the seths of Murshidabad who represented a most influential banking and financial house, advanced money to both farmers of revenue and nawabs of Bengal, and wielded great political influence at the time of the advent of the English in the province.[87]

With regard to the social origins of this class, N.C. Sinha says:

The trading classes of the mid-eighteenth century were a pre-eminently non-feudal community. They were not sprung from the landed capital, nor did they invest in land. The Jagatt Seths had no landed estates, the Arunji Nathji would not invest in land grants from the Company and a class of the Chetties would prefer to be petty traders than land-holders. The cause of this aversion to land lay in the fact that the national economy provided a far better field of investments than land. There was a widespread and highly developed textile industry whose variegated products sold in the markets of Europe.[88]

Thus, in the seventeenth and eighteenth centuries there were many industries in India – the textile being the most important – that could compare favourably with the most flourishing industries of Europe of that period. For example, Delhi, Agra, Meerut, Lucknow, Lahore, Patna, Ahmedabad, Dacca and many other Indian towns became great industrial centres.[89] How could these towns have become so great if they depended, as mentioned earlier, only on the favour of the court? As Henry Maine has rightly observed, these industries sometimes outgrew the needs of the court:

Some peculiar manufacture had sometimes so firmly established itself as to survive the desertion, and these manufacturing towns sometimes threw out colonies.[90]

Usually a particular industry flourished in a particular city – for example, muslins at Dacca, silk at Murshidabad, chintzes at Lucknow, *dhotis* and *dopattas* at Ahmedabad, shawls at Srinagar.[91] The cotton manufacturers, were of course, the most widespread; next to them in importance were the manufacturers of silk cloths.[92] The towns in Bengal, especially Dacca, Murshidabad, and Malda, excelled in the production of both textiles and silk.[93] The muslin of Dacca was the finest and best known of all these: a Manchester manufacturer, when he could not rival its fineness, said deprecatingly that it was but 'a shadow of a commodity'.[94]

According to Edmund Burke:

> there are to be found [in India] a multitude of cities not exceeded in population and trade by those of the first class in Europe: merchants and bankers who have once vied in capital with the Bank of England, whose money had often supported a tottering state and preserved their governments in the midst of war and desolation; millions of indigenous manufacturers and mechanics.[95]

Thus we find, just before the rise of the British, a new bourgeoisie that was coming into its own in the emerging trading cities of India.

This efflorescence of trade and industry, which started with the discovery of the sea route to India from Europe, continued until the victory of British power. The towns which were centres of administration were transforming gradually into flourishing trade centres. Merchant capital also took the fundamental step towards manufacturing industry by separating the producers from the products.

> The merchant capitalist advanced funds to the weavers with which they bought the necessary material and supported themselves while at work. Thus, when they handed over their products to the merchant capitalist, they were no longer owners of their own produce. The product was alienated from the producer. The merchant-capitalist derived not the usual profit out of buying cheap and selling dear; he was already exploiting the labour power of the producer.[96]

Under such circumstances, it was not impossible that the Indian bourgeoisie could have triumphed and caused the birth of industrial capitalism.

The development of the new form of commerce and industry was also working as a disintegrating force in the village community in some parts of India. The production of the village artisans, particularly in Bengal and other advanced areas, was no longer geared to meet the needs of the village; it was undertaken for foreign markets.[97]

> His production was no longer the property of the community to be exchanged by himself into other necessities produced by equally independent members of the community. Arts and crafts, which centuries ago had arisen as a part of the village economy within the bonds of castes, had long ceased to be the exclusive concern of the isolated villages, but was taken from one province to another in order to be sold and resold by a prosperous trading class with considerable capital accumulated in its hand. The principal industries had been commercialized and their base had been removed from the village confines to the towns, hundreds of which flourished all over the country. Still confined to the caste guilds in so far as labour was concerned, the social and economic control of the industrial products had gone out of the hands of the artisan. Instead of completely controlling production and distribution as before, the craftsman was supplied with raw materials by the trading middleman, who took the finished products out of the former's hand, not to distribute it according to the needs of the community, but to sell it for profit.[98]

In this connection, the following extraction from Marx's *Grundrisse* is very significant:

> In the periods of the dissolution of pre-bourgeois relations, there sporadically occur free workers whose services are bought for purposes not of consumption, but of production; but, firstly, even if on a large scale, for the production only of direct use value, not of values; and secondly, if a nobleman e.g. brings the free worker together with his serfs, even if he re-sells a part of the worker's product, and the free worker thus creates value for him, then this exchange takes place only for the superfluous [product] and only for the sake of superfluity, for luxury consumption is thus at bottom only a veiled purchase of alien labour for immediate consumption or as use value. Incidentally,

wherever these free workers increase in number, and where this relation grows, there the old mode of production – commune, patriarchal, feudal etc. – is in the process of dissolution, and the elements of real wage labour are in preparation.[99]

From the point of view of organization, the merchant capitalist introduced an even more significant innovation. The products were often procured in a semi-finished state and the final processing was carried out in workshops by craftsmen working as wage labourers.[100] So this class of traders could be viewed as the advance guard of the coming Indian industrial bourgeoisie which might have developed into the modern capitalist class had not its normal growth been obstructed. The defeat of the rising bourgeoisie of India at the hands of the more developed bourgeoisie of England sealed India's fate.

But how could the bourgeoisie grow without weakening the state? In fact, India's social structure was undergoing a significant change at this period. As M.N. Roy says:

> In the later part of the eighteenth century, there came into existence in India a prosperous trading class with considerable capital accumulated in its hands. This trading class was largely responsible for undermining the foundations of feudalism [office-prebend] in the days of the decay of the Moghul power. All the big landowners, as well as the rulers of the various independent states that sprang up on the ruins of the Moghul Empire, were heavily indebted to this class of usurious traders.[101]

B.N. Ganguly has more succinctly described how a new kind of feudalism was emerging on the ruins of the central authority of the state:

> So long as there was a strong central authority, the revenue farmers were mere government officials. But when, after the death of Aurongzeb, the authority of the king began to wane, the local officers and assignees declared themselves independent of the central authority. Since time immemorial, the right to demand and collect revenue, had been, in the minds of the Indian rural population, regarded as an attribute of sovereignty. The revenue farmers made use of this popular idea and began to

exercise not only rights of ownership of land but also magisterial and administrative powers.[102]

Thus we find, in India's land relations, a significant change taking place at this period; it was a transition from prebendalization to feudalization. According to Weber, prebendal organization of office means:

> Payments which are somehow fixed to objects or which are essentially economic usufruct from lands or other sources. They must be compensation for the fulfillment of actual or fictitious office duties; they are goods permanently set aside for the economic assurance of the office. The transition from such prebendal organization of office to salaried officialdom is quite fluid.[103]

Moreover, as has been hinted by Weber, prebendalization can either transform itself into pure bureaucracy with the development of the money economy or into landlordism with the consolidation of power by the tax farmers. In the case of England, France and other West European nations, 'the sale of office' was gradually replaced by pure bureaucracy; in India the bureaucrats were transforming their 'office prebends' into hereditary estates.

In the development of capitalism in the West, the bourgeoisie at first sided with the crown or the state because feudal relations hindered its growth; in the East, the state was the greatest obstacle which had to be overcome to attain emancipation. How obstructive was the hold of the bureaucracy on the bourgeoisie can be judged from the following description:

> It is mentioned that Mir Jumla once demanded Rs 50,000 from the merchants of Dacca. On refusal they were threatened with death by being trampled by elephants and compromised for Rs 25,000 while the bankers of the city appeased his wrath by paying Rs 300,000 without much further ado. Occasionally, however, the mercantile community could protest successfully against the exactions of a governor or high administrative officer by hartal or suspension of business.[104]

So it was not surprising that this rising merchant class tried to undermine the authority of the state. They did this by forming an alliance with the tax farmers, or office-prebend holders metamorphosed into landlords. However, the weakening of the state did not lead to the consolidation of power by the bourgeoisie. Before the bourgeoisie could form its own state, the internecine warfare among the feudal lords and the consequent decline of the central authority created a power vacuum into which the British stepped.[105]

Thus, the emerging bourgeoisie of India was defeated by the established bourgeoisie of England which enjoyed the backing of its own state power. The Indian nascent bourgeoisie might have succeeded in overcoming the obsctacles of state power and rising feudal elements if they could have succeeded in keeping the country independent a little longer.

For Marx, three factors were necessary for the indigenous development of capitalism in any country:

> First, a rural social structure which allows the peasantry to be set free at a certain point; second, the urban craft development which produces specialised, independent, non-agricultural commodity production in the form of crafts; and third, accumulation of monetary wealth derived from trade and usury.[106]

From the above analysis of the social economy of India just before the rise of British power, it is clear that India satisfied the second and the third conditions, but her rural structure, except in very few places, was far from the state of dissolution which could lead to the large-scale alienation of the peasants from the soil. The forces of production and their relationships were thus the main stumbling-blocks on which the urban bourgeoisie floundered. Their weakness *vis-à-vis* the state also stemmed from this.

3   The victory of the British and its impact on the evolution of social classes in India

Prolegomena

In this chapter the impact of British rule on the evolution of India's social economy and social classes, and the role played by the state in this process, will be examined.

First an attempt will be made to analyse how the establishment of the colonial state in the service of a metropolitan mercantile bourgeoisie led to the disappearance of the rising merchant bourgeoisie of India and to the ruthless exploitation of its artisan industry. Then it will be explained how the success of industrial capitalism in establishing its hegemony over state power in England caused a metamorphosis in the task of the colonial state, which reduced India from being an exporter to becoming instead an importer of manufactured commodities. In short, India was turned into a supplier of primary products for the metropolitan capital, and a market for its finished goods. The process was accompanied by the conversion of Indian agriculture into a source of primitive capital accumulation for the metropolitan centre. However, the various measures, including legislation, which were adopted by the colonial state, did not result in any fundamental change in the organization of production in Indian agriculture. The process of integrating India into the world capitalist market required the creation of new relations of production, and new state organizations. As a consequence new social classes and social categories came into existence. However, due to the obstructed growth of industries (but not their total absence) and the failure of the capitalist class to establish its control over agriculture, the public official and other professions related to the state remained, as in the pre-colonial period, the most important sources of employment and power. Thus, during the colonial period, despite the emergence of an industrial bourgeoisie and a proletariat, as will be discussed below, the basis of the hegemony of the state remained substantially unaltered.

The colonial state and the decline of incipient capitalism

The victory of British power in 1757 killed indigenous capitalism in its nascent stage. The trade which was being carried on by the East India Company, and for which England had to pay huge amounts of bullion to Indian traders and manufacturers, was transformed into 'organized plunder'.

The artisans were forced to accept whatever price the company and its agents paid them. (Company agents also had their own native employees, known as *gomasthas*, who traded in the name of the company.) The plundering was so merciless that even the English-appointed Bengali Nawab protested to the Company's governor in Calcutta:

> They forcibly take away goods and commodities of the ryots, merchants, etc., for a fourth of their value; and by ways of violence and oppression, they oblige the ryots, etc., to give five rupees for goods which are worth but one rupee.[1]

An English merchant, 'who saw things with his own eyes', has presented a vivid picture of how the artisans were being turned into 'bond slaves of the company':

> Inconceivable oppressions and hardships have been practised towards the poor manufacturers and workmen of the country, who are, in fact, monopolised by the Company as so many slaves. Various and innumerable are the methods of oppressing the poor weavers, which are duly practised by the Company's agents and gomasthas in the country; such as by fines, imprisonments, floggings, forcing bonds from them, etc., by which the number of weavers in the country has been greatly decreased .... Upon the gomastha's arrival at the aurang or manufacturing town, he fixes upon a habitation, which he calls his Kachari, to which by his peons and harkaras he summons the brokers, together with the weavers, whom he makes to sign a bond for the delivery of a certain quantity of goods, at a certain time and price, and pays

them a part of the money in advance. The assent of the poor weaver is in general not deemed necessary, for the gomasthas, when employed on the company's investment, frequently make them sign what they please.[2]

Until the beginning of the industrial revolution in England, the main interest of the East India Company was not to turn India into a market, but to monopolize Indian exports. Indian merchants were prohibited from buying from local producers, and forced to purchase goods at higher prices from the company and its servants. Thus ended the days of prosperity of the Indian merchants. Henceforth they were allowed to exist only as the agents of the company and their employees in the form of *gomasthas* and *baniyans*.[3]

The 'plunder of Bengal', however, helped capital formation in England on an unprecedented scale and ushered in the Industrial Revolution. Brooks Adams has given a very vivid picture of how it happened:

Very soon after Plassey the Bengal plunder began to arrive in London, and the effect appears to have been instantaneous, for all the authorities agree that the 'industrial revolution', the event which has divided the nineteenth century from all antecedent time, began with the year 1760. Prior to 1760, according to Baines, the machinery used for spinning cotton in Lancashire was almost as simple as in India; while about 1750 the English iron industry was in full decline because of the destruction of the forests for fuel .... Plassey was fought in 1757, and probably nothing has ever equalled the rapidity of the change which followed. In 1760, the flying shuttle appeared, and coal began to replace wood in smelting. In 1764 Hargreaves invented the spinning jenny, in 1776 Crompton contrived the mule, in 1785 Cartwright patented the powerloom and, chief of all, in 1768 Watt matured the steam engine, the most perfect of all vents of centralising energy .... In themselves inventions are passive, many of the most important having lain dormant for centuries, waiting for a sufficient store of force to have accumulated to set them working. That store must take the shape of money, and money not hoarded but in motion. Before the influx of the Indian treasure, and the expansion of credit which followed, no force sufficient for this purpose existed; and had Watt lived fifty years earlier, he and his invention must have perished together. Possibly since the world began, no investment has ever yielded the profit reaped from the Indian plunder, because for nearly fifty years Great Britain stood without a competitor. From 1694 to Plassey (1757) the growth had been relatively slow. Between 1760 and 1815 the growth was very rapid and prodigious.[4]

He goes on to describe how the circulation of money capital suddenly increased many times in England:

For more than sixty years after the foundation of the Bank of England, its smallest note had been for 20 pounds, a note too large to circulate freely, and which rarely travelled far from Lombard Street. Writing in 1790, Burke said that when he came to England in 1750, there were not 'twelve bankers shops' in the provinces, though then (in 1790) he said, they were in every market town. Thus the arrival of the Bengal trade not only increased the mass of money, but stimulated its movement; for at once, in 1759 [Bengal was conquered in 1757] the bank issued 10 and 15 pound notes and in the country private firms poured forth a flood of paper.[5]

Thus the plunder of Bengal was a major source of 'the primitive capital accumulation', to use an expression of Marx. André Gunder Frank gives the role of primitive capital accumulation for the industrial revolution in Europe to Bengal and other major regions of Latin America.

There surely are no major regions in Latin America which are today more cursed by underdevelopment and poverty; yet, all of these regions, like Bengal in India, once provided the life blood of mercantile and industrial capitalist development – in the metropolis.[6]

Christopher Hill, the historian notes:

Where did the capital for the Industrial Revolution come from? Spectacularly large sums flowed into England from overseas – from the slave trade, and, especially from the seventeen-sixties, from organized looting of India.[7]

Karl Marx has summarized how and where the capital was formed for the industrial revolution:

> The discovery of gold and silver in America, the extirpation, enslavement and entombment in mines of the aboriginal population, beginning of the conquest and looting of the East Indies, the turning of Africa into a warren for the commercial hunting of black skins, signalised the rosy dawn of the era of capitalist production. These idyllic proceedings are the chief momenta of primitive accumulation.[8]

We have already observed that American gold and silver was pouring into India via Europe for payments for Indian products. A major part of this huge capital was tapped from the 'plunder of India'. During the decade 1747–56, according to Brooks Adams, £562,423 bullion on average was exported to India annually, but after 1757 bullion export to India ceased: British trade with India was financed from the wealth collected in India itself.

It has already been mentioned that the typical aim of the East India Company[9] was to make a profit by securing a monopoly trade in the goods and products of India which found a ready market in England and Europe. Prior to 1757 the difficulty the company faced was that it had to pay in silver or gold because the British industries (which were still undeveloped) could not offer much in exchange for Indian goods.[10] So the British had to conduct their transactions in silver which they 'obtained by the sale of the slaves in the West Indies and Spanish America'.[11] As Knowles says:

> The English trade with India was really a chase to find something that India would be willing to take, and the silver obtained by the sale of the slaves in the West Indies and Spanish America was all important in this connection.[12]

It may be pointed out here that for more than two and a half centuries (1500–1757) the balance of trade was always in favour of India. Trade consisted mainly of the export of cotton and silk goods in exchange for bullion.[13] However, the merchant capitalists of the East India Company made huge profits from selling the Indian commodities in England and Europe. As Macaulay says:

The company enjoyed during the greater part of the reign of Charles II, a prosperity to which the history of trade scarcely furnished any parallel and which excited the wonder, the cupidity and the envious animosity of the whole capital (London) .... the gains of the body (the East India Company) were almost incredible .... the profits were such that in 1676 every proprietor received as a bonus a quantity of stock equal to that which he held. On the capital thus doubled were paid, during five years, dividends amounting to an average of 20 per cent annually.[14]

In 1677 the price of the stock increased to 245 for every 100. In the 1680s it rose to 500. However, towards the end of the seventeenth century, according to Brooks Adams, Europe, including England, was on the brink of a contraction of money, due partly to the constant bullion drain to Asia. Part of this huge amount was paid to the Indian manufacturers and traders. Throughout the seventeenth century, and until the middle of the eighteenth, wealth poured into India from various European countries.[15]

However, this trend was reversed when the company captured political power after the battle of Plassey. Since then, 'methods of power could be increasingly used to weigh the balance of exchange and secure the maximum goods for the minimum payment'.[16] From the very beginning of the East India trade, the purchase of commodities by means of bullion was disliked by merchant capitalists since they regarded gold and silver as the only real wealth and were loath to part with them.

L. Scrafton, a member of Clive's Council, declared in 1763, on the basis of the plunder after Plassey, that it had been possible to carry on the whole of India's trade for three years without sending out one ounce of bullion:

These glorious successes have brought nearly three millions of money to the nation [Britain]; for, properly speaking, almost the whole of the immense sums received from the Soubah (Bengal) finally centres in England. So great a proportion of it fell into the company's hands, either from their own share, or by sums paid into the treasury at Calcutta for bills and receipts, that they have been enabled to carry on the whole trade of India for three years together, without sending out one ounce of bullion.

Vast sums have been also remitted through the hands of foreign companies, which weigh in the balance of trade to their amount in our favour with such foreign nations.[17]

According to a report of the Company's governor, Verelest, during the three years 1766–68, India's exports amounted to £6,311,250, while her imports amounted to only £624,375.[18] Thus, ten times as much was taken out of the country as was sent into it. The deficit in the balance of trade was paid from revenues collected in India, which was termed the company's 'investment'. The House of Commons Select Committee reported, in 1783:

> A certain portion of the revenues of Bengal has been for many years set apart in the purchase of goods for exportation to England, and this is called the investment.... When an account is taken of the intercourse, for it is not commerce, which is carried on between Bengal and England, the pernicious effect of the system of investment from revenue will appear in the strongest point of view. In that view, the whole exported produce of the country, so far as the company is concerned, is not exchanged in the course of barter, but it is taken away without any return or payment whatever.[19]

The whole situation was stated more clearly by Burke:

> This new system of trade, carried on through the medium of power and public revenue, very soon produced its natural effects. The loudest complaints arose among the natives, and among all the foreigners who traded in Bengal. It must have unquestionably thrown the whole mercantile system of the country into the greatest confusion ...
> In all other countries, the revenue, following the natural course and order of things, arises out of their commerce. Here, by a mischievous inversion of that order, the whole foreign maritime trade, whether English, French, Dutch or Danish, arises from the revenues; these are carried out of the country without producing anything to compensate so heavy a loss.[20]

The Indian trade on the basis of Indian revenue was made possible because Clive, the governor of the company, obtained a charter in 1765 from the tottering Moghul emperor who handed over the revenue administration of the Subah of Bengal to the company. Although the Moghul emperor had no power, his charter gave the company a legal status. This kind of revenue-farming[21] was first put into practice in Bengal in 1765. It was extended to other parts of India as these came under the Company's rule before its demise was forced through the British Parliament, in 1858, by the industrial bourgeoisie.[22]

There was also another means for extracting resources from India which came to be known as the 'Indian debt'. The total Indian debt was a little over 7 million pounds in 1792: it rose to 10 million in 1799. Then came Lord Wellesley's wars, and the Indian debt stood at 27 million in 1807; in 1858, the year the company's rule was merged with the Crown, it stood at 69.5 million.[23] Moreover, India was debited with expenses incurred in England: India became liable for her own conquest by the company. She was also charged with the cost of the Afghan and Chinese Wars and other wars outside her boundaries.[24]

It is impossible to state exactly how much India had been drained since the battle of Plassey in 1757. According to W. Digby:

> Estimates have been made which vary from 500,000,000 pounds to nearly 1,000,000,000 pounds. Probably between Plassey and Waterloo the last mentioned sum was transferred from Indian hoards to the English Bank.[25]

Again, the excess of Indian exports (over imports) during this period reached the enormous total of nearly 5,000,000,000 pounds.

> If one could follow the money in all the ramifications through which, in India, it might have passed, its fertilising effect in every one of the five hundred and forty thousand villages, its accumulating power (money begets money) fructifying in a land where its expenditures would have led to an increase in substance, it would, even then, be impossible to put into words the grievous wrong which has been done to India.[26]

As a result of this unprecedented organized economic drain from India, the rising merchant and artisan classes were completely wiped out.[27] However, as we have already observed, the destruction of the Indian industries eased the way for the emergence of the industrial revolution in England, which was mainly agricultural until the middle of the eighteenth century.

> In 1750 there had been only two cities in Britain with more than 50,000 inhabitants – London and Edinburgh; in 1801 there were already eight, in 1851 twenty-nine, including nine over 100,000. By this time more Britons lived in town than in country, and almost a third of Britons lived in cities over 50,000 inhabitants.[28]

England favoured with coal and iron mines, and with easy credit emanating from the Indian plunder, soon dominated the world market.

The commercial basis was already well established in Britain. Socially, conditions were ripe for the advance to industrial capitalism. A huge unattached labour force was ready to be tapped as the industrial proletariat. Still, the transition to the industrial capitalist stage required 'an initial accumulation of capital on a much larger scale than was yet present in England of the middle eighteenth century'.[29]

The resource transfer from India was one of the primary hidden 'sources of capital accumulation' on which industrial England was built up. There is also no doubt that the transformation of merchant capital into industrial capital stemmed from the desire to 'manufacture foreign imports at home'.

> This vast and growing circulation of goods did not merely bring to Europe new needs, and the stimulus to manufacture foreign imports at home. 'If Saxony and other countries of Europe make up fine China', wrote the Abbé Raynal in 1777, 'if Valencia manufactures Pekins superior to those of China; if Switzerland imitates the muslins and worked calicoes of Bengal; if England and France print linens with great elegance; if so many stuffs, formerly unknown in our climates, now employ our best artists, are we not indebted to India for all these advantages? [Within a few years he would have failed to mention the most successful imitators of the Indians, Manchester.] More than this, it provided a limitless horizon of sales and profit for merchant and manufacturer. And it was the British who – by their policy and force as much as by their enterprise and inventive skill – captured these markets.[30]

India's transformation into an arena of primitive capital accumulation

Once the industrial revolution was achieved in England the task before the British power was to transform India from being an exporter of cotton goods to the whole world to being an importer of these goods – in short, to make her into a market for British industrial capital.[31]

As Hobsbawm says, 'Whoever says Industrial Revolution says cotton, ... the cotton industries of Lancashire and Manchester.'[32] In fact, the industrial revolution could not have triumphed so easily without destroying the Indian cotton industry.[33]

> The cotton manufacture was a typical by-product of that accelerating current of international and especially colonial commerce .... Its raw material, first used in Europe mixed with linen to produce a cheaper version of that textile ('fustian'), was almost entirely colonial. The only pure cotton industry known to Europe in the early eighteenth century was that of India, whose products ('calicoes') the Eastern trading companies sold abroad and at home, where they were bitterly opposed by the domestic manufacturers of wool, linen and silk. The English woollen industry succeeded in 1700 in banning their import altogether, thus accidentally succeeded in giving the domestic cotton manufacturers of the future something like a free run of the home market. They were as yet too backward to supply it, though the first form of the modern cotton industry, calico-printing, established itself as a partial import substitution in several European countries .... For the home market it produced a substitute for linen or wool and silk hosiery; for the foreign market, so far as it could, a substitute for the superior Indian goods, particularly when war or other crises temporarily disrupted the Indian supply to export markets.[34]

Although the industrial bourgeoisie in England succeeded in prohibiting the import of Indian textiles and silk into England, the East India Company continued to export Indian products to various countries of Europe.[35] Even in decline – because of the destruction wrought by the merchant bourgeoisie – the Indian industries remained superior to the British, especially in textile manufacture which became the primary industry in the industrial revolution of

England.[36] So this superiority had to be destroyed if the rapidly growing manufacturers in England were to find markets.[37]

The first step in this direction was taken in 1769. With the rise of the power of the British bourgeoisie in Parliament came the first parliamentary interference in the company's affairs. It was decided that the company should, during each year of the term, export British merchandise, exclusive of naval and military stores, to the amount of £380,837.[38] So the directors of the company desired in a letter to the Governor of Bengal, dated 17 March 1769, that the manufacture of raw silk should be encouraged. In 1783 the House of Commons' Select Committee on administration of justice in India remarked:

> This letter contains a perfect plan of policy, both of compulsion and encouragement, which must in a considerable degree operate destructively to manufacturers of Bengal. Its effect must be to change the whole face of that industrial country, in order to render it a field of the produce of crude materials subservient to the manufacture of Great Britain.[39]

Despite the fact that the mercantile bourgeoisie was carrying out the orders of the industrial bourgeoisie, it – in particular, the monopoly companies – appeared to be a nuisance and hindrance to the rapid development of the industrial bourgeoisie. So an ideological offensive was launched against the East India Company's administration in India by Adam Smith, the theoretical mentor of the rising industrial bourgeoisie of England. He demanded that the opportunities to trade in India should be opened to all.[40] However, this could not be done without undermining the mercantile basis of the company's rule. It is interesting to note how the governor of the company, Warren Hastings, the spokesman of the mercantile school, denied the possibility of developing India into a market.[41] It is no wonder that Warren Hastings (Governor-General of India from 1772 to 1785) was attacked by England's great parliamentarians – Pitt, Fox, Burke, and Sheridan – the representatives of the rising industrial bourgeoisie (see note 35).

As a result of the actions of the industrial bourgeoisie and their parliamentary representatives, British manufactured goods were forced into India through the agency of the company's Governor-General and its commercial residents, while Indian manufactures were kept out of England by prohibitive duties. It was observed that, as early as 1769, the directors desired the manufacture of raw silk to be encouraged in Bengal, and that of silk fabrics discouraged. It was also laid down that the silk-winders should work only in the company's factories and be prohibited from working outside 'under severe penalties by the authority of the government'.[42]

Although the mandate had its desired effect, and the manufacture of cotton and raw silk declined, India was not de-industrialized until 1813. Indian textiles and silk goods were still superior to British products. However, the representatives of the British industrial bourgeoisie in Parliament were determined to promote British industries at the sacrifice of Indian industries. The export of British manufactures to India became a life and death issue for British industrial capital when Napoleon Bonaparte banned the import of British commodities into Europe (see note 36).

In 1813 an enquiry was made in the House of Commons to ascertain how India could be developed as a market for the rising British machine industry.[43] It was found that only by imposing prohibitive duties – not on the basis of the technical superiority of British machine industry – could India be transformed into a British market.

It is also a melancholy instance of the wrong done to India by the country on which she has become dependent. It was stated in evidence (in 1813) that the cotton and silk goods of India up to the period could be sold for a profit in the British market at a price from 50 to 60 per cent lower than those fabricated in England. It consequently became necessary to protect the latter by duties of 70 and 80 per cent on their value or, by positive prohibition. Had this not been the case, had not such prohibitory duties and decrees existed, the mills of Paisley and of Manchester would have been stopped in their outset, and could scarcely have been again set in motion, even by the power of steam. They were created by the sacrifice of the Indian manufacturer. Had India been independent, she would have retaliated, would have imposed preventive duties upon British goods, and would thus have preserved her own productive industry from annihilation. This act of self-defence was not permitted her; she was at the mercy of the stranger. British goods were forced upon her without paying any duty, and the foreign manufacturer employed the arm of political injustice to keep down and ultimately strangle a competitor with whom he could not have contended on equal terms.[44]

Henry St George Tucker wrote in 1823, only ten years after the date of the Parliamentary enquiry:

> the cotton fabrics, which hitherto constituted the staple of India, have not only been displaced in this country but we actually export our cotton manufactures to supply a part of the consumption of our Asiatic possessions. India is thus reduced from the state of a manufacturing to that of an agricultural country.[45]

Thus, on the basis of one-way free trade, and the prevention of direct trade between India and Europe or other foreign countries, the de-industrialization of India was made complete. Marx describes this, and the importance of India as a market for British industrial capital, thus:

> Till 1813, India had been chiefly an exporting country, while it now became an importing one; and in such a quick progression that already in 1823 the rate of exchange which had generally been 2s 6d per Rupee, declined to 2s per Rupee. *India, the great workshop of cotton manufacture for the world since immemorial times,* became now inundated with English twists and cotton stuffs. After its own produce had been excluded from England, or only admitted on the most cruel terms, British manufactures were poured into it at a small or merely nominal duty, to the ruin of the native cotton fabrics once so celebrated. In 1780, the value of the British produce and manufactures amounted to only 386,152 pounds, the bullion exported during the same year to 15,041 pounds, the total value of exports during 1780 being 12,648,616 pounds. So that Indian trade (export) amounted to only 1/32nd of the entire foreign trade. In 1850, the total exports to India from Great Britain and Ireland were 8,024,000 pounds, of which the cotton goods alone amounted to 5,220,000 pounds, so that it reached more than 1/4 of the foreign cotton trade. But, the cotton manufacture also employed now 1/8 of the population of Britain and contributed 1/12 of the whole national revenue.

After each commercial crisis, the East India trade grew of more paramount importance for the British cotton manufacturers, and the East India Continent became actually their best market. At the same rate at which the cotton manufacturers became of vital interest for the whole social frame of Great Britain East India became of vital interest for the British cotton manufacture.[46]

The irony of the situation is that the heavy hand of the state fell upon India at a time when the ideological slogan of the industrial bourgeoisie was the non-interference of the state in economic affairs. Neither Adam Smith nor Ricardo had anything to say when the policy of free trade was reversed in the case of India. The representatives of the industrial bourgeoisie knew when it was wise to remain silent. However, in 1844, a great German economist, Friedrich List, pointed out the injustice which had been perpetrated in India:

Had they sanctioned the free importation into England of Indian cotton and silk goods, the English cotton and silk manufactories must, of necessity, soon come to a stand. India had not only the advantage of cheap labour and raw material, but also the experience, the skill, and the practice of centuries. The effect of these advantages could not fail to tell under a system of free competition. But England was unwilling to found settlements in Asia in order to become subservient to India in the manufacturing industry. She strove for commercial supremacy, and felt that of two countries maintaining free trade between one another, that one would be supreme which sold manufactured goods, while that one would be subservient which could only sell agricultural produce. In the North American colonies, England had already acted on these principles in disallowing the manufacture in those colonies of even a single horse-shoe nail, and still more, that no horse-shoe nails made there should be imported into England. How could it be expected of her that she would give up her own market for manufactures, the basis of her future greatness, to a people so numerous, so thrifty, so experienced and perfect in the old system of manufacture as the Hindus?

Accordingly, England prohibited the import of the goods dealt in by her own factories, the Indian cotton and silk fabrics. The

prohibition was complete and pre-emptory. Not so much as a
thread of them would England permit to be used. She would
have none of these beautiful and cheap fabrics, but preferred to
consume her own inferior and costly stuffs .…

Was England a fool in so acting? Most assuredly according to
the theories of Adam Smith and J.B. Say, the theory of values.
For according to them, England should have bought what she
required where she could buy them cheapest and best; it was
an act of folly to manufacture for herself goods at a greater
cost than she could buy them at elsewhere, and at the same time
give away that advantage to the Continent.[47]

This makes it clear that, while British political economists were
propounding the principles of free trade in the latter half of the
eighteenth and early nineteenth centuries, they were not ready to
apply them in the case of India until Britain had crushed her
industries. (The other great colony of the British Empire, the
United States of America, was able to develop its manufacturing
power – although primarily it was an agricultural country in the
eighteenth century – by protectionism after its independence in
1776.) As E.J. Hobsbawm points out, the enthusiastic proponents of
laissez-faire conveniently ignored their own theories in the case of
India:

The one exception was India. Its abnormality leaps to the eye. It
was, for one thing, the only part of the British Empire to which
laissez-faire never applied. Its most enthusiastic champions in
Britain became bureaucratic planners when they went there, and
the most committed opponents of political colonization rarely,
and then never seriously, suggested the liquidation of British
rule .…

India was an increasingly vital market for the staple export,
cotton goods; and it became so because in the first quarter of the
nineteenth century British policy destroyed the local textile
industry as a competitor with Lancashire.[48]

After the industrial tide had turned in favour of Britain, British
cotton manufactures exported to India rose from less than one million yards in 1824 to 64 million yards in 1837.[49] During the same period,
the export of Indian cotton goods fell rapidly, never to rise again.

The impact of this process of de-industrialization on the Indian economy was devastating. Prosperous territories, towns and market places lay in ruins. The great manufacturing towns of Dacca, Murshidabad, Surat, and Malda became desolate. In 1757, Clive described the city of Murshidabad as more extensive, populous and prosperous than the city of London. Montgomery Martin reported to the Select Committee:

> The decay and destruction of Surat, of Dacca, of Murshidabad and of other places where native manufactures have been carried on, is too painful a fact to dwell upon. I do not consider that it has been in the fair course of trade; I think it has been the power of the stronger exercised over the weaker.[50]

Marx reported this wrecking of the Indian economy as follows:

> From 1818 to 1836, the export of twist from Great Britain to India rose in the proportion of 1 to 5,200. In 1824, the export of British muslins to India hardly amounted to 100,000 yards, while in 1837 it surpassed 64,000,000 yards. But at the same time, the population of Dacca decreased from 150,000 inhabitants to 20,000. This decline of Indian towns, celebrated for their fabrics, was by no means the worst consequence.[51]

He further commented in *Capital*:

> English cotton machinery produced an acute effect on India. The Governor General reported in 1834-35: 'The misery hardly finds a parallel in the history of commerce. The bones of cotton weavers are bleaching the plains of India.'[52]

As India was transformed into a market by British industrial capital, her huge imports had to be matched by exports of raw materials. In fact, throughout the whole of the nineteenth century and until the 1930s, India had a comfortable surplus of exports over imports. Even after she was reduced to the status of an agricultural country, a large transfer of capital occurred from her pre-capitalist agriculture. Table 3.1 shows the nature of India's trade in the twenty-five years preceding the First World War.

After the First World War, India's trade surplus declined considerably due to the growing impoverishment of her economy, but still the balance of trade was in her favour (Table 3.2).

TABLE 3.1 Foreign trade, 1874–99 (in millions of rupees)

Quinquennial Average	Exports	Imports	Excess Export
1874–79	630	380	250
1879–84	790	590	200
1884–89	880	610	270
1889–94	1,040	710	330
1894–99	1,070	740	330

Source: M.N. Roy, *The Future of India's Politics* (London: R. Bishop, n.d.), p. 14.

TABLE 3.2 Foreign trade in commodities, 1900–40 (in millions of rupees)

Years	Imports	Exports	Excess Export
1900–01			
1904–05	836.2	1,310.1	473.9
1910–11			
1913–14	1,530.5	2,283.0	752.5
1919–20			
1923–24	2,540.4	2,863.4	323.0
1935–36			
1939–40	1,502.2	1,808.5	306.3

Source: H. Venkatasubbiah, *The Foreign Trade of India, 1900–1940* (New Delhi: Indian Council of World Affairs, Oxford University Press), pp. 28–9.

Thus, India's imports were always less than her exports. This favourable balance of trade, however, did not indicate India's growing prosperity. The excess exports were always siphoned off to England to serve the imperial cause. Moreover, over 80 per cent of India's exports consisted of raw materials and foodstuffs. The unpaid excess exports thus led to the growing impoverishment of the peasants, and to a primitive capital accumulation which, however, did not make possible the introduction of the capitalist mode in agriculture.

Furthermore, while approximately 70 per cent of India's exports went to countries outside the Empire, roughly 70 per cent of her imports came from Britain. These imports (i.e. British exports) – the amount of surplus labour which the owners of capital in England extracted from British labourers[53] and which throughout the nineteenth and early twentieth centuries constituted the bulk of British exports to India – formed the major part of British capital.[54] Cotton goods constituted the lion's share of British exports,[55] and India was one of the major importers of British cotton goods (see Table 3.3).

TABLE 3.3 British cotton piece-goods exports, 1880–1914 (in million yards)

Years	Total	India
1880	4,496	1,813
1890	5,124	2,190
1900	5,034	2,019
1913	7,075	3,000

Source: A. Redford, *Manchester Merchants and Foreign Trade*, vol. II, Manchester, 1956.

Thus Britain was able to use India's surplus with other countries to pay for her exports to India. However, very little of the British capital formed from this triangular trade was invested in India. As Barbara Ward says:

Before the First World War, all Britain's investments, public and private, in India amounted to not much more than 10 per cent of British investments, the bulk of which had gone to the temperate lands.[56]

In fact, it was the investment of British capital in the U.S.A. in the nineteenth century that laid the base for further development of that country on the industrial path. That is why Braudel says that the victory of Britain at the battle of Plassey was not only significant for the social evolution of England, it was significant for the emergence of new forces of production in the world at large.

When civilisations clash, the consequences are dramatic. Today's world is still embroiled in them. One civilisation can get the better of another: this was the case with India following the British victory at Plassey which marked the beginning of a new era for Britain and the whole world.[57]

The new land system under the British

The process of changing India into a market and supplier of primary products which could be exported to other countries necessitated the restructuring of her land relations on a commercial basis. The new land system superseded the traditional right of the village community. Under the village community system, land was not a commodity, and it could not be alienated without the approval of the village community. But under the new system land was transformed into a commodity which could be disposed of in the market like any other. As has already been mentioned, the village community in the economically advanced areas such as Bengal had shown signs of weakening before the British conquest.

However, British intervention did not allow India to undergo the natural transition from a conglomeration of thousands of atomistic little republics to a unified economic and political national unit. Her economy had to suffer the aberrations of the existing Asiatic mode of production as well as the semi-feudal and semi-capitalist system imposed by the colonial state (see below).

India's agriculture was gradually commercialized, but it did not undergo the capitalist mode of production. Marx has described the historical significance of capitalism in the sphere of agriculture:

> It is one of the great outcomes of the capitalist mode of production, that it transforms agriculture from a merely empirical and mechanically perpetuated process of the least developed part of society into a consciously scientific application of agronomics, so far as this is at all feasible under the conditions going with private property; that it detaches property in land on the one side from the relations between master and servant, and on the other hand totally separates land as an instrument of production from property in land and landowners .... The rationalizing of agriculture on the one hand, and thus rendering it capable of operation on a social scale and the reduction *ad absurdum* of private property in land on the other hand, these are the great merits of the capitalist mode of production. Like all its other historical advances, it brought these also by first completely pauperizing the direct producers.[58]

This was true in the case of western nations where the feudal mode of production was replaced; in the process, the cultivators were pauperized. But in the case of India, British capital was not interested in introducing the capitalist mode of production.[59] Its interest lay in the capitalistic penetration of India: the share of commodity extraction from agriculture had to be considerably increased without disturbing fundamentally the mode of production itself. To this end new land tenure systems were brought into being without undermining the traditional concept of the state as the supreme landlord. This change in the land system under the colonial government has been succinctly described by Wadia and Merchant:

> When the East India Company acquired political control, they took over the traditional system .... It was assumed that the State was the supreme landlord. In the place of the traditional share of the Government in the produce paid by the village communities as a whole, there was introduced a system of fixed payments in cash assessed on land which had no reference to good or bad harvests. In most cases the assessment was individual, whether levied directly on the cultivator or on landlords appointed by the State. The land revenue was considered as a rent rather than tax. Under British rule, the system of assessing and collecting revenue varied according to the varying circumstances of different provinces and to suit administrative convenience ....
>
> Land tenures in India may be defined as the system of rights and responsibilities of individuals owning or cultivating the land, *vis-à-vis* the state, regarding the payment of revenue. The principal land tenure in India may be classified: (1) on the basis of the relation between the holder and the Government as Zamindari and Ryotwari; (2) on the basis of the duration of the tenure as permanent and temporary. The Zamindari system makes the zamindar the holder of all lands from the government. He is responsible for the land revenue, the land being cultivated by tenants. Under the Ryotwari system the land is held directly by the ryot or occupant who is in most cases individually responsible to Government for land revenue. The Zamindari Settlement is ordinarily known as the Permanent Settlement, though there was another type known as Temporary Zamindari system....
>
> The Ryotwari Tenure is characterized by the following features: (a) The principle of the state ownership of all lands

including waste lands underlies the system. (b) The holder of the land is a mere occupant, having the right to use, bequeath, transfer and relinquish the occupancy of the holding. He holds the land so long as he pays the land revenue .... (c) Every holder of land is individually responsible for the payment of land revenue. (d) The assessment is fixed for a period of 20 or 30 years and is periodically revised under a survey settlement. The successive settlements gave an opportunity to the Government to raise the land revenue.[60]

The Permanent Settlement was first introduced in Bengal by Lord Cornwallis in 1793 and later extended to parts of Bihar, Orissa and Madras. Temporary settlements of the *zamindari* variety were made in U.P., the Central Provinces, and West Punjab. The *Ryotwari* system prevailed in Southern Madras, Bombay, Berar, East Punjab and in some areas of Assam and Coorg.[61]

It has been claimed by many (including Marxists) that by introducing the *zamindari* system, the British created a feudal class in India. But nothing could be further from the truth. The *zamindars*, or the landlords, brought into being by the fiat of the state, had no independent power base. Unlike Europe, where a naturally grown pre-existing feudal class fought with the emerging bourgeoisie for the control of the state, the *zamindars* (landlords) in India were the creation of a state which represented the interests of the metropolitan bourgeoisie. Though the inherited state apparatus of the Moghuls became subservient to the metropolitan interest, it remained supreme over the indigenous social classes. That is why Marx termed the *zamindari* system a caricature of English landed property and wondered what kind of landlord was the *zamindar*.

> a curious sort of English landlord was the zamindar, receiving only one-tenth of the rent, while he had to make over nine-tenths of it to the Government. A curious sort of French peasant was the ryot [in Ryotwari areas] without any permanent title in the soil, and with the taxation changing every year in proportion to his harvest.[62]

With profound insight, Marx analysed the character of the tenurial system, the state's supremacy and the method of extracting the surplus:

Thus, in Bengal, we have a combination of English landlordism, of the Irish middleman system, of the Austrian system, ... transforming the landlord into the tax-gatherer and of the Asiatic system making the State the real landlord. In Madras and Bombay we have a French peasant proprietor who is at the same time a serf and a metayer of the State. The drawbacks of all these various systems accumulate upon him without his enjoying any of their redeeming features. The ryot is subject, like the French peasant, to the extortion of the private usurer; but he has no permanent title in his land like the French peasant. Like the serf he is forced to cultivation, but he is not secured against want like the serf. Like the metayer he has to divide his produce with the State, but the State is not obliged with regard to him, to advance the funds and the stock as it is obliged to do with regard to the metayer. In Bengal as in Madras and Bombay, under the zamindari as under the ryotwari, the ryots – and they form 11/12ths of the whole Indian population – have been wretchedly pauperized; and if they are, morally speaking, not sunk as low as the Irish cottiers, they owe it to their climate, the men of the South being possessed of less wants, and of more imagination than the men of the North.[63]

Marx makes it clear that, while he was aware that the new land systems would fundamentally change the nature of production in land, he was also aware that it was the state which would be the biggest beneficiary from the change and would remain supreme over the social classes that were being created through the transformation of land into a commodity:

The zamindari and the ryotwari were both of them agrarian revolutions, effected by British ukases, and opposed to each other; the one aristocratic, the other democratic; the one a caricature of English landlordism, the other of French peasant proprietorship; but pernicious both combining the most contradictory character – both made not for the people, who cultivate the soil, nor for the holder, who owns it, but for the government that taxes it.[64]

The new land systems soon began to show results, by transforming Indian agriculture into a sphere of primitive capital accumulation for the industrialization of the metropolitan centre (a process already discussed above).

With the passage of time, the *zamindars* degenerated into a selfish parasitic class of absentee landlords. Many *zamindars* also leased out their interests, and the middlemen leased out in turn, thus creating a long chain of rent receivers and rent payers who intervened between the state and the actual cultivators (see chapter 7). These people, the *zamindars* and the intermediary rent receivers, could spend the surplus produced by the cultivators, not on the improvement of agriculture, but on luxury goods imported from Great Britain.

As stated above, under the *ryotwari* system the settlement was made directly with the cultivator; he was recognized as the owner of the land he tilled. The *Ryotwari* had this advantage over the Permanent Settlement from the ruler's point of view: being subject to periodical reassessment it secured the entire spoils for the government.[65]

One of the reasons, as explained earlier, for the introduction of the new land regulations was to replace production for village use by that for the market. As the rural economy was partially monetized and the rate of rent gradually increased, the peasant's need for cash also increased. He was thus forced to produce not only for home consumption but also for the market.

Moreover, the government's insistence on a regular repayment of rent, irrespective of the quality of the harvest, led to the peasants' increasing indebtedness. With the growing burden of land revenue, their dependence on credit also rose. The nearest person the peasant could approach for a loan was the village moneylender. But with the commercialization of agriculture and the introduction of the British legal system, which recognized the absolute right of alienation of land, a significant change occurred in the function of the moneylender. He could now appropriate land for non-payment of a loan, something which would have been impossible under the village community system.

The transformation of agriculture on the basis of private property in land, without a corresponding introduction of the capitalist mode of production, created a situation in which the peasants' burden of debt increased steeply and landownership began to pass from the cultivators to the moneylenders. This process of commercialization is described by D.R. Gadgil:

The commercialization of agriculture had progressed most in those tracts where the crops were largely grown for export out of the country. This was so in the Burma rice area, the Punjab wheat area, the jute area of Eastern Bengal and the Khandesh, Gujerat and Berar cotton tracts.

These circumstances were the payment of the government assessments and interest of the moneylenders. To pay these two dues, the cultivators had to rush into the market just after the harvest, and to sell a large part of their produce at whatever price it fetched.[66]

As a result of this commercialization of agriculture a large class of parasitic landowners, moneylenders and land speculators came into existence and more and more people were drawn to these sources of income. Furthermore, since British rule destroyed the urban industries many uprooted people with no other employment fell back on agriculture, which in this way became the only source of livelihood for most of the people in India.

Thus the legendary poverty of India today – in contrast to its legendary riches which in the past had attracted adventurers from the West – is the result of colonial rule. Paul Baran's classic description of the wretchedness of the subjugated people possibly fits no other country better than India:

the peoples who came into the orbit of the Western capitalist expansion found themselves in the twilight of feudalism and capitalism enduring the worst features of both worlds, and the entire impact of imperialist subjugation to boot. To oppression by their feudal lords, ruthless but tempered by tradition, was added domination by foreign and domestic capitalists, callous and limited only by what the traffic would bear.... Their exploitation was multiplied; yet its fruits were not to increase their productive wealth; these went abroad or served to support a parasitic bourgeoisie at home. They lived in abysmal misery, yet they had no prospect of a better tomorrow. They existed under capitalism, yet there was no accumulation of capital.[67]

Referring to India, Baran adds:

it should not be overlooked that India, if left to herself, might have found in the course of time a shorter and surely less tortuous road towards a better and richer society. That on that road she would have had to pass through the purgatory of a bourgeois revolution, that a long phase of capitalist development would have been the inevitable price that she would have had to pay for progress, can hardly be doubted. It would have been, however, an entirely different India (and an entirely different world), had she been allowed – as some more fortunate countries were – to realize her destiny in her own way, to employ her resources for her own benefit, and to harness her energies and abilities for the advancement of her own people.[68]

The emergence of trading town and a new indigenous bourgeoisie

The material base which the British established had the worst features, as pointed out by Baran, of feudalism and capitalism – and, we may add, of the existing Asiatic mode of production. It has been shown that, as a result of the decay of urban industries, many old cities fell into oblivion in the late eighteenth and early nineteenth centuries. However, new trading cities established by the British began to emerge after the second half of the eighteenth century. Very few of these cities had any industrial activity: most were commercial towns needed for the capitalist penetration of India. Some of them were offshoots of the railway system established by the British. Lord Dalhousie's famous minute on railways clearly shows why their establishment became indispensable, if India was to be made a market for British goods and a source of raw materials:

> The commercial and social advantages which India would derive from their establishment are, I truly believe, beyond all present calculation.... England is calling aloud for cotton which India does already produce in some degree, and would produce sufficient in quality and plentiful in quantity, if only there were provided the fitting means of conveyance for it from distant plains to the several ports adopted for its shipment. Every increase of facilities for trade has been attended, as we have seen, with an increased demand for articles of European produce in the most distant markets of India.[69]

Therefore the cities that were growing at this period were the centres which were being used for the exploitation of the Indian market.[70] As Gadgil has pointed out:

We have no reason to suppose that the urban population in India was in any way growing between 1800 and 1872. The only cities to which any growth at this time can be ascribed were the ports of Calcutta, Bombay and Madras and a few places in the interior like Cawnpore; but, on the other hand, there was certainly a great decrease to be accounted for in the population of a large number of old towns, e.g., Dacca, Murshidabad, Lucknow, Tanjore, etc. Indeed, considering that modern industry was almost non-existent in India at this time... it seems more probable that the percentage of the urban population in India was bigger at the beginning of the century than in 1872. In 1872 the percentage of urban population was 8.7 per cent.... In Western countries the percentages of the urban population towards the beginning of the nineteenth century were: England and Wales 21.3, Scotland 17.0, France 9.5, Prussia 7.25, Russia 3.7, U.S.A. 3.8.[71]

Bombay, Calcutta and Madras were major ports through which Indian cotton, wheat, rice, jute, tea, indigo, rubber, etc. were exported to other countries, and through which textile products, hardware and manufactured goods from England were imported. The other important cities were Delhi, Amritsar, Lucknow, Ahmedabad, Bangalore, etc. These were also important railway junctions connecting the whole country through a vast network of railways. Marx thought the railways would be the forerunners of modern industry in India. He wrote:

I know that the English millocracy intend to endow India with railways with the exclusive view of extracting at diminished expense the cotton and other raw materials for their manufactures. But when you have once introduced machinery into the locomotion of a country which possesses iron and coal, you are unable to withhold it from its fabrication.... The railway system will, therefore, become in India truly the forerunner of modern industry.[72]

British capitalists, for the extraction of raw materials and commercial penetration, had to invest in railways, tea, coffee, jute, coal, iron ore, and other mining industries.[73] The Indian bourgeoisie, who, collecting and transporting raw materials and delivering British manufactures to the hinterland, as agents or businessmen also owned capital, could not be excluded. As commercial penetration grew, the Indian trading class was gradually drawn into industrial activities, but their basic capital was formed from commerce.

British capital was mainly invested in those areas of the Indian economy which did not come into conflict with metropolitan industrial interests, and was confined to such enterprises as railways, coal mines, jute mills, tea, coffee and sugar plantations – industries related to the production and export of raw materials. Later, British investments in steel, cement and chemicals were ancillary to the railways and other raw material industries. For the period 1850–1914, the total British investment in India was 500 million pounds. However, there was little capital export from Britain to India. Only for the seven years 1856–1862 was there an excess of exports over imports totalling 22.5 million pounds.[74] Normally India's exports, as has been explained, were always in excess of her imports.

There were three important industries in India by 1880 – jute, coal and cotton (excluding the railways which were owned by the government). There were twenty jute mills, fifty-six coal mines and fifty-six cotton mills.[75] The first two were mainly owned by the British, and it was only in the cotton industry that Indian merchants played a priming role. Why did Indian entrepreneurship play this important role in the development of the cotton industry? They knew from their experience as traders of British cotton goods that the country had a big market for textiles: local industry had declined in the first half of the nineteenth century. Moreover, since the market consisted of private Indian consumers, the discriminatory purchasing policy, as applied in the purchase of railway stores, could not be effective here.

Once started, Indian entrepreneurs expanded their activities into other fields. As Marx had hinted, Indian capitalists came into their own, independent of their British counterparts. In this emergence of the Indian industrial bourgeoisie during British rule, capital was first accumulated in trade (even in money-lending and landownership) and later invested in industry. This process was further facilitated by a system unique to India known as the managing agency system.

The managing agency system was the progeny of an older system known as the 'agency house'. In the late eighteenth and early nineteenth centuries, company servants engaged in private trade. There were also many free merchants trying to gain a foothold in the lucrative East India trade. At first there were frequent conflicts between these two groups. Later, however, the successful free merchants were joined by the company servants who brought their past gains with them into their joint enterprises. Agency houses thus emerged which attracted capital: this could be invested both in commerce and industry. They did not import any capital from England. By 1790 there were fifteen agency houses in Calcutta:

> The most prominent among them were messrs. Ferguson, Fairlie and Company; Paxton, Cockrell and Delisle; Lambart and Ross; Colvins and Bazell; and Joseph Baretto. They controlled the country trade, financed indigo and sugar manufacture, cornered the government contracts, ran three banks and four insurance companies at Calcutta and speculated in public securities.[76]

By the 1820s the agency houses had invested capital in indigo cultivation, cotton, screws, and clocks. In 1826, six of the big agency houses went bankrupt when the price of indigo fell on the London market.[77] By the middle of the 1830s the other agency houses had met the same fate.

The failure of these early agency houses was primarily due to their dependence on a limited number of exports and agricultural commodities. Moreover, the nature of the organization was such that it had very little capacity for shock absorption. Whenever there was a crisis, the panicky partners rushed to withdraw their capital, thus accelerating their collapse.

> On the ruins of these agency houses a new organisation of British capitalist enterprise arose – the managing agency system – which ushered in the industrial development of India and with it a new age.[78]

The managing agency system no longer depended on the savings of the company's servants. The managing agents used to take charge of the construction of buildings, purchase of machinery, securing of technical personnel and marketing, but their most important function was to supply the capital. Generally, the managing agents gathered capital from persons who had money but no knowledge about running industries. They also promoted the joint stock companies and arranged for financing by acting as guarantors of the concerns. The remuneration of the agency was a commission either in terms of gross profits, total sales or total production. The managing agencies, at first predominantly British, built up vast interests by a process of amalgamation, absorption and expansion.

> From the start, the lack of modern industry encouraged the agencies to seek self-sufficiency, each developing its own sources of raw materials, its own services, and a substantial market within its own operations. Martin Burn's steel output went largely into its railway interests, alternatively into its constructional engineering activities, which found further support in its cement interests, and so on. Andrew Yule's jute mills required electricity and coal supplies which in turn required engineering facilities, transport and the host of ancillary materials and services to be found within that complex.[79]

Thus the managing agency system provided economies of scale and the establishment of modern finance capitalism in India was made through their agency. This process also saw the rise of cartels and trusts.

The industries which could not depend upon huge sources of capital, on banks, insurance companies or investment trusts, were severely handicapped: the industries owned by the Indians were in this category.

The overwhelming influence of British finance capital on the Indian economy, in fact, was the greatest disadvantage Indian industrialists suffered in their competition against the British. The British managing agents were more powerful than their Indian counterparts, could furnish large capital sums and could borrow advantageously if necessary from such places as the London market. Moreover, British finance capital worked through the banking system in conjunction with the government's financial and exchange policy.

There were British and foreign exchange banks, as well as Indian joint stock banks, the weakest in the group. This weakness, to a great extent, emanated from government policy. While foreign finance capital operated in India unfettered, Indian capital had to function under various vexatious rules and regulations imposed by the government.

The Indian Industrial Commission stated in 1919:

> The lack of financial facilities is at present one of the most serious difficulties in the way of extension of Indian industries.[80]

Buchanan, an American historian of Indian economics, wrote in 1934:

> Events of the last decade tended to increase this difficulty [the lack of finance]. Comparisons with western countries in terms of banks or banking capital per capita are meaningless, but even as compared with Japan, India is ridiculously backward. Whereas in 1926 India had, excluding the Imperial Bank of India, 73 banks with a total paid-up capital, surplus and reserves of Rs 119,200,000 ($42,912,000); Japan had on June 30, 1927, excluding the Bank of Japan, 1,513 banks with paid-up capital, surplus and reserves of Yen 2,850,324,000 ($1,425,162,000).[81]

Thus it is no wonder that the Indian industries were starving from capital shortage.

Although there was no dearth of British capital,[82] it was never invested into sectors which could have affected Britain's export market in India. This was expressed in a statement by the British economist George Paish to the Royal Statistical Society:

> One of the most noteworthy characteristics of the British investor is his objection to place capital in any enterprise or in any country for the matter of that, the development of which appears to be against the interest of the motherland.[83]

Thus, whatever industrialization took place in India, it had to battle against intense opposition from British finance capital, both in the political and financial fields. The British metropolitan industrialists were opposed to Indian capital spilling into sectors other than the development of raw materials and extractive industries. In these circumstances the only area in which Indian capital made some headway was the cotton industry. However, even in this field Indian industrialists had to face stiff opposition from Manchester. When the weak Indian cotton industry began to emerge in the 1860s and 1870s there was a demand in England for the removal of import duties on cotton goods (into India) which (in the absence of Indian cotton industries) had been imposed for revenue purposes. The Manchester Chamber of Commerce presented a memorandum to this effect in 1874 and a resolution was adopted in the House of Commons in 1877. Lord Salisbury, in forwarding this resolution, noted with alarm that:

> five more mills were about to begin work [in India], and it was
> estimated that, by the end of March 1877, there would be
> 1,231,284 spindles employed in India.[84]

The infant Indian industries needed tariff protection from the well-established industries of the West. But in the name of free trade, protection was always denied them.[85] Not only that; in 1896 a 3½ per cent import was levied on imported cotton cloth for revenue purposes. To neutralize the effect of this duty, a 3½ percent duty was levied on all cloth made in the Indian mills. This duty was imposed at the insistence of Manchester and Lancashire industrialists. To quote Lord Curzon:

> ever since India was ordered to abolish her custom tariffs
> in 1875, it has been in the main in response to Lancashire
> pressure that the successive readjustments of this policy have
> been reintroduced.[86]

In 1902, at a large public meeting in London, an Indian economist protested that it would be wrong to compare India's industrial development with that of Japan, where protection was being adopted as rapidly as the treaty powers would permit. An Under-Secretary of State for India was in the chair, and expressed the apparent conclusion of nearly all present as follows:

> everybody was agreed that no stone should be left unturned to
> enable India to produce, as far as possible what she now
> imported. But the primary consideration of the matter must not
> be forgotten, that India had for centuries past been an

agricultural country, and he did not see how the government of any country could suddenly change all that had gone before, merely by a desire to do so.... The timid opponents might have suggested that Japan was not being changed from an agricultural country 'merely by a desire' but by definite governmental action.[87]

Many important British officials, including Lord Curzon, were in favour of rapid industrialization of India. They could foresee that India would decline as a market unless her economy was improved. An Indian Civil Service officer said that the British Indian Government should follow Japan's lead and that 'the native character was well adopted to the factory system' yet 'almost nothing ... had been done to restore the decaying industries of India, and launch her people on new careers'.[88] Another official wanted 'duties to encourage Indian arts and manufactures and insisted that the question of protection for India'[89] should be decided, not on English grounds or by English people in England, but 'by the government in Calcutta in the interests of India alone'.[90]

For development, Indian industries needed not only money and protection, but also technical know-how. However, the government of India did very little to import technical knowledge. This attitude of the metropolitan government towards India's industrialization was described by the American economist Buchanan as follows:

> A governing group which understood its people and really cared for their welfare should make an effort to teach them better ways of earning a living. This the government of Japan tried to do and as a result the Japanese are about two generations in advance of India. While Indian craftsmen are literally starving, unemployed, Japanese of the same group are learning to operate modern machinery. Often this was set up by the government itself for demonstration to both capitalists and labourers; and as soon as possible the home market was preserved to the home producers. There have been anomalies in the Japanese protective system but it has 'worked'.[91]

As a result, whatever progress Indian industrialists made before independence, they made without any help from the colonial state.

In fact, in the nineteenth and early twentieth centuries, despite many impediments raised by the state, which operated in the interests of the metropolitan bourgeoisie. Indian industries came into being.

The emergence of the proletariat and the rise of a new middle class

The social class with the most progressive potential that arose under British rule was the proletariat. As was noted above, large-scale industrialization started in earnest in India after 1880. By 1894, the size of the industrial labour force, i.e. workers employed in factories, was of the order of 350,000. The major industries at that time were textiles and jute. Table 3.4 shows the numerical growth of organized industry and the proletariat since 1894.

One should note that, compared to India's population, the size of the industrial proletariat was remarkably small. The 1931 Census Report commented:

> The number of workers employed in organised industry is extraordinarily low for a population the size of India's, and the daily average number of hands employed by establishments in British India to which the Factories Act applies is only 1,553,169...[92]

TABLE 3.4 The workers employed in organized industry

Year	No. of factories	Average daily number of workers
1894	815	350,000
1919	3,440	1,171,000
1939	10,466	1,751,000

Data obtained from annual Statistical Abstracts (the figures are not strictly comparable as the definition of 'factory' was modified over time).

This was quite natural: as explained above, the industrial revolution in England destroyed the artisan classes both in England and India. But while in England the pauperized artisans, along with the ex-propriated peasants, were absorbed into the expanding industries, in India agriculture became their sole source of livelihood. As a result, the number of landless workers continued to increase and very few of them could be employed in industries. According to an International Labour Organization report of 1938:

> The total number of agricultural labourers which was given as 21.5 million [including underemployed] in 1921 was shown by the census of 1931 to be over 31.5 million, of whom 23 million were estimated by the Indian Franchise Committee in 1931 to be landless, while the total number of non-agricultural labourers, as estimated by the Franchise Committee, was 25 million.[93]

This vast industrial reserve army kept the wage level of industrial workers depressed to the 'vital minimum' below which reproduction of the labourer was not possible. Table 3.5 indicates that there had been no increase in the real wages of factory workers during more than half a century (1880 to 1938). Later it will be seen that the condition of the industrial proletariat has not improved much in post-independent India either.

TABLE 3.5 Changes in the economic condition of industrial workers, 1880–1938

Years	Money wages	Cost of living	Real wages
1880–89	87	69	127
1890–99	94	85	112
1900–09	107	97	111
1910–19	135	143	98
1920–29	211	207	103
1930–38	184	143	129

Source: Jurgen Kuczynski, 'The Condition of the Industrial Worker in the English Colonies' (second half of the chapter on India), included in V.B. Singh (ed.), *The Economic History of India*, p. 611.

An industrial bourgeoisie, as has been shown came into existence in India in the second half of the nineteenth century; the commercial bourgeoisie was, of course, already on the scene. At the same time, a new middle class consisting of government employees, lawyers, doctors and other professionals began to form in the British-established towns. This class was mainly recruited from the traditional 'literati' class which had been serving the administrative apparatus of the Moghuls and its potentates. It should not be forgotten that even when in decline the central authority (under the Moghuls) and its agents exerted vexatious control over the rising bourgeoisie.

In Indian tradition, public employment continued to be more valued than any other occupation. It should be noted that throughout the Orient these occupations, although they enjoyed considerable state patronage, were subservient to the state. Like the mandarins in China, the literati in India were dependent on the state.

> In the absence of a national system of education, however, the scholarly professions were dependent on royal favour or private munificence. Abul Fazal cites a number of instances in which learned men had either to lose their *jaigirs* or their very life for a show of independence. Abdul Qadir, whose duty it was to say daily prayers at the audience hall of Fatehpur Sikri, where scholars assembled for debates and discussions, had his considerable *jaigir* cancelled because he refused to say prayers at the private residence of Akbar. Maulana Alauddin ... happened to occupy a seat at a *darbar* [audience hall] in front of that of a leading officer of government. When asked to go back, he retorted: 'Why should not a learned man stand in front of fools?' The result was that he had to leave the hall to which he never returned again. Mir Nurullah, an eminent jurist and for a long time *qazi* of Lahore, offended the emperor by a 'hasty word' for which he was executed.[94]

Despotism was thus all pervasive. But public officials and the literati, being nearer to the state, had more social prestige and political power than members of other professions.

This situation did not change, even under British rule, because its cause was rooted in the social milieu. The education system, the mechanism through which these classes – public officials and literati – were formed can best be understood if it is contrasted with that of the West. The Western 'merchant capitalists' of the fifteenth and sixteenth centuries established schools with an emphasis on the education of the laity to suit their growing requirements for geographical and scientific knowlede. These in time broke down the ecclesiastical monopoly of the educated professions. The Indian educated class, 'which the British aimed at creating, was to be a class of imitators, not an originator of new values and methods'.[95] The West encouraged education to satisfy the needs of a developing economy. Max Weber, in his *General Economic History*, has shown what an important role Western education (in particular the process of rationalization) has played in the development of the capitalist economy.[96] Unlike the West, India, under the British, proceeded to encourage the type of education which would produce a class intended to 'develop' the economy in the interest of the metropolitan bourgeoisie. Moreover, the traditional bias in India for administrative jobs and against commercial and industrial occupations led to the gearing of the educational machinery to satisfy the needs of the public service, thus perpetuating the old emphasis on literary education.[97]

It must also be noted, in the analysis of the Indian educated middle class, that such a class had a structurally different origin from that of the West. This phenomenon probably persuaded Bernier to pronounce that there was no middle class in India:

> In Delhi, there is no middle state. A man must be either of the highest rank or live miserably.[98]

There was, however, a class of literati in India that, unlike in the West, did not emerge from the rising bourgeoisie, but was a 'parasitic class' subsisting on state patronage.

> The Indian middle class historically had ... a different origin from that of its counterpart in the West. There, the middle class was mainly composed of merchants and industrialists together with intellectuals and people belonging to the learned professions; these people did not depend upon agriculture for their livelihood, but some of them might purchase estates for the sake of prestige and profit. The middle class in India, on the other hand, had its roots in the agrarian system of the country and it largely lived on the profits of agricultural industry.[99]

The various professional classes that emerged in the West were rooted in the expanding bourgeois economy. They developed gradually with the economy. Speaking of the non-existence of similar professional classes in pre-British India, Moreland says:

> There were at this time no lawyers, very few if any professional teachers, no journalists or politicians, no engineers, no forms of employment corresponding to modern railways ... and if we remove these from middle classes as they exist today, we shall find that there is little left, beyond the families dependent on the various public offices.[100]

The public officials and literati were, in fact, the nuclei from which grew the educated middle class in India. Public offices, both in pre-British India and under the British, were the instruments through which the economy was channelled. He who had control over public offices had control over the economy. This was due to the fact that the bourgeoisie, until very late, did not constitute any political element in the Indian body politic, and hence did not or could not play the role of its European counterpart.

The professional middle classes were created by the British to meet her administrative needs. The British government had to organize a huge and extensive state machinery to administer the country. It was not possible to staff this huge machine by bringing in educated people from Britain other than to fill the upper posts. Moreover, the capitalist penetration of the country needed youths educated in the English language. So, in 1835, English was made the medium of instruction of higher learning and the official language by Lord William Bentinck, then the Governor-General of India.[101]

It should be pointed out, however, that the Christian missionaries – inspired by a proselytizing spirit – had laid the foundation of modern education in India long before the government took any step in that direction. But their attempts were feeble and could not satisfy the growing needs of the colonial economy. Another source of English education were the British liberals. They thought that by 'Anglicizing' the Indians, they would lead them towards the path of light. Some Indians, like Rammohan Roy, who is regarded as the pioneer of modern education in India, shared this view.[102] It is interesting to note that most of the articulate Orientalists were not Indians:

The curious fact is that the Orientalists were almost all Englishmen in the service of the Company, whereas almost all Indians of repute were Anglicists.[103]

As a true representative of the bourgeoisie (though not belonging to that class), Rammohan expressed very succinctly why English learning was necessary for the Indians:

> If it had been intended to keep the British nation in ignorance of real knowledge, the Baconian philosophy would not have been allowed to displace the system of the schoolmen which was best calculated to perpetuate their ignorance. In the same manner, the Sanskrit system of education would be the best calculated to keep this country in darkness if that had been the policy of the British legislature.[104]

However, despite the attempts of the Christian missionaries and the liberals, English could not secure many adherents until it was made the administrative language in 1835. It is also noteworthy that the students who pioneered the learning of English had, in most cases, a comprador background:

> It is the Hindus of Calcutta, the Sircars [i.e., the agents] and their connexions and their descendants and relations of Sircars of former days, those who have risen through their connexions with the English and with public offices, men who hold or seek employments in which knowledge of English is a necessary qualification. These are the classes of persons to whom the study of English is as yet confined.[105]

How great was the lure of public offices for the Indian literati could be guessed from the fact that, in the 1830s, according to Adam's report, more Hindus in Bengal were learning Persian than were Muslims.

> With regard to scholars, there are only 9 Hindu to 149 Musalman students of Arabic and consequently 2087 Hindus to 1409 Musalmans who are learning Persian. The small comparative number of Arabic students who are Hindus and the large comparative number of Persian scholars of the same class seem

to admit of only one explanation, viz, that the study of Persian has been forced by the practice of government. [106]

Persian was the cultural language of the upper class Muslims and the official language until 1835. Hindus were learning Persian because, as agents of the employees of the East India Company, they were more prosperous than the Muslims. But their prosperity depended on their access to the government.

So the middle class which emerged in India on the basis of English education was not a result of the growing economy; it was an offshoot of British rule. The colonial state had no intention of making education universal: its interests were best served by keeping the Indian middle class elitist in nature as in the past. The rationale was expressed by Macaulay thus:

> We must at present do our best to form a class who may be interpreters between us and the millions whom we govern; a class of persons, Indian in blood and colour, but English in taste, in opinions, in morals and in intellect. [107]

At the same time, this class would develop India's resources in the form of raw materials for the metropolitan industries and secure an increasing demand for metropolitan goods. As the Educational Despatch clearly states, the advancement of English education

> will teach the natives of India the marvellous results of the employment of labour and capital, rouse them to emulate us in the development of the vast resources of their country, guide them in their efforts, and gradually but certainly, confer upon them all the advantages which accompany the healthy increase of wealth and commerce; and at the same time, secure to us a large and more certain supply of many articles necessary for our manufacturers and extensively consumed by all classes of our population, as well as an almost inexhaustible demand for the produce of the British labour. [108]

English education was thus found useful for the economic as well as political requirements of the British rule in India. Although the state policy of the government, and such well-intentioned persons as Trevelyan and Adam, was to broaden its scope, it was found practicable to limit it to the upper and middle classes. To quote Trevelyan:

> It was absolutely necessary to make a selection, and they therefore selected the upper and middle classes as the first object of their attention, because, by educating them first, they would soonest be able to extend the same 'advantages' to the rest of the people.[109]

It was believed that by educating these classes first, because of their previous monopoly of education, it would be easier to educate the masses through them. But this 'infiltration theory of education' did not succeed because the British capitalist economy failed to expand in the colony; but the middle classes created by the British rule expanded more than the demand. So the middle classes were concerned more with getting employment than with educating the masses.

In the West, the concept of middle-class education became universal with the growth of capitalism. It was rooted in the freedom of opportunity, the concept of *laissez-faire*, the antithesis of mercantilism or a monopolist concept of the economy and education. As a distorted form of capitalism was implanted on India's social structure, which to a great extent remained embedded in 'the Asiatic mode of production', it was natural that the middle classes in India (as well as in other Asian countries except Japan, which had become an industrial nation) should remain elitist. When Gunnar Myrdal, in a recent economic survey of the Indian sub-continent, criticizes the 'educated unemployed' of India for their contempt for manual work, he fails to take into consideration the institutional framework of this attitude. The concept of the dignity of labour is a capitalist concept which was not to be found anywhere in the world before the rise of capitalism. Both the Greek and Roman philosophers, including Plato and Aristotle, considered manual work as detrimental to intellectual growth. This attitude was a natural corollary of the slave mode of production.

Furthermore, as has already been observed, because of the obstructed growth of industries and excessive pressure on agriculture, very few opportunities were left in non-agricultural fields in India, and there was tremendous competition among the English-educated middle class for the public offices and occupations that came into existence as a result of British rule.

From the foregoing discussion it emerges that the rise of colonial power in India hindered the possibility of the transformation of the nascent capitalism of pre-British India into industrial capitalism. The spread of trade and industry – that in the process of gradual evolution could have led to the birth of a unified capitalist economy out of the decay of atomistic village economies – was aborted by the ruin of Indian industry. Agriculture, to a great extent, was commercialized and village land was transformed into a commodity by the colonial state, thus facilitating the transfer of resources from India to the metropolitan centre. This process of capitalist penetration of agriculture, which stopped short of the transition to a fully-fledged capitalist mode of production, resulted in the creation of a social formation which was partly Asiatic, partly feudal and partly capitalist, where the state still remained independent of any class control. Due to the obstructed growth of industries, the bourgeoisie remained too weak to make the state functionaries subservient to its own interests. This weakness of the bourgeoisie became even more manifest after independence.

4 Socialism in India: an ideology of state hegemony

Prolegomena

In the second and third chapters the reasons why the state in India, during the pre-British and British periods, remained independent of class control are discussed. It was the result of a unique development of productive forces determined by geography, that in turn conditioned the development of the relations of production. The hegemony of the state, *vis-à-vis* the social classes, was at the root of the weakness of Indian polity. Unlike the West, the Indian bourgeoisie could not depend on the state to advance its own interests. In fact the state and major social classes – revenue and money interests – were antagonists. This was the reason why the rising Indian bourgeoisie, in spite of its immense economic power, was defeated by the British bourgeoisie which was backed by its own state.

It has also been seen how the colonial state, as an agent of the metropolitan bourgeoisie, encouraged the development of a comprador, indigenous bourgeoisie, but when the native bourgeoisie gradually began to acquire power, its further development was thwarted by various fiscal policies. The further weakening of the Indian bourgeoisie stemmed from its failure to exercise its own control over the state in the sense that the colonial (metropolitan) state neither governed nor ruled in its interests.

Now it is time to examine how the weakness of the bourgeoisie encouraged the state to take an active, participative role in the industrialization of the nation; the bourgeoisie's reaction to this state participation; and how this role was legitimated by the state in the name of 'socialism'.

Economic conditions on the eve of independence and the weakness of the bourgeoisie

At the time of independence the Indian bourgeoisie was too weak to initiate large-scale industrialization on its own. How weak it was can be guessed from the fact that in the year 1 April 1948 to 31 March 1949, the share of industry in the national income was only 17 per cent, while that of agriculture was 48 per cent. Even the income from commerce, communication and transport exceeded that of industry: it was 19.5 per cent.[1] Again, in industry itself, the share of organized industry was only one-fifth of the total. According to the First Report of the National Income Committee, while large-scale industry produced goods worth Rs 100 crores (in 1948–9), the share of small enterprises (artisan and small-scale industry) amounted to Rs 500 crores.[2] The bulk of consumer goods, such as coarse clothes, utensils, etc., was supplied by the unorganized industries, much of which was not even monetized. Of the Indian rural economy, 45 per cent was not monetized in 1952.[3] This 45 per cent of the rural economy, of course, depended on artisan industries with whom the cultivators had a barter relationship. The weakness of the bourgeoisie could also be gathered from the fact that while in every one of the capitalist countries the proportion of people in industry had been increasing at the cost of agriculture, in India the reverse was the case (see below, Table 4.2).

Another way of assessing the strength of the bourgeoisie could be based on its size. In this respect, too, we find that in 1950–51, tax-paying income recipients constituted only 0.6 per cent of all income recipients and they commanded only 4.7 per cent of all total disposable incomes.[4] Moreover, a person was taxable at the meagre income level of Rs 4200[5] (approximately $840) per year. If, from those liable to pay income tax the taxable salary earners and professionals are deducted (for which we do not have any data), the size of the bourgeoisie proper would be even smaller. In addition to this, another significant characteristic of the weakness of the bourgeoisie in India was that its average income was not far above the average income of other groups.[6]

Thus, in the absence of bourgeoisie development and industrial employment opportunities (the reasons for which were discussed in chapter 3), dependence on agriculture continued to increase. Table 4.1, compiled from various census reports, presents a comparative

TABLE 4.1 Distribution of the labour force

	1901	%	1911	%	1921	%	1931	%
	Population (in millions)							
Agriculture, forestry and fishing	64.1	68	70.2	72	69.6	73	72.1	72
General labour	5.3	6	2.6	3	2.8	3	3.7	4
Manufacture, mining and construction	9.9	11	9.6	10	8.9	9	9.1	9
Trade	5.0	5	5.4	5	5.5	6	5.6	6
Transportation and other services	9.0	10	9.3	10	8.7	9	9.5	9

Source: *Census of India: 1901*, vol. I, part 2, table XV; *1911*, vol. I, part 2, table XV; *1921*, vol. I, part 2, table XVII; *1931*, vol. I, part 2, table X.

TABLE 4.2 The percentage distribution of workers, 1931, 1951

	1931	1951
Agriculture and mining	71.2	73.0
Industry	16.3	13.0
Commerce	6.0	6.1
Transport	1.7	2.0
Public force and administration	1.2	2.6
Professions and liberal arts	1.6	1.9
Domestic service	2.0	1.4

Source: V.K.R.V. Rao, *Papers on National Income and Allied Topics,* vol. II (Bombay: Asia Publishing House, 1962), p. 8.

view of the changing nature of the occupational structure in India from 1901 to 1931. It is noteworthy that the number of people employed in the various sectors remained more or less constant in all four enumerations.

Using a different method of enumeration, the *Census of India, 1951*, pointed out that

notwithstanding an element of unavoidable uncertainty, this may probably be relied upon as evidence that dependence on

agriculture for employment did not decrease during these twenty
years (from 1931 to 1951), but probably increased though to a
small extent only.[7]

The enumeration of the Papers on National Income (see Table 4.2)
supports this assertion.

However, the condition of agriculture was dismal, particularly
with respect to food crop production. While the population in India
increased from 279.4 million in 1891 to 388 million in 1941,[8] food
crop production, according to George Blyn's calculation, declined
from 73.9 million tons in 1893–4 to 69.3 million tons in 1945–6.[9]
During the same period, however, non-food crop production registered a considerable increase. The output ratio of non-food crops,
which was approximately 22:100 in 1893–4, rose to 44:100 in 1945–
6.[10] Most of these non-food crops were commercial crops and raw
materials which were exported to pay for the finished goods imported into India. The export of raw cotton increased from 178,000 tons
in 1901–2 to 762,133 tons in 1936–7.[11] As can be seen from Table
4.3, despite the increase in the production of non-food crops, the
per capita output of all crops declined considerably, not to speak of
the miserable decline in the *per capita* food output.

TABLE 4.3 Estimates of average annual *per capita* output of food and
non-food crops, 1893–4 to 1945–6

	Output in index units per capita		Output of food crops, pounds per capita
	Food crops	*All crops*	
1893–94 to 1895–96	100	100	587
1896–97 to 1905–06	95	97	560
1906–07 to 1915–16	91	97	547
1916–17 to 1925–26	90	98	538
1926–27 to 1935–36	78	90	461
1936–37 to 1945–46	68	80	399

Source: George Blyn, *Agricultural Trends in India*, p. 117.

The pressure on Indian agriculture and the consequent wretched
condition of the peasant was noted by the Royal Commission on
Agriculture (1928):

The overcrowding of the people on the land, the lack of alternative means to secure a living, the difficulty of finding any avenue of escape ... combine to force the cultivator to grow food whenever he can and on whatever terms he can.[12]

At independence, then, the state in India was confronted with a dismal and deteriorating economic situation. In addition to this there was a widespread demand for economic development, employment and income, promised to the people by the nationalist leaders at the time of the freedom movement.

The state functionaries, therefore, wanted to improve the economy through industrialization which they thought would alleviate the excess pressure on agriculture, create more jobs, and raise the productivity of the land. Moreover, without modern industry which could provide irrigation, electricity, pumps, fertilizers, power tillers, tractors, etc., no modern agriculture was possible.

The state's policy on industrialization and the reaction of the bourgeoisie

The organized private industrial sector, as has already been pointed out, was too weak to undertake large-scale industrialization on its own. It not only lacked the means, it also lacked the will to invest in sectors that required long gestation periods. Only the state had the means to do that. Furthermore, just after independence (and even before it), the private sector appeared quite willing to let the state play an important part, at least in the initial stage of industrialization. Private capital interests in India were fully aware that in an age of advanced capitalism dominated by the giant multinational corporations of the West and Japan, their very survival was at stake without some sort of state protection. Even in the West, after the depression of the 1930s, the concept of unfettered competitive capitalism without any state intervention had been abandoned.

After the Second World War many mechanisms of state intervention, such as state control of the banking system, government participation in the development of new technology, the creation of a trained labour force suitable for the adoption of the new technology, the nationalization of private enterprises, etc., were resorted to in order to infuse new life into post-war capitalism in the advanced capitalist countries.[13] These steps were taken over and above the Keynesian prescriptions to reduce business risks and speed up the process of investment.

Under such changed situations in the world economy, it was quite natural that the weak Indian bourgeoisie should also seek help from the state to further its own interests. During the closing year of the Second World War a blueprint for the industrialization of India after the War – known as the Bombay Plan – was drawn up by a few industrialists headed by Tata and Birla, with this purpose in view.

The plan called upon the state to play an active role in laying the groundwork for the future industrialization of India. It also proposed that the state should have both preventive as well as positive functions to accelerate economic growth. It unequivocally stated that 'An enlargement of the positive as well as the preventive functions of the state is essential to any large-scale economic planning.'[14]

The Bombay Plan pointed out three areas of state intervention – ownership, management, and control – and for obvious reasons opted for the last one:

> State control appears to be more important than ownership or management. Mobilization of all the available means of production and their direction towards socially desirable ends is essential for achieving the maximum amount of social welfare.[15]

With respect to social overheads, the Bombay Plan agreed to state ownership with reluctance but added,

> if later on private finance is prepared to take over these industries, *state ownership must be replaced by private ownership* (emphasis added).[16]

Even in cases of state ownership, it suggested that the management of the concerns should be vested in private capitalists:

> It does not invariably follow that all the enterprises owned by the state should also be managed by it.[17]

Although it is clear that the Bombay Plan called upon the state to operate actively in the economy in the interests of the bourgeoisie, the call itself was a big departure from what is normally regarded as the subjective preference of the capitalist class – the independent capitalist path of development or *laissez-faire*. One may pertinently ask: why did the Indian bourgeoisie not seek the collaboration of foreign capital instead of asking for state intervention? There are two answers to this question. First, on the morrow of independence, the capitalist class was genuinely apprehensive that a call for foreign private capital to operate in India would have meant the loss of a sheltered market for itself,[18] for which very purpose it had joined the independence movement. Second, it could not be expected that foreign private capital would be interested in developing only the slow-yielding infrastructure industries, which the Indian bourgeoisie considered essential for its own development and aggrandizement.[19]

It may be noted here that the very concept of economic planning on the part of the bourgeoisie was a novel step, if not a revolutionary one, because until then the concept was associated with socialist, or more precisely Soviet, planning.

India was probably the first country outside the soviet and socialist blocs to undertake long-term economic planning[20] under which the basic industries were to be owned by the state. Even before the Bombay Plan, a National Planning Committee of the Congress Party was appointed as early as 1938, under the chairmanship of Jawaharlal Nehru, who became the first Prime Minister of free India. Planning was defined by this Committee

> as the technical coordination, by disinterested experts, of consumption, production, investment, trade and income distribution, in accordance with social objectives set by bodies representative of the nation. Such planning is not only to be considered from the point of view of economics and the rising standard of living but must include cultural and spiritual values, and the human side of life.[21]

The National Planning Committee represented different social groups and interests.[22] The Committee included fifteen members of the Congress who were assisted by the representatives of the governing bodies of each province.[23] Non-Congress provincial governments and many large princely states also participated in its deliberations. In the words of Nehru, the composition of the Committee was as follows:

Toward the end of 1938 a National Planning Committee was
constituted at the instance of the Congress. It consisted of fifteen
members [from the Congress] plus representatives of provincial
governments and such Indian states [native princely states] as
chose to collaborate with us. Among the members were well-
known industrialists, financiers, economists, professors,
scientists, as well as representatives of the Trade Union Congress
and the Village Industries Association. The Non-Congress
provincial governments (Bengal, Punjab and Sind), as well as
some of the major states (Hyderabad, Mysore, Baroda,
Travancore, Bhopal) co-operated with the committee. In a sense
it was a remarkably representative committee cutting across
political boundaries as well as the high barrier between official
and non-official India.... Hard-headed big business was there as
well as people who are called idealists and doctrinaires, and
socialists and near-communists. Experts and directors of
industries [i.e., government officials concerned with industries]
came from provincial governments and states.[24]

The big business interests joined in the deliberations of this committee because they were afraid that its decisions would go against
their interests. Nehru adds:

Big business was definitely apprehensive and critical [of the
committee], and probably joined up because it felt that it could
look after its interests better from inside the committee than
from outside.[25]

It was decided by the National Committee that the defence
industry must be owned and controlled by the state. Regarding
other key industries, the majority members were of the opinion that
they should be state owned; the minority members, acting as depu-
ties for the business interests, opined that state control would be
sufficient.[26] The opinion of the majority prevailed. Its other important recommendations were: public utilities to be state owned; all
businesses to be licensed and regulated by a public authority; banking to be licensed and regulated; and a national board to be formed
to supervise insurance.[27]

A very significant factor emerges from the aim, composition and
deliberation of the Planning Committee. The aim of planning, as

has been pointed out, was to realize 'social objectives' set by 'bodies representative of the nation'. It soon became clear that the 'bodies representative of the nation' were predominantly comprised of literati and officials. Thus the presence of capitalist interests was futile because of its inherent weakness, and this presence could not resist the Planning Committee's determination to monopolize for the state the ultimate say in the future industrialization of India.

It may be noted, in this connection, that the projected intervention of the state in the production processes of India was quite different from its intervention in production in the advanced capitalist countries, as pointed out by Klaus Offe:

> Due to lack of capitalist class cohesiveness, the state takes on responsibility for managing crises through production policy. With no class-originated policy guidelines, the state itself is forced to devise decision rules that reproduce private capital accumulation.[28]

In the case of India, there was a distinct class-originated policy guideline that reluctantly agreed to have some sort of state control in key industries, but not state ownership.[29] Even state control was acceded to, because the bourgeoisie was too weak to undertake on its own the development of the infrastructure.

The bourgeoisie demanded from the state a base for quick private capital accumulation but that demand did not originate from the 'lack of class cohesiveness' or 'specific bottlenecks, externalities or crises due to breakdowns in private capital investment'[30] – which are endemic to the system (capitalism) in advanced capitalist countries.[31]

In India the state intervened, not because it was delegated power to intervene on behalf of the bourgeoisie resulting from crises in the process of capital accumulation or from its lack of cohesiveness, but because the latter was too weak. Despite protests from the bourgeoisie, the state in India could take the decision to own and manage the basic industries because it was independent of bourgeois control, and its freedom to act in the economic field could not be thwarted by the lack of support from the bourgeoisie (such as non-investment or withdrawal of investment).

After independence, the decisions of the National Planning Committee were adopted in a modified form in the Industrial Resolution Policy (I.R.P.) which the Government of India published on 6 April

1948. A brief compendium of the important points of the Resolution is given below:

State Enterprise v. Private Enterprise: It was stated that the State must play a progressively active role in the development of industries. The ability to achieve the main objectives should determine the immediate extent of State responsibility and the limits to private enterprise. It was realised that under the existing conditions the mechanisms and the resources of the State might not permit it to function forthwith in industry as widely as might be desired. It was, therefore, felt that for some time to come the State should contribute more quickly to the increase of national wealth by expanding its present activities wherever it was already operating, and by concentrating on new units of production in other fields, rather than on acquiring and running existing units [the existing units mainly consisted of jute and textile industries]. It was stated that in the meanwhile, private enterprise properly directed and regulated, had a valuable role to play.

Allocation of spheres: In order to implement this policy industries were classified as under:

(a) Industries reserved for the exclusive monopoly of the Government of India: In this category were included the manufacture of arms and ammunition, the production and control of atomic energy, and the ownership and management of railway transport.

(b) Industries reserved for State initiative: The State was defined as including Central, Provincial and State Governments as well as public authorities like Municipal Corporations. State initiative meant that the State would be exclusively responsible for the establishment of new undertakings in certain industries, though it was further laid down that in those cases where the state itself found it necessary in the national interests to secure the cooperation of private enterprise, it would do so subject to such control and regulation as the central government might prescribe. The industries in this category were:

(i) coal;

(ii) iron and steel;

(iii) aircraft manufacture;

(iv) shipbuilding;

(v) manufacture of telephone, telegraph, and wireless apparatus, excluding radio receiving sets; and (vi)　mineral oils.

So far as the existing private enterprise in the above industries was concerned the inherent right of the state to acquire any existing industrial undertaking was emphasised.

So far as the management of a State enterprise was concerned, it was laid down that as a rule it would be through the medium of public corporation under the statutory control of the Central Government, which would assume such powers as might be necessary to insure this policy. But it was mentioned that government had decided to let existing undertakings in these fields develop for a period of ten years.... At the end of this period the whole matter was to be reviewed and a decision taken in the light of circumstances obtaining at the time. Compensation on a fair and equitable basis would be given if the state decided to acquire any unit.

(c) Private Enterprise: Industrial activities other than those indicated above would normally be open to private enterprise. It was, however, laid down that the state would also progressively participate in this field; and that it would not hesitate to intervene if the progress of an industry under private enterprise was unsatisfactory.

Foreign Capital: It was proposed to introduce legislation for regulating the conditions under which foreign capital might participate in Indian industries. Each individual case of such participation was to be scrutinised and approved by the Central Government. As a rule it would provide that the major interest in ownership and effective control should always be in Indian hands. Power would, however, be taken to deal with exceptional cases in a manner calculated to serve the national interest.

Cottage and small-scale industries: The role of these industries in the national economy was emphasised and though they fell within the provincial sphere, the Government of India agreed to investigate how far and in what manner these industries could be coordinated and integrated with large-scale industries; for example, how the textile mill industry can be made complementary rather than competitive, to the handloom industry. The creation of a Cottage Industry Board at the centre, as well as of a Cottage and Small-scale Industries Directorate was envisaged. The encouragement to these industries by means of industrial co-operatives was suggested.

Labour–Capital Relations: The Government of India accepted the resolution of the Industries Conference which among other things laid down: 'That the system of remuneration to capital as well as labour must be so devised that, while in the interests of the consumers and the primary producers, excessive profits should be prevented by suitable methods of taxation and otherwise, both will share the product of their common effort, after making provision for payment of fair wages to labour, a fair return on capital employed in the industry and reasonable reserves for maintenance and expansion of undertaking.'

In accepting this resolution the Government observed that labour's share of the profits should be on a sliding scale normally varying with production.[32]

We have quoted in detail the main features of the Industrial Policy Resolution of 1948 because they embodied the directive principles for the future industrialization of India. The Second Industrial Policy Resolution of 1956 was in many ways a reiteration of the first.[33] But it made a few important points of departure. It declared, as its avowed goal and principle, the establishment of a 'socialist pattern of society' which did not find any mention at all in the first Resolution.

The Second Industrial Policy Resolution categorically declared that all industries of *basic and strategic importance*, or in the nature of public utility services, should be in the public sector. It also included policies to undertake state trading on an increasing scale. All industries were classified into three categories on the basis of their strategic importance to the state.

The industries in the first category were made the exclusive monopoly of the state. Those in the second category were to be progressively state-owned, and new undertakings in this category were to be initiated by the state. The private sector was given a secondary role to supplement the endeavours of the state. All the remaining industries, falling under the third category, could be developed by the private sector, but it was declared at the same time that it would be open to the state to start any industry even in this category.

The first category (Schedule A) included:

arms, ammunition, and allied items of defence equipment;
iron and steel;

heavy castings and forgings of iron and steel;

heavy plant and machinery required for iron and steel production, mining, machine tool manufacture, and such other basic industries as may be specified by the Central Government;

heavy electrical plants including large hydraulic and steam turbines;

coal and lignite;

mineral oils;

mining of iron ore, manganese ore, chrome ore, gypsum, sulphur, gold and diamonds;

mining and processing of copper, lead, zinc, tin, molybdenum, and wolfram;

minerals specified in the schedule to the Atomic Energy (Control of Production and Use) Order, 1953;

aircraft;

air transport, railway transport, shipbuilding;

telephones and telephone cables, telegraph and wireless apparatus (excluding radio receiving sets);

generation and distribution of electricity.

The second category (Schedule B) consisted of:

all other minerals except 'minor minerals' as defined in Section 3 of the Mineral Concession Rules 1949;

aluminium and other non-ferrous metals not included in Schedule A;

machine tools;

ferro-alloys and tool steels;

basic and intermediate products required by chemical industries such as the manufacture of drugs, dyestuffs and plastics;

antibiotics and other essential drugs;

fertilizers; synthetic rubber;

carbonization of coal;

chemical pulp;

road transport and sea transport.

What is obvious is that the above lists indicate that all basic and strategic industries were to be brought under state production. This was done in the name of 'socialism', although the term was conspicuously absent in the First Industrial Policy Resolution.

The nature of state socialism in India

The social economy of India on the eve of independence made the intervention of the state inevitable; and state initiative in large-scale industrialization until then was associated, even in enlightened circles, with the ideology and practice of socialism.

Although the term 'socialist pattern of society' was first officially used in the Second Industrial Policy Resolution, it had already been adopted in a non-official resolution in the Indian Parliament in 1954.[34] The urgency in adopting these resolutions lay in the partial failure of the First Five Year Plan – embarked on in April 1951 – to enlarge the industrial sector and to shift the ever-swelling population from agriculture to industry.[35] Although the First Industrial Policy Resolution provided resolutions which were sufficient to enable the state to develop industries on its own, the incorporation of the term 'socialist pattern of society' reinforced the purpose and gave the functionaries of the state a better ideologial base to work on.[36]

Agriculture had failed to generate, during the First Five Year Plan – thus belying the expectations of the planners – the necessary surplus for the expansion of other sectors. This failure was readily confessed in the Second Five Year Plan:

> There has not been any marked change in the occupational pattern in India over the last three or four decades.... Broadly speaking, agriculture and allied pursuits continue to absorb about 70 per cent of the working force; mining and factory industry absorb about 2.6 per cent of the working force; small enterprises including construction, take up some 8 per cent; about 7 per cent of the working force is engaged in transport, communication and trade; public administration, professions and liberal arts and domestic services account for over 10 per cent. This means that the secondary and tertiary sectors have not grown rapidly enough to make an impact on the primary sector; nor has the primary sector itself thrown up surpluses which would create conditions favourable for expansion elsewhere.[37]

In short, the development of industrialization needed a big push which would lead to a significant change in the occupational structure, the removal of the burden on agriculture, and an improvement in the standard of living.[38] The state of the economy at the end of the First Five Year Plan made it imperative for the state to play a more vigorous and active role in enlarging industrial production and this could be readily undertaken and vindicated on the grounds of establishing a 'socialist pattern of society'.

The 'socialist pattern of society', or 'socialism', that was underlined in the Second Industrial Policy Resolution and the Second Five Year Plan rested on three cardinal resolutions:

(i) the productive forces of the country should be rapidly expanded, and in this endeavour the basic and strategic industries should be owned and controlled increasingly by the state;

(ii) unorganized (cottage and village) and small-scale industries should be given preference over, and be provided with more facilities than, the large-scale private sector industries;[39]

(iii) to reduce disparities in income and wealth, the concentration of economic power in the hands of a small number of persons should be resisted. To accomplish this and to make business conform to the 'social and economic policy' of the state, economic activity should be regulated and controlled by various legislative and fiscal means.[40]

What emerges from the above scheme is that the essence of Indian socialism that began to take a concrete form after the Second Five Year Plan lay not in the establishment of an egalitarian society based on social ownership, but in the rapid growth of productive forces mainly, but not exclusively, through the state sector. Private business was not eliminated, but its activities were curbed and its role was defined in order to complement the state sector. It is clear that the emphasis was more on production than distribution.

However, this was not the goal of Nehru, the socialist, in 1933. He wrote then in a booklet entitled *Whither India?*

The nationalist answer is to prefer home interests to foreign interests, but beyond that it does not go. It tries to avoid disturbing the class division or the social status quo. It imagines that various interests will somehow be accommodated when the country is free. Being essentially a middle class movement, nationalism works chiefly in the interests of that class. It is obvious that there are serious conflicts between various interests in a country, and every law, every policy, which is good for one

interest may be harmful for another.... Appeals are issued for
unity between different classes and groups to face the common
national foe, and those who point out the inherent conflict
between landlord and tenant, or capitalist and wage labourer,
are criticised.[41]

Rejecting the appeal for class collaboration to stand against the
common enemy, Nehru's answer was: 'India's immediate goal can
only be considered in terms of the ending of the exploitation of her
people.'[42] This meant, for him, not only political independence but
also economic emancipation of all the people. However, as the first
Prime Minister of India he began to speak in a different voice only
five months after independence.

Production became for him, then, the first priority. Now he
wanted to minimize the inherent conflict between the owners of the
means of production and the sellers of labour power in order to
ensure continued production:

Capital may want a certain prize, labour may want a certain
prize; the consumer, the producer, everybody naturally wants to
benefit himself or his group.... It is not necessary to give up the
hope of getting the prize, but rather to put first things first, that
is, to preserve the prize and then either in a friendly way come to
future decisions or, if you like, have a conflict; but when the
conflict endangers the prize itself, then obviously this is an
exceedingly unfortunate and foolish way of approaching a
thing.[43]

The question is: why this transformation? To find an answer to
this question, let us examine briefly what alternative courses of
action were open to him. He could either urge the Congress Party,
which he headed, to usher in a full-scale socialist revolution, thereby
dissolving the existing social formation which was a complex of
various modes of production – partly Asiatic, partly feudal, and
partly capitalist. Or he could let the existing social structure continue whereby the state, as the single most powerful organ, would
have a great amount of leverage to mould the future development of
society. He opted for the second alternative.

The choice was dictated by two factors. First, the Indian National
Congress, which was the largest political party and which had won

India's freedom, was composed of various social strata – the educated middle class, the professionals, small businessmen, small landlords, rich and poor peasants;[44] all these could not easily be brought together shortly after independence in order to unleash a social revolution. Moreover, the socialist core of the party was very small.[45] The leadership was predominantly made up of intellectuals of petit-bourgeois origins.[46]

Second, the party derived its mass support mainly from the peasants with smallholdings[47] whose aversion to any kind of social change had been noted by Marx long ago.[48] In the case of India this was further reinforced by the village communal life, as well as the caste system. In short, the configuration of social forces, despite the poor and declining condition of the economy, was not favourable for a social revolution at this juncture.[49]

Thus, at independence, Nehru and his Congress party were confronted with a situation in which the state had considerable leverage, free from any dominant class hegemony, to plan and determine India's future social development. By manipulating the state machinery in curbing the private and expanding the public sectors, it would be possible, so Nehru thought, to establish in India a socialist society without having recourse to the violent overthrow of the existing structures. After all, a social revolution is always fraught with unforeseen consequences.[50] His strategy was, therefore, one of creeping socialism which, with increasing production in the state sector, would minimize the concentration of wealth and income in the hands of a few capitalists, and at the same time would implicitly provide assurance for the workers' needs.

But the system Nehru visualized did not include any change in the 'ownership pattern'. He said:

> Obviously, most persons who believe in a socialist pattern must believe in the public sector growing all the time. But it does not necessarily mean that the private sector is eliminated even at a much later stage. In regard to the private sector and the public sector, I think the criteria should be basically two. One is to have as much production as possible through all the means at our disposal, and the second is prevention of accumulation of wealth and economic power in individual hands. If we have only the first one, it may lead subsequently to unsocial, undesirable and harmful consequences. Therefore we must aim right from the

beginning and all the time at the prevention of this accumulation of wealth and economic power.[51]

He also added:

socialism involves higher grades of production, more production and more wealth being produced and equitable distribution.[52]

In brief, the equitable distribution should be gradually effected through the diminution of the private sectors and the expansion of the public sectors; the idea was that economic benefits would automatically flow from this process to the less fortunate. What is clear, however, is that what Nehru envisaged in mixed-economy socialism was the gradual enhancement of the state's economic (as well as political) power without changing the 'ownership pattern'.

The state would not – as proclaimed by Marx and Lenin, and put into practice in the socialist countries – restructure society by breaking up the existing 'ownership pattern' and replacing it with 'social property'.[53] The state, here, was not the instrument to abolish class relations which emanate from private property.

From the foregoing discussion it may be concluded that the hegemonical role of the state, in India, both in economics and politics, was determined by factors generated from the depths of society itself. The 'socialistic form', or the name 'socialism', was given only to legitimate what was already there, weak social classes dominated by a strong state which wanted to further consolidate its position by strengthening its economic power. The aim, indeed, was to make the state independent of economic subservience to the capitalist class (see chapter 6). This could be done only by bringing under its own ownership and control the basic and strategic industries, so that the state in India, unlike that in the developed capitalist countries, would not have to depend on the private capitalists' investments which therein determine both the volume of capital accumulation and its partial appropriation through the mechanism of taxes, public debt, etc. (i.e. social capital and social expenses as explained by James O'Connor in his *The Fiscal Crisis of the State*). In short, the Indian state was not a capitalist state.[54]

The state in India manifested itself over almost all social classes, the bourgeoisie, the peasants and the workers. If it had any relationship on the basis of inputs with any class, it was, to some extent, with the petit-bourgeoisie. However, in terms of output, it would be very difficult to locate the state in any class because, as it appears, its policies were (and are) principally directed towards the augmentation of its own power and not the power of any social class (see below, chapter 6).

However, it must be borne in mind that the classes and their relationship with the state do not remain static. In the modern world, in every country, the bourgeoisie and the proletariat – in Third World countries other forces as well, such as the feudal elements, rural bourgeoisie, etc. – are engaged in a perpetual struggle to determine in their own favour the nature of both inputs (structure) and outputs of the state. At the same time, in countries like India, with its myriad bureaucratic structures, where the state has enjoyed autonomy from any class control for so long, it is natural that it would try to resist the hegemonic domination of the bourgeoisie.

5 The artisan and small-scale industries in India's social economy and their relationship with the state

Prolegomena

In the last chapter we saw that the state in India, following independence, after the indigenous bourgeoisie became free of metropolitan competition and restraints, could maintain its hegemonic position free of any class control. The state could do this because the economic strength of the indigenous bourgeoisie was insufficient at a time when the socio-economic situation, in the form of conditions of employment and standard of living of the masses, demanded a quick pace in industrial progress. The state undertook the task and could monopolize to itself the basic and strategic industries, these being still undeveloped and unoccupied by the indigenous capitalist class.

As we noticed, this was done in the name of establishing a socialist pattern of society, which further augmented the power of the state in manipulating the development of social classes, and in particular in curbing the bourgeoisie. Because the ownership pattern was not abolished, however, the bourgeoisie continued (and still continues) to grow despite all these checks. Simultaneously it waged (and still wages) a relentless struggle to gain control over the state in terms of both inputs and policy formulations (see chapter 6). To understand the dialectic of this interaction, it is necessary to have a clear idea of the structure of Indian industry because the state, in its attempts to restrict the growth of the power of the capitalist class, not only developed the public sector, with which it eventually wanted to wipe out the private sector, but also imposed detailed regulations on the private sector (see chapter 4), and encouraged small-scale production and artisan industries (most of which are unorganized household enterprises) to emerge as serious competitors to the big private enterprises.

In this chapter an attempt will be made to first categorize the different types of industries (although the categories tend to overlap as will be indicated below) that are found in India, and then see how state action in encouraging village and small-scale industries and in delimiting the area of development for large-scale private industry has led to the failure of growing capitalism to integrate the pre-capitalist sectors, and also how this in turn has further buttressed the continued existence of the post-Asiatic social formation, leading to the maintenance of the state's independence and hegemony.

The organized industries can be classified into three subgroups: industries organized by the state sector; industries organized by the large-and medium-scale private sectors (both of which hereafter will be called large-scale industry); and small-scale private sector industries which come under the jurisdiction of the Factory Act, the definition of which has changed from time to time.

Unorganized industries normally described as small-scale enterprises fall into three categories: the first is engaged completely in the production of use values employing family members almost exclusively and seldom hiring labourers; the second is involved in the creation of both use and exchange value employing both family members and hired labourers; and the third, usually known as small-scale industry, produces exclusively for the market employing wage labour as well as modern means of production. Almost all units in the first category are located in villages (rural areas) and cater to the needs (use values) of village members. The exchange of products takes place not on the basis of market forces or market principles, but on the basis of local customs. The units in the second category can be found in both urban and rural areas and their market is mostly regional. Production in the third category, which is predominantly located in urban areas, is oriented to meet the demands of both national and international markets. In fact, the third category, small-scale industry, is organized on the basis of the capitalist principle.

Some of the units in the third category expand enough to come under the jurisdiction of the Factory Act, and are listed under organized industry. In fact, the third category in organized industry and the third category in unorganized sector overlap in respect of mode of production to such an extent that it is theoretically difficult to distinguish between the two. In this discussion, therefore, both will be included under the term 'small-scale industry' and the units of the other two categories in the unorganized sector will be referred to as 'artisan industries'. It may be pointed out here that the government documents refer to both artisan industries and small-scale industries as 'small-scale enterprises' – a very confusing term –, thereby blurring their distinct modes of production. In this chapter the main features of the artisan and small-scale industries will be analysed, while the next chapter will be devoted to the analysis of the state sector and large-scale private sector industries.

The state and artisan industries

The first and second categories of unorganized industry have one characteristic in common: they use traditional techniques of production. In these categories the investment of physical capital per unit of labour is very low and, hence, productivity is low too. Yet as was noted in chapter 4, the share of unorganized industry (mainly composed of these two categories), on the eve of independence, constituted two-thirds of the total industrial production.

In terms of employment, it was estimated in the census of 1951 that more than 16 million out of 21 million non-agricultural rural labourers were engaged in household enterprises.[1] From Table 5.1 it can be seen that even after fourteen years of independence, household industry employed more people than organized manufacturing industry (including both public and private sectors).

Though it has not been possible to ascertain from the 1971 census what is the *real* share of household industry in employment in industry as a whole,[2] the White Paper on National Accounts Statistics, released by the Central Statistical Organisation, provides information which indicates that the ratio of the workforce in different sectors of industry has not altered very much since 1960–61. According to the Central Statistical Organisation, while the share of industry in the overall domestic product was 19.9 per cent in 1960–61, it has increased to 22.8 per cent in 1975–76. An increase of only 3 per cent, it can easily be inferred, would not radically transform the distribution of labour between various sectors of industry.

In the unorganized sector, the primary sector takes up the biggest portion and it is split up into millions of small atomistic units. These units are scattered among six hundred thousand Indian villages. The eminent statistician V.K.R.V. Rao has described the nature of

TABLE 5.1 Distribution of labour, 1961

	1961 %
Agriculture	69.5
Mining, fishing, quarrying, livestock, forestry, fishing, hunting and plantations, orchards and allied activities	2.8
Manufacturing – household industry	6.2
Manufacturing – other than household industry	4.4
Construction	1.1
Trade and commerce	4.0
Transport, storage and communications	1.6
Other services	10.4
Total	100.0

Source: *The Census of India, 1961.*

these units (in order to point out the difficulties involved in computing the income from the primary sector) as follows:

> Agriculture accounts for the employment of the major portion of the active labour force and constitutes practically half of the gross national product. Statistics of output of agricultural commodities are not completely accurate in any country in the world, as by the very nature of the industry, it is not possible to have a census of production comparable to that of manufactures. In India, however, the difficulties are specially great. The number of production units run into many millions (it is estimated that the number is nearly sixty million), most of them do not keep any accounts, a large portion of the output is not sold for cash, being either consumed by the producer and his family or exchanged in barter...[3]

Household industries of the first category are adjuncts and dependent on the above form of agriculture (in chapter 2 there is a detailed discussion on how the unity of agriculture and industry provided the base of the Asiatic mode of production). This kind of agriculture, in turn, cannot operate without some kind of internal industry within the village, which provides it with the basic tools, the instruments of production, and services. Only when these prerequisites are met do the villages in India become self-generating and self-sustaining. The village artisans, who produce these tools, are not only employees of the village, along with other service sector servants such as barbers, priests and teachers, they are an integral part of the village.

The unity of agriculture and industry make these villages complete as both production and consumption units and this unity, in turn, makes them self-reproductive and unchangeable. In this connection we again recall what Marx considered as the basic characteristics of the Asiatic mode and the reasons for its stability:

> The chief part of the products is destined for direct use by the community itself, and does not take the form of a commodity. Hence, production here is independent of that division of labour brought about, in Indian society as a whole, by means of the exchange. It is the surplus alone that becomes a commodity, and a portion of even that, not until it has reached the hands of the state, into whose hands from time immemorial a certain quantity of these products has found its way in the shape of rent in kind.[4]... This dozen of individuals [the blacksmith, the carpenter, the barber, etc.] is maintained at the expense of the whole community.... The whole mechanism discloses a systematic division of labour; but a division like that in manufactures is impossible, since the smith and the carpenter, etc., find an unchanging market, and at the most there occur, according to the sizes of the villages, two or three of each, instead of one. The law that regulates the division of labour in the community acts with the irresistible authority of a law of nature, at the same time that each individual artificer, the smith, the carpenter, and so on conducts in his workshop all the operations of his handicraft in the traditional way, but independently, and without recognizing any authority over him. The simplicity of the organization for production in these self-sufficing communities that constantly reproduce themselves in the same form ... this simplicity supplies the key to the secret of the unchangeableness of Asiatic Societies.... *The structure of the economic elements of society* remains untouched by the storm clouds of the political sky.[5]

We have already seen that even today the predominant mode of industry in India is the traditional household industry. Let us now see to what extent this form still corresponds to the Asiatic mode of production, and what changes have taken place in it under the impact of the expanding market forces.

In 1956 the Planning Commission of the Government of India undertook a study to obtain detailed information on the economic conditions of the village artisans. The sample villages were taken from Assam, Punjab, Travancore-Cochin, Madras, Saurashtra, Madhya Bharat and Vindhya Pradesh, thus covering almost all four corners and the central regions of India.[6] The crafts which were inquired into were those of weavers, carpenters, blacksmiths, cobblers, tanners, potters, brick makers, masons, stone workers, oilmen, tailors, bamboo and cane workers, and coil and rope makers. The study found that 81.5 per cent of carpenters, 97.1 per cent of blacksmiths, 81.8 per cent of masons, 95.9 per cent of weavers and 100 per cent of potters among the artisan households were pursuing their ancestral occupations.[7] Most of the equipment they used was the indigenous type, the only exception being that of the tailors.[8] Forty-five per cent of the artisan households had their market exclusively within the village; most of the remainder sold goods both in and outside their village.[9] There were very few cases of households, only 6 out of 401, producing goods for sale exclusively outside the village. The percentage of households selling goods exclusively within the village was highest in the case of blacksmiths (66 per cent). Pottery and carpentry ranked next in this respect. In fact, out of the 401 artisan households covered in the survey, only 175 were found to be producing goods for sale. In case of sale, the entries for direct sale to consumers without any intermediary constituted 88 per cent of the total, while those for sale through merchants were only 11 per cent.[10]

The reason for this slow 'commoditification' of artisan-produced goods, particularly that of producers' goods, can be easily attributed to the social economy of the village communities. The village cultivators, as explained before, depend exclusively on village artisans for the supply of production tools as well as their servicing. In return, the artisans are customarily paid fixed remuneration in kind or cash.

In this connection it should be borne in mind that all village artisans do not receive equal remuneration. The amount is determined both by the nature of their service to the community as well as their caste status. The caste status of occupations also varies from region to region. Local forces of production, to some extent, condition what castes enjoy what status, but there is seldom any occupational group in any village which is beyond the pale of caste.[11]

It is not necessary here to discuss the caste system in detail, but it should be pointed out that the caste system, by making occupations primarily hereditary,[12] provided a strong support for the stability of the existing mode of production.

However, despite caste and community restrictions, in the first half of the eighteenth century a few segments of Indian industry – particularly weaving, both cotton and to some extent silk – were on the verge of bursting their bounds and developing into the capitalist mode under the impact of international demand (see chapter 3). But before this could happen India was colonized and became an importer rather than an exporter of textile goods.

With the opening in 1498 of the sea route to India from Europe, and with the growing demand for Indian products in Europe – because of the fineness of Indian textiles – the market for Indian products suddenly expanded to such an extent that the quantitative change within the sphere of circulation was about to bring in a qualitative change in the area of production itself. The leading agent of this transformation was the merchant capitalist. In the West the producer himself, the rural artisan, as he was not bound by the guild, could accumulate enough capital to expand his production and gradually absorb circulation as a mere phase of production.[13] But in India the rural artisan, like his compatriots in the urban centres, was circumscribed by guild-like caste regulations. Under these circumstances only the merchant castes in India could operate as the vehicles of change. Although their position in the social structure was not very high, because of their inherited weakness due to their subservience to the state, they were structurally assigned the job of accumulating money through the exchange of commodities. In pre-capitalist societies, as Marx notes,

> merchants' capital appropriates to itself the overwhelming
> portion of the surplus product, either in its capacity as a mediator
> between societies, which are as yet largely engaged in the
> production of use values and for whose economic organisation
> the sale of that portion of its product which is transferred to the

circulation, or any sale of products at their value, is of minor importance; or, because under those former modes of production, the principal owners of the surplus product, with whom the merchant has to deal, are the slave holder, the feudal landlord, the state (for instance, the oriental despot)[14] and they represent the wealth and luxury which the merchant tries to trap.[15]

As was discussed in detail in the second chapter, the merchant capitalist of India, particularly of Bengal and Gujarat, was able to concentrate huge capital sums, primarily as a middleman for the international trade of Indian textile and silk goods. He also took the significant step of bringing in the workers under a common roof;[16] this was over and above the 'putting out' system (known as *dadni* in India) under which the merchant advanced some money or provided the raw materials to the weavers and later bought the finished products from them at a fixed price deducting the amount advanced or the cost of raw materials.[17] The former system (workers producing under a common roof) was definitely a step towards the introduction of the capitalist mode of production in the sense that the merchant capitalist was gradually transforming himself into an industrial capitalist.[18]

While the operation of the former system was restricted only to urban centres, the second system could be found in both urban and rural areas. The gradual dissolution of the once mighty Moghul State in the eighteenth century (before the rise of British power in India) led to the pauperization of a large number of people which included not only soldiers and other state employees but also craftsmen who depended on state patronage. These floating masses of people made it possible to develop full-scale wage labour on the basis of which an incipient industrial capitalism was slowly emerging in different urban centres, many of them one time seats of Moghul administration.[19]

Thus, while manufacture was establishing its sway in many urban centres during the eighteenth and early nineteenth centuries, the products of the village artisan, too, were being slowly brought into the sphere of circulation by merchant capital. However, this was being done without a corresponding change in the mode of production. The village weaver was still tied to the community through the relation of clientship and service (and also to some extent through the mechanism of caste). He was an independent producer outside the domination of capital, but his independence was limited by his obligation and calling to the village. However, the very process of bringing his products into circulation had the effect of separating such products from the customary mode of payment.

Merchants' money was thus able to sever the weavers' commodities, but not the weavers' dependency on the community; the products became freely floating but not the producers. This was one of the fundamental reasons why the merchants' capital in India failed to operate as a solvent of the existing mode of production in rural areas. It subjected the weavers' production, even that of the village artisans, 'more and more to exchange value by making enjoyments and subsistence more dependent on the sale than on the immediate use of the products'.[20] It 'increased the circulation of money'; it 'seized no longer upon the mere surplus production' but corroded production itself 'more and more, making entire lines of production dependent upon it'.[21] However, as Marx pointed out, whether a new mode of production would be able to dissolve the old mode or what new mode would emerge on its dissolution does not depend on commerce but on the internal solidity of the old mode and its articulation. In India's case, although urban industries were on the verge of capitalist development as a result of international demand for their products, the rural industries – on the basis of which capitalism grew in England outside the debilitating effect of urban guilds – continued to operate within the framework of the village community and caste calling, and could present a solid rock of stability on the level of production relations on which all waves of commerce had to founder.

Even afterwards, as Marx noted, when the penetration of the Indian market by industrial capitalism started in earnest, through cheap products from Manchester and Sheffield, British commerce was unable to undermine completely the solidity of the Asiatic mode which was based on the unity of industry and agriculture.

> The obstacles presented by the internal solidity and articulation of pre-capitalistic, national, modes of production to the corrosive influence of commerce is shown in the intercourse of the English with India and China. *The broad basis of the mode of production is here formed by the unity of small agriculture and domestic industry. . . .* The English commerce exerts a

revolutionary influence on these organisations [the village communities] and tears them apart only to the extent that it destroys by the low prices of its goods the spinning and weaving industries, which are an archaic and integral part of this unity. *And even so the work of dissolution is proceeding very slowly....* On the other hand, Russian commerce unlike the English, leaves *the economic basis of Asiatic production* untouched (emphasis added).[22]

In 1853, long before these lines from the third volume of *Capital*, Marx had written:

We know that the municipal organisations [i.e. village *panchyats* formed on the caste principle] and the economical basis of the village communities have been broken up, but their worst feature, the dissolution of society into stereotyped and disconnected atoms, has survived....

The British have broken up *the* self-sufficient inertia of the villages, railways will provide the new want of communication and intercourse. 'Besides, one of the effects of the railway system will be to bring into every village affected by it such knowledge of the contrivances and appliances of other countries, and such means of obtaining them, as will first *put the hereditary and stipendiary village artisanship* of India to full proof of its capabilities, and then supply its defects' (emphasis added).[23]

However, it seems from our earlier extract from *Capital* that Marx modified his views and admitted that the process of dissolution even in respect of the economic basis had been far from complete and had been subverted only to the extent of the spinning and weaving industry. Nearly a century later we find that the situation in the Indian villages has changed very little.[24] Villages in India today are still stereotyped little entities, with more or less the same self-perpetuating economic base, at least in terms of unity between cultivation and producers' goods. In 1956, the Programme Evaluation Organisation under the Planning Commission, whose investigation of the condition of village artisans has already been referred to, observed:

The system of customary payments in kind or cash in lieu of

services rendered by artisans and others, is a distinctive feature of the Indian rural society.... In two crafts, masonry and weaving, it is entirely absent.... *The system is the strongest in blacksmithing followed by carpentry.* Nearly all the blacksmiths and about 62 per cent of carpenters follow the customary payment system. The services of these two categories of artisans are most essential for cultivation purposes, because without ready and timely availability of these, cultivation would suffer seriously. No other class of artisans is as indispensable to the cultivator as these two. This leads one to venture the thought that the system is best preserved at the point where the cultivator's productive activities and his economy are most vitally affected and is comparatively weak in the case of artisans catering merely to his consumption requirements (emphasis added).[25]

This indicates that, although under the impact of commerce weaving and to some extent other consumer products[26] have been separated from the customary mode of payment and brought under the rule of the market, the basic features of the Asiatic mode of production in India have retained their vitality, and this underlies a kind of organic integration between cultivation and producers' industries, manifest in the prevailing customary payment basis in respect of tools of cultivation.

It is also noteworthy that even in the case of weaving, which Marx thought had been destroyed as a component of the village whole, it was found that

> all the producers (in the craft) in Erode-Madras and
> Manavadar-Sourashtra produce for sale both in and outside the
> village. But in Arunachal-Assam where there is a large number
> of female weavers, about one-third of the producers are
> producing exclusively for disposal within the village.[27]

Weaving is, thus, still a living part of the village economy in India, though its dependence has been removed from the village confines.

The industrialization policy of the Government of India, since independence, has been directed toward shoring up these village artisan industries as well as the small-scale industries to make them viable competitors against large-scale private industries. This deliberate policy, in conjunction with the agrarian reforms[28] (see chapter

7), has resulted in the further buttressing of the Asiatic mode in rural areas, despite the tremendous impact on it from the capitalist development flowing from urban centres.[29]

The government's policy has been, in short, the following: what consumer goods can be produced by cottage industries (and household enterprises of the first category) should only be produced by them; what they cannot produce, small-scale industry will; what neither small-scale nor cottage industry can produce will be left open to private large-scale industry. This policy, as mentioned earlier, was given a clear exposition in the Industrial Policy Resolutions of 1948 and 1956.

Following the first Industrial Policy Resolution which promised household industries 'safeguards against intensive competition by large-scale industries', the First Five Year Plan (1950–55) included provisions to protect them by the reservation of spheres of production. Limitation was also placed, by the mechanism of licensing, on the expansion of large-scale industries. A number of agencies were set up by the Central Government to help household industries. These were the Khadi and Village Industry Board, All India Handicrafts Board, All India Handloom Board, the Central Silk Board, and the Coir Board.[30]

In the Second Industrial Policy Resolution (1956) the policy of strengthening the village and small industries and increasing their competitiveness *vis-à-vis* large private industries was further emphasized.

> The state has been following a policy of *supporting cottage and village and small scale industries by restricting the volume of production in the large-scale sector, by differential taxation, or by direct subsidies.* While such measures will continue to be taken whenever necessary, the aim of the state policy will be to ensure that the decentralized sector acquires sufficient vitality to be self supporting and its development is integrated with that of large-scale industry. The state will, therefore, concentrate on measures designed to improve the *competitive strength* of the small-scale producer (emphasis added).[31]

This policy of consolidating the village artisan and small-scale industries at the cost of large private industries got further impetus from the report of the Karve Committee (1955). The committee was appointed to recommend schemes for the development of village and small-scale industries and to suggest means for the best utilization of resources to be allotted in the plans for this purpose. The committee's terms of reference included the objective

> that the bulk of the increased production during the Plan period of the consumer goods in common demand has to be provided by the village and small scale industries.[32]

The committee accordingly recommended that 'a ceiling should be imposed on the growth of large-scale consumer goods'.[33] This, they thought, would have the effect of channelling the growing demand for consumer goods to the household and small-scale sector. It is significant that the committee also recommmended a proposal to provide the basis for establishing an essentially decentralized society (in other words, to keep society dispersed and divided into separate small villages as had been the situation for centuries), although its terms of reference did not include any such objective.[34] Was this a subconscious attempt on the part of the committee to legitimize the state of the economy, or to subvert the growth of capitalist centralization? Or did it spring from the desire to implement the Gandhian ideology which regarded village industries, particularly the 'Ambar Chakra', i.e. hand spinning and weaving, as the panacea for all economic ills in India? Whatever might have been the motives, almost all recommendations of the Karve Committee – for example, the non-issuing of licenses for additional spindleage in the large private industries till the results on the Ambar Chakra are known[35] – had two effects. First, they helped to sustain and nourish the pre-capitalist mode and second, created as a result a built-in resistance in the economy against the spread of modern capital goods, even those produced in the state sector. The Reserve Bank of India's review of the Karve Committee's report minced no words in criticizing the overemphasis placed on village artisan industries by the government as a regressive attempt to support a pre-capitalist mode of production.

> Perhaps the most serious drawback of the Report is the lack of reference or regard in the formulation of its proposals, to fundamental economic trends or forces. ... For example, the decline of hand-pounding of rice, as of hand-grinding of wheat, is

an incidence of the commercialisation of agriculture.... The need for large-scale, increasingly mechanised operations has grown with the inexorable course of this process of commercialisation. Maybe, then, it is commercialisation which is the villain, and a halt ought to be put to any furtherance of that vicious process! But let us not forget that the 380 million of India's population could not survive on a basic pattern of self-sufficiency of production of the type when hand-pounding and hand-grinding were in their hey-day. In the circumstances, self-sufficiency remains an utterly inadequate basis for a worthwhile rate of increase of production; and the vital shortcoming of such philosophy as one can discern behind the Committee's proposal is that it appears to be rooted logically in a self-sufficient economy.[36]

It can be added that the Karve Committee would not deny the truth in this accusation, but would argue that its main concern was not so much production, but the maintenance and increase of the level of employment without disturbing the existing structure of the economy. It was opposed to big industry, and consequently to capitalist and post-capitalist modes of production, because 'the process of adoption of modern techniques involves *changing the structure of economic society*'.[37]

The state and small-scale industries

Now we turn from the artisan industries to small-scale industries which, along with the former, were required by the Industrial Policy Resolutions and Plans to provide the major portion of consumer goods. In fact, in terms of organization and techniques of production, small-scale industry has closer affinity with its large- and medium-scale counterparts than with village household industries. Small-scale industries use modern machines to produce modern products. They employ more wage labourers than family hands; raw materials are procured from long distances, even from abroad. The investment of capital per unit of labour is many times higher here than in the artisan industries; and goods are manufactured entirely for sale.

The government's definition of small-scale industry is primarily based on capital investment. However, the definition has undergone changes during the last twenty-five years. In 1953, all undertakings with a capital investment up to Rs 100,000 were designated as small-scale.[38] In 1956 the ceiling was raised to Rs 500,000.[39] In 1966 a new definition was adopted:

> Small scale industries will include all industrial units with a capital investment of not more than Rs 7.5 lakhs [Rs 750,000] irrespective of the number of persons employed. Capital investment for this purpose will mean an investment in productive plant and machinery only.[40]

Although Indian planners lump together artisan and small-scale industries under the common name of 'small-scale industries', the two are distinct in many respects, as enunciated above. However, there may be a reason for including them in one category: the petty commodity production in the rural sector under government patronage has the potential to develop into small-scale industry, but the odds, as has already been noted, are more against them. To refresh the memory it may be mentioned that household industries have not yet been able to leave the confines of the village, while most small-scale industries are situated in towns. Nevertheless, it may be quite possible for some of the better-off small rural producers to migrate to nearby towns and establish their own workshops.

Because of the many types of assistance provided by central and state government agencies (see below) the rate of growth in small-scale industry has been spectacular since the beginning of the Second Five Year Plan. During its course, despite shortages of certain basic raw materials like pig iron, steel and non-ferrous metals, the growth rate in certain small-scale industries such as sewing machines, electric fans, bicycles, builders' hardware and hand tools, varied from 25 to 50 per cent and, in some cases, was even higher.[41] In 1960, small industries accounted for 'over 92 per cent of all registered factories and ... employed over 1,330,000 persons, or 38 per cent of total employment'.[42] This growth rate steadily increased during the Third and Fourth Five Year Plans. According to a recent survey (1976), conducted by the Small Industries Development Organisation,

> the share of the small scale units' production in the total production has risen more than 40 per cent and *this trend is likely to become stronger in the years to come* (emphasis added).[43]

The survey reports that the continuous growth of the small sector is indicated by the rise in the value of fixed capital investment from Rs 10,540 million in 1972 to Rs 13,200 million in 1975.[44] The number of registered factories in the small-scale sector had been increasing during the same period at an average rate of 17 per cent per year.[45] In 1976 the small-scale industries in the factory sector alone provided employment for two million persons.[46] Quantitative growth apart, the small-scale industry has also been able to expand its sphere of production to many non-traditional items including engineering goods.

In the export field, too, small-scale industry is emerging as a competitor with large-scale industry. In 1971–2 it exported goods worth Rs 1,550 million. The amount rose to Rs 6,000 million in 1975–6. For the same year, its share in total export was estimated at 15 per cent.[47]

In short, the increasing importance of small-scale industries in the Indian economy is an undeniable fact and, to a great extent, at the cost of large-scale private industry. One of the noteworthy aspects of Indian small-scale industry is that many items exclusively reserved for it[48] could easily, and probably more efficiently, have been produced by private large-scale industry. The productivity in large-scale industry, as pointed out in a survey conducted by the Central Statistical Organisation in 1967, is definitely higher per unit of labour than in small-scale industry (this is not only due to more capital investment per unit of worker: see below).

In the normal course of capitalist development – as we find in the developed industrialized nations – this trend would have meant the ruin and constriction of small-scale production. But in India, instead, small-scale industry has been able to sustain and in most cases increase its total employment as well as its share in the national income. This has been due to two reasons. First, while large-scale industry is regulated and controlled by an elaborate licensing system and other means such as controls on profit, restriction on the expansion of output, import limitations on raw materials, fixing of prices, etc. (see chapter 6), small-scale industry is not encumbered by any restraints. Second, while the tax burden on large-scale industry is quite extensive, small-scale industry enjoys subsidies, tax-holidays and priority in the allocation of raw materials. These government measures have obstructed the free development of capitalist forces, leading to the enlargement of the small-scale capitalist sector instead of the gradual absorption of this sector into large-scale industry.[49]

Furthermore, to encourage small-scale industry, the government has provided assistance in respect of technology, credit and marketing. During 1972–3 the Small Industries Development Organisation[50] gave technical assistance to 100,413 entrepreneurs.[51] The National Small Industries Corporation, which was set up in 1955, procured machinery for small-scale industries on a hire-purchase basis on concessional terms. During 1972–3 the agency delivered machines worth more than 90 million to various small-scale units.[52] It also assisted the small-scale sector in obtaining orders from many government departments and agencies; the total value of these orders amounted to Rs 370 million in 1972–3.[53] Until 31 March 1973, 585 industrial estates were set up in various parts of the country to accommodate small industrial units in a more congenial atmosphere where specialization, externalities in the form of easier transportation, marketing facilities, procurement of raw materials, etc., could be provided.[54]

These government measures have induced many merchants, moneylenders and upper strata of the rural artisan class, some elements of the petite-bourgeoisie (such as unemployed engineers, university and college graduates) to invest money in small-scale industry and to become entrepreneurs.[55] The *Economic Times* describes this broadening of the small-scale entrepreneurial base as follows:

> A large number of new modern small-scale industries have come into existence and a new entrepreneurial class has come into being, which is drawn from various walks of life and different levels of society. The government's development programme for small-scale industries has been responsible for stimulating the growth of over 300,000 new enterprises, many of which have the potentiality to grow into medium industries.[56]

However, despite the fact that subsidized small-scale industry involves more capital expenditure in the form of market subsidies, supply of machines on concessional terms, creation of risk-bearing funds, establishment of industrial estates and loss of tax (which could have been realized from large industries if they were allowed to operate in the products reserved for the small-scale sector), the government's main argument in favour of small-scale industry is that it generates more employment. This argument has been aptly repudiated by P.N. Dhar and F.H. Lydall in research conducted on behalf of the Institute of Economic Growth in 1961:

> The principal argument put forward in favour of small
> enterprises is that they 'give employment'. This, although true, is
> irrelevant, since the problem facing India is how to save capital
> and other scarce resources, not how to use abundant
> resources. . . . Within the modern sector of manufacturing
> industry – with which we are primarily concerned – available
> evidence suggests that small factories use more capital and more
> labour per unit of output than large factories. The difference in
> the output – capital ratios is particularly marked when account is
> taken of the fact that large factories can more easily be organized
> on a multi-shift basis than small factories. From the point of view
> of saving capital, medium or large multi-shift factories give the
> best results, and small factories usually the worst.[57]

Moreover, they argue,

> It is obvious that, if one wants to increase employment, there is no
> need to search for industries (or sizes of firms) that require a
> large amount of employment per unit of output. Employment as
> such can be 'created' by adding on extra workers at any point one
> likes in the productive (or non-productive) process. The
> important problem, in other words, is not how to absorb surplus
> resources, but how to make best use of scarce resources.[58]

Other government arguments in support of small-scale enterprises, according to Dhar and Lydall, are social and political in nature. The social argument is that small-scale enterprises are less exploitative and more inclined towards equal distribution of income. In fact, the reverse is true. 'In general, wages in small firms are lower than in large firms'.[59] Besides, small-scale enterprises tend to be more exploitative in over-populated countries like India where labour is so cheap. Unlike large-scale enterprises, workers are not protected here by unions, and are very often forced to work beyond their normal hours.[60] Extraction of absolute surplus value is definitely higher in small-scale enterprises than in large industries.

The 'political arguments' seem to be more cogent and express the real reason why the government is more favourably disposed towards small-scale industry. The argument is: the existence of a large number of small-scale industries 'is a guarantee of the maintenance of democratic institutions, *an obstacle to the domination of trade unions, and a barrier to communism'.*[61] It may also be added that their existence undermines capitalist concentration, and creates a favourable situation for the state to maintain its hegemony over the two contending classes, the bourgeoisie and the petite-bourgeoisie.

From the foregoing discussion we find that industrialization in India is not a uniform process. It is not treading the same path which was followed by industrial capitalism. In the West the capitalist mode overcame the pre-capitalist mode and in the course of its further development large-scale enterprises gradually swallowed up small-scale industry. Wherever small-scale enterprises survived, they usually did so either as ancillary to large-scale industry or in areas which were not technically viable for the operation of the large-scale sector. In India, on the other hand, the free development of capitalist concentration has been thwarted and small-scale industry shored up as a competitor with large-scale industry. Moreover, in India the capitalist mode and the pre-capitalist mode which, in fact is the partially dissolved Asiatic mode, co-exist, the former in urban and the latter in rural areas. The special characteristic of the Asiatic mode, as has been mentioned as well in chapter 1, is its integral unity between agriculture and artisan industry. The Asiatic mode in India has persisted and been strengthened because after independence the change that occurred in Indian agrarian relations failed to bring agriculture under the rule of capital (see chapter 7). The abolition of the *zamindari* did not basically alter the agrarian scene characterized by small peasant holdings whose insignificant needs for producers' goods could only be met from the customary source: poverty meant dependence on local artisans even for consumer articles such as earthen utensils, etc.

In the West the industrial revolution occurred when the capitalist class had been able to integrate the whole economy – agriculture and industry – under the capitalist mode of production. The demand for capitalist agriculture was met by capitalist industry and vice versa. Agriculture ceased to support independent industry beyond the capitalist sphere. In India, on the other hand, industrial capitalism has been established only in the urban sector; its reproduction cycle is thus totally different from that in rural artisan industry. In rural areas the reproduction of pre-capitalist industry is most often simple reproduction. While the average rate of profit determines the nature of investment in various sectors of capitalist urban industry, rural artisan industry depends on the purchasing capacity of the village cultivators. Thus there is no continuum between the rural and urban industrial spheres.

6 The state and the growth of the public and private sectors

Prolegomena

The public sector was the most important mechanism through which the state in India has been able to maintain its independence and contain the aspirations of the bourgeoisie which is still engaged in a relentless struggle to take control over it. Unlike the situation in the developed countries, the public sector in India was not an appendage to the capitalist sector. As was noted in chapter 4, the public sector was developed to curtail the economic power of the private corporate sector and to strengthen the state's economic muscle by concentrating in its own sphere the development of the basic and strategic industries.

The means whereby the state accomplished this task in order that the public sector should occupy the commanding height of the economy involved four principles. First, the development of basic large-scale industries was restricted to the state (see chapter 4). Second, private sector investments (in this chapter, private sector means large-scale private industries) and expansions were controlled through a licensing mechanism (see below). Third, the state also determined the growth of the private sector through import quotas, allocations of foreign exchange, price fixing, capital issues, and other governmental measures. Fourth, the state monopolized to itself all financial resources through the nationalization of large banks and insurance companies, thus opening an abundant access to capital to public sector enterprises while limiting access to the private sector.

In this chapter the mechanisms employed by the state to control and regulate the development of the private sector will be examined, as also the relative growth of the public and private sectors, and the contributions of the public and private sectors to the national income, saving and capital formation. This information will throw light on the state's ability to preserve its independence.

The main thrust of the argument will be that the state sector in India, unlike in the West, is not operating to provide social capital or social expenses for monopoly capital to grow. On the contrary, it is trying to liberate itself fiscally, as well as economically, by developing its own enterprises.

Measures of state control

In accordance with the Industrial Policy Resolution of 1948, an act known as the Industries (Development and Regulations) Act, was passed in 1951.[1] This act provided the state with virtually unlimited powers to control and regulate private industries. Under its provisions all industries above a certain size (listed in the first Schedule to the Act) are required to obtain a licence from the Licensing Committee before they can begin operations; no new unit can be set up or old plants be expanded without a prior licence from the state. The government is empowered to refuse a licence or invalidate an existing one on various grounds.

The act also authorizes the government to examine the working of any industrial undertaking and issue instructions. In the case of a violation of these instructions, or mismanagement, the State can take it over. On the strength of this act the government can fix prices, regulate the channels of distribution, forbid production of certain commodities and prescribe the volume of production.

In addition to the Industries (Development and Regulations) Act of 1951, the Companies Act was brought into being in 1956 (and amended later) to further regulate and control the private sector.[2] According to A.H. Hanson, the Companies Act 'constituted one of the most detailed and stringent codes of business legislation to be found anywhere in the world'.[3] One of its main purposes was to restrict the practice of a managing agency system which had been facilitating the growth of monopolies.

Chapter 2 has shown how the managing agency system in the formative period of industrial development in India promoted the joint stock companies by providing capital, technical know-how, marketing facilities, etc. Later on the system gave birth to an Indian variety of trust through the interlocking of funds and directorships.

Moreover, managing agents often charged client companies 20 to 50 per cent of their profits as remuneration for their managerial services. In addition, some managing agents also charged 'office allowance', and 'extra remuneration for extra services' (such as for procurement of machines from abroad, etc.).[4]

Through the provisions of the 1956 Companies Act attempts were made to contain this trend towards the concentration of economic power in a few hands. The following provisions are important in this regard:

  (i) that overall managerial remuneration shall be limited (clause 198);

 (ii) that government approval shall be required for the appointment of any managing or whole-time director (clause 269);

(iii) that no person shall be a director of more than twenty companies (clause 275);

(iv) that no person, except with the permission of the government, shall be appointed managing director of more than two companies (clause 316);

 (v) that no managing director shall be appointed for more than five years at a time (clause 317);

(vi) that the government, at its discretion, shall have the power to order a special audit of a company's accounts and, on receipt of the auditor's report, take such action on it as is considered 'necessary in accordance with the provisions of this Act or any other law for the time being in force' (clause 233A).

The Industries (Development and Regulations) Act of 1951, along with the Companies Act of 1956 (as amended), were formidable tools in the hands of the government to keep in check the rise of the bourgeoisie. The government's licensing committee was formed in 1952 with representatives from all ministries dealing with economic affairs.[5] This committee was the final clearing authority for all licence applications submitted to the government. However, before an application could be placed before the licensing committee for approval, it would have to be passed by another government bureau – the Director General of Technical Development (D.G.T.D.).

The task of this bureau is to examine the technical implications of all applications that seek permission to establish new industrial units or expand old ones. The Ninth Report of the Estimates Committee has described its functions as follows:

The D.G.T.D. makes a technoeconomic appreciation of the applications for industrial licensing, indicating inter-alia:
a) if there is need for more capacity for the item of production proposed in the application, also keeping in view import substitution and export possibilities;
b) if the scheme of manufacture is technically sound;
c) whether the capacity asked for by the entrepreneur is commensurate with the capital goods to be installed, taking into consideration the capital goods which the party may already possess;
d) whether the scheme as submitted or as further modified in the light of discussion with D.G.T.D. will ensure reaching the maximum possible indigenous content within a reasonable time;
e) whether the plant to be installed and/or method of manufacture to be adopted is modern and economic;
f) whether the location lends itself to economic viability and disposal of effluents.[6]

Based on these basic considerations, the D.G.T.D. recommends to the Licensing Committee either acceptance or rejection of the application.[7]

The other hurdles a prospective investor must cross before he can set up an industry include clearance from the Capital Issue Committee, the Capital Goods Committee, the Controller of Imports and Exports, and the Reserve Bank of India. In the case of foreign collaboration, the approval of the Foreign Agreements Committee is also needed.

The Capital Issue (Control) Act of 1947 makes it obligatory to obtain permission from the government for the issue of all types of shares and debentures. All joint stock companies of India and abroad (issuing stocks in India) fall under the jurisdiction of this act. The act empowered the government to limit the concentration of investment in any industry.[8]

After the receipt of approval for issuing stocks, the next step for an entrepreneur is to obtain a capital goods licence from the Chief Controller of Imports and Exports who is to find out whether the goods and equipment can be procured from indigenous sources. If the items are not available in India, the entrepreneur may get approval to import them.

Under the Foreign Exchange Regulation Act and the Import and Export (Control) Act of 1947, however, no commodity can be imported from abroad without prior permission from the Controller of Import and clearance from the Reserve Bank of India. So the kind of capital goods and where they can be procured depend upon the amount and denomination of foreign exchange released.

The Essential Commodities Act of 1955 gave authority to the government to fix prices on almost all products. In 1966, the Administrative Reform Commission advised the government to set up a 'Commission on Prices, Cost and Tariff to undertake the following functions:

Cl. 321.1 (a) determination of prices of industrial products and industrial raw materials and intermediates with a view to assisting the government in evolving a rational price policy;
(b) conducting studies on the costs of production of selected industrial products and locating the areas in which reductions in costs are feasible and necessary, and making recommendations for the achievement of such reduction; and
(c) conducting inquiries relating to tariff protection and making recommendations to government on the basis of such inquiries.[9]

Furthermore, it was suggested,

Cl. 321.3: The commission should be invested with the powers similar to those enjoyed by the Commissions of Inquiry Act, 1952.[10]

In most cases the prices of industrial goods in India used to be fixed by the Tariff Commission;[11] since 1970 they are being regulated on the basis of advice from the Bureau of Industrial Costs and Prices. This Bureau was constituted in January 1970, in accordance with the recommendation of the Administrative Reforms Commission. The operation of price controls in India is not uniform in respect to all industries or products. In respect to some products the government determines the factory, wholesale and retail prices; in others, factory and wholesale prices; and in some only the factory prices. However, price control is applicable evidently only in the case of large-scale factories.

In brief, what should be the role of the government in the economic administration or physical control of the organized private sector has been succinctly described by the Administrative Reforms Commission in its delineation of the subjects to be looked after by the Ministry of Commerce and Industry.

> Cl. 311: The subjects of Commerce and Industry should be combined into a single Ministry of Commerce and Industry. This ministry should be responsible for formulating broad policies and strategy for industrial and commercial development in the public as well as private sectors. It should, however, not be in any administrative control of any public sector industrial undertakings.[12]

The state's functionaries and private corporate capital

Thus we find that the state's controls over the organized private sector are varied and extensive, and they are exercised primarily through the executive branch of the state and especially through the bureaucracy.[13] In order to understand the operation of private sector industry (organized) in India, it is necessary to assess the private sector's (organized) relationship with the state. Stanley A. Kochanek, an American scholar, has made a thorough study of the patterns of business access to the government. In his view

> Business lacks direct elite representation and has been unable, so far, to influence the selection of the top political leadership. And so business is forced to rely on indirect influence through formal and informal channels to government decision-makers. Because business played a behind-the-scenes role (so far as it played any role at all) in the freedom movement, the post independence political leadership was drawn predominantly from the urban intellectual elite which had all along dominated the leadership of the Congress party. As one senior civil servant put it, 'By training and background, the political leadership in India has no background in modern business. Perhaps the only exception was T.T. Krishnamachari. No other minister has had that kind of background. This has resulted in a lack of rapport between the political leadership and business.'[14]

Kochanek further maintains that the process of access to the higher bureaucracy has been even more precarious:

> Indian business did not enjoy that rapport with the colonial bureaucracy that English business easily maintained. Thus, there were no long-term personal contacts, no long established strategies of access to fall back on when bureaucracy became, after independence, a center of power in its own right, by virtue of its pivotal position in a planned and controlled economy.[15]

The most important factor which limited the influence of the private sector on the bureaucracy could be traced to the tradition of bureaucracy that developed during the days of the British Raj. In fact, the British administrative system in India was built upon the model of the earlier Moghul administration. When the British replaced the Moghuls as the rulers of India in the eighteenth century, they did not at first introduce any fundamental change in the administrative system they inherited. As has been said by the historian Percival Spear, 'The British found the wreck of this [former] system and admired it even in decay.'[16] Without going into details of how the Indian bureaucracy evolved in the nineteenth century[17] from this wreck, which remained more or less unchanged even in independent India, it can be said that the fundamentals of both Moghul and British administrations had a great deal in common. Both concentrated on the collection of revenue, law and order, and dispensation of justice.[18] Even the British retained Akbar's revenue division of the country into *subas, sarkars, parganas,* and *mahals.* Under the British, the district officer, who was designated as the collector of revenue, had as much power as that of a Moghul *subadar* or *fouzdar*:

> Local administration under British rule was built around the position of the collector. Based on a system developed by the Moghul rulers, the post was created to give the civilians more power in overseeing the Empire. The English first utilized it in 1769. Abolished in 1773, it was finally reinstituted in 1781. By 1790, it had developed the essential form it was to maintain until the 1930s. Because of the nature of its responsibilities, the position was central to the structure of the ICS (Indian Civil

Service), and a contributor to the status of the ICS in India. It was to become the keystone of British rule and, perhaps more importantly, the symbol to the people both in India and in England of that rule.[19]

The Indian Civil Service (often called 'the greatest civil service') was not developed on the model of the English Civil Service; rather, it differed from the 'home government' or the English Civil Service in several important respects. In the home government, the civil servants in most cases executed the policies adopted by the politicians. In India, the civil servants were responsible not only for executing but also for formulating the policies.[20] The English civil servant was employed in a civil capacity. Unlike the Indian civil servant, he was not a holder of political or judicial office. Indian civil servants were trained in a literary generalist tradition, which aimed at imparting virtues of Platonic guardianship. As true guardians, they were educated in methods designed to hold India in a benevolent but tight grip.[21]

The Indian Civil Service had a dual role. On the one hand it determined the policy of the government in the secretariat; on the other it served as the executive arm of the government in the field. It was also provided by law that one-third of High Court and Supreme Court judges should be civil servants.[22] Thus it had all-pervasive power: why? H.F. Goodnow, in a recent book on the Civil Service of Pakistan, thinks that the British, to maintain their rule in India,

> had to occupy the important positions, and all offices held by natives must be supervised by a British officer. The simplest type of organizational pyramid was established. The District Officer was delegated extensive power within his district. The tougher or more volatile problems might be reviewed by his senior at division headquarters or even by the governor of the province. At the top was the Governor-General. It was a very simple hierarchy – at least in the beginning. As the problems became more complex, the size of the Governor's staff was increased; ultimately it became a secretariat.[23]

In Goodnow's view the British, in their anxiety to control violence, gave the civil service unlimited power. This argument is partially true and touches only the surface. L.S.S. O'Malley has given the real reason underlying the power of the civil servants; it was rooted in the social economy of India:

> One very important distinction between them (i.e., the Indian civil servants) and the civil servants elsewhere is that they are the local representatives of a government which is not only the supreme administrative authority, but also the *supreme landlord*. Its position as such has been inherited from previous governments. *In India the right of the state to a share in the produce of the soil has been recognised* from time immemorial. This right takes the form of payment of land revenue, which historically is older than private rent (emphasis added).[24]

So we find that even under the British, civil servants derived their power as the representatives of the state which was the supreme landlord or owner of the soil. As has already been observed, the patrimonial bureaucrats of Moghul India, such as the *fouzdars* or *subadars*, had unlimited power[25] because they were agents of a state whose power, unlike in Europe, was never curtailed by the development of feudal or bourgeois classes in the proper sense of the terms.[26] The nobility, i.e. the revenue collectors (*fouzdars, subadars*, etc.), had no independent existence outside the state or the grace of the sovereign. Their remuneration was paid from the share of the state's revenue. They had no independent claim to rent, as was the case in feudal Europe. In brief, in India the state's control was so complete that there was no scope for centrifugal forces to develop to challenge its power.

It is noteworthy that even under the British the bureaucracy was recruited from the traditional literati classes which, unlike in Europe, had little organic relationship with trade and industry. As B.B. Misra points out:

> Except for the educated and salaried employees in business, the bulk of the Indian professional classes excluded those engaged in trade and industry, who in England constituted powerful groups among the educated classes. Moreover, except during the three most recent decades, the increase in the number of Indian lawyers and public servants, doctors and teachers, writers, scholars and members of other recognised professions was due to

educational, judicial and administrative development rather than to technological or industrial progress. In fact, from the peculiar circumstances of their growth the professional classes in India *continued to comprise* those who also ranked high in the hierarchy of caste (emphasis added).[27]

These higher caste people (in the pre-British period), as can be recalled from the discussion in chapter 2, were mostly hangers-on to the state or community; they were seldom related to production directly. In the British period, too, in the absence of large-scale industrialization, the educated middle class from which the Indian component of the bureaucracy was recruited failed to establish a link with the producing classes. That is why V. Subramaniam characterizes it as a 'derivative middle class';[28] and he also finds the reason for its different development from its counterpart in the West in the very nature of class formation in India under British rule.

> It is unlike the natural middle class of Western Europe or America which evolved naturally through social evolution without foreign conquest. This natural middle class has two balancing wings: the economic wing of distributors, rentiers, small-scale industrialists and such other types of petit bourgeoisie, and a professional wing of lawyers, civil servants, school teachers, etc. Each wing supports the other – commercial lawyers are needed to sort out differences in commerce and commerce is needed to pay for the lawyers. In a colonial situation, however, this derivative middle class develops only the professional wing because the rulers will not allow a commercial or industrial wing to develop too soon.[29]

S. Kochanek also holds the same view and argues that the Indian bureaucracy is independent because economic interests have failed to colonize it. He says:

> A final factor which limits intervention in the bureaucracy has been the inability of modern economic and social interests to colonize the bureaucracy. The bureaucracy is independent, enjoys a very high social status and is, above all, committed to accomplishing its own institutional missions.[30]

Thus the Indian bureaucracy is recruited from the traditional literati castes (who evolved as the ideologues of the Asiatic Mode of Production), and having no connection with trade and industry, has little interest in advancing the cause of private capital. In fact the bureaucracy, as well as the people in general in India, share a common distrust if not contempt towards private business. In a simple survey of the people's attitudes toward business, Taub found that 'most of the community viewed businessmen as greedy and dishonest'. Furthermore, most respondents

> who answered the question 'Is the government achieving the proper balance between the public and private sector?' (68.6%), said that the government should take on more responsibility in the business areas; that is, the public sector should be enlarged. Turning to the question of whether businessmen are hampered by too many rules and regulations, 53 of the 63 people who answered the question (84.1%) thought that businessmen needed to be controlled in every sphere by rules that limit their behavior.[31]

Turning to the bureaucrats' attitudes towards business, Taub noted that their demand for their control of business stemmed from I.C.S. tradition as well as self-interest:[32]

> The IAS has a tradition, inherited from the ICS, of controlling whatever means are related to their goals. In this context, attitude against free enterprise seems inevitable. The officer who made the following statement spoke for many when he observed that 'resources in the private sector are not available to the planners. That is, they have no control over them. Several attempts are being made to regulate private business through licensing policy and control of some materials. But this is neither enough nor the proper way'.[33]

The growth of private corporate capital and the monopoly houses

The state control measures over private capital, however, have not been successful in curbing its expansion, though they might have slowed down its pace of development. This fact is adequately demonstrated by the growth of the monopoly houses in the last two decades. P.C. Mahalanobis's Committee on the Distribution of Income and Levels of Living reported in 1964 that, in 1960–61, the total number of companies each having a paid-up capital of less than Rs 5 lakhs (half a million) constituted 86% of the total number of companies, but their share in the total paid-up capital was only 14.6 per cent. At the same time, companies each having a paid-up capital of Rs 50 lakhs (5 million) and above constituted only 1.6 per cent of all companies but owned 53 per cent of the total paid-up capital[34] (see Table 6.1).

R.K. Hazari, in a study on the structure of the corporate private sector, found that twenty selected complexes or groups dominate it.[35] He defined a corporate group as consisting of units or companies which are subject to the policy decisions of a common source. Each company is a separate legal entity but policy decisions on investment, production, sale, profits, etc., originate from a common authority and are coordinated by it. The controlling authority very often does not own the majority of shares in every company, but, through intercorporate investment, acquires control over a number of companies with little investment. It was found by Dr Hazari that the twenty groups had an interest of one kind or another in 983 companies with a share capital of Rs 236 crores in 1951, and 1,073 companies with a share capital of Rs 352 crores (1 crore = 10 million) in 1958. Table 6.2 illustrates how the twenty groups increased their share capital, net capital stock and gross physical stock of all non-government companies from 1951 to 1958.

Further, it can be seen from Table 6.2 that four groups controlled more than 25% of all share capital and net as well as gross capital stock.

It was thus realized by the functionaries of the state that, despite the operation of the Industries (Development and Regulations) Act, the growing concentration of economic power in the hands of a few has continued. To find out the lacunae in the Industries Act, Dr Hazari was made an honorary consultant of the Planning Commission in 1966. In a detailed report[36] he pinpointed how the big industrial houses were able to subvert the intent of the Industrial Act. What they did was to submit a number of applications for a licence on each product. In this way they could appropriate the licensable capacity of any industry. His indictment was particularly severe on Birla applications:

TABLE 6.1 Number and amount of paid-up capital of non-government companies at work by size classes of paid-up capital

Size class of paid-up capital (Rs lakhs)	Companies				Paid-up capital			
	number		% of total		Rs crores		% of total	
	1951–2	1960–1	1951–2	1960–1	1951–2	1960–1	1951–2	1960–1
below 5	26,785	22,363	91.8	86.0	202.0	185.1	25.0	14.6
5–50	2,170	3,222	7.4	12.4	337.2	409.7	41.6	32.3
50–100	148	238	0.5	0.9	107.6	157.9	13.3	12.4
100 and above	80	185	0.3	0.7	162.6	517.0	20.1	40.7
all classes	29,183	26,009	100.0	100.0	809.4	1,269.7	100.0	100.0

Source: Department of Company Law Administration (unpublished): cited as Table 4.3 in Mahalanobis Committee's *Report on Distribution of Income and Levels of Living.*

TABLE 6.2 Share of twenty groups in share capital, net capital stock and gross physical stock of all non-government public companies (public companies only)

Groups	Share capital		Net capital stock		Gross capital stock		Difference in percentage share between 1951 and 1958		
	1951	1958	1951	1958	1951	1958	share capital	net capital stock	gross capital stock
Total non-government companies	100.0	100.0	100.0	100.0	100.0	100.0			
20 complexes	38.97	47.96	36.48	45.05	37.05	44.85	8.99	8.57	7.80
10 complexes	29.35	34.53	26.99	32.62	27.21	31.83	5.18	5.63	4.62
4 complexes	22.13	26.75	20.55	26.60	21.20	25.20	4.62	6.05	4.00

Source: *Report of the Committee on Distribution of Income and Levels of Living*, p.41.

It is to some extent legitimate to infer that Birla enterprise, justifiable or not in terms of ultimate performance, does tend to pre-empt licensing capacity in many industries. The sheer pressure to multiple applications for each product must be such as to yield positive results for at least two or more applications.[37]

Another committee – the Industrial Policy Licensing Committee – was appointed by the government of India in 1967 to inquire into the actual operation of the licensing system. The committee submitted its report in July 1969. Its observations were more or less similar to those of the Hazari Committee. It found that the two biggest industrial houses, Tata and Birla, did not always use the licences which they pre-empted. The number of licences not acted upon were 164 for the Birla enterprise and 47 for that of Tata. The Birla enterprise also was severely reprimanded by the Industrial Licensing Policy Inquiry Committee (I.L.P.I.C.):

> From our aggregative analysis and case studies, we have found that among the Houses which were responsible for various forms of pre-emption, the most prominent is the House of Birla. They held the largest number of unimplemented licenses, made repeated attempts to obtain a large number of licenses for many products, created excess capacities and tried to have them regularised afterwards and also produced more than authorised capacities.[38]

According to I.L.P.I.C., there were 73 large industrial enterprises with assets of Rs 5 crores or more each, which controlled over 1,125 units in 1964. In addition to this, 60 large concerns were identified with assets above Rs 5 crores. Of the 73 industrial houses, 20 were designated as 'large Industrial Houses', the criterion being the possession of assets of Rs 35 crores or above. In 1966 the government of India granted 7,445 licences to the private corporate sector, 2,800 of which were chanelled to the large industrial houses.

From the reports of the I.L.P.I.C. and Hazari Committee it became clear that the impressive gains by the large industrial houses were based on middle-class consumer goods industries catering to the urban population. In 1970 a new industrial policy was announced by the government, incorporating most of the recommendations of the I.L.P.I.C. This did not alter the Industrial Policy Resolution of

1956, but divided all industries into a number of sectors: public, private, joint, core, heavy industry, middle-scale and co-operative sectors. Under the new licensing system the large industrial houses were debarred from investment or expansion of investment in the middle sector, which consists mainly of consumer goods industries, other than for maintaining a minimum level for economic operation. However, they could invest in the core sector and the non-core heavy industries sector (requiring Rs 5 crores or more in investment), excluding those reserved for the public sector in schedule A of the 1956 Industrial Policy Resolution. The addition of the core and heavy industries sectors in the new industrial policy was motivated by two considerations: curtailing the concentration of economic power in the large industrial houses, and the economic growth of the country. The industries in the core and non-core heavy industries sectors need heavy investment: compared to middle sector industries there is a longer gestation period and profits are not so easy. The core sector consists of industries such as synthetic rubber or certain chemicals which are important because of their links to other industries. The government declared that it would release inputs for these industries on a priority basis for growth reasons.

It was also decided under the new industrial policy that the public sector should establish industries beyond the areas reserved for it in the Industrial Policy Resolution of 1956, particularly in the short-gestation consumer goods sector, thus removing at the same time both the government's and the consumer's dependence on the private sector.

Further, it was found by each and every committee that the reasons for the quick expansion of the large industrial houses lay also in their greater ability to take loans from state financial institutions and private banks. The Mahalanobis Committee on Distribution of Income reported:

> The growth of the private sector in industry and especially of the big companies has been facilitated by the financial assistance rendered by public institutions like the Industrial Finance Corporation (IFC), the National Industrial Development Corporation, etc. Thus as on 30th June, 1963, loans had been approved by the IFC for a total sum of Rs 127.7 crores. The number of concerns to which loans had been sanctioned was 244; 143 of these concerns were given loans of less than Rs 50 lakhs

each, the total amounting to Rs 32.7 crores, while 101 concerns were given loans exceeding Rs 50 lakhs, the total being Rs 94.9 crores. Loans exceeding Rs 1 crore each were given to 22 concerns and accounted for Rs 34.8 crores.... Lending by NIDC which totalled Rs 3 crores up to March, 1963, would also generally be to bigger companies.[39]

The I.L.P.I.C. also noted that the 20 larger industrial houses received 17 per cent and the 73 large industrial houses 44 per cent of all assistance provided by the financial institutions to the corporate sector for the period 1956 to 1966. Loans were advanced on the criterion of efficient use. Large concerns enjoying economies of scale could more fruitfully use the loans than small establishments, and were thus automatic choices for these grants. But the whole idea of large industrial enterprises expanding on the basis of finance provided by the government was repugnant to the functionaries of the state and contrary to their professed goal of establishing a socialist pattern of society.

The I.L.P.I.C. headed by an I.C.S. officer, provided an easy solution to this dilemma (efficiency v. non-concentration of economic power): governmental institutions should own and control the concerns they assist up to the amount they provide. Thus the I.L.P.I.C. recommended that government financial institutions should be entitled to convert their loans into equity and also have the prerogative of actively participating in planning and management.

In short, existing private enterprises in which investments of government financial institutions are predominant should be for all practical purposes considered as the public sector and the government should have the final say in planning and top appointments in these concerns, which would be known as the 'joint sector'. The 'joint sector', the committee thought, would be able to prevent the concentration of economic power in industries classed under schedules B and C of the 1956 Industrial Policy Resolution, particularly in those industries which require heavy investments, by letting the government provide the bulk of the funds and reserving to itself the final control.[40]

As was expected, the 1970 new industrial policy came under heavy attack from large industrial concerns. J.R.D. Tata of the House of Tata, which then occupied the top position in terms of assets and sales, submitted a memorandum to the Prime Minister in

May 1972, protesting at the exclusion of the large industrial houses from the middle sector, and suggesting some fundamental revisions in the joint sector. The following extract from the memorandum underlines the anxiety felt:

> Finally, we come to the most important factor inhibiting investment, which is government's industrial policy introduced in February, 1970, to prevent the growth of the larger houses with a view to avoiding the further growth of economic power....

The memorandum further contends that this policy, by

> drastically curbing the growth of companies forming part of large houses and foreign controlled companies which between them represent over 50 per cent of organised private industry's total physical assets, automatically deprives the private sector of half of its investment and growth potentiality.[41]

As the banks were the other most important source of finance for the private sector, another significant step taken by the state in 1969 to bring the corporate sector under its control was the nationalization of fourteen major commercial banks (with deposits of Rs 50 crores or more), many of which belonged to the larger industrial houses, and through which they could use the small savings of the people to expand their industrial empires. The Mahalanobis Committee reports:

> Analysis of the bank credit thus made increasingly available for the financing of industrial expansion during the last few years shows that the main beneficiaries have been the big and medium enterprises....
> The dependence of private industry on banks for financing its expansion is confirmed by a purposewise analysis of advances by scheduled banks.[42]

With the banks nationalized (along with other organized financial institutions, most of which were already state-owned), the state acquired a 'tremendous power of intervention, in every type of business enterprises, both large and small, and a widespread power of control and planning over the entire economic field'.[43]

It was not an exaggeration, therefore, when S. Kochanek says:

> One official estimated that 75 per cent of the decisions affecting business are made by the bureaucracy. The colonial raj has thus given way to what has been called 'the permit, license, quota raj' and its princes are the top bureaucrats.[44]

Moreover, he adds:

> The bureaucracy has in its hands such tremendous power to regulate and control business that business is afraid to offend government by intervening excessively or tactlessly. Business is too dependent upon administrative actions to risk antagonizing government to the point of retaliation. There is too much that the bureaucracy in a controlled economy can do, or fail to do, in the way of regulatory, licensing, and enforcing actions. The majority of businessmen, therefore, still come to government as supplicants. Only the largest have begun to approach government in the manner of the self-confident industrialist; and threats, even on the part of the most powerful industrialists lack credibility.... Thus, for example, government did not take seriously the threat by the drug industry to stop production of particular drugs if price controls were imposed. Nor does government quake when business talks of a strike in the capital market. Because most businessmen receive large portions of their funds from government credit agencies, this threat, too, lacked credibility.[45]

Thus it was not unexpected that the large industrial houses have not been able to expand as rapidly in recent years as they had been doing before the nationalization of banks in 1969 or the imposition of new restrictions on their investments in the new industrial policy of 1970.[46] Table 6.3 indicates their rate of growth since 1963–4.[47]

Table 6.3 also shows that, in terms of expansion of assets, the rate of progress of the twenty larger industrial houses has been uneven. While in 1966–7 the Tatas topped the list, since 1972–3 the Birlas have outgrown them both in assets and sales.

Needless to say, in the Indian economy where private ownership has not been abolished, the growth of the private sector will continue unabated (if there is no recession or other economic constraint), despite all state attempts to curb it; but its rate of growth,

TABLE 6.3 Big business houses in India

| | Total assets (Rs crores) | | | | Percentage increase | | |
	according to M.I.C. 1963–4	L.P.I.C. 1966–7	E.T. 1972–3	Estimate 1975–6	1975–6 over 1972–3	1972–3 over 1966–7	1966–7 over 1963–4
Birla	282.9	446.9	725.8	1064.6	46.7	62.4	58.0
Tata	375.0	520.0	685.5	974.6	42.2	31.7	38.8
Mafatlal	39.5	106.5	218.9	284.3	29.9	105.5	169.6
J.K. Singhania	54.5	63.8	136.8	224.1	63.8	114.4	17.1
Scindia	46.3	63.9	127.0	217.1	70.9	98.7	38.0
Thapar	63.3	85.3	132.0	204.1	54.6	54.7	34.7
Bangur	62.5	97.9	139.9	195.9	40.0	42.9	56.6
Shri Ram	50.3	73.2	137.8	186.9	35.6	88.2	45.5
Sarabhai	33.8	56.7	129.5	182.5	40.9	128.4	67.8
I.C.I.	36.9	49.0	146.0	181.5	24.3	198.0	32.8
Kirloskar	19.1	45.9	114.4	177.1	54.8	149.2	140.3
A.C.C.	76.9	91.3	137.2	169.1	23.3	50.3	18.7
Parry	11.7	72.7	111.2	148.1	33.2	53.0	521.4
Mahindra	20.1	42.5	83.1	143.9	73.2	95.5	111.4
Bajaj	16.7	40.3	94.8	143.2	51.1	135.2	141.3
Killicks	38.3	51.4	93.7	139.4	48.8	82.3	34.2
Walchand	52.7	83.1	99.6	135.1	35.6	19.9	57.7
Modi	11.3	19.4	62.3	116.1	85.4	221.1	71.7
Larsen & Toubro	n/a	29.4	54.3	113.5	109.0	84.7	
Kasturbhai Lalbhai	33.9	49.3	85.8	109.2	27.3	74.0	45.4

Source: *M.I.C.: Monopolies Enquiry Committee*; L.P.I.C.: *Licensing Policy Enquiry Committee Report*; E.T. estimate: *Economic Times* estimate (*Economic Times*, 14 February 1977).

direction, and decisions about who should get the opportunity to expand, depend to a great extent on state patronage. It was not by virtue of more efficiency that the Birlas went ahead of the Tatas in both total assets and sales; their success lies in their greater ability to secure a larger number of licences and more loans from the nationalized banks and state financial institutions. While in 1973 outstanding loans to the Birlas from the nationalized banks stood at Rs 77.3 crores, those to the Tatas amounted to Rs 50 crores.[48] The Birlas' ability to acquire the lion's share of licences issued to the private corporate sector has already been mentioned. In fact, in respect to capital–output ratio, the Tatas were not inferior to the Birlas, but, for the reasons mentioned, the Birlas could outgrow them.

The public sector's growing command over the economy

The main mechanism through which the state has been able to maintain its hegemony over the private corporate sector is through the expansion of the public sector. In the last two decades the public sector has risen to a commanding height in the economy, mainly as a result of larger investments in the public sector since the Second Five Year Plan (see Table 6.4).

TABLE 6.4 Public and private sector investments (in Rs crores)

	Total actual outlay	Private sector actual outlay	%	Public sector actual outlay	%
Second Plan	6,750	3,100	45.9	3,650	54.1
Third Plan	10,400	4,100	39.4	6,300	60.6
Fourth Plan	22,635	8,980	39.7	13,655	60.3

Source: Relevant Plans.

In the Second Five Year Plan the total outlay amounted to Rs 6,750 crores; of this, the public sector's total share (including irrigation, power, etc.) came to Rs 3,650 crores. In the Third Five Year Plan, the total outlay was Rs 10,400 crores and in the Fourth Five Year Plan Rs 22,635 crores. Of these, public sector investments accounted for Rs 6,300 crores and Rs 13,655 crores respectively. The expected outlay for the Fifth Five Year Plan is Rs 53,411 crores. Of this amount, the public sector has been allocated Rs 37,250 crores and the private sector Rs 16,161 crores. The share of investments in industry and minerals in the public sector is expected to rise to Rs 8,939 crores in the Fifth Five Year Plan.

As a result of this huge investment in the public sector, the number of public sector enterprises in operation increased from only 5 in 1950 to 129 in March 1975; the investments comprising equity and loan capital in these enterprises also increased from Rs 29 crores in 1950 to Rs 7,261 crores in 1974–5 (see Table 6.5). Thus, it was not at all surprising that eight public sector companies, each having more than Rs 100 crores in total assets, were twice the size of the top twenty larger industrial houses put together (see Tables 6.3 and 6.6). While the total assets of the top twenty-eight public sector concerns, according to an estimate of the *Economic Times* in March

TABLE 6.5 Growth in investments in the central public sector

	Total investment (Rs crores)	Number of enterprises
At the commencement of the First Five Year Plan	29	5
At the commencement of the Second Five Year Plan	81	21
At the commencement of the Third Five Year Plan	953	48
At the end of the Third Five Year Plan (31.3.66)	2,415	74
As at 31.3.67	2,841	77
As at 31.3.68	3,333	83
At the commencement of the Fourth Five Year Plan (31.3.69)	3,902	85
As at 31.3.70	4,301	91
As at 31.3.71	4,682	97
As at 31.3.72	5,052	101
As at 31.3.73	5,571	113
As at 31.3.74	6,237	122
As at 31.3.75	7,261	129

Source: *Annual Report on the Working of Industrial and Commercial Undertakings of the Central Government, 1974–75*, vol. I.

TABLE 6.6 Total assets and net sales of top twenty-eight undertakings of the central government

	Total Assets	*Net Sales*
	Rs *crores*	
1 Hindustan Steel	1,270.6	851.9
2 Bokaro Steel	1,081.1	52.7
3 Fertiliser Corp. of India	907.2	159.7
4 Bharat Heavy Elec.	836.2	171.7
5 Shipping Corp. of India	680.9	211.6
6 Food Corp. of India	650.6	1,871.4
7 Indian Oil	608.1	1,856.3
8 Hindustan Aeronautic	386.0	115.2
9 Central Coalfields	340.9	96.0
10 Heavy Eng. Corp.	292.1	53.1
11 O.N.G.C.	280.7	133.8
12 Coal Mines Authority	261.1	194.1
13 Damodar Valley	249.5	48.5
14 Indian Petrochemicals	225.4	36.3
15 Air India	222.8	187.4
16 Hindustan Copper	220.3	28.4
17 Bharat Aluminium	196.0	10.5
18 Indian Iron	172.3	98.3
19 State Trading Corp.	171.6	956.0
20 F.A.C.T.	171.0	53.4
21 Neyveli Lignite	138.5	33.7
22 N.M.D.C.	150.9	21.9
23 M.M.T.C.	148.3	642.8
24 Bharat Electronics	129.0	54.8
25 H.M.T.	123.1	83.5
26 Mogul Lines	118.9	21.2
27 Hindustan Petroleum	115.2	281.2
28 Indian Airlines	102.5	92.2
Total	10,250.8	8,417.6

Source: *Economic Times*, 12 March 1977.

1977, amounted to Rs 10,250 crores (see Table 6.6), the aggregate assets of the top twenty business houses was Rs 5,110 crores. Moreover, in the private sector there were only two industrial houses which had assets exceeding Rs 300 crores (Table 6.3), while in the public sector there were nine such enterprises (Table 6.6). It is also noteworthy that, in the private sector, the number of houses with assets of more than Rs 100 crores was twenty, while in the public sector it was twenty-eight. The comparison between the larger industrial houses and the big concerns in the public sector clearly brings out their relative strength.

The bulk of investments in the public sector are made by the central government in the form of equity capital and long-term loans. State (provincial) governments have also been allowed to participate in the equity capital. The general principle followed by the government is to maintain an approximate parity between equity and long-term loans. In the total government investments of Rs 7,261 crores up to 1974–5, the equity capital amounted to Rs 3,839 crores and long-term loans to Rs 3,422 crores.[49] Since the nationalization of fourteen large commercial banks in 1969, the public sector enterprises have been

> empowered to have cash credit arrangements with the nationalised banks. It is open to each enterprise to deal with one public sector bank or a consortium of public sector banks depending upon operational convenience and the extent of cash credit requirements.[50]

Until 31 March 1975 public sector enterprises had outstanding loans with the nationalized banks under cash credit arrangements of Rs 1,028 crores.[51] These funds were available to the public sector enterprises over and above the investment of Rs 7,261 crores mentioned earlier. To meet working capital needs these enterprises can take short-term loans from the central government. The duration of such loans is two to three years, but under special circumstances they can be extended to five years, but no longer. Outstanding short-term loans to public sector enterprises at 31 March 1975, totalled Rs 174.95 crores.[52]

The government's income from public sector enterprises is realized by means of dividends on equity capital and interest on loans. The rate of interest charged is shown in Table 6.7. The high rate indicates that these loans are a good source of income for the state.

The duration of a long-term loan is fifteen years inclusive of the period of moratorium when, under certain circumstances, the principal or loan cannot be repaid. This repayment starts one year after the commencement of production.

The performance of the public sector enterprises, on the basis of profits, was not very commendable until 1971. In fact, until then,

TABLE 6.7 Rate of interest charged on public sector undertakings

	Industrial and Commercial enterprises		Financial institutions	
	until 31.7.74	*from* 1.8.74	*until* 31.3.74	*from* 1.8.74
Up to 1 year	7.0	9.5	4.75	6.25
Exceeding 1 but not exceeding 4 years	7.0	9.5	5.25	6.75
Exceeding 4 but not exceeding 9 years	7.5	10.0	5.75	7.25
Exceeding 9 but not exceeding 15 years	8.0	10.5	6.25	7.75
Exceeding 15 but not exceeding 30 years	–	–	6.5	8.0

Source: *Annual Report on the Working of Industrial and Commercial Undertakings of the Central Government, 1974–75.*

many units were making losses. But the utility of public sector enterprises cannot be measured in terms of profits only. Their social returns should also be taken into consideration – such as providing consumer goods or construction materials to the poorer sections at a subsidized rate, or keeping more people on payrolls than is required. Thus by providing employment they can function as the agents of social harmony.

Moreover, one of the reasons for the low returns on investment in public sector enterprises was due to the long gestation period of the basic and heavy industries: many enterprises took long periods to reach their capacity utilization. However, since 1971–2 their performance has been genuinely impressive; they have achieved a considerable growth rate in turnover, profitability, internal resource mobilization, employment, capacity utilization and foreign exchange earnings. The turnover of all running concerns increased from Rs 3,310 crores in 1970–71[53] to Rs 6,776.69 crores in 1973–4, and further increased to Rs 10,217.19 crores in 1974–5 (see Table 6.8). Gross profit (before interest on loans) was Rs 559.21 crores in 1974–5, compared with Rs 339.59 in 1973–4 (Table 6.8), and Rs 146 crores in 1970–71. The rate of return (gross profit) increased from 6.4 per cent in 1973–4 to 8.4 per cent in 1974–5.

In net profits, too, public sector enterprises have recorded a tremendous growth rate since 1970–71. While in this year the net profit of the public sector enterprises was only Rs 20 crores, it was Rs 155.92 crores in 1973–4 and Rs 322.34 crores in 1974–5 (see Table 6.8). The total foreign exchange earned by public enterprises

TABLE 6.8 Consolidated profit and loss account for public sector enterprises for the year 1974–5

Previous Year†		1974–75 (Rs crores)		
		Production Enterprises	Service Enterprises	Total
	To opening stock of finished goods and work-in-progress:			
736.05	Finished goods	509.64	665.76	1,175.40
297.01	Work-in-progress	401.50	1.94	403.44
2,453.42	To purchase of finished goods	1,140.62	3,274.46	4,415.08
1,317.44	To consumption of raw materials, stores and spares	2,242.82	118.97	2,361.79
773.30	To salaries, wages, welfare and other benefits to employees	879.78	163.96	1,043.74
75.92	To repairs and maintenance	72.15	29.49	101.64
1,443.76	To power, fuel, royalties, freight, handling charges, removal of overburden and other expenses	354.39	569.27	923.66
258.85	To depreciation, amortization of development expenditure	255.70	49.06	304.76
38.01	To write-off of development, commissioning and deferred revenue expenditure	28.23	1.54	29.77
333.59	To gross profit brought down	364.33	194.88	559.21
7,727.35		6,249.16	5,096.33	11,318.49
	By sales/operating income:			
6,776.69	Gross sales and other operating income	5,909.91	4,307.28	10,217.19
17.22	Less commission and discount	9.15	11.02	20.17
6,759.47		5,900.76	4,296.26	10,197.02
563.42	Less excise duty	847.65	0.01	847.66
6,196.05		5,053.11	4,296.25	9,349.36
	By closing stock of finished goods and work-in-progress:			
1,132.09	Finished goods	770.58	770.54	1,541.12
399.21	Work-in-progress	425.47	2.54	428.01
7,727.35		6,249.16	5,069.33	11,318.49

(*continued*)

(Table 6.8 *continued*)

Previous Year†		1974–75 (Rs crores)		
		Production Enterprises	Service Enterprises	Total
	To interest on loans:			
111.30	(i) from Central Government	112.53	20.84	133.37
13.93	(ii) from foreign parties	5.74	13.71	19.45
8.97	(iii) from other parties	5.17	10.76	15.93
61.10	(iv) from banks as cash credit	55.80	37.04	92.84
(10.39)	(v) Less interest capitalized	(14.47)	(0.39)	(14.86)
184.91		164.77	81.96	246.73
84.26	To provision for tax	70.79	58.14	128.93
0.12	To share of loss on partnership account	–	–	–
155.92	To net profit (of undertakings carried down)	254.20	68.14	322.34
425.21		489.76	208.24	698.00
333.59	By gross profit brought down	364.33	194.88	559.21
91.62	By net loss (of undertakings carried down)	125.43	13.36	138.79
425.21		489.76	208.24	698.00

† 1973–74 figures for 115 undertakings retained as such.

Source: *Annual Report on the Working of Industrial and Commercial Undertakings of the Central Government, 1974–75.*

amounted to Rs 1,091.50 crores in 1974–5 compared with Rs 675.06 crores in 1973–4.[54] Many units of the public sector considerably improved their production capacity in 1974–5:

> The number of units where capacity utilisation has been higher than 75% increased from 41 in 1972–73 to 45 in 1973–74 and to 54 during the year 1974–75 indicative of sustained improvement over these three years.
> The number of units where capacity utilisation ranged between 50% to 75% increased from 16 in 1972–73 to 23 in 1973–74 and to 27 during the year 1974–75.
> The number of units recording less than 50% capacity

utilisation decreased from 25 in 1972–73 to 16 in 1973–74 and remained the same in the year 1974–75.[55]

For the state to maintain its independence from the bourgeoisie it was imperative that the state sector should generate resources in order to be able to gradually expand the public sector. This aim was categorically stated in the Industrial Policy Resolution of 1956:

> Public enterprises will augment the revenues of the State and provide resources for further development in fresh fields.[56]

In this task, too, the public sector enterprises have been gradually improving their performance. In the third plan period, internal resources generated by public sector enterprises amounted to Rs 287 crores; the fourth plan target was Rs 1,265 crores. There was a shortfall of only 0.4 per cent, the amount generated being Rs 1,260 crores (see Table 6.9).

TABLE 6.9 Gross internal resources generated by public sector enterprises (in Rs crores)

		Depre-ciation	Retained profits	Total
(i) Plan target		896	369	1,265
(ii) Actual resources generated:				
Year	No. of enter-prises			
1969–70	47	146	48	194
1970–71	55	149	55	204
1971–72	68	169	46	215
1972–73	75	193	67	260
1973–74	84	233	154	387
	Total	890	370	1,260
(iii) Achievement of plan target		99.3%	100.0%	99.6%

Source: *Annual Report on the Working of Industrial and Commercial Undertakings of the Central Government, 1974–75.*

Over and above the internal resource mobilization for their own expansion, the public sector enterprises have been substantially contributing to the Central Government exchequer by way of income tax, excise and other duties, and interest payment on loans and dividends (see Table 6.10), thus fiscally liberating the state from dependence on the private corporate sector.

TABLE 6.10 The contribution of public sector enterprises (in Rs crores)

	Dividends	Interest on Central Government loans	Income tax	Excise duty	Total
Fourth Plan					
1969–70	12	104	19	347	482
1970–71	14	104	23	394	535
1971–72	15	121	41	438	615
1972–73	16	124	63	514	717
1973–74	13	111	84	563	771
Total	70	564	230	2,256	3,120
Fifth Plan					
1974–75	20	133	129	848	1,130

Source: *Annual Report on the Working of Commercial and Industrial Undertakings of the Central Government, 1974–75.*

The state's increasing control over the economy can also be seen from the income, savings, and capital formation of the public and private corporate sectors in the national economy. According to the White Paper on National Accounts Statistics for the period 1960–61 to 1974–5, released by the Central Statistical Organization, in 1977, the income of the organized sector in 1960–61 amounted to Rs 3,409 crores; of this, the public sector's share was Rs 1,422 crores compared with the private sector's earnings of Rs 1,987 crores (see Table 6.11). In 1974–5 the public sector's income surpassed that of the private sector; it was Rs 9,603 crores compared with the private sector's income of Rs 7,790 crores (see Table 6.11). The C.S.O. also provides recent data on savings. In the total net savings for 1975–6, the household sector's contribution came to 73 per cent, the public sector's to 22, and the private corporate sector's to only 5 per cent. It should, however, be borne in mind that the major portion of the

TABLE 6.11 Distribution of incomes among various sectors (percentages)

	Net Domestic product	Primary sector	Secondary sector	Tertiary sector	Organized sector	Unorganized sector	Organized public and private sector Public enterprises and administrative depts.	Private enterprises
Total Rs crores								
1960–61	13,335	6,965	2,549	3,821	3,409	9,926	1,422	1,987
1974–75	58,485	29,167	11,592	17,726	16,853	41,632	9,063	7,790
Employees' Compensation								
1960–61	33.7	25.4	47.8	39.5	66.7	22.4	71.3	55.6
1974–75	32.9	20.0	52.3	41.8	70.8	17.7	73.7	57.7
Interest								
1960–61	3.2	3.3	4.4	2.3	5.8	2.3	13.6	3.9
1974–75	4.5	3.2	10.5	2.7	9.1	2.6	13.9	8.5
Rent								
1960–61	5.2	2.9	1.3	11.9	1.3	6.5	0.4	2.1
1974–75	3.3	2.2	1.4	6.2	1.5	4.0	1.3	2.3
Profits and Dividends								
1960–61	6.7	2.7	19.2	5.6	26.2	—	14.7	38.4
1974–75	5.4	2.3	14.3	4.5	18.6	—	11.1	31.5
Mixed income of self-employed								
1960–61	51.2	65.7	27.3	40.7	—	68.8	—	—
1974–75	53.9	72.3	21.5	44.8	—	75.7	—	—

Source: *White Paper on National Accounts Statistics, 1960–61 to 1974–75.*

household sector belongs to the unorganized primary and secondary sectors. In fact, since 1970–71, the public sector's share has been about half of the total net capital formation (see Table 6.12).

TABLE 6.12 Public sector net product and related data at current prices (Rs crores)

	1970-1	1973-4	1974-5
1 Net domestic product – total	34,746	49,720	58,485
2 Net product of public sector	5,048	7,217	9,063
3 Share of public sector –			
(2) as % of (1)	14.5	14.2	15.5
4 Net savings – total	4,499	6,764	8,500
5 Net savings of public sector	830	1,158	1,969
6 Share of public sector savings			
to total – (5) as % of (4)	18.4	17.1	23.4
7 Net capital formation – total	4,893	7,156	9,576
8 Net capital formation of			
public sector	2,346	4,062	4,771
9 Share of public sector capital			
formation to total –			
(8) as % of (7)	47.9	56.8	49.8
10 Distribution of factor incomes			
of public sector:			
(a) Compensation to employees	4,052	5,927	7,430
	(80%)	(82%)	(82%)
(b) Operating surplus	996	1,290	1,633
	(20%)	(18%)	(18%)

Source: *The White Paper on National Accounts Statistics, 1960–61 to 1974–75.*

The factor incomes of the public and the private sectors are also of importance in determining the sources of capital formation in these sectors. Apparently, in this regard, the private sector is in a more advantageous position. According to the Central Statistical Organization's data, in 1974–5 as much as 73.7 per cent of the income of the public sector was spent on employees' compensation and 13.9 per cent on interest on loans. Only 11.1 per cent was retained for dividends and profits. During the same period, the private sector earned as dividends and profits 31.5 per cent, while it paid only 57.7 per cent as employees' compensation (see Table 6.11). But the moot point is: while profits, dividends and interest of public enterprises can be reinvested for the expansion of the same industry or for the establishment of other industries, the profits of the private sector are distributed as dividends among shareholders; a significant portion of these dividends are spent on consumption. Thus, the private sector's superiority in mobilizing resources might be more illusory than real.

Now we turn to employment. Here too the state sector is the largest employer (in the organized sector). Its employment is double the size of the private sector's employment as shown in Table 6.13.

TABLE 6.13 Estimated employment in the public sector and private sector, 1974 and 1975 (thousand persons)

	Public sector		Private sector (including small-scale industries)	
	1974	*1975*	*1974*	*1975*
Agriculture, hunting, forestry and fishing	324	340	806	818
Mining and quarrying	606	694	134	123
Manufacturing	1,027	1,019	4,179	4,108
Gas, electricity and water	537	507	42	39
Construction	997	956	121	127
Wholesale and retail trade and restaurants and hotels	449	53	318	309
Transport, storage and communications	2,313	2,362	77	79
Financing, insurance, real estate and business services		492		168
	6,232		1,118	
Community, social and personal services		6,444		1,032
Total	12,484	12,868	6,794	6,804

Source: Compiled from *The Pocket Book of Labour Statistics, 1977.*

In short, as a result of huge investments and rapid expansion during the last two decades, the public sector has attained the commanding heights of the economy in all facets.

It should be borne in mind that the public sector in India, unlike in the West, has expanded at the cost of the private sector. It is not an appendage to monopoly capital to provide 'social capital' or 'social expenses' for the expansion of the private corporate sector. Because of the weakness of the bourgeoisie at the time of independence, the autonomy of the state enabled the state managers to pursue vigorously the goal of augmenting state capital. They not only actively participated in the productive spheres of the economy, but restricted the private sector's operation in basic industries. In fact, state sector enterprises in most vital areas of the economy are monopoly concerns. In the West these sectors normally belong to the 'natural territory' of private monopoly capital. Their monopolization by the state in India clearly indicates its independence from the control of the bourgeoisie. Moreover, the monopolization of productive capital and internal resource mobilization have virtually fiscally liberated the state from dependence on the private corporate sector. This independence has been further reinforced by the state's emergence as a financial capitalist through the nationalization of insurance companies, banks and other financial institutions. The state's control over finance along with its predominance in basic industries have made the private corporate sector totally dependent on it for the supply of finance[57] as well as basic inputs.

The difference between the state sectors in India and the West can best be understood from the following extract from James O'Connor's *The Fiscal Crisis of the State*, where he briefly pinpoints the essential characteristics of the state sector in the West:

> In American capitalist society, state investments are normally confined to indirectly productive projects. Obviously it is in the interest and within the reach of monopoly capital to seize all profit-making opportunities for itself and to resist the encroachment of state capital on its own 'natural territory'. Indirectly productive investments (i.e., social capital) increase private profits and expand monopoly capital's natural territory. Monopoly capital also wants the state to remain dependent on tax revenues and thus fiscally weak – to reduce the possibility that a popular government would reorder the allocation of material resources. Finally, it is ideologically important for private capital to monopolize profit-making activities in order to perpetuate the myth that the state is too incompetent to manage directly productive capital.
>
> Monopoly capital employs many and varied methods and techniques to prevent the state from acquiring and managing

directly productive capital. Economic domination gives the owning class ideological domination as well – that is, the entire legal system is based on the interests of the monopoly capital. This means that the equity financing of state enterprise often is ruled out, which denies an enterprise a financial cushion and exposes it to real risks when interest charges on loan capital exceed earnings. The pinch can be especially painful if state enterprise is managed on the principle of balanced budget pricing (i.e., if it is forced to set prices at levels that will just cover costs, no more, no less). For example, unable to raise equity capital and forbidden to generate internal surpluses, British nationalized enterprises increased their debt five times over through 1961. At that time the government modified its financial policies, but one legacy of British nationalization is still a swollen debt structure.... In Europe many state enterprises are allowed to issue marketable equity stock. But the legal framework within which these enterprises operate mitigates against their self-actualization. In Austria, France and Germany nationalized industries have an indeterminate status in law[58] – and in some cases there are no statutes governing their operation...

European governments normally have responded to *general or specific economic and political crises* by setting up mixed enterprises or decreeing nationalization, not by providing indirect subsidies, underwriting investment, and so on. In France (except for the nationalized railroads), *the first major group of enterprises coming under public ownership were victims of the financial crisis of the 1930s....*[59]

During the Great Depression there was little resistance to the nationalization of directly productive industries; in Italy (as in most European countries) the state supported the banks and evolved 'mixed companies' to protect the value of private bank shares. In the context of European capitalist development it was natural for the state to give massive support, including outright purchase, to private capital – not to remove capital from the private sphere, but to keep productive activities in operation.

It was not until immediately after World War II that the British Government nationalized industries that had been particularly hard hit by the Great Depression. Nationalization rescued most of the industries (particularly rail transport and coal) from bankruptcy...

Because of its largely conservative character, European state enterprise has not promoted the fiscal liberation of the state, but rather has strengthened private capital. Many state enterprises – especially the nationalized sector in Britain, the Italian state railways and some French state corporations (e.g. coal production) are forbidden by law to generate profits or are otherwise financially hamstrung....

Even when state industries generate surpluses, the surpluses typically are not available to the state treasury because *the enterprises normally are not managed by government representatives, but rather by autonomous administrations....*[60]

Another factor confining the state fiscally is that a great part of productive state capital consists of backward industries that under the best of circumstances cannot generate a large surplus year in and year out. As for the dynamic industries monopolised or participated in by state capital, legislation and administrative rulings limit the state's ability to develop an overall industrial policy that might finance the general state budget. For example, British laws have been amended to prohibit nationalized firms from producing equipment for their own use (emphasis added).[61]

Thus we find that, in the U.S.A., state enterprises are confined to indirectly productive projects which cannot, or are not allowed to, generate profits, because they depend on loan capital rather than on equity financing; in most cases they operate on a 'no loss and no profit' basis. The main purpose served by these state enterprises is to provide the support for the expansion of the private monopoly capital. But as the state enterprises do not generate any internal surplus, the state's fiscal dependence on the private corporate sector remains unchanged. In the U.S.A. as well as in Europe, the state sector began to emerge as a result of the Great Depression of the 1930s, in Europe mainly through the process of nationalization of bankrupt companies. Although in Europe some state enterprises could issue equity capital and earn profits and dividends, the environment of private capital or the capitalist ideology did not let them do themselves justice.

Although European state enterprises are different in appearance from those in the U.S.A., in operation they are identical. Failure to generate surpluses in the state sector make the state budgets in

Europe equally dependent on tax revenue from the private sector. Even in France – eulogized by Shonfield as the leader in capitalist planning – where the state bureaucracy has played a relatively more independent role (for various historical reasons) than in any other capitalist country, planning has been essentially a 'conspiracy' between it and big business interests. And the task of planning has been mainly to generate business confidence so that the private sector does fight shy of investing.

In India, on the other hand, the state sector was not developed as a response to the financial crises of private capital. It developed because the bourgeoisie was weak. From the beginning state capital aimed at expediting industrial growth through the augmentation of its own capital, very often at the cost of private capital formation. The gradual expansion of public enterprises and the monopolization of the sources of finance enabled the state to maintain its independence in the capital market, and also enabled it to generate a cultural environment conducive to the growth of state capital. As has been noted above, this cultural environment was highly suspicious of private capital. If the state had become dependent on private capital, the cultural environment would have changed, as in the U.S.A. and Western Europe, and would have become critical of the expansion of the state apparatus and supportive of the private corporate sector's enlargement. In India the overall cultural environment, hostile to the business community, shows that the continuing struggle of the bourgeoisie to take control of the political and ideological superstructures has not yet been crowned with success.

It should, however, be noted in this connection that the state's ownership of the basic means of production has not led to any improvement in the real income for the working population in industry (see Table 7.12). Nor has the state been able to transfer the increasing burden of population from agriculture to industry (see chapter 7). The strong state in India which maintains its hegemony over the social classes is thus not founded on a strong social economy. This is the paradox in the character of the state and its social formation; the reasons for this paradox will be discussed in detail in the next chapter.

7 The social economy of Indian agriculture and its effect on industrialization and the state

Prolegomena

In the last two chapters the process of industrialization and the nature of the development of the bourgeoisie and the state's role in this process have been discussed. However, no analysis of the social economy, class formation, and industrialization of a country is possible without an analysis of its agrarian structure, particularly if the country is primarily agricultural, as India is. As was noted earlier, according to an estimate by the Central Statistical Organisation about 50 per cent of India's G.N.P. today comes from the primary sector, and 70 per cent of her population is employed in it. So it is of fundamental importance to know what is the mode of production in agriculture in India and how the surplus that is being generated in this sector is being appropriated and used.

This examination is of particular significance because the industrialization of a country is dependent on its agricultural sector in three ways: for raw materials, for the supply of labour (especially in the formation period of industrialization), and for the farm sector's demand for industrial products. In this chapter an attempt will be made to analyse these issues, and to explain why the capitalist class has failed to bring agriculture, as a whole, under its control. This failure has important ramifications, not only in respect to the development of the Indian economy, but also in terms of the political power of the capitalist class.

The impact of the colonial heritage on the modes of production in Indian agriculture

In chapter 2 it was pointed out that, prior to the rise of British power in India, the rural economy was characterized by self-sufficient villages based on an organic unity between agriculture and artisan industries. The village surplus was extracted by the state in the form of revenue. The British inherited this system from the Moghuls, but introduced major changes to increase revenue, as this then constituted the primary source of income of the state (see chapter 3). In some parts of India, they established the *zamindari* system whereby 'private landlords' were created, and the state bestowed on them some but not all of the benefits of private ownership of land. The *zamindars* and the subordinate tenants (created by the former) acted as intermediaries between the state and the tillers. In other parts, *ryotwari* or temporary land settlement was introduced whereby the state collected revenue directly from the peasants. In the *ryotwari* areas, the tillers were given the right to inherit, mortgage and sell the right of occupancy, but they were not given exclusive private property rights in the land (in the western sense of the term).

In both systems the state remained the supreme landlord (see chapter 2). These tenurial changes, however superficial they might have been in changing the organization of production, had the effect of transforming land into a commodity. This process facilitated the reduction of India's agriculture into a continuous source of primitive capital accumulation for the metropolitan centre (see chapter 3 and below). The peasants' need for cash to pay the increasing land revenue to the *zamindars* or to the state made him an easy victim of usurers, whose rates of interest ranged from 100 to 300 per cent.[1] As land became the only source of livelihood (in the absence of industrialization), and as it could be alienated as a commodity for the non-payment of revenue or the moneylenders' interest, etc., it became a common practice for the small and even middle peasants to rush to the market immediately after the harvest to pay the state's rent and moneylenders' interest, in order to be able to cling to their miserable patches of land.

The situation was further exacerbated by the deteriorating land/man ratio and increasing intermediary rent-receiving interests (see below). These rentiers were parasites; many of them lived in cities thriving on the rents collected from the direct producers. Referring to the debilitating effect of this kind of rent on production, Marx wrote:

> This rent may assume dimensions which seriously threaten the reproduction of the conditions of labour, of the means of

production. It may render an expansion of production more or less impossible, and grind the direct producers down to the physical minimum of means of subsistence. This is particularly the case, when this form is met and exploited by a conquering industrial nation, as India is by the English.[2]

Rents in India continued to be collected on the basis of the earlier mode of extraction, but on a far bigger scale (see below).

Thus, the existing mode of production, with some changes in property relations, was ideally suited to meet industrial capital's demand for markets as well as raw materials. The growing number of rentiers meant not only more surplus extraction but also that industrial capital found in them, at least for the time being, an expanding market.[3] Similar was the role played by usury. According to the census of 1921, the number of people living on rent was 3.7 million; it went up to 4.1 million in the 1931 census. The Simon Commission Report of 1930 noted:

> In some districts the sub-infeudation has grown to astonishing proportions, as many as fifty or more intermediary interests having been created between the zamindar at the top and the actual cultivators at the bottom.[4]

Khan Bahadur S.M. Hussain, a member of the Floud Commission, estimated that in 1793 the net income of the *zamindars* in Bengal amounted to Rs 20 lakhs; in 1940 their income was Rs 832 lakhs, an increase of more than 4,000 per cent.[5]

To this exploitation was added the exploitation of usury. In the Indian villages there was a class of moneylenders long before British rule was established. In the past they performed, in a limited sense, a necessary economic function by providing loans to the cultivators in times of need. This changed drastically under the new legal system introduced by the British. They could now expropriate the cultivators' land for the non-repayment of loans – a practice virtually unknown under the village community system. Moreover, customary limits on interest also became extinct. As Nanavati and Anjaria point out:

> With the increasing adoption of the cash nexus and the introduction of the British system of jurisprudence which laid down rigid laws of property and contract, the human basis of

creditor debtor relationship in the village was destroyed. Consequently, new opportunities for exploitation were opened up for the moneylender.... The rule of Damdupat which prohibited him from receiving a sum double the sum lent became extinct. The new laws of Indian Contract Act and Civil Procedure Court were always in favour of the moneylender and enabled him not only to secure his exorbitant claims but attach the debtor's cattle and implements and even to arrest and imprison him. The Registration of Documents Act (1864) and the Transfer of Property Act (1882) enabled claims to be systematically recorded and led to the growth of mortgages in number and value. Any appeal to the law by the farmer was therefore sure to lead to his own destruction. In the words of Sir Malcolm Darling, 'by 1880 the unequal fight between the peasant and moneylender has ended in a crushing victory for the latter. For the next thirty years the moneylender was at his zenith and multiplied and prospered exceedingly to such good effect that the number of bankers and moneylenders and their dependents increased from 55,263 in 1868 to 193,890 in 1911.'[6]

The Famine Commission reported in 1880 that one-third of the peasants were in deep debt; and another third in debt but with the power to redeem their debt.[7] Table 7.1 indicates how the rural debt in India continued to grow.

TABLE 7.1 Rural debt in India

Name of committee	Year of enquiry	Character of debt
Famine Commission	1880	One-third of peasants in debt but can repay the debt, another third in deep debt with little possibility of redeeming the debt.
Famine Commission	1901	About one-quarter of cultivators lost their land to moneylenders in Bombay. Only one-fifth free from debt.
Central Banking Enquiry	1929	Rs. 900 crores (total amount of rural debt).
Agricultural Credit Department	1937	Rs. 1,800 crores (total amount of rural debt).

In a study of a south Indian village by N.S. Subramaniam (Congress Economic and Political Studies, No. 2, 1936), we get a clearer picture of the mechanism and the degree of exploitation of the Indian peasantry.[8] The study was conducted in a village named Nerur in the district of Trichinpoly, with a population of 6,200. The net income of the village from agriculture amounted to Rs 212,000 after deducting all cultivation expenses. Net income from other sources (artisans' incomes, salaries and wages remitted to the village earned outside, etc.) was estimated at Rs 24,000. Total income from all sources thus came to Rs 236,000. From this income

the following outgoings of the village were noted: land revenue, irrigation and allied cesses, Rs. 30,000; rent to owners of land outside the village, Rs. 70,000; interest on debt (calculated at the lowest rate of 8 per cent), Rs. 40,000; rentals to government for toddy and arak shops, tree taxes, rent to tree owners, Rs. 12,000. This makes a total of Rs. 152,000 for government revenue, taxation, rent and interest. Together with minor outgoings of Rs. 4,000, the total payments from the village of Rs. 156,000 leave a balance for the village of Rs. 80,000 or under Rs. 13 a head. It will be seen that each inhabitant of this village earns an average of 38 rupees or 2 pounds 17 shillings for the year. After the tax collector, landlord, and moneylender have taken their share, he is left with under 13 rupees or 19 shillings to live on for the year. He is left with one-third; two-thirds are taken.[9]

Thus, in the case of most small and medium peasants, two-thirds of the products had to be brought into circulation to pay for rent and interest. From these surpluses India's exports were made and they also formed the basis from which the import needs of the consuming classes in the cities were met (see chapter 3). In this way the products of the Indian peasantry were brought into the domain of the world capitalist market.

However, the peasant's mode of production did not change. He continued to cultivate his land in the same way he had been doing for centuries. The implements of cultivation – the plough, the spade, etc. – were, and still are, the same as they had been in the past. The most important source of power to supplement human labour was, and still is, the bullock. Yet the method of cultivation was not inferior to that prevailing in Europe in the nineteenth century. Nor was the cultivator slothful and lazy. But his growing poverty prevented him from investing in inputs necessary for increasing the productivity of his land and labour. Dr J.A. Voelcker, consulting chemist to the Royal Agricultural Society, was appointed to investigate agricultural techniques in India in 1880, and reported as follows:

> At his best the Indian Ryot or cultivator is quite as good as and in some respects the superior of, the average British farmer; whilst at his worst, it can only be said that this state is brought about largely by an absence of facilities for improvement which is probably unequalled in any other country, and that the Ryot will struggle on patiently and uncomplainingly in the face of difficulties in a way that no one else would....
>
> But to take the ordinary acts of husbandry nowhere would one find better instances of keeping land scrupulously clean from weeds, of ingenuity in device of water raising appliances, of knowledge of soils and their capabilities, as well as the exact time to sow and to reap, as one would in Indian agriculture, and this is not at its best alone, but at its ordinary level. It is wonderful too, how much is known of rotation, the system of mixed crops and of fallowing. Certain it is that I, at least, have never seen a more perfect picture of careful cultivation, combined with hard labour, perseverance and fertility of resource, than I have seen in many of the halting-places in my tour.[10]

Similarly Sir John Russell wrote:

> The Indian ryot compares favourably with any of the peasant populations I have met in different parts of the world.[11]

The Indian peasant's poverty did not stem from his indolence or lack of knowledge, but from the fact that his economy was incorporated into the world capitalist system without his having the benefits of the capitalist mode of production in agriculture. His surplus was extracted and exchanged for commodities from abroad to satisfy the consumption of the indigenous rentiers and other parasites; it was not ploughed back into agriculture in the form of industrial inputs.

One must remember that the same capital flow which expropriated English peasants from their soil and dragged them off to become cogs in machines, also drove the Indian town artisans back to the village to become a drain on its agriculture. The same capitalist class which used machines in England to extract surplus value from its labour debarred their introduction into India because it suited their interests better to let Indian peasants produce the surplus in the form of raw materials, rent, interest, etc. If the metropolitan centres are what they are today as a result of capitalist production, India and other Third World countries are what they are today because of capitalist exploitation. If it is the flow of capital which has concentrated approximately 70 per cent of the inhabitants of North America and Western Europe in industry, it is the same capital flow which has forced approximately 70 per cent of the people of India and other Third World countries into agriculture.

Thus, with the growing burden of people on the land (in the absence of occupational opportunities in industry), the land/man ratio began to decrease with the natural increase of the population. Dr Harold Mann, Director of Agriculture in Bombay, wrote in 1917:

> It is evident from this that in the last 60 or 70 years the character of the land holdings has changed. In the pre-British days, and in the early days of the British rule, the holdings were usually of a fair size, most frequently, more than 9 or 10 acres, while individual holdings of less than 10 acres were hardly known. Now the number of holdings is more than double, and 81 per cent of these holdings are under 10 acres in size, while no less than 60 per cent are less than 5 acres.[12]

It is evident that the above process of diminution of holdings could not lead to the development of capitalist farming. Poor peasants who operated small patches of land could hardly afford the advanced techniques of production or modern scientific inputs. Moreover, as has been noted, their surpluses were drawn away in the form of rent and interest. How the size of holdings continued to decrease in India can be gathered from Table 7.2, which was computed on the basis of a study of 72 villages in the Borsad Taluka in Gujarat. A similar picture emerges from the evidence before the Agricultural Commission in 1927; it was based on a study of a district (area 1 million acres) in Bombay (see Table 7.3). In the process of enquiry, the government witness significantly added:

> These figures referring only to a period of five years appear to me to show a very marked increase in the number of agriculturists cultivating holdings up to 15 acres, which except in a very few soils is not an area which can economically employ a pair of bullocks. . . . There is also a drop in the holdings of 25–100 acres, which means a decrease in the comparatively substantial agriculturist class who can with luck lay by a little capital [Thus, instead of an increase in the size of holdings as in the capitalist countries, Indian agriculture witnessed a reverse process].[13]

TABLE 7.2   Increase in the number of small holdings

Size (in acres)	1901 Number	%	1921 Number	%	% change since 1901
5 and under	7,740	58	19,740	82	+ 125
6 to 25	5,107	38	3,916	16	− 23
26 to 100	570	4	432	2	− 3
101 to 500	30	–	29	–	–
Total	13,447	100	24,117	100	+ 79

Source: P.A. Wadia and K.T. Merchant, *Our Economic Problem*, p. 210.

The increase in the number of small holdings, it seems, continued unabated. Just after independence in 1950 the nature of the distribution of holdings by size in different states is reflected in Table 7.4.

From these tables it can be seen that although the small and medium peasants operated most of the holdings, there were a few landholders who, owning more than twenty-five acres of land, were in a position to adopt capitalist farming. Why did they not do this? The simple answer is that they could earn more by letting out the land to poor tenants and sharecroppers than by cultivating the land themselves.

It was found in a study conducted in a co-operative farm in West Bengal in 1959 that the average cost of production of an acre of land on the basis of the capitalist method of employing wage labour was Rs 290 and output amounted to Rs 332; the profit was thus Rs 42 or 14 per cent of the outlay.[14] A landowner in West Bengal could easily

TABLE 7.3 Change in the number of holdings

Average holding (in acres)	*Number of holdings* 1917	1922
Under 5	6,272	6,446
5 to 15	17,909	19,130
15 to 25	11,908	12,108
25 to 100	15,532	15,020
100 to 500	1,234	1,117
Over 500	20	19

Source: *Report of the Royal Commission on Agriculture*, Vol. II, Part I of Evidence, 1928, p. 292.

TABLE 7.4 Distribution of holdings according to size, 1950 (in acres)

	Average size of holding	*% of holdings to the total:* Below 5	Below 10	Below 15	Below 25
Madras	4.5	82.0	89.0	n.a.	n.a.
Punjab	10.0	63.7	80.0	87.9	93.7
U.P.	n.a.	81.2	93.0	n.a.	99.1
Bengal	4.4	71.3	88.3	n.a.	n.a.
Bombay	13.3	41.9	60.9	72.5	85.2
Mysore	6.2	65.9	86.7	n.a.	n.a.
Assam	4.8	66.4	87.4	n.a.	n.a.
Orissa	4.9	79.2	89.5	94.3	97.8

Source: *Agricultural Legislation in India*, vol. II, 'Consolidation of holdings', p. 11.

lease out his land at that time to a sharecropper and legally demand 40 per cent of the produce from the tenant, who would contribute both labour and capital. Why, then, should the landowner invest his capital in cultivation?

It was further found from various N.S.S. (National Sample Survey) studies that poor farmers (below the five acre size group) who rented land at such an exorbitant cost did so just to eke out a living.[15] In a deteriorating land/man ratio, where the threat of total pauperization haunts the peasant, it is quite natural for him to ensure his minimum income through the ownership of a small piece of land and supplement his income by renting land from other sources. As access to land secures the bare minimum for himself and his family, a peasant would agree to surrender to the landowner whatever he produces on that land above the bare subsistence level.[16] Thus the income a landowner in India derived from his ownership or monopolization of land was not the ground rent that a capitalist tenant pays to the landlord. Capitalist ground rent is the surplus over the average rate of profit on capital invested by the capitalist tenant. In cases where the tenant is the owner, he pockets the surplus or the ground rent. In India the surplus appropriated by the landowners and the state through sharecropping or other means, either in cash or kind, is pre-capitalist ground rent. Marx explains this kind of rent as follows:

> By money rent we mean here – for the sake of distinction from the industrial and commercial ground-rent resting upon the capitalist mode of production, which is but a surplus over the average profit – that ground rent which arises from a mere change of form or rent in kind, just as this rent in kind is but a modification of a labour rent. Under money rent, the direct producer no longer turns over the product but its price to the landlord (who may be either the state or a private landlord).

Marx also explains the basis of this kind of absolute rent:

> [the direct producer] has to perform for his landlord, who is the owner of the land, of his most essential instrument of production, forced surplus labour, that is, unpaid labour for which no equivalent is returned.[17]

In India this forced surplus labour was paid not only to the landlords but also to the moneylenders, traders and rich peasants. The poor peasants had to turn to these sources for their cash requirements to pay their ever-increasing rents. Moreover, interest on usury capital was not capitalist interest; it was forced labour which was obtained from the direct producers just to let them reproduce themselves on the barest minimum biological level.

During the colonial period in India the property relations which were imposed were not bourgeois relations of property, because these can only emerge when there are bourgeois relations of production.[18] By introducing a restricted form of private property in land, the English introduced into India (see chapter 3) a base for the future development of bourgeois property which could develop only with the development of the capitalist mode of production. That was why Marx hailed the introduction of private property in land in India as the greatest desideratum. This, he thought, would lay the foundation for the future development of the capitalist mode of production. At the same time he ridiculed the land systems established by the colonial government as a caricature of British landlordism and French peasant property. British landlordism was then founded on capitalist ground rent, while the French peasant was normally a small peasant proprietor outside the debilitating effect of the feudal mode of production.

In India, by letting the state appropriate the major portion of rent (nine-tenths in the permanent settlement areas) and also by letting it determine the future appropriation on an arbitrary basis (in the *Ryotwari* areas) and at the same time enabling the landowners to usurp the major portion of the surplus over and above the state's demands, a kind of feudalism was grafted onto the Asiatic system (a point clearly made by Marx in his characterization of the British-introduced land systems in India – see chapter 3). While the revenue farmers in the Asiatic systems were granted only a portion of the state's revenue as their remuneration and could not raise their demand over the customary level, the new system, by bestowing 'ownership rights' on the subordinate landlords below the supreme landlord (the state), enabled them to appropriate the major portion of the peasants' surpluses, in fact even part of their normal wages, by the constant threat of ejection from the land. The extraction of surplus was done through two modes: the Asiatic and the feudal. The peasant had to satisfy the ever-growing needs of the state as well as the needs of the private landlords, not to speak of the usury which can be found as a cancerous appendage in any pre-capitalist formation.

Merchant capital mediated between this formation of Asiatic and feudal modes and advanced industrial capital. As a result banking, credit, and commerce penetrated the pre-capitalist formation and acted as a corrosive influence on its constituent modes. But the extension of the market or the development of merchant capital, and, hence, the expansion of the circulation of commodities, cannot by itself make possible the transition of one mode of production into another. As Marx says:

The extent to which production ministers to commerce and supplies the merchants, depends on the mode of production. It reaches its maximum under a fully developed capitalist production, in which the product is primarily produced as a commodity, not for direct subsistence. On the other hand, on the basis of every mode of production, commerce promotes the production of surplus products destined for exchange, for the purpose of increasing the enjoyments of the wealth of the producers (who are here understood to be the owners of the products). Commerce impregnates production more and more with the character of a production for exchange.

The metamorphosis of commodities, their movements, consist, 1) materially of an exchange of different commodities for one another; 2) formally, of a conversion of commodities into money by sale, and a conversion of money into commodities by purchase. And the functions of merchants' capital resolve themselves into these functions of buying and selling commodities. It promotes merely the exchange of commodities, which must be conceived at the outset as being something more than a bare exchange of commodities between direct producers. Under slavery, feudalism, vassalage, so far as primitive organisations are concerned, it is the slave holder, the feudal lord, the tribute collecting state who are the owners and sellers of the products. The merchant buys and sells for many. In his hands are concentrated purchases and sales, and purchase and sale cease consequently to be dependent on a direct necessity of the buyer (as a merchant).... all development of merchants' capital tends to give to production more and more the character of a production for exchange and to impregnate the products more and more with the character of commodities. But the development of merchants' capital by itself is incapable of bringing about and explaining the transition from one mode of production to another.[19]

Marx further maintained that the impact of commerce on a pre-capitalist mode of production may or may not change the nature of its organization of production but can change conceivably its purpose:

In the antique world the effect of commerce and the development of merchants' capital always result in slave economy; or, according to what the point of departure may be, the transformation may simply turn out to be the transformation of a patriarchal slave system devoted to the production of direct means of subsistence into a similar system devoted to the production of surplus value. However in the modern world it results in the capitalist mode of production.[20]

But this is not always so in many colonial economies. In India, as we have already pointed out, the impact of merchant capital resulted in the increasing production of surplus value but on the basis of the same mode of production. The reason why the mode of production did not change could be found in the nature of accumulation and its investment. The surplus generated in Indian agriculture did not lead to an accumulation here; the accumulation was taking place in the metropolitan centre via merchant capital which tapped the increasing resources extracted by the rentiers and usury capital. (Included in it, too, was the unequal exchange between primary and industrial products.)

As has been noted, there was no return to the peasant sector equivalent to what was being taken out. In short, neither the rentiers nor the state ploughed the surplus they commanded back into agriculture to encourage further accumulation. The difference between an Indian and an English or German landowner was that the former failed to transform himself into a capitalist farmer. As a rentier, his needs as a consumer had been continuously exploited by merchant capital, and via merchant capital the process led to capital formation in the metropolitan centres. The cycle of production in Indian agriculture remained simple reproduction: despite the introduction of private property in land it was not transformed into extended reproduction.

It must also be borne in mind that, although merchant capital operates as the main form of capital in pre-capitalist social formations, it is subordinate to the industrial capital of the metropolitan countries. While it was dominant in India (in the absence of developed industrial capital), its operations were subordinate to and determined by the latter. Hence merchant capital, in the service of metropolitan industrial capital, transformed the goal of the appropriation of the surplus in Indian agriculture without changing its form. Although the extracted surplus satisfied the immediate needs of the rentiers, usurers, etc., it was finally being absorbed for the extended reproduction of industrial capital in the metropolitan areas.

This is the way in which India was integrated into the world capitalist market through the medium of merchant capital. If one understands the Marxian analysis of merchant and industrial capital and their interaction with pre-capitalist formations, one need not indulge in a futile search for a colonial mode of production as has been done by Hamza Alavi.[21] The hegemony of the capitalist formation over the pre-capitalist one has been clearly spelled out by Marx in *Capital*.

Social formation and the social classes in post-Independence Indian agriculture

If we turn from the colonial period to the post-Independence period, do we observe a great transformation in Indian agriculture? Has the social formation undergone a change? What are the changes – if there are any – in the class configuration of Indian agriculture after independence? An attempt will be made to answer these questions in the following pages. The answers are relevant in the light of perspectives raised at the beginning of this chapter.

At the time of independence the masters of the countryside in most parts of India were the semi-feudal landlords or the intermediary rent-receiving interests. One of the first and foremost of the new state's decisions was to abolish these intermediaries between the state and the tillers. These intermediaries, as has been noted, were mainly created by the colonial state and their power was mainly derivative in nature. They had no independent power base on the strength of which they could protect and safeguard their interests when the colonial state withdrew.

A new constitution for independent India was adopted in 1950, and under it land reform legislations came under the jurisdiction of the states.[22] However, in 1951 the central government provided a broad framework for tenancy legislations to be adopted by the states in conformity with local requirements. The salient features of the guidelines were: abolition of intermediaries; transfer of land to the tillers and as many owner cultivators as possible; fixing of a ceiling on the size of holdings; reduction of rent by fixing upper limits, and security of tenure to the cultivators.[23]

As a result of legislation enacted by the states to implement these recommendations, the intermediaries – those who collected rent on behalf of the state – were more or less eliminated in most parts of India by 1956.[24] This, however, did not lead to any revolutionary change in India's agrarian structure. The main objective of the tenancy legislation was to remove the intermediaries between the state and the tillers.

Land which was under 'personal cultivation' of the intermediaries did not come under the jurisdiction of the new law. The lacunae in the law enabled many intermediaries (but not all) to retain the land they cultivated 'personally' (either by employing hired labourers or cropsharers or by letting out to tenants without permanent rights). Of course, a ceiling was imposed on owner-cultivated land, but the ceiling did not contribute much to the redistribution of land, as many erstwhile intermediaries and rich peasants could easily bypass the laws by transferring ownership to other members of their family.[25]

With regard to rent, laws were passed to delimit what the land-owners could exact from the producers. In West Bengal and Tamil-nadu, a landowner was legally allowed to demand 40 per cent of the produce even though the cropsharer (i.e. the cultivator) supplied inputs; in Bihar, the landowner's share could not exceed seven-twentieths of the gross product; in Punjab, Jammu, and Kashmir, the maximum was one-third; in Assam, Karnataka, Tripura, Orissa and Manipur, one-fourth; and in Maharastra and Rajasthan one-sixth.[26]

These rent laws could hardly be regarded as beneficial to the direct producers, i.e. the tenant farmers or the cropsharers. The fourth Five Year Plan recognized the inadequacy of the statutes enacted by various states, and stated that:

> The rents as fixed by law are still high in Andhra area, Jammu and Kashmir, Tamilnadu, Punjab and West Bengal and should be brought down to the level recommended in the Plans – to one-fourth or one-fifth of the gross produce.[27]

Even the small concessions which were granted to the direct producers in the tenancy legislation could not be implemented in the situation of the acute land hunger prevailing in India. Poor cultivators could hardly be expected to assert their legal rights in the courts of law. As the Third Five Year Plan pointed out:

When there is pressure on land and the social and economic position of the tenant is weak, it becomes difficult for them to seek the protection of law. Moreover, resort to legal processes is costly and generally beyond the means of tenants. Thus, in many ways, despite the legislation, the scales are weighted in favour of the continuance of existing terms and conditions.[28]

In fact, in certain respects the terms and conditions under which tenants could lease their lands worsened. The ban on the leasing of land to permanent tenants while at the same time allowing the system of sharecropping, transformed open tenancies into concealed ones (i.e. from contractual to oral tenancy).

Despite legislation by the states during the last two decades, the concentration of landholding did not show any fundamental change. The data collected by N.S.S. in 1954–5 and by the Agricultural Census in 1970–1 give us an idea of the trend in land concentration.

According to N.S.S. data (8th round, July 1954–April 1955), the number of marginal farmers who cultivated less than 2.49 acres of land constituted 45.2 per cent of total households and accounted for 5.9 per cent of the total worked area. Small farmers owning 2.5 acres to 4.99 acres of land comprised 15.5 per cent of households and controlled 10.6 per cent of the total area. Farmers belonging to the 5 to 9.99 acres medium-sized group held 19 per cent of worked land and numbered 14.3 per cent of households. Well-to-do farmers in the 10 to 19.99 acres group constituted 8.5 per cent of households and worked 22.5 per cent of the total area. Rich landowners who had 20 acres and over made up only 5.6 per cent of households but total land under their ownership amounted to 41.9 per cent of the cultivated area.

According to the All-India Report on Agricultural Census (1970–71), which is not strictly comparable to the N.S.S. data, but which nevertheless enlightens us about the trend in the concentration of land, the following picture emerges (see Table 7.5). Marginal farmers belonging to the group working less than 1 hectare or 2.5 acres (approximately) constitute 50 per cent of the total operational holdings and they own 9 per cent of the area. Small farmers (1–2 hectares or 2.5–5 acres) constituting 19 per cent of holdings have 11.9 per cent of the area. The medium-sized group owning 2 to 4 hectares (5 to 10 acres) comprise 15.2 per cent of operational holdings and own 18.5 per cent of the area. The well-to-do peasants in the range 4 to 10 hectares (10 to 25 acres) account for 11.3 per cent of operational holdings but own 29.7 per cent of the area. Rich farmers belonging to the group owning 10 hectares or more (25 acres or over) constitute 3.9 per cent of the operational holdings but own 30.9 per cent of the total area under cultivation.

The classification of farmers into marginal, small, medium, well-to-do, and rich has been made here not only on the basis of land-holdings but also on the basis of work done by members of the farmer's family on their own farms or on others' farms, and also on their command over agricultural inputs such as cattle, buffaloes, ploughs, etc. (land, cattle and draught animals were adopted by Lenin as categories to differentiate the peasantry in Russia).

Farm management studies indicate that there is a positive correlation between the size of holding and other farm input endowments. Later studies conducted by the N.S.S. in the 1970s (the 26th round) confirm the validity of this finding. The viability of holdings also depends upon the size of the family. However, the smaller the size of holding the greater is the possibility that the farmer and members of his family will seek other sources of income or sell their labour power to other farmers.[29] On many occasions marginal and small landholders find it more convenient to lease out their land and seek employment in secondary or tertiary sectors.

The main distinction between a marginal farmer (owning up to 2.5 acres) and a small farmer (2.5 to 5 acres) is that, while a marginal farmer or his family members are very often forced to sell their

TABLE 7.5 Size distribution of operational holdings, 1970–1

Size group	Number (000s)	%	Area (000ha)	%
Marginal (less than 1 ha)	35,682	50.6	14,545	9.0
Small (1 – 2 ha)	13,432	19.0	19,282	11.9
Semi-medium (2 – 4 ha)	10,681	15.2	29,999	18.5
Sub-total: small and semi-medium (1 – 4 ha)	24,113	34.2	49.281	30.4
Medium (4 – 10 ha)	7,932	11.3	48,234	29.7
Large (10 ha and above)	2,766	3.9	50,064	30.9
All categories	70,493	100.0	162,124	100.0

Source: Government of India, Ministry of Agriculture and Irrigation, *All India Report on Agricultural Census, 1970-1*

labour power to others and in the process convert the household's status into that of an agricultural labourer's household, members of small-farmer households sell their labour power to other farmers but this seldom leads to a change in their family status. A study undertaken by Sheila Bhalla on the household origin of agricultural labourers in three regions of Haryana makes this point very clear (see Table 7.7 and compare Table 7.6).

However, small households in the size group 2.5 to 5 acres are very poor in the sense that they do not even possess two draught animals, the minimum requirement for the cultivation of any plot of land. Many of them share draught cattle or rent them from others.[30]

TABLE 7.6 Employment on and outside the farm on the basis of landholding (in 8-hour days)

Size group (in hectares)	Employment on the farm	Employment outside the farm
Andhra Pradesh (West Godavari) 1957–60		
0 – 0.51	89	104
0.51 – 1.01	126	68
1.01 – 2.02	154	60
2.02 – 3.03	186	43
3.03 – 4.05	177	42
4.05 – 6.07	189	15
6.07 – 8.09	214	10
8.09 and above	191	–
Orissa (Sambalpur) 1957–60		
0.01 – 1.01	49	94
1.01 – 2.02	94	49
2.02 – 4.05	122	16
4.05 – 8.09	135	3
8.09 and above	198	0
Rajasthan (Pali) 1962–63		
0.01 – 1.01	84	122
1.01 – 2.02	127	69
2.02 – 3.03	192	92
3.03 – 4.05	138	62
4.05 – 6.07	178	39
6.07 – 8.09	193	11
8.09 – 10.12	162	15
10.12 and above	185	14

Source: *Farm Management in India*, April 1966.

TABLE 7.7 Household origin of male permanent agricultural labourers by main income source of household and acreage class

	Region A	Region B	Region C
Total Permanent	72,240	37,744	4,820
(1) From landless agricultural labour households	54,984	25,363	4,820
(2) From agricultural labour households with land	6,765	8,022	–
(i) 0 – 2.5 acres	6,765	7,120	–
(ii) 2.5 – 5.0 acres	nil	nil	–
(iii) 5 – 10 acres	nil	nil	–
(3) From households whose main income is source cultivation	10,491	4,359	–
(i) 0 – 2.5 acres	2,723	953	–
(ii) 2.5 – 5.0 acres	2,723	953	–
(iii) 5 – 10 acres	3,960	1,062	–
(iv) 10 – 15 acres	1,676	–	–

Source: S. Bhalla, 'New relations of production in Haryana agriculture'.

Their *per capita* expenditure is below subsistence as is the case with members belonging to marginal households.[31]

Medium households (5 to 10 acres) are self-sufficient in resource position and can employ their family labour moderately and provide them with an above average subsistence.[32] The well-to-do households (10 to 25 acres) have near total independence in terms of resource endowments (in the Indian context). These farms have more than three draught cattle, which gives them more elbow room than the medium peasants who become dependent on others in case one of their draught cattle falls sick or dies.[33] However, after critically examining the F.M.S. surveys, we find that this group is left with little surplus after incurring all expenditures including the cost of production of cultivation and family expenses.[34] In other words, this group seldom has any accumulation to reinvest in agriculture for extended reproduction.

Finally, there is a minority of rich households, each cultivating an area of 25 acres or more.[35] Their command over land is matched by their command over other farm resources. The value of their investment in livestock for each household is nearly four times that of a small peasant's; and that in implements of cultivation is also three to four times higher.[36] Their farms are normally not only self-sufficient but also generate a surplus (after meeting all expenses including the family's) which can be used for ploughing back into agriculture. Needless to say, these farmers depend to a great extent on outside labour to cultivate their land.

This description of the differentiation among the peasantry in India is not wholly satisfactory because various factors have not been taken into consideration: the cropping pattern, the nature of the soil (wet or dry, irrigated or not, etc.), or family size. However, this classification of the peasantry on the basis of size of land holding is not far off reality as is proved by the fact that the resource position of peasant households is closely related to amount of land owned.

What is clear from this class analysis of the peasantry is that, while 4 per cent of rural households own about 30 per cent of land, 50 per cent of rural households are nearly destitute and own only about 9 per cent of total land. Of the rest, the condition of the 19 per cent of rural households that own 12 per cent of land is pitiable; the remaining 27 per cent just manage to maintain a tolerable level of living on the remaining 48 per cent of land.

The important question is: what is the effect of this kind of social classification on the forces of production? Could the capitalist mode of production emerge in this social structure? As noted above, 96 per cent of rural households do not generate any surplus, so very few among them (perhaps some among the medium or well-to-do households) have the potential to grow as capitalist farmers. Approximately 70 per cent of land, therefore, has little possibility of being brought under capitalist agriculture.

What about the 4 per cent of households that hold 30 per cent of the land? This question has already been answered. In the face of the tremendous land hunger of the marginal and small peasants, there is no reason why the rich peasants should invest in capitalist farming if their capitalist profit does not exceed the pre-capitalist ground rent (which varies from 40 to 60 per cent of produce) which can easily be extracted from the sharecroppers or the attached farm servants. A farmer would agree to invest an extra amount of capital only when that would give him an extra amount of profit over and above the pre-capitalist ground rent: a possibility if the productivity of the land can be increased substantially in a sudden leap. This has been achieved in a noticeable way only in Punjab and Haryana due to the large size of holdings and availability of irrigation water.

The new inputs – known as the techniques of green revolution: a complex of new varieties of seeds, fertilizers, pesticides, and improved equipment – can raise the productivity of the land if the supply of water is constant and adequate.[37] Unfortunately, water in the required quantities is not plentiful except in Punjab, Haryana and some areas in Andhra, U.P., Rajasthan and Tamilnadu. Moreover, in most of India the small size of the average holding makes it very difficult for farmers to employ modern methods of cultivation or the techniques of the green revolution. Even the rich peasants in the 25-acre and above size group seldom own land in a single plot: holdings are fragmented and dispersed throughout the village.[38] On these tiny plots the use of small machinery or scientific cultivation is uneconomic, and the best practicable way to maximize income is to lease holdings to sharecroppers or engage attached farm servants.

It may be pointed out in this connection that what owners extract from attached farm servants is more in the nature of pre-capitalist ground rent than capitalist profit. This is one of the reasons why human labour is disproportionately high compared with mechanized techniques in Indian agriculture. The majority of these farm servants is recruited from marginal landholders or landless agricultural labourers.[39] Landowner profits are derived not as a result of increasing labour productivity from more capital investment, but through the payment of barest reproduction remuneration to farm servants, both in kind and cash, and the forcible appropriation of the major part of the surplus produced by them.

Another reason why landowners do not want to introduce technological improvements in land, despite possible economic gain to themselves, has been pointed out by Amit Bhaduri:

> Indeed, in certain circumstances, the semi-feudal landowner ... may be put off from a big improvement because it makes the kisan [peasant] free from perpetual debt and destroys the political and economic control of the landowner over his kisan, even though on exclusively economic grounds it may be profitable to him.[40]

It is not at all certain whether even on economic grounds he would gain. As noted above, the landowner might decide to invest his capital in usury because here the rate of return may be higher than in agriculture.

Another important reason for the perpetuation of the pre-capitalist mode of production in India, noted by Marx long ago, has received little attention from the analysts of Indian agriculture. This is the unity of agriculture and industry, or the mutual patron – client relationship between the cultivators and rural artisans – the phenomenon characterized by Marx as the determining features of the Asiatic mode of production. As most cultivators are marginal or small peasants, their needs for producers' goods are mostly met by the village artisans. The cultivators secure their equipment from (or get it repaired by) the artisans at the time of ploughing and sowing, and pay them for their services in cash or kind on a customary basis after the harvest. This practice is also prevalent among the medium and well-to-do peasants. As they are obliged to pay customary dues to the artisans, whether they take their services or not, and most of them are left with virtually no surplus before another crop, it is very natural that they should seek implements from the artisans. Bijan Sen, in his field survey, came across a rich farmer in West Godavari district who owned forty acres of fertile land and was in a position to use developed instruments of cultivation; but instead, he 'employed simple wooden ploughs and other implements replaced annually by the village carpenter in exchange for a bag of rice'.[41]

This instance clearly indicates that even rich peasants in India are reluctant to adopt advanced methods of technology because of this traditional dependence on village artisans. (Chapter 3 describes in detail how the carpenters, blacksmiths, etc. are paid on a customary basis for the services they render to the cultivators.) The interdependence between cultivators and village artisans is also indicated by the fact that even in 1952 45 per cent of the Indian economy was not monetized.[42] Furthermore, as noted in chapter 5, about 16 million people were engaged in artisan industries at that time, and in 1974 the number increased to approximately 20 million.[43] Today, in a village of, say, 300 people, there are about ten artisans to serve the villagers' needs of producer as well as consumer goods.

The dependence of India's agriculture on its artisans can also be indirectly derived from the fact that, according to Ashoke Rudra's calculation made on the basis of data collected by the Indian Statistical Institute, 'In 1960–61 inputs from industry amounted to no more than 1.1% of total production of agriculture proper'[44] (see Table 7.8).

TABLE 7.8 Dependence of agriculture on industries for current inputs (1960–1) (figure in rupees crores at 1959–60 prices)

Input from sectors	Output sectors			
	Planta-tions	*Animal husbandry*	*Agriculture proper*	*Forestry*
Packing materials: jute textiles and wooden products	4.3		2.9	
Chemical fertilizers	6.3		24.0	
Petroleum products	0.4		18.2	
Food industries	–	55.0	–	
Chemicals	1.6	19.0	5.9	
Electricity	0.2		7.8	
Coal	0.6		0.4	
Other industries	11.4		8.9	9.0
All industries	24.8	74.0	68.1	9.0
Agriculture proper	–	97.0	507.7	–
Total of all inputs	24.8	171.0	575.8	9.0
Output	196.0	1,130.0	6,071.0	180.0
Proportion of industrial inputs to outputs (%)	9.4	6.5	1.1	5.0

Source: A. Rudra, *Relative Rates of Growth of Agriculture and Industry*, p. 16.

Table 7.8 indicates that the total inputs expended came to Rs 575.8 crores for the output of Rs 6071 crores. Out of this, industry constituted only Rs 68.1 crores, the bulk of which was again expended on fertilizers. There is no separate column for agricultural implements; this is included under the heading 'other industries' and amounted to only Rs 8.9 crores. The insignificant contribution of modern implements by organized industry underlies agriculture's dependence on the traditional tools of production included under the heading 'agriculture proper'. In recent times the use of thrashers and power pumps has increased considerably in the green revolution zones, but the main impediment against their use in other areas, as explained above, is the mode of production. The nature of surplus extraction leaves very little in the hands of the marginal and small peasants. They can invest almost nothing for extended reproduction in the form of machinery, etc., and have to depend on the village artisans[45] for their implements. Even the rich peasants, as we noted, preserve their capital for investment in moneylending, trade, etc., and try to squeeze out as much as possible from the sharecroppers or attached farm servants.

The continued existence of village artisans or, in other words, the interdependence of agriculture and village artisan industry provides a formidable base for the persistence of the pre-capitalist technique of production in Indian agriculture. The partially dissolved Asiatic mode of production (in the form of interdependence between agriculture and the artisan industry) reinforces the semi-feudal mode of production and vice versa; the semi-feudal mode of production buttresses the semi-Asiatic mode of production by keeping capital away from the domain of agriculture.

The continuous one-way outflow of surplus from agriculture without even a small return – particularly in the form of producers' goods – that was its characteristic during pre-colonial and colonial days has remained unchanged. During the colonial period the extracted surplus led to capital formation in the metropolitan centres via the consumption of the rentier classes. The same kind of pre-capitalist ownership (changed in form but not in essence) has led to capital accumulation in the organized sector of India's industry (through import substitution), but has retarded the development of capitalist agriculture.

So, unlike the agriculture of economically developed countries, the organic composition of Indian agriculture is characterized by little use of constant capital. Because of this, while the productivity of labour in the organized industrial sector (both public and private) is increasing, the productivity of labour in agriculture is virtually stagnant. The pre-capitalist nature of technology is also responsible for the identical labour productivity in big and small farms.[46] Interestingly, the productivity per acre of land is sometimes higher in the small farms than it is in the big farms.[47]

In Europe, while capitalism was expanding, it brought under its sway both the agricultural[48] and industrial sectors. It was not an accident that approximately 4,000 capitalist landlords owned the major portion of arable land in England in the late eighteenth century.[49] Similarly, the Junker landlords of Prussia cleared their land for its capitalist transformation.[50]

These changes in the relations of production in agriculture in the West were accompanied by changes in the forces of production. New inputs were introduced which began to increase the productivity of labour in agriculture.[51]

One of the primary motivations for the development of capitalist agriculture in the West was provided by the development of industries, with their consequent expanding demand for labourers, raw materials, and food. The basis for this was the emerging capitalist social division of labour between agriculture and industry. The expropriated paupers in agriculture were gradually absorbed into the ever-growing industries. The increasing number of wage labourers in industries created a home market for its agricultural products. The law of development of the industrial population at the expense of agricultural population as enunciated by Marx (and employed by Lenin in his analysis of the development of capitalism in Russia) is based on the fact that

> in industry variable capital increases absolutely (the increase of variable capital implies an increase in the number of industrial workers and an increase in the total commercial and industrial population), whereas in agriculture the 'variable capital' required for the exploitation of a certain piece of land decreases absolutely.[52]

In India, industry (both public and private) cannot expand at a very rapid rate, not only because of the lack of necessary capital, but also because, as we noted above, its consumer base is very thin. The base is composed of the upper strata of rural society who are mainly rentiers, moneylenders and traders, and the upper echelons of state employees, the commercial bourgeoisie and successful professionals. Most of these groups are parasites, and as such their demand for industrial goods remains more or less static. Thus the natural increase in population in agriculture can hardly be reduced by the increase of employment in industries (see Table 7.13).

What is more, as India is a late starter in industrialization, the organic composition of her industry is very high. This restricts the possibility of large-scale absorption of variable capital (or workers) into industry at a rapid pace, even if its rate of development becomes brisk. The large-scale growth of capitalist agriculture is, therefore, hindered by the extreme weakness of the internal market for agricultural goods in the absence of the fast expansion of the industrial population.

Industry provides a stimulus to the development of capitalist agriculture as follows: it creates a demand for agricultural goods, which leads to the expropriation of the peasants from their land through economic means such as buying up their land and squeezing them out through competition, or through extra-economic means of forcible ejection. The absorption of these landless peasants as wage workers into industries creates a demand for agricultural goods. As a result, the rise in the income of agriculture leads to an increase in the investment of constant capital which leads to the further decline of employment in agriculture, leading to a renewed spurt of pauperization or the expansion of the industrial reserve army. However, the increase in income in agriculture leads to an increase in the demand for industrial goods; the expansion of industries, in turn, creates employment for a sizeable section of the pauperized cultivators – as the industrial proletariat.

The expropriation of peasants from their land expands the internal market in another way. The expropriated peasants must now buy their means of subsistence which they previously produced on their own land. To do so, they sell their labour power to the capitalist farmers who pay them a wage with which they procure their means of reproduction which, of course, is less than what they produce for the buyer of their labour power. However, their means of subsistence is no longer in the form of use value, but appears as exchange value and thus leads to an expansion of the internal market for agricultural produce.

Moreover, as a consequence of the decline in the variable capital (i.e. workers), the marketable surplus of agriculture increases continuously and this surplus is released to feed the growing industrial population. However, in India, this process is disrupted in various ways. As agriculture is predominantly pre-capitalist, the major portion of produce is consumed by agriculture itself (see Table 7.9).[53] It is estimated that about two-thirds to three-quarters of the total annual foodgrains are retained by farmers for their domestic consumption and other requirements (payments to the hired labourer, rent of land, seeds, etc.); only one-third to one-quarter of the produce is marketed.

Moreover, despite the slow growth of industry, the intersectoral terms of trade may move in favour of agriculture due to a slight fall in production resulting from flood or drought or from any other fortuitous reason in one or two states.[54] In fact, during the last decade, the prices of agricultural commodities have registered a greater increase than those of industrial products (see Tables 7.10 and 7.11).

TABLE 7.9 Marketable surplus in
India (as percentage
of production)

Crop	Marketable surplus as percentage of total production
Rice	31
Wheat	37
Jowar	24
Bajra	26
Maize	24
Gram	24

Source: *Farm Management in India*,
April 1966.

This shift in the terms of trade in favour of agriculture reduces real wage rates in industry (see Table 7.12), and this, in turn, leads to a decline in the demand for manufactured goods. The ensuing slow growth of industry results in a slower absorption of rural paupers into industry.

The overpressure of the population hinders the growth of capitalism in agriculture in another way. As employment outside of agriculture is too uncertain, peasants try to cling to their land at any cost. V.S. Vyas found, on the basis of surveys of the land market in Gujarat, that

the alternative before the small farmers was not migration to urban areas to be absorbed in the urban industrial work force but in supplementing their incomes by auxiliary occupations like agricultural labour and dairying considerably weakened the compulsion to sell off the land.[55]

Finally, the development of capitalist industry, as well as capitalist agriculture in India, is constrained by the small buying power of her rural population, as 50 per cent of them live below the poverty line and 20 per cent just on the verge of it.

The non-development of the capitalist mode of production meant, for India and other colonized countries, an absolute increase in the variable capital in its agriculture which would have been reversed in the case of capitalist development. It has been argued by main-

TABLE 7.10 Index numbers of wholesale prices (1961–2 = 100)

	General index	Change over previous year/month (per cent)	Index for manufactures	Change over previous year/month (per cent)	Index for agricultural commodities	Change over previous year/month (per cent)	Prices of manufactures as per cent of prices of agricultural commodities
Average of months							
1962–63	103.8	—	103.2	—	102.3	—	100.9
1966–67	149.9	+13.9	175.3	+ 7.1	166.6	+17.6	75.2
1967–68	167.3	+11.6	129.1	+ 3.0	188.2	+13.0	68.6
1968–69	165.4	− 1.1	132.8	+ 2.9	179.4	− 4.7	74.0
1969–70	171.6	+ 3.7	139.7	+ 5.8	194.8	+ 8.6	71.7
1970–71	181.1	+ 5.5	149.7	+ 7.2	201.4	+ 3.4	74.3
1971–72	188.4	+ 4.0	160.5	+ 7.2	199.6	− 0.9	80.4
1972–73	207.1	+ 9.9	168.8	+ 5.2	219.7	+20.0	76.8
1973–74	254.2	+22.7	189.3	+12.1	280.6	+27.8	67.8
1974–75	313.0	+23.1	240.7	+27.2	350.8	+25.1	69.5
1975–76							
April	309.2	—	247.7	− 0.1	339.9	+ 0.8	74.2
May	313.2	+ 1.3	247.2	− 0.1	338.8	− 0.3	73.0
June	312.3	− 0.3	247.1	—	339.4	+ 0.2	72.8
July	309.2	− 1.0	248.6	+ 0.6	330.1	− 2.7	75.3
August	311.2	+ 0.6	247.5	− 0.4	332.6	+ 0.8	74.4
September	309.7	− 0.5	247.4	+ 0.2	324.8	− 2.3	76.3
October	308.4	− 0.4	247.9	—	316.4	− 2.7	78.5
November	303.1	− 1.7	247.3	− 0.2	370.8	− 2.7	80.3
December	294.4	− 2.9	246.8	− 0.2	297.3	− 3.4	83.0

Source: 'Economic Survey', Government of India, for 1975–6 and 1970–1.

TABLE 7.11 Consumer price index numbers, 1961–75 (1960 = 100)

	Industrial workers								Urban non-manual employees	
	All India				Bombay	Calcutta	Delhi	Madras	General index	% Change from previous period
	Food index	% Change from previous period	General index	% Change from previous period						
1961	109	—	104	—	103	101	103	103	103	—
1966	164	+10.1	151	+10.2	143	144	147	141	142	+ 9.2
1967	192	+17.1	172	+13.9	158	159	168	150	157	+10.6
1968	196	+ 2.1	177	+ 2.9	166	171	178	151	161	+ 2.5
1969	190	– 3.1	175	– 1.1	173	181	182	156	165	+ 2.5
1970	200	+ 5.3	184	+ 5.1	180	185	195	169	173	+ 4.8
1971	203	+ 1.5	190	+ 3.3	188	194	209	178	178	+ 2.9
1972	216	+ 6.4	202	+ 6.3	198	216	218	197	189	+ 6.2
1973	262	+21.3	236	+15.8	224	279	250	221	212	+12.2
1974	342	+30.5	304	+28.8	275	288	324	281	259	+22.2
1975	357	+ 4.4	321	+ 5.6	303	297	336	325	—	—
January	368	—	326	—	298	289	342	327	280	—
February	365	– 0.8	325	– 0.3	300	279	335	326	278	– 0.7
March	359	– 1.6	321	– 1.2	301	275	335	323	277	– 0.4
April	361	+ 0.6	323	+ 0.6	303	280	339	325	278	+ 0.4
May	366	+ 1.4	327	+ 1.2	308.	287	337	325	281	+ 1.1
June	363	– 0.8	328	+ 0.3	309	285	341	328	283	+ 0.7
July	361	– 0.6	324	– 1.2	305	285	341	337	280	– 1.1
August	357	– 1.1	321	– 0.9	303	293	332	334	280	—
September	354	– 0.8	319	– 0.6	301	296	333	330	280	—
October	350	– 1.1	316	– 0.9	305	301	336	320	280	—
November	346	– 1.1	315	– 0.3	303	304	334	322	—	—
December	330	– 4.6	306	– 2.9	296	287	328	304	—	—

Source: Government of India, Ministry of Labour, *Indian Labour Journal*, March 1976, p. 610.

TABLE 7.12 Index numbers of real earnings of employees
earning less than Rs 400 per month in manufacturing industries for 1962-71 (1961 = 100)

Year	Index number of money earnings	All-India C.P.I. numbers (base shifted to 1961 = 100)	Index number of real earnings
1962	106	103	103
1963	109	106	103
1964	114	121	94
1965	128	132	97
1966	139	146	95
1967	151	166	91
1968	160	171	94
1969	170	169	101
1970	180	178	101
1971	187	183	102

Source: Government of India, Ministry of Labour, *The Indian
Labour Year Book 1972*, p. 28.

stream economists that, if Japan could develop with a small peasant
agriculture, why not India or other Third World countries? The
simple fact is that, due to capitalist development, the number of
workers (i.e. the variable capital) in agriculture is decreasing in
Japan,[56] or for that matter in any developed capitalist country,
while it is increasing in all pre-capitalist economies (see Table 7.13).

The growing number of people in agriculture, as we noted above,
helps to sustain the pre-capitalist mode of production in agriculture,
and this further acts as a brake on the rapid growth of industries. In
the pre-capitalist mode of production, as has been explained above,
there is little scope for the use of constant capital where small
cultivators predominate. Also, there is less incentive on the part of
rich peasants to reinvest capital (which can earn more profit in usury
or trade). As Marx stressed,

> In the case of colonists and independent small producers in
> general, who have no command at all over capital or at least
> command it only at a high rate of interest, that part of the product
> which stands in place of wages is their revenue, whereas it
> constitutes an investment of capital for the capitalist. The

colonist, therefore, regards this expenditure of labour as the indispensable prerequisite of his product, which is the thing that interests him first of all. As for his surplus labour, after deducting that necessary labour, it is evidently realised in a surplus-product; and as soon as he can sell this, or even use it for himself, he looks upon it as something that cost him nothing, *because it cost him no materialised labour*. It is only the expenditure of materialised labour which appears to him as an outlay of wealth. Of course he tries to sell as high as possible, but even a sale below value, below the capitalist price of production still appears to him as a profit, unless this profit is claimed beforehand by debts, mortgages, etc.[57]

TABLE 7.13 Number of male workers in agriculture in some countries (in 000s)

	Number of farms	Number of male workers in agriculture		
	1960	1955	1960	1965
Argentina	472	1,411	1,295	1,334
Australia	252	433	395	392
Austria	402	369	297	267
Belgium (and Luxemburg)	269	266	215	174
Brazil	3,350	7,566	8,698	8,911
Canada	481	625	484	420
Ceylon	1,174	1,131	1,263	1,255
Chile	174	496	512	533
Colombia	1,210	1,704	1,612	1,957
Denmark	197	338	303	273
Finland	388	201	187	173
France	1,994	2,969	2,395	2,205
Germany, Fed. Rep.	1,678	1,780	1,477	1,273
Greece	1,156	1,083	1,101	1,096
India	48,882	66,165	86,847	91,339
Ireland	360	393	343	316
Israel	70	90	77	80
Italy	4,294	5,129	3,898	3,364
Japan	6,057	5,745	4,897	4,405
Libya	146	n.a.	n.a.	n.a.
Mauritius	22	55	56	57
Mexico	1,365	4,778	5,287	5,998
Netherlands	77	451	387	351

(Table 7.13 *continued*)

	Number of farms	Number of male workers in agriculture		
	1960	1955	1960	1965
New Zealand	301	117	112	109
Norway	434	118	103	95
Pakistan (and Bangladesh)	12,155	17,233	18,464	23,206
Paraguay	161	191	231	248
Peru	870	711	758	797
Philippines	1,639	3,305	3,959	4,183
Portugal	n.a.	1,060	1,075	1,047
South Africa	110	1,351	1,415	1,493
Spain	3,008	3,868	3,023	3,442
Surinam	16	n.a.	12	n.a.
Sweden	265	274	225	201
Switzerland	185	267	233	219
Syria	418	420	477	508
Taiwan	808	1,095	1,116	1,320
Turkey	3,410	4,122	4,469	4,907
U.A.R.	2,946	3,960	4,046	4,509
U.K.	306	961	877	799
U.S.A.	3,711	4,584	3,542	3,088

Source: Y. Hayami and V.W. Ruttan, *Agricultural Development: An International Perspective*, p. 321.

The small peasant is very often forced to sell below the capitalist price of production, particularly at a time when there is too much supply in the market. So whatever profit there is does not usually accrue to the small cultivators but to traders, moneylenders and rich peasants who, for reasons explained above, are seldom interested in ploughing it back to develop agriculture on capitalist lines.

It is the low organic composition of capital that distinguishes the productivity of Third World countries from those of advanced capitalist nations. Table 7.14 indicates the differences in yields between Japan and some Third World countries.

The difference in productivity between Japan and India can easily be traced to quantity of fertilizers used in these countries. The per-hectare consumption of fertilizer in India was only 16 kg while it was 400 kg in Japan in 1971–2.[58] The use of farm machines per hectare is also greater in Japan than in India.[59]

TABLE 7.14 Comparative paddy yields, 1971 (figures in 100 kg per hectare)

Country	Yield
Bangladesh	16.9
India	17.1
Burma	16.9
Philippines	17.2
Thailand	19.7
Japan	52.5

Source: Report No. 455ABC, *Bangladesh Development in a Rural Economy*, vol. I, Document of the International Bank for Reconstruction and Development, 1974, p. 54.

Thus the development of capitalism in a country leads to a higher organic composition of capital in that country; in other words, capitalists increasingly tend to invest more in constant capital than in variable capital. Marx brings out this point as follows:

> for the capitalist the investment of both variable and constant capital represents an outlay of capital. The relatively larger outlay of the capitalist reduces the cost price, and in fact the value of commodities, provided other circumstances remain the same. Hence, although the profit arises only from surplus-labor, consequently only from the employment of variable capital, still it may seem to the individual capitalist that living labor is the most expensive element of his cost of production, which should be reduced to a minimum above all others. This is but a capitalistically distorted form of the correct view that the relatively greater use of past labor, compared to living labor, signifies an increase in the productivity of social labor and a greater social wealth.[60]

It is, therefore, the higher productivity of labour that leads to an accumulation of capital. Further, the productivity of labour in industry is higher than that in agriculture (see below). The underdevelopment of Third World countries stems primarily from the non-development of capitalism or the low productivity of social labour with consequently little or no increase in social wealth.

What is more, the low productivity of labour or the non-development of production accounts for what appears to be the overpressure of population in most Third World countries, particularly in Asia.

Theories of modernization and social productivity of labour in Third World countries

Many scholars and journalists who seek their inspiration from Malthus (as is evident in the spate of articles in newspapers and journals all over the world) believe that the major reasons for the underdevelopment of such countries as China, India, Indonesia, Bangladesh, Pakistan, Egypt, etc., lie in their rapid population increase. However, if we compare Asia's population growth with that of Europe for the last three centuries, we find that, in fact, Asia's share of world population declined from 60.6 per cent in 1650 to 54.5 per cent in 1933. In the same period, Europe's share increased from 18.3 per cent to 25.2 per cent.[61] In 350 years, from the beginning of 1600 to 1951, the population of India increased approximately three and a half times. The population of England increased nearly ten times for the period 1700 to 1951. According to Moreland, India's population at the beginning of the seventeenth century stood at 100 million; it rose to 356 million in 1951. England's population rose from 4.5 million in 1700 (Finliason's report in the preface of the 1931 census) to 43 million in 1951.

From the first census taken in India in 1871 to that of 1911, India's population increased 18.9 per cent. For the same period, Europe's average increase was 45.4 per cent.[62]

Even today the average national density per km^2 is lower in India than in many developed countries. While India has 186 people per km^2, Japan has 303, West Germany 247, Pakistan 90, Netherlands 337, Italy 186, and England 326.[63] Moreover, India has more arable land, i.e. land under cultivation,[64] than any other country in the world with the possible exception of the U.S.S.R., the U.S.A., and China. However, in almost all the developed countries, the yield per hectare is two to three times higher than it is in India because of the more advanced mode of production.

It is significant that the population increase in Europe started to decline only after the first decade of the twentieth century when a major transformation in the standard of living of the masses coincided with a major breakthrough in medicine.

According to Gregory King's estimation, at the end of the seventeenth century (1695) the *per capita* income in England and Holland was sixty dollars, and fifty dollars in France (in 1952–4 dollars). 'In the eighteenth century western countries', says L.J. Zimmerman, 'were certainly not richer than the rest of the world.'[65] On the basis of data collected by Phyllis Dean, he has made an estimate of the rise of *per capita* income in the United Kingdom from the beginning of the eighteenth century (see Table 7.15).

The *per capita* income in most of the West European countries reached 400 dollars at the beginning of the twentieth century. This rise in income, with the control of disease, made it possible for the people in these countries to limit their family size. It can be seen

TABLE 7.15 *Per capita* income in the United Kingdom, 1695–1960

	Per capita income in 1952–54 dollars
1960	910
1957	860
1952–54	780
1946–52	720
1935–44	680
1925–34	550
1915–24	480
1905–14	480
1895–1904	450
1885–94	390
1875–84	310
1870	260
1860	260
1850	240
1839	180
1820	150
1812	110
1800	110
1744	70
1695	60

Source: L.J. Zimmerman, *Poor Lands, Rich Lands*, p. 105.

from Table 7.15 that the *per capita* income in England almost doubled in the forty years from 1870 to 1905. Unlike the dispossessed urban workers of Victorian times – whose wretched conditions roused the anger of Dickens, Marx, and Carlyle – the labourers of Western Europe and North America of the early twentieth century had an income far above subsistence level. Thus, the fertility decline came to these countries gradually in a social environment of a rising standard of living, rising urbanization, rising productivity of labour, and widespread education.

Furthermore, the industrialization of the economy of the developed countries enabled them to shift the major part of their population from agriculture to industry and tertiary sectors, and from rural to urban areas. The following table shows the changing percentage of employment in the primary sectors in a few developed countries of the world.

TABLE 7.16 Changing percentage of employment in primary sectors

	1830	1870	1910	1960
Great Britain	23	15	8	4
United States	71	51	32	9
Sweden	63	56	48	14
France	63	50	41	25
Japan	—	82	63	33

Source: L.J. Zimmerman, *Poor Lands, Rich Lands*, p. 8.

At the beginning of the eighteenth century almost all countries of the world – with the exception of Great Britain, Holland and India – had about 80 per cent of their people employed in agriculture.[66] Table 7.16 shows that the dependence on agriculture decreased gradually in the industrializing countries, but it continued to increase in India. According to the census reports of India, the proportion of people dependent on agriculture was 61 per cent in 1891, rose to 66 per cent in 1901 and to 73 per cent in 1921.

When the British took control of political power in India in the middle of the eighteenth century the land/man ratio was so favourable that it was labour which was a scarce element. Kingsley Davis recognized that India's lack of economic development must be attributed in considerable measure to its colonization:

> The British had an opportunity to transform the economy of India. Things were in a shambles from the breakup of the Moghul regime; population was not too dense; rich resources were available; and the strength of the British Raj was beyond challenge. But the British pursued the short-run advantage of a crude specialization of function as between industrializing England and rural India.... Though their own economy was being transformed by the use of fossil fuels and machinery, they assumed all along that agriculture would remain India's principal economic activity. Since machinery and fossil fuels were not applied anywhere to tillage until the twentieth century, the emphasis on agriculture was singularly unpropitious for India's economic development. Agriculture was the one thing hardest to modernize.[67]

Although the population in India rose very slowly throughout the eighteenth, nineteenth and early decades of the twentieth centuries, its cumulative effect in the absence of alternative employment (in industry) had a very adverse result on the land/man ratio. This was further aggravated by the transfer of labour from manufacturing industries to the cultivation of land (see above for the deterioration of the land/man ratio).

The situation further deteriorated with the rapid rise of the population in the 1930s as more and more diseases such as malaria, cholera, plague, etc. were brought under control. India, which had been a food surplus economy throughout the nineteenth century – despite the increasing overpressure on agriculture – became a food importing economy in the 1940s.

However, this population increase might have been averted if India had been allowed to industrialize in the nineteenth century. Notestein argues that the decline in fertility is closely associated with changes in ways of living and thinking which again are products of industrialization.[68] Moreover, India's inability to industrialize in the nineteenth century affected its economic growth in another way. The productivity of labour, as has been found in surveys of various countries, is definitely higher in the secondary and tertiary sectors than in agriculture because the organic composition of capital increases more rapidly in these sectors than in agriculture. Table 7.17 illustrates the productivity of labour in the primary, secondary and tertiary sectors.

TABLE 7.17   Production per labourer in the primary, secondary and tertiary sectors (*c.* 1953)

	Productivity per labourer in dollars		
	Primary sector	*Secondary sector*	*Tertiary sector*
North America	2,860	5,530	5,200
Oceania	4,150	2,360	2,430
Northwest Europe	1,050	1,700	1,590
Southeast Europe	310	1,280	720
Latin America	360	1,120	1,480
Japan	400	1,100	1,020
Near East	280	690	680
Southeast Asia	170	370	380

Source: L.J. Zimmerman, *Poor Lands, Rich Lands*, p. 49.

The transfer of people from agriculture to industry in the modern economies of Europe and North America not only provided new employment to the rapidly rising population in these countries, but also ensured a very fast growth rate in G.N.P. by increasing the *per capita* productivity of labour.[69] It may be noted here that the early stages of industrialization normally accompany a rapid growth in the population which later slows down with the progressive improvement in the standard of living of the masses. This was the case with all industrially developed countries, including Japan.

So we find that the population problem is the result of slow economic growth or non-industrialization. The main defect in the Malthusian prognosis is that he thought that the population would increase at a faster rate than capital and technology. Economic history conclusively proves that a very high rate of population increase was more than compensated for by a higher rate of capital growth and technical development in the industrially developed countries. This, in turn, resulted in a rise in the standard of living in these countries.

Now we turn to the question of whether India had the technology or capital to ensure a rapid economic development. Until the early nineteenth century, India had technological superiority (in urban centres) over Great Britain in the textile industry which was the basis of the industrial revolution in England. In other industries, too, Indian technology was equal if not superior to western technology. As M. Weiner says,

> There is evidence that ... India was equal and possibly ahead of Western countries in its technology and volume of manufactures. Indian textiles in particular were superior to what was then produced in the West.[70]

There was also no shortage of capital. The South American gold and silver which was accumulated in India in exchange for its manufactures throughout the sixteenth, seventeenth, and eighteenth centuries provided a significant part of the capital for England's industrial revolution after India's defeat in the battle of Plassey.[71]

Even after India was reduced to being an agricultural country there occurred a tremendous capital transfer on the basis of primitive capital accumulation in its agricultural sector. Eighty per cent of India's total exports consisted of raw materials and foodstuffs. Her imports were always less than her exports. This favourable balance of trade, however, was used in the imperial cause. The excess exports did not augment the capital accumulation in India nor raise her social productivity.

It may be contended that, even if India had capital, she did not have the developed industrial technology of the West. Notwithstanding India's technical superiority over Europe in the early eighteenth century, one may say that it was the developed machine technology which propelled the industrial revolution in the West. The simple fact is that technology, science or knowledge can never be kept hidden for long. Numbers, decimals and negative numbers were invented in India and they were instrumental in emancipating mathematics from the bondage of Roman numerals. It was a similar case with Arabic algebra and alchemy. Without these vital inventions there was little possibility of any advancement in science. Gunpowder was discovered in China; it opened up a new horizon in technological development. None of these inventions or discoveries could be kept secret for long. They were diffused all over the world. Thus, knowledge could never be claimed as the exclusive property of any individual nation. It is the product of cumulative endeavours of men and, therefore, a universal heritage.

England tried desperately to keep secret her new machines. She was successful only for a few years. As S.A. Hetzler says,

> England, early recognizing the importance of mechanical inventions, jealously hoarded this knowledge by forbidding the export of machinery or machine designs, or the migration of artisans knowledgeable of machine construction. Inevitably, all three diffused, and with a lag of, perhaps, a couple of decades, the factory method spread to western and central Europe and the United States.[72]

The machine also reached Japan – the only country in Asia not colonized or semi-colonized – in the later part of the nineteenth century.

Despite the independent discovery of the factory method, the early separation of labour from capital and the introduction of the putting-out system and its close association with Britain, India failed to benefit from the industrial revolution and technical inventions. What was the secret behind India's failure and Japan's success?

Was it due to ideological factors that India lagged behind Japan? Many social scientists think so. Most of them draw their inspiration directly or indirectly from Max Weber. However, Weber thought differently. In his view, both Japan and India were traditional societies and had social institutions which impeded their development towards capitalism. These were mainly caste in India and clan in Japan. India and Japan were also handicapped by the absence of a 'bourgeois estate' and a 'city commune'.[73] Yet Japan entered the orbit of capitalist development on the very basis of clan organization or family ties. India failed to do so in spite of the fact that the caste organization was extremely responsive to new demands imposed on it by the emerging society in the seventeenth and eighteenth centuries.[74] As we know from the literature, the egalitarian reform movements in religion during this period, particularly Vaishnavism among the Hindus and Sufism among the Muslims, greatly undermined the rigidity of social stratification. New universalistic codes came into existence to regulate and channel the process of social mobility and social mobilization.

However, it is a common practice among modernization theorists to classify world societies into traditional/modern, organic/mechanical, status/contractual, etc., and to consider these categories as explanatory of reality. The argument goes like this: backward societies are traditional, therefore they are backward. The only redeeming feature of these tautological theories lies in their meticulous attempt to bring out the characteristics of traditional societies. But such characteristics reflect the nature of social relations in these societies; they do not inform us why these types of social relations came into being in the first place. In the absence of an historical analysis of social structures, most of the studies in the sociology of development fail to explain how particular cultures, modern or traditional, evolve.

It must be borne in mind that, unlike his followers, Weber always tried to find out the material basis of tradition and ideology. His historical studies of religions of China and India are replete with discussions of economic factors. He agreed with Marx that the reason for the specific stability of Asiatic peoples could be found in their forces of production. It is also interesting to recall that even in his study of the role of protestantism in the rise of capitalism, he wanted to know how 'Protestant asceticism was in turn influenced in its development and its character by the totality of social conditions, especially economic'.[75]

On the other hand, it is not true that Marx did not recognize the role of values and traditions in economic development and social change. His characterization of the 'Asiatic society' clearly indicated that he considered the prevailing social institutions of Asia as positive hindrances to social change. Writing on India, he concluded that the railway system would be the forerunner of modern industry in India and modern industry in turn 'will dissolve the hereditary divisions of labour, upon which rests the Indian castes, those decisive impediments to Indian progress'.[76] He also believed that British rule, by introducing modern transportation and communications, would 'release the desires and efforts indispensable to social advance'.[77]

Marx was fully aware of how traditions (such as castes) could obstruct social change. He also knew the importance of 'desires and efforts' – 'n Ach' of McLelland – for social progress, but he did not think they could emerge in the psyche in a vacuum without a material base being.[78] Marx believed that the material base was laid by the British when they had introduced railways, the electric telegraph, a free press, political unity, and private property in land into India.

British rule, according to Marx, had a double mission to accomplish: 'one destructive, the other regenerative – the annihilation of the old Asiatic society'.[79] Thus, for Marx, colonialism was a destructive but progressive force. In this, Marx differed from Marxist writers like Gunder Frank. Marx was optimistic that British rule would unintentionally create objective conditions for India's independence and self-development. In the process of creating these conditions the bourgeoisie would drag 'individuals and peoples through blood and dirt'.[80] However, he was convinced that the Indians

> will not reap the fruits of the new elements of society scattered among them by the British bourgeoisie ... till the Indians themselves shall have grown strong enough to throw off the English yoke altogether.[81]

In this prognosis, too, Marx was correct.

However, it seems that Marx could not foresee that colonial rule would be able to continue for a long time without transforming the entire colonial economy. With profound insight he showed that market exchange does not always act as a dissolvent of the old modes of production. The corrosive power of market exchange depends on the solidity or stability of the old mode. The major mechanism of colonial exploitation – the exchange of commodities between two modes, the capitalist and the pre-capitalist – was based on the preservation of the old pre-capitalist modes which did not disintegrate, as he expected, after the introduction of market exchange.

In certain cases, the old mode or modes were strengthened by the nature of colonial capitalist exchange. Marx thought that railways, electricity and the introduction of manufactured goods, etc., would destroy entirely or substantially the pre-capitalist modes of production in the colonies. This did not happen. His fear about the resisting force of the pre-capitalist modes was proved true rather than his optimism.

André Gunder Frank's mistake also emanated from the fact that he viewed the colonial economy as a capitalist economy. That was why he suggested[82] that capitalism advanced in the colonies in times of war, depression, etc., when colonial ties were weakest. Although this is true, it was simply not mercantile exchange which facilitated colonial exploitation. The main mechanism was the perpetuation and exploitation of the pre-capitalist mode for the benefit of the rising capitalist system. The jute and cotton production in India was carried on by pre-capitalist modes, but they were used in the jute and textile industries in Dundee and Manchester to augment their capital.

It should be kept in mind, however, that the weakness of the modes of production in the colonies, in most cases, was not the result of colonial rule. Rather, colonial rule exploited the inherited weakness of the indigenous modes for its own benefit. This kind of exploitation, however, was inherent in the nature of the integration of world economy by capitalism. It did not result from the villainy of any particular colonial rulers or the foolishness of the native people. The victimizers and the victims were both prisoners of the system. The colonizers could not introduce a large-scale capitalist mode of production into the colonies without inflicting self-injury.

For the colonizing countries, the exploitation of its own labour force and raising its productivity through accumulation depended, to a great extent, on transforming the colonized countries into markets; they could not let the colonized countries industrialize, at least in the formative phase of the industrial revolution, and thus lose these markets. This, however, led to an international division of labour between the colonizing and colonized countries. Marx describes the process vividly in the following words:

> By ruining handicraft production in other countries, machinery forcibly converts them into fields for the supply of its raw material. In this way East India was compelled to produce cotton, wool, hemp, jute and indigo for Great Britain.... A new and international division of labour, a division suited to the requirements of the chief centres of modern industry springs up, and converts one part of the globe into a chiefly agricultural field of production, for supplying the other part which remains a chiefly industrial field.[83]

It is this international division of labour, rooted in the colonial past, that is still responsible for the stagnation of erstwhile colonial economies like India. The productivity of the Indian working population, most of whom are engaged in agriculture, is next to nothing compared to the productivity of an industrial or even an agricultural labourer in a developed capitalist country.

As has already been seen, the more the number of people working in agriculture – this phenomenon is the characteristic of a pre-capitalist economy – the less is that country's productivity of labour. For this reason the theory of unequal exchange is correct when it states that, in the exchange of commodities between the developed and developing countries, unequal amounts of consumed labour are exchanged. But the reason it gives is incorrect. According to the theory of unequal exchange, a labourer in the developing country gets a lower return for his labour than his counterpart in the developed world because of the pricing mechanism. The unequal prices for the same amount of labour are administered through the better bargaining position of the metropolitan centres because of their monopoly control of trade.[84] Our contention is that unequal prices are not the real reason for the underdevelopment of Third World countries.

Even if and when prices are equal, there will be unequal exchange of labour between the developed and developing countries because of the low application of constant capital in the developing countries. The same commodity or the same unit of product in the developing countries will contain more labour than in the developed countries because in the former the productivity of labour will remain low as a result of less use of constant capital.[85] Moreover, in the developed capitalist countries, the productivity of social labour and consequently social wealth is far greater because the productivity of labour in the industrial sector is significantly higher than in the agricultural sector.

The small peasantry as the basis of state autonomy

From the foregoing discussion we can conclude that capitalism in India has not yet been able to bring agriculture under its complete sway. The production of agriculture is still being carried on in a more or less unchanging, wretched, pre-capitalist form, when the cultivator works for himself as well as when he works for the landlord. This is both the result and cause of his low productivity and poverty. The pre-capitalist character of Indian agriculture, remaining dependent on its pre-capitalist industry, has failed to bring an end to the atomistic fragmentation of production. This kind of small peasant farming is again inseparably related to the isolation of the producers. It is this isolation and insularity of the small peasants that is at the root of the autonomy of the state, in India.

As explained in chapter 1, Marx traced the autonomy of the oriental despotic state to the indifference and apathy of its most numerous class – the peasants in the villages – which reproduced itself and the economy in an isolated manner far removed from the state to which its social surplus was provided. Engels, too, pointed out that the apathy of the peasants was the foundation of Russian despotism, as well as of the corruption of parliamentary practices in some countries:

> The peasant has so far largely manifested himself as a factor of political power only by his apathy, which has its roots in the isolation of rustic life. This apathy on the part of the great mass of the population is the strongest pillar not only of the parliamentary corruption in Paris and Rome but also of Russian despotism.[86]

Lenin, in his study of the development of capitalism in Russia, found that

> in spite of the difference in the forms of landownership, the same thing can be applied to the Russian peasant as was said about the small French peasant by Marx...[87]

in 'The Eighteenth Brumaire'. Similar small-peasant characteristics are present among Indian peasants, too, despite their differences. The common element among these three peasant societies is that, as regards their mode of life and interests, they are a class (= class-in-itself), but 'in so far as ... the identity of their interests begets ... no political organization'[88] (because of the small peasants' isolation, apathy, and insularity), they do not form a class (= class-for-itself). This lack of political will on the part of the small peasants, when they constitute the most numerous class in society, provides a basis for the state to assume autonomy from the rule of other dominant and contending classes by claiming that it represents the interests of the peasants. This was the background of the state autonomy of Bonapartism, as was enunciated by Marx:

Only under the second Bonaparte does the state seem to have
made itself completely independent.... And yet the state power
is not suspended in mid air. Bonaparte represents a class, and the
most numerous class of French society at that, the small-holding
(parzellen) peasants.... The small-holding peasants form a vast
mass, the members of which live in similar conditions but without
entering into manifold relations with one another. Their mode of
production isolates them from one another instead of bringing
them into mutual intercourse. The isolation is increased by
France's bad means of communication and by the poverty of the
peasants. Their field of production, the small holding, admits of
no division of labour in its cultivation, no application of science
and, therefore, no diversity of development, no variety of talent
no wealth of social relationships. Each individual peasant family
is almost self-sufficient; it itself directly produces the major part
of its consumption and thus acquires its means of life more
through exchange with nature than in intercourse with society. A
small holding, a peasant and his family; alongside them another
small holding, another peasant and another family. A few score
of these make up a village, and a few score of villages make up a
department. In this way, the great mass of the French nation is
formed by simple addition of homologous magnitudes, much as
potatoes in a sack form a sack of potatoes. In so far as millions of
families live under economic conditions of existence that
separate their mode of life, their interests and their culture from
those of the other classes, and put them in hostile opposition to
the latter, they form a class. In so far as there is merely a local
interconnection among these small-holding peasants, and the
identity of their interests begets no community, no national bond
and no political organisation among them, they do not form a
class. They are consequently incapable of enforcing their class
interests in their own name, whether through a parliament or
through a convention. They cannot represent themselves, they
must be represented. Their representative must at the same time
appear as their master, as an authority over them, as an
unlimited governmental power that protects them against the
other classes and sends them rain and sunshine from above. The
political influence of the small-holding peasants, therefore, finds
its final expression in the executive power subordinating society
to itself.[89]

India had been, and is, a country of small peasants. These peasants cannot represent themselves; they must be represented. Previously, i.e. in pre-British days, as Marx pointed out, 'the despot here' appeared 'as the father of all lesser communities, thus realizing the common unity [the unity of small peasants] of all'.[90] All post-independent governments[91] claim that they represent the interests of small peasants and vow to protect them against the other classes. Thus it is not at all surprising that twelve points of Mrs Gandhi's twenty-point programme vouched to safeguard and enhance the interests of the small peasants, and three of the remaining points aimed at curtailing the economic power of the big landlords and private corporate capital.[92] In the same way the slogan of the Janata government is that it furthers rural interests, particularly of small peasants, and it will not let big industries expand.

Like the Bonapartist state, the autonomy of the state in India emerges from the fact that the power of the landlords is non-existent on the political level and the bourgeoisie is too weak; the state can claim that it is representing the interests of the small peasants and seek, on their behalf, to contain the bourgeoisie. However, the power of the feudal lords was not destroyed, because in India they never flowered in the form they had in France; the bourgeoisie was weak because their growth was obstructed; the small peasant was a social force as a class-in-itself but not as a class-for-itself. That is why the state in India, like the Bonapartist state, could pretend to represent their interests without, in fact, doing so. There is another similarity. Bonaparte, as Marx says,

> looks on himself as the adversary of the political and literary [ideological] power of the middle class [bourgeoisie]. But by protecting its material power [existing relations of production in the form of property rights], he generates its political power anew. The cause must accordingly be kept alive; but the effect, where it manifests itself, must be done away with.... As against the bourgeoisie, Bonaparte looks on himself ... as the representative of the peasants and of the people in general, who want to make the lower classes of the people happy within the frame of bourgeois society.[93]

All post-colonial governments in India consider themselves the champions of the cause of the lower classes against the bourgeoisie;

but they, like Bonaparte, want the lower classes to be contented within the framework of the existing relations of property. They too, like Bonaparte, attack the effect (concentration of wealth) but not its cause or the material base (private ownership). An important deviation, however, in India, is the attempt to concentrate basic industries in the state sector.

However, without substituting private ownership for social ownership, the bourgeoisie has not been, and cannot be, subjugated. The ceaseless struggle of the bourgeoisie to bring the state apparatus under its direct control, therefore, continues unabated (more about this in the conclusion).

There is, however, one fundamental difference between the Bonapartist autonomy and the autonomy of the state in India. While the Bonapartist form of state was a temporary phenomenon in France and Germany (in the form of Bismarckism), the autonomy of the state in India had, and has, at least until now, a more permanent base in its villages formed of small-holding peasants. The base had been grounded on a stubborn, but now slowly dissolving, Asiatic mode of production.

8 Conclusion

In the preceding pages a comprehensive analysis has been made of the evolving social economy and its relationship to the state, in which it is shown that the state in India, because of the nature of the evolution of its social formation, has been able to play an independent role *vis-à-vis* the social classes. This contention is so contrary to the 'traditional Marxist class theory of the state', in which the state is inevitably a means of class hegemony, that it will be elaborated on the basis of Marx's and Engels's own writings. In fact, the Marxian theory of the state, which was never expounded in a complete form in any of his works but remained central to almost all his writings, is much more complex and subtle than simply representing the state as an instrument of the rule of the dominant class. The state, of course, in his view, is the focus of the class struggle, but the exercise of state power cannot mechanically or automatically be traced to the dominant class or classes.[1] Marx makes it very clear that it is quite possible for one class to exercise state power in the interests of another class.[2] According to Marx, what determines the nature of polity and how state power is exercised depends on the nature of the social formation, particularly on its dominant mode of production, as the dominant mode controls other modes of production for its own reproduction. To put it another way, the autonomy of the state or the state's subservience to any class depends on the nature of the development of classes or class configurations which, in turn, are the result of the unfolding of the social formation. The point, to be noted here, is that classes are not, in most cases, passive elements: they play a definitive role in the evolution of the mode or modes of production which constitute the social formation.[3]

There have been many scholarly works which have endeavoured to show the operation of this dialectic in bringing out the state's role as the instrument of class rule where the exercise of the state power is directed to reproduce the dominant mode of production. However, there appears to be no concrete work, till now, which has attempted to relate the autonomy of the state with the evolution of classes and social formations as has been attempted, with many limitations, in the preceding pages. For Marx and Engels, the autonomy or the independence of the state and its role, however, was an important problem to be analysed in the evolution of any social formation. Their preoccupation with Bonapartism is a typical example of this concern.

In the following pages the analysis will be concluded by probing into what is meant by the independence or autonomy of the state in Marxism (particularly with reference to precapitalist formations), and then by relating it to the exposition of the modes of production, the social classes and the state in India contained in the preceding chapters. This would serve two purposes: first, it would focus upon the broad theoretical background of the empirical analysis; and second, it would enable the findings to be presented succinctly and abstractly in the conclusion.

According to Miliband there are two views of the state in Marxist political theory. The first view, he says,

> finds its most explicit expression in the famous aphorism of the Communist Manifesto: 'The executive of the modern state is but a committee for managing the common affairs of the whole bourgeoisie,' and political power is 'merely the organised power of one class for oppressing another.' ... This is the classical Marxist view of the subject of the state and it is the only one which is to be found in Marxism/Leninism. In regard to Marx himself, however, and this is also true to a certain extent of Engels as well, it only constitutes what may be called a primary view of the state ... for there is to be found another view of the state in his work.... This secondary view is that of the state as independent from and superior to all social classes, as being the dominant force in society rather than the instrument of the dominant class.[4]

While Miliband points out one exception to the state as the instrument of class rule, as in the Bonapartist state, David McLellan recognizes a few such exceptions.

Marx does admit exceptions to his general description of the
state as an instrument of class domination, and especially in two
of his most striking analyses of contemporary events – The Class
Struggles in France and the Eighteenth Brumaire of Louis
Bonaparte.... In relatively backward countries, where classes
were not fully developed, Marx thought that the state could play
an independent role; also in the European absolute monarchies
in the transition between feudal and bourgeois classes.[5]

The other major exception, adds McLellan,

in Marx to the idea of the state as an instrument of class
domination occurs in Asian societies – in India, China, and to
some extent Russia.[6]

Here, Marx

saw a despotism which, being mainly based on the absence of private
property in land did not serve the interests of a particular class.[7]

What Miliband calls the primary view of the state, in Marxism, we
find in Marx's and Engels's own writings that, even according to
that view, the state is not and does not become the instrument of
class rule unless and until estates have been replaced by classes. Till
then, even in modern societies, the state might be able to preserve
its independence.

The independence of the state is only found nowadays in those
countries where the estates have not yet completely developed
into classes, where the estates, done away with in more advanced
countries, still have a part to play, and where there exists a
mixture; countries, that is to say, in which no one section of the
population can achieve dominance over the other. This is the
case particularly in Germany. The most perfect example of the
modern state is North America.[8]

As the Marxian theory of the state is based on the theory of social
classes and class struggles, the state, according to Marx, does not
mechanically become an instrument of class rule; the state is transformed into an apparatus of class rule as and when a particular class

emerges victorious over other classes. That is why North America provides the best example of a class state because here, as Marx points out,

> the state, in contrast to all earlier national formations was from the beginning subordinate to bourgeois society [and] to its production.[9]

On the contrary, in most national structures of Europe, the bourgeoisie, at first, had to fight (against other classes, notably the feudal lords and state power) for its survival and then to assert its authority through the capture of the latter:

> Each step in the development of the bourgeoisie was accompanied by a corresponding political advance of that class. An oppressed class under the sway of feudal nobility, an armed and self-governing association in the mediaeval commune; here independent urban republic (as in Italy and Germany), there taxable 'third estate' of the monarchy (as in France), afterwards, in the period of manufacture proper, serving either the semi-feudal or the absolute monarchy as a counterpoise against the nobility, and, in fact, corner-stone of the great monarchies in general, the bourgeoisie has at last, since the establishment of Modern Industry and of the world market, conquered for itself, in the modern representative State, exclusive political sway.[10]

Before the bourgeoisie could conquer state power for itself, there were about two centuries of absolute monarchy in which no class could positively claim to be politically dominant. Under such a situation, as Engels points out,

> warring classes balance each other so nearly that the state power, as ostensible mediator, acquires, for the moment, a certain degree of independence of both. Such was the absolute monarchy of the seventeenth and eighteenth centuries, which held the balance between the nobility and the class of burghers.[11]

Marx describes the social base of the absolutist state as follows:

> Modern histories have demonstrated that *absolute monarchy* appears in those transitional periods when the old feudal estates

are in decline and the medieval estate of burghers is evolving into the modern bourgeois class, without one of the contending parties having as yet finally disposed of the other. The elements on which absolute monarchy is based are thus by no means its own product; they rather form its social prerequisite, whose historical origins are too well known to be repeated here. The fact that absolute monarchy took shape later in Germany and is persisting longer, is explained solely by the stunted pattern of development of the German bourgeois class. The answers to the puzzles presented by this pattern of development are to be found in the history of trade and industry.[12]

In Marx's and Engels's theory of the state (unlike the mechanical interpretation of the state – always operating in the interest of a particular class in so-called Marxism), the state always tries to acquire some kind of independence from being in the services of any social class[13] whenever that opportunity emerges in the struggle of contending classes.

Thus, absolute monarchy now attempts, not to centralise, which was its actual progressive function, but to decentralise. Born from the defeat of the feudal estates and having the most active share in their destruction itself, it now seeks to retain at least the semblance of feudal distinctions. Formerly encouraging trade and industry and thereby at the same time the rise of the bourgeoisie class, as necessary conditions both for national strength and for its own glory, absolute monarchy now everywhere hampers trade and industry, which have become increasingly dangerous weapons in the hands of an already powerful bourgeoisie.[14]

The emergence of an absolute monarchy, thus, would not have been possible in the absence of a class struggle between the nobility and the burghers for the capture of state power. As Engels says, 'The basic precondition for the monarchy [absolute] … was the struggle between the nobility and the bourgeoisie in which the monarchy held the balance.'[15]

It needs to be pointed out in this connection that, for Marx, state power is not suspended in the air; it reposes, primarily, in the bureaucracy:

If in a speech I call for arming against the state power, is it not
self-evident that I am calling for violent resistance to officials?
The *existence* of the state power is embodied precisely in its
officials, the army, the administration and the courts. Apart
from this, its physical embodiment, it is but a shadow, an idea, a
name. The overthrow of the government is impossible without
violent resistance to its officials. If in a speech I call for
revolution, it is superfluous to add: 'offer violent resistance to the
officials' (emphasis is Marx's).[16]

Thus, according to Marx, state power embodies, to a great extent,
bureaucratic power: the independence of the state for Marx, therefore, implies the independence or autonomy of the bureaucracy
from class control. Once the bureaucracy acquires this independence, it does not naturally feel inclined to surrender its coveted
power to an emerging class which wants to take over the state. As
Marx points out with respect to his concrete study of the political
situation in Prussia,

the absolute monarchy in Prussia, as earlier in England and
France, will not let itself be amicably changed into a bourgeois
monarchy. It will not abdicate amicably. The princes' hands are
tied both by their personal prejudices and *by a whole
bureaucracy of officials, soldiers and clerics – integral parts of
absolute monarchy who are far from willing to exchange their
ruling position for a subservient one in respect of the bourgeoisie*
(emphasis added).[17]

Thus, contrary to traditional Marxist lore, according to Marx's
own analysis of the contemporary German situation, the bureaucracy in itself was power to be reckoned with. The bourgeoisie
could not automatically reduce the bureaucracy to an apparatus of
its own class rule without a struggle, because the bureaucracy itself
had political ambitions; it did not want to substitute its ruling
position with that of a subservient one. The bureaucracy, to preserve its own independence, tried to contain the bourgeoisie as
much as possible. As long as the bourgeoisie did not bring the state
apparatus under its own political domination, as Engels points out
in his analysis of 'The Constitutional Question in Germany', the
bureaucracy was a positive barrier to the growth of the bourgeoisie.

bureaucracy...very soon becomes an unbearable fetter for the bourgeoisie. Already at the stage of manufacture official supervision and interference become very burdensome; factory industry is scarcely possible under such control. The German factory owners have hitherto kept the bureaucracy off their backs as much as possible by bribery, for which they can certainly not be blamed. But this remedy frees them only from the lesser half of the burden; apart from the impossibility of bribing all the officials with whom a factory owner comes into contact, bribery does not free him from perquisites, honorariums to jurists, architects, mechanics, nor from other expenses caused by the system of supervision, nor from extra work and waste of time. And the more the industry develops, the more 'conscientious officials' appear – that is, officials who either from pure narrow-mindedness or from *bureaucratic hatred of the bourgeoisie*, pester the factory owners with the most infuriating chicaneries. The bourgeoisie, therefore, is compelled to break the power of this indolent and pettifogging bureaucracy. From the moment the state administration and legislature fall under the control of the bourgeoisie, *the independence of the bureaucracy ceases to exist*, indeed from this moment, the tormentors of the bourgeoisie turn into their humble slaves. Previous regulations and decrees, which served only to lighten the work of the officials at the expense of the industrial bourgeoisie, give place to new regulations which lighten the work of the industrialists at the expense of the officials (emphasis added).[18]

Engels makes it clear in his study that the social formation which prevailed at that time in Prussia, that enabled the bureaucracy to put obstacles in the way of the growth of the bourgeoisie, was substantially pre-capitalist though it was being gradually eroded by encroaching capitalism.[19] In this social set-up the bourgeoisie, though striving to capture political power, was too weak to do so.

While in France and England the bourgeoisie has become powerful enough to overthrow the nobility and to raise itself to be the ruling class in the state, the German bourgeoisie has not yet had such power.[20]

Engels then adds,

The present political system in Germany is nothing more than a compromise between the nobility and the petty bourgeoisie, which amounts to resigning power into the hands of a third class: the bureaucracy.[21]

In Engels's analysis, the petty bourgeoisie (i.e. small-scale producers) and the nobility, in a situation of equilibrium of power, could live side by side and leave the administration in the care of an independent bureaucracy, but the bourgeoisie can do so only at its own peril.

The conditions under which nobility and petty bourgeoisie can exist side by side are absolutely different from the conditions of life of the bourgeoisie and only the former are officially recognised in the German states.[22]

The German states recognized the nobility and the petty bourgeoisie, in the sense that these states, ruled by the bureaucracy, enacted laws to protect the interests of the petty bourgeoisie in the towns against the nobility, as well as laws to safeguard the interests of the nobility in the countryside.[23] The bourgeoisie or the industrial capitalist class had no such protection; in fact, they were daily being tormented by various state control measures or rules by a pettifogging bureaucracy. Further, as Engels tells us emphatically, the bourgeoisie could not develop and could not 'make his class the first in society and state' without transforming agriculture into a capitalist agriculture.

The bourgeois cannot in any way leave the regulation of property relationships in the countryside to the discretion of the nobility, for the complete development of his own interests requires the fullest possible industrial exploitation of agriculture too, the creation of a class of industrial farmers, free saleability and mobilisation of landed property.[24]

But,

laws are framed first of all in the interests of the judicial bureaucracy who administer the assets, and then in the interests of the non-bourgeois as oppsed to the bourgeois.[25]

Thus, Marx and Engels make it clear from their studies of Germany that a state could become autonomous when classes in it have stunted growth, or when no class is in a position to take the lead over other classes. In these situations, the bureaucracy becomes the ruling class. The bureaucrats may rule under the political banner of a king, a prince, or a party, but once they attain independence, they try to preserve it by playing off one class against the other (such as feudal lords against burghers under the absolute monarchy), or by containing the growing strength of the class that endangers their ruling position (as was the case with the emerging bourgeoisie in Germany), or by furthering the interests of other classes as opposed to the rising class.

The following are the reasons for this discussion of Marx's and Engels's own writings on the independence of the state. First, they show that, contrary to orthodox Marxism, the view propounded in this book on the state's independence from class hegemony is endorsed by Marx's and Engels's own analyses of social conjunctures.[26] They show how certain social conjunctures enable the state to preserve its independence from class hegemony. Second, the point to be made was that Marx and Engels, unlike Poulantzas, show that the actions of state functionaries are not rigidly determined by the structure of the social economy but are dependent on how they view it. Moreover, Marx and Engels, in contrast to Poulantzas, point out how the state adopts various measures to maintain its hegemony and to contain the rising classes. Third, Marx's and Engel's discussion of the social conjunctures which make possible the independence of the state provides us with an analytical perspective to compare and expound the distinguishing characteristics of the nature of the state's hegemony in India and the social formation on which it is based.

Chapter 2 describes in detail the specific kind of autonomy of the state in the Orient – oriental despotism – under the Asiatic mode of production. It was shown that the state was superior to all classes in India, as in other parts of Asia, because a feudal class could not emerge here as land belonged to the state through the village community. The absence of the feudal class hindered the growth of the bourgeoisie. Unlike in Western Europe, the bourgeoisie could not advance its own interests in the towns by helping the monarch against the feudal lords. The state in Asia, therefore, unlike the absolute monarchies in Europe, did not have to balance the bourgeoisie against the feudal lords to attain and retain its independence. The state was independent here as it was founded on a mode of production which did not enable any class to grow strong. There is, however, one common element wherever the independence of the state from class control is found: the predominance of the small-scale peasantry or the failure of the capitalist class to bring agriculture under its domain. This is so under the absolute monarchies, the Bonapartist state, or the German bureaucratic states, as well as under oriental despotisms.

The analysis in chapter 3 shows that the British inherited in India the state structure from their predecessors – the Moghuls – and introduced many changes in it without fundamentally altering the base of the state – the mode of production. Chapters 3 and 7 described how primitive capital accumulation took place on the basis of the existing mode, through the mechanism of merchant capital which remained subservient to the industrial capital of the metropolitan centre. As a result, the extracted surplus did not lead to capital accumulation in India but in the metropolitan centres. This further deteriorated the condition of agriculture (as a consequence of the lack of capital) and the small peasants became poorer (due to overpressure on agriculture). The continuance of the small peasantry, thus, provided the base for the preservation of the independent state.

The colonial state was superior to all indigenous classes not only because it represented the metropolitan capitalist class but also due to the fact that the old base of the despotic state was perpetuated. This fact did not escape Engels's sharp observation which, like Marx's, could always apprehend the reality behind the appearance. Engels wrote in a letter to Kautsky in 1884:

> It would be a good thing for somebody to take the pains of elucidating the state socialism now rampant by using the example of it in Java where its practice is in full bloom. All the material for that will be found in Java, or How to Manage a Colony, by I.W.B. Money, Barrister at Law, London 1861, 2 Vol. Here it will be seen how on the basis of the old community communism the Dutch organised production under state control and secured for the people what they considered a quite comfortable existence. The result: the people are kept at the stage of primitive stupidity and 70 million marks (now surely more) are

annually collected by the Dutch national treasury. This case is highly interesting and can easily be turned to practical use. Incidentally it is proof of how today primitive communism furnishes there as well as in India and Russia the finest and broadest basis of exploitation and despotism.[27]

Engels knew very well about the existence of private legal owner-ship of land in India (where the permanent and *ryotwari* land tenure settlements were introduced in the late eighteenth and early nine-teenth centuries), and in Russia, yet he characterized the agriculture in these countries as primitive communism because the small pea-sants were, despite some differences, basically equal in poverty. However, as in Java, so in India and Russia, these small peasants provided their surplus to the state, over which neither the peasants nor any indigenous class had any control. The despotism or the independence of the state thus resulted from its power to exact surplus on a broad basis.

Another very important point to be noted in the above-quoted letter from Engels is his attack on state socialism. State socialism, advocated by Ferdinand Lassalle (against whom Marx and Engels waged a bitter struggle) and encouraged by Bismarck at that time, was based on the theory that 'the state is the manager of economic life'.[28] This enabled the state – as Engels pointed out by citing the instance of Java – to control and exploit the economy without making any improvement in the condition of life of the direct producers. Hence, Engels was trying to warn Kautsky that the Lassalleian type of state socialism would only enhance the des-potism of the Bismarckian state, by letting it control the productive forces and by playing off the proletariat against the bourgeoisie. His message: the proletariat should not be taken in by the term 'socialism' and, thus, strengthen the hands of a bureaucratic state. The main features of the Bismarckian state, as specified by Engels time and again, were its bureaucratic character and autonomy, derived from its ability to balance the power of one class with that of another.

the state as it exists at present in Germany is also the necessary product of the social basis out of which it has developed. In Prussia – and Prussia is now decisive – there exists side by side with a landowning aristocracy which is still powerful, a comparatively young and markedly very cowardly bourgeoisie, which up to the present has not won either direct political domination as in France, or more or less indirect as in England. Side by side with these two classes, however, there exists a rapidly increasingly proletariat, which is intellectually highly developed and which is becoming more and more organised everyday. We find, therefore, in Germany alongside of the basic condition of the old absolute monarchy, an equilibrium between the bourgeoisie and the proletariat. But both in the old absolute monarchy and in the modern Bonapartist monarchy [Marx and Engels viewed Bismarckian monarchy as Bonapartist monarchy] the real governing power lies in the hands of a special caste of army officers and state officials. In Prussia this caste is supplemented partly from its own ranks, partly from the lesser aristocracy owning the entailed estates, more rarely the higher aristocracy and least of all from the bourgeoisie.[29]

It was, therefore, in the interests of the bureaucracy (both civil and military) to keep the bourgeoisie out of political power, and whenever it showed any political ambition, Bismarck reined it in by playing off the proletariat.[30] This kind of state socialism – one from above – Engels cautioned the working class, would not better their life but strengthen the bureaucratic state *vis-à-vis* the bourgeoisie.[31]

The similarity between Indian socialism and the state socialism that was advocated by Lassalle in Germany is obvious. An attempt has been made in chapters 4 and 6 to show how the socialism that is acted upon in India is really in the interests of a bureaucratic state which, through the monopolization of basic productive forces and state control measures, has kept the bourgeoisie in check and has maintained its own independence from class hegemony. There are, however, a few interesting similarities, as well as differences, between Bismarck's Germany and India on the eve of independence. In both, the bourgeoisie was young and weak. In addition, in Germany the bourgeoisie was too scared of the proletariat to make a bid for political power in the aftermath of the 1848 revolution and the Paris Commune of 1871. In India, however, no such menace of political take-over by the proletariat was imminent. Still, the Indian bourgeoisie was weaker than their counterpart in Germany for the following reasons. In Germany, the feudal lords were transforming themselves into bourgeois farmers. The decomposition of village industry (which was never in the form of India's village artisan industry) had been accomplished long ago. So there it was a matter of time when the bourgeoisie with the complete subjugation of the economy (and with the removal of political threat from the proletariat), would place the state under its own domination.

In India, on the other hand (as delineated in detail in chapters 5 and 7), artisan industries are still important components of the village economy. These provide an important basis for the persistence of the existing social formation in India composed of partly Asiatic, partly feudal and partly capitalist modes of production. The state's support for artisan as well as small-scale industry (petty bourgeoisie) is avowedly to delimit the concentration of economic power in the hands of the big bourgeoisie. This is over and above the extensive state control measures (discussed in detail in chapter 6), that are positive restraints on the free development of the bourgeoisie. Furthermore, the overpressure of population in agriculture (as explained in chapter 7), is the result of India's integration in the world capitalist economy without a corresponding change in its mode of production. The overpressure of population in agriculture, the dire poverty of the rural population, the failure of agriculture to generate considerable surplus for industrialization, the constricted internal market for industries as well as agriculture, the inefficiency of industry to create more jobs to absorb the rural surplus population – all these (enumerated in chapter 7) have raised almost insurmountable obstacles on the path of the bourgeoisie to colonize agriculture, without which its conquest of the economy remains incomplete, and, hence, also its hegemony over state power. In Germany the bourgeoisie was not encumbered by such a village artisan industry, nor by an agriculture groaning under a pre-capitalist social formation more stubborn than feudalism. Finally, in Germany as well as in France, the Bonapartist states could not create, despite a few creditable attempts in the context of that period, state sectors which are in India formidable weapons (as has been shown in chapter 6) for the state to free itself from its dependency on the bourgeoisie.

However, in none of these countries – despite the accumulation of capital in India on an extended reproduction basis in the state sectors – had or has the cause of the expansion of the bourgeoisie, i.e., the private ownership of property, been replaced by socialist ownership. This is the reason why the bourgeoisie in India, as in Germany and France, continues and continued to grow. Everyday the ranks of the bourgeoisie are swelling in India; everyday some members of the petty bourgeoisie, whose cause the state espouses to keep the bourgeoisie in check, are increasing the ranks of the bourgeoisie. These newly recruited members day by day strengthen the hand of the bourgeoisie in its struggle to bring the state apparatus under its own rule. How long the state apparatus in India will be able to maintain its ruling position *vis-à-vis* the bourgeoisie depends on how long the latter will take to transform agriculture into a capitalist sector; how long the numerous petty bourgeoisie will be able to maintain an identity separate from the bourgeoisie; and how long the state will be able to balance them. Under the present economic situation in India, it seems improbable that the victory of the bourgeoisie over the state apparatus can be achieved in the near future. The social formation that prevails in agriculture seems to be too ossified or stubborn to be dissolved without a shake-up of a fundamental nature in the social structure. The situation in agriculture, as has been explained, poses a problem for industry too, if it is to be able to absorb the surplus labour from agriculture.[32] While unemployment is increasing in both rural and urban areas, the average size of farm, as has been noted, is decreasing at the same time. The pauperization of the rural peasantry is matched by the rising number of the *lumpenproletariat* in urban areas (2.6 million in 1971). The condition of the employed proletariat has also worsened (see Table 7.12).

Thus, the socialism from above that has been imposed by an autonomous state in India has been totally unsuccessful in alleviating the condition of the people and the producing classes. The danger that looms for the state in this failure is also a danger for the bourgeoisie. Even if the bourgeoisie and the functionaries of the state can foresee the impending catastrophe, it seems they can do virtually little within the existing social formation to arrest it. One should not, however, feel discouraged.

The gathering of the storm over India's political sky is beckoning a new future to her. After the storm is over, a new dawn will emerge. I would like, therefore, to conclude my study with a quote from John G. Gurley, Professor of Economics at Stanford University:

> For centuries, China was a door mat for preying capitalist
> nations, and her record was, for long, dismal compared to
> Japan's. But these differences are now rapidly disappearing.

India was once economically superior to Britain, then became an exploited colony. In the meantime, Britain, as the kingpin, has come and gone, India is slowly re-emerging, gathering strength, augmenting the revolutionary forces against the old powers. Uneven development has been the rule for centuries as nations have moved into and through the capitalist to the socialist mode of production. One has to have some conception of where the world is going to be able to speak wisely about the present, but perhaps transitory, superiorities.[33]

Notes

Introduction

1 Henri Lefebvre, *The Sociology of Marx*, p. 159.
2 Marx/Engels, *Correspondence*, pp. 480–1.
3 The term 'functionaries of the state' henceforth will be used to mean both the politicians and the bureaucrats who are in charge of the apparatuses of the state.
4 K. Marx, 'Perspectives for the new coalition government', *New York Times*, 28 January 1853.
5 K. Marx, 'The Eighteenth Brumaire of Louis Bonaparte', p. 170; K. Mark, *Capital*, vol. I, p. 789.
6 'The history of all hitherto existing society [all written history] is the history of class struggles. Freeman and slave, patrician and plebeian, lord and serf, guildmaster and journeyman, in a word, oppressor and oppressed stood in constant opposition to one another, carried on an uninterrupted, now hidden, now open fight, a fight that each time ended, either in a revolutionary reconstitution of society at large, or in the common ruin of the contending classes' (Marx and Engels, *Selected Works*, pp. 35–6).
7 K. Marx, *Capital*, vol. III, p. 703 (and see preceding note).
8 See J. O'Connor, *The Fiscal Crisis of the State*.
9 See R. Miliband, *The State in Capitalist Society*; N. Poulantzas, *Political Power and Social Classes*.
10 Michael Burawoy has raised a couple of pertinent questions regarding Poulantzas's theory of the state. 'The weakness of the structuralist view of the state, as it is presently formulated, is its functionalism. How is it that the state does what it is supposed to do? How does it secure and protect its relative autonomy?' ('Contemporary Currents in Marxist Theory', *American Sociologist*, no. 1, 1978). I have tried to answer the above questions in my study. I have tried to show with concrete examples how the state secures and protects its autonomy and what the state does at particular socio-historical conjunctures and why.
11 In this connection, it should be noted what Engels explained as the materialist conception of history: 'According to the materialist conception of history the determining element in history is ultimately the production and reproduction in real life. More than this neither

Marx nor I have ever asserted. If therefore somebody twists this into the statement that the economic element is the only determining one, he transforms it into a meaningless, abstract and absurd phrase. The economic situation is the basis, but the various elements of the superstructure – political forms of the class struggle, and its consequences, constitutions established by the victorious class after the battle, etc – forms of law – and then *even the reflexes of all these actual struggles in the brains of the combatants*: political, legal, philosophical theories, religious ideas and their further development into systems of dogma – also exercise their influence upon the course of the historical struggles and in many cases preponderate in determining their form' (F. Engels, 'Letter to J. Bloch', 21 September 1890; emphasis added).

12 T. Bamat, 'Relative state autonomy and capitalism in Brazil and Peru', *Insurgent Sociologist*, Spring 1977.
13 Ibid.
14 Ibid.
15 H. Alavi, 'Bangladesh and the crisis of Pakistan', p. 303; also see 'The state in post colonial societies'.
16 H. Alavi, 'Bangladesh and the crisis of Pakistan', p. 305.
17 The present study does not, however, claim that the weak development of the social classes was exclusive to the Asiatic mode of production. Recent studies on some African countries indicate that social classes were weak in these social formations too. See, for example: Claude Meillassoux, 'A class analysis of the bureaucratic process in Mali'.

2 The mode of production and social formation in pre-British India

1 H. Pirenne, *Economic and Social History of Medieval Europe*, pp. 42–5.
2 Ibid., pp. 82–3; K. Takahashi, 'A contribution to the discussion', in R. Hilton (ed.), *The Transition from Feudalism to Capitalism*, pp. 81–3.
3 C. Hill, *Reformation to Industrial Revolution*, pp. 146–54.
4 Pirenne, *Economic and Social History*, p. 54; see also H. Pirenne, *Medieval Cities*; M. Weber, *The City*; H. See Pirenne, *Modern Capitalism*.
5 Leo Huberman, *Man's Worldly Goods*, p. 48; Hilton, 'A comment', in *Transition*, pp. 114–15.
    Adam Smith (*The Wealth of Nations*, Book III, ch. 3) has this to say: 'The inhabitants of merchant towns imported refined manufactured goods and expensive articles of luxury from rich countries, and thus offered incentives to the vanity of the large landowners, who eagerly bought these goods and paid large quantities of raw materials from their lands for them. Thus the commerce of a large part of Europe during this period consisted in an exchange of the raw materials of one country for the manufactured products of some industrially developed country. As soon as this taste became general and created a considerable demand,

the merchants, in order to save the expenses of freight, began to establish similar manufactures in their own countries.'

6 See H.J. Habakkuk, 'English landownership, 1680–1740'; G. Lefebvre, *The Coming of the French Revolution*, p. 14; M. Dobb, *Studies in the Development of Capitalism*, p. 193; M. Weber, *General Economic History*, p. 94; Pirenne, *Economic and Social History*, p. 84.

7 Marx, *Capital*, I, pp. 784–5; J.D. Chambers, 'Enclosure and labour supply in the industrial revolution'; Hill, *Reformation*, pp. 146–54.

8 Marx, *Capital*, I, pp. 784–804.

9 Marx, *Grundrisse*, pp. 253, 505; *Capital*, I, p. 163; E. Mandel, *From Class Society to Communism*, p. 38.

10 Marx, *Grundrisse*, p. 508.

11 Marx, *Capital*, III, p. 389.

12 Ibid., p. 390.

13 M.N. Roy, *India in Transition*, pp. 91–2.

14 See L. Huberman, *Man's Worldly Goods*, pp. 56–60; A. Toynbee, *Lectures on the Industrial Revolution of the 18th Century in England*.

15 G. Lefebvre, 'Some observations', in R. Hilton (ed.), *The Transition*, pp. 125–6; also see R.M. MacIver, *The Modern State*; Marx, *Capital*, I, p. 789.

16 Marx/Engels, 'Manifesto of the Communist Party', in *Selected Works*, p. 37; R.H. Tawney, 'Harrington's Interpretation of His Age', pp. 211–16.

17 E.J. Hobsbawm, *The Age of Revolution*, pp. 79–86; P. Zagorin, 'The English Revolution, 1640–1660'.

18 There was, however, another class of artisans in the towns in India which catered primarily to the needs of the court. With the expansion of trade with Europe, their external market expanded, but their attempt to colonize the internal market proceeded slowly, although in Bengal and certain advanced areas the village artisan industry began to dissolve. It should be noted here that Marx later traced to the interdependence of agriculture and artisan industries rather than to irrigation the base of the Asiatic mode of production and the reason for its greater stability than other precapitalist modes of production.

19 L. Krader, *Asiatic Mode of Production*; B. Hindess and P. Hirst, *Pre-Capitalist Modes of Production*; G. Lichtheim, 'Marx and the Asiatic Mode of Production'; D. Thorner, 'Marx on India and the Asiatic Mode of Production'.

20 Marx, *Critique of Political Economy*, p. 29 n.

21 Engels, 'Letter to Marx, 6 June 1853' in Marx/Engels *Correspondence*.

22 'The distinction is based on the fact that in the cultural evolution of Egypt, western Asia, India and China, the question of irrigation was crucial. The water question conditioned the existence of bureaucracy, the compulsory service of the dependent classes, and the dependence of the subject classes upon the functioning of the bureaucracy of the king. That the king also expressed his power in the form of a military monopoly is the basis of the distinction between the military organization of Asia and that of the west. In the first case the royal official and army officer are from the beginning the central figure

of the process, while in the west, both were originally absent. (Max Weber, *General Economic History*, p. 237). It should be noted here that Marx later traced to the interdependence of agriculture and artisan industries rather than to irrigation the base of the Asiatic mode of production and its reason for greater stability than other pre-capitalist modes of production.

23 In Europe, after the disintegration of the Roman Empire, the fiefs became the social, political and economic units. The legal basis of the military and political power of the feudal lords was their control over the land.

24 Azizul Huque, *The Man Behind the Plough*, p. 214.

25 I. Habib, *The Agrarian System of Mughal India*, pp. 256–60.

26 F. Bernier, *Travels in Mughal India*, p. 224.

27 M. Weber, *The Religion of India*, p. 71.

28 Marx, *Economic and Philosophical Manuscripts of 1844*, p. 61.

29 Ibid.

30 Ibid.

31 K. Takahashi, 'A contribution to the discussion', in Hilton (ed.) *Transition*, pp. 80–4; Lefebvre, 'Some observations' in ibid., pp. 125–6.

32 It should be borne in mind that the merchant capital in its initial period was dependent on the surplus extracted by the feudal lords from the peasants and serfs, and also on the resources created in petty production.

33 R.H. Tawney, *The Agrarian Problem in the Sixteenth Century*, pp. 257–8; P.J. Mantoux, *The Industrial Revolution in the Eighteenth Century*, p. 177.

34 G. Lefebvre,'Some Observations', in Hilton (ed.), *Transition*, pp. 123–4; Huberman, *Man's Worldly Goods*, p. 109; Tawney, *Agrarian Problems*, pp. 406–8; F.M.L. Thompson, 'The social distribution of landed property in England since the sixteenth century', p. 515.

35 Weber, *General Economic History*, p. 94; Marx, *Capital*, III, pp. 927–9.

36 Marx, *Pre-Capitalist Economic Formations*, p.69; Parliamentary Papers, *The Fifth Report from the Select Committee on the Affairs of the East India Company, 1812*, p. 85; R.D. Bandopadhya, *Banglar Itihas*, vol. 1, pp. 55–70.

37 K.S. Shelvankar, *The Problem of India*, p. 78.

38 In this sense, the state was the supreme landlord, but not the king. He only represented the interests of the community.

39 R. Mukerjee, *Democracies of the East*, p. xxiii.

40 Marx, *Capital*, I, pp. 784–805; Hilton, *Transition*, pp. 113–16.

41 Habakkuk, 'English landownership, 1680–1740', pp. 15–16.

There was a crisis of feudalism in Europe in the fourteenth and fifteenth centuries. 'At this time of contracting demand for agricultural products, urban wages and hence industrial prices were rising, because of the shortage of labour bred by population decline. This in turn raised the cost of agricultural labour while reducing rents (insofar as they were fixed while nominal prices were inflating). This led to what Marc Bloch has called the 'momentary impoverishment of the seigniorial class'.... The economic squeeze led to increased exactions on the peasantry which were then counterproductive, and resulted in peasant flight. One path to the restoration of income for the nobility, one often efficacious for the wealthiest stratum, was to involve themselves in new and remunerative carriers with the princes. It was not however sufficient to counteract the effects of recession and therefore to stem the decline of the demesne. And it may incidentally, by removing seigniors from residence, have encouraged disinterest in management. What then happened to the large estates? They were sold or rented for money to the principal groups ready and able to engage in such a transaction, the better off peasants, who were in a position to obtain favorable terms' (Immanuel Wallerstein, *The Modern World System*, p. 26).

Duby, on the other hand, maintains: 'We must be constantly on our guard against considering the abandonment and regrouping in the fourteenth century of all the fields into a few coherent village territories subject to strict agrarian constraints as signs of economic malaise, agricultural failure or a too sudden decline in the population. On the contrary, these topographical transfers reflect a critical phase in the growth of the cereal economy, postponed for a century or two, but quite comparable in their development and nature to those of which the Ile de France was the scene in the thirteenth century. Thus, in North Western Germania the lords enclosed their woods whose value was increasing. They surrounded them with hedges, shut out the peasants' swine and henceforth forbade periodic heat-burning' (*Rural Economy*, p. 309, cited in I. Wallerstein, *The Modern World System*, p.26).

42 Marx, *Capital*, III, pp. 917–19.
43 D. D. Kosambi, who is often quoted in support of the argument that there had been private property in land in India, makes it very clear that the private ownership in land in India was not in the nature of bourgeoisie property in land. He says: 'The question of private property in land [in ancient India] makes no sense if regarded from the modern bourgeois point of view, namely the right to buy and sell. In the first place, most of the actual cultivators had emerged from a tribal stage where land was only territory, while primitive slash-and-burn cultivation had made individual plots useless till the day of the plough and cattle-manure fertilization. Secondly, the holding, even in the sense of mere right of cultivation, was a privilege as well as proof of membership in a community. Finally, within a village community that produced virtually no commodities, land would have no purchaser, while uncleared waste or marginal land was still to be had for the cultivation. The only conditions were payment of taxes to the king and perhaps of a nominal adoption fee to the previous village community, unless the settlers could form a separate community of their own. This state of affairs continued almost to the end of the Moghul period, with local variations' (*An Introduction to the Study of Indian History*, p. 323).
44 M. Bloch, *Feudal Society*; Pirenne, *Early Democracies in the Low Countries*, pp. 46–7.

45 Marx, *Capital*, III, p. 919.
46 Ibid., I, p. 392.
47 However, this tendency on the part of the revenue collectors to appropriate the land of the peasants was not altogether absent. 'This first appears in the *Ain* where it cautions revenue officials against entering peasant holdings (*raiyat-kashta*) as 'personally cultivated land' of *modadi-maash* holders, in their records. The second is one of the twelve decrees issued by Jahangir on his accession. It prohibits the revenue officials themselves from forcibly converting the land of the peasants (*zamin-i-raiyat*) into their own holdings (*Khud Kashta*)' (Irfan Habib, *The Agrarian System of Mughal India*, p. 115).
48 Ibid., p. 154.
49 Ibid., p. 153.
50 See Parliamentary Papers, *The Fifth Report from the Select Committee on the Affairs of the East India Company, 1812*; G.C.M. Birdwood, *The Industrial Arts of India*, p. 137; D. R. Gadgil, *The Industrial Evolution of India*, p. 10.
51 Marx, *Capital*, I, pp. 392–4.

Irfan Habib's description of the village system of Moghul India points out how the division of labour within the village was made the basis of caste: 'Almost every craft within the village, carpentry, pottery, etc., would be the business of a separate caste, possibly represented there by no more than one family. The need for self-sufficiency was the economic cause which made the presence of certain primary crafts imperative for each village. But even if the separation of trades was originally "spontaneously developed", it was "crystallised and finally made permanent by law", the law of the caste system. Once this had been achieved, every village became a single economic and social unit apart, a single community, able, when any increase in its population occurred, to reproduce from itself another on the same pattern' (Irfan Habib, *The Agrarian System of Mughal India*, p. 122).

Kosambi describes how the Brahmin provided the ideological basis of the village economy and, thus, that of the Asiatic mode of production: 'The Smriti foreshadows complete victory of the village, with consequences far deadlier than any invasion. The hide-bound caste system became rigid only within stagnant villages whose chief intellectual product the Brahmin, was stamped with incurable rusticity elevated to religious dogma. For an orthodox Brahmin, travel beyond the traditional limit of *arya-desa* entailed penance; residence was forbidden.... This mentality killed history. It mattered little which kind ruled over relatively changeless village.... The passage of years had little meaning compared with the vital round of the seasons, because the villagers produced almost all they needed every year, to consume it (but for that portion expropriated for taxes) by the time of the next harvest. As a result, Brahmin scholars joined (still engage in) bitter theological controversy about the tithi (lunar date) of a festival even like Rama's legendary conquest of Lanka, without troubling themselves as to the year' (D.D. Kosambi, *An Introduction to the Study of Indian History*, p. 258).

52 Weber, *The Religion of India*, p. III.
53 Gadgil, *The Industrial Evolution of India*, p. 10.
54 Marx, *Pre-Capitalist Economic Formations*, p. 67.
55 Ibid.
56 The Russian sociologist Kovalevsky pointed out that three of the four characteristics of Germano-Roman feudalism were present in India. But Marx refused to accept Kovalevsky's characterization of India as a feudal society and asserted: 'Kovalevsky forgets among other things serfdom, which is not of substantial importance in India. (Moreover, as for the individual role of feudal lords as protectors, not only of unfree but of free peasants,… this is unimportant except for the Wakuf Estates devoted to religious purposes.) Nor do we find that "Poetry of the soil" so characteristic of Romano-German feudalism (cf. Maurier) in India, any more than in Rome' (cited in E.J. Hobsbawm's introduction to Karl Marx, *Pre-Capitalist Economic Formations*, p. 58).
57 K.S. Shelvankar, *The Problem of India*, p. 80.
58 For example, the enclosure movement in England, i.e., transforming the arable land into pasturage (for the production of more valuable wool with the rise of the wool industry) by the feudal lords led to the expropriation of the peasants from the soil. These landless peasants formed the industrial reserve army from which the wage workers for the industries in England were recruited. In other parts of Europe, too, such as France and Germany, many landlords took control of their land and uprooted the peasants. In India the nobility or the revenue collectors could not do so because their right was confined to the right of revenue collection only.
59 Marx, *Pre-Capitalist Economic Formations*, p. 70.
60 Ibid., pp.70–1.
61 Ibid.
62 Ibid., p. 83.
63 Gadgil, *The Industrial Evolution of India*, p.11.
64 Huberman, *Man's Worldly Goods*, pp. 55–6.
65 Marx, *Pre-Capitalist Economic Formations*, pp. 77–8.
66 Gadgil, *The Industrial Evolution of India*, p. 6.
67 See B.B. Dutt, *Town Planning in Ancient India*; J. Sarkar, *Economics of British India*, pp. 55–6.
68 H. Maine, *Village Communities in the East and West*, p. 119.
69 Marx, 'Letter to Engels, 2 June 1853' in Marx/Engels *Correspondence*.
70 A.B. Hibbert, 'The origins of the medieval town patriciate', pp. 15–27; see also Pirenne, *Early Democracies*, p. 20.
71 Huberman, *Man's Worldly Goods*, pp. 73–4; see also Pirenne, *Medieval Cities*.
72 Cited in Ramakrishna Mukherjee, *The Rise and Fall of the East India Company*, p. 4.
73 Pirenne, *Economic and Social History of Medieval Europe*, pp. 50–2; Huberman, *Man's Worldly Goods*, pp. 72–6.
74 Ibid., pp. 27-37; Pirenne, *Economic and Social History*, pp. 50–5.
75 D. Harvey, *Social Justice and the City*, p. 252.

76 Weber, *The Religion of China*, p. 13.
77 In breaking the power of the great feudal lords in the Wars of the Roses, the English king had to depend on the support of the rising bourgeoisie: 'the "Tudor Revolution in Government", as Dr Elton called it, was a consequence of social changes which were increasing the importance of the House of Commons *vis-à-vis* the House of Lords, which secularized the monasteries, which led to enclosure for sheep-farming and to a society in which wealth came to be measured in £.*s.d.*, rather than in military followings. Indeed, by the end of the Wars of the Roses, with the growing importance of gunpowder, money was needed even to raise private armies. The dependence of the Tudors on the gentry [i.e., the bourgeoisie in agriculture] and the greatest merchants ... explains why Henry VIII said that he never stood so highly in his estate royal as in the time of Parliament' (Christopher Hill, *Reformation to Industrial Revolution*, p. 29).

The situation was similar in France. 'This history of the Capetian monarchy had in fact been largely the story of its struggle against the aristocracy. Sometimes the royal power had won out, as under Francis I and Henry II to go back no further, or under Henry IV and Richelieu. Sometimes the aristocracy had regained the advantage, through the wars of religion, the minority of Louis XIII or the Fronde. Under Louis XIV the conflict seemed to be over, and the nobility saw itself at last even subjected to direct taxation.... Saint-Simon had complained of Louis XVI, that the monarch surrounded himself with nothing but "vile bourgeoisie" ' (George Lefebvre, *The Coming of the French Revolution*, p. 16).

78 Habib, *Agrarian System*, pp. 317–18.

Moreland characterizes the Indian nobility as follows: 'We have officers posted to their charges by the king, and transferred, removed or punished, at his pleasure, administering their charges under his orders, and subjected to the strict financial control of the Revenue Ministry. None of these features has any counterpart in the feudal system of Europe.... The use of feudal terminology was presumably inspired by the fact that some of the nobles of the Delhi Kingdom occasionally behaved like feudal barons, that is to say, they rebelled, or took sides in disputed successions to the throne; but, in Asia at least, bureaucrats can rebel as well as barons, and the analogy is much too slight and superficial to justify the importation of feudal terms and all misleading ideas which they connote. The Kingdom was not a mixture of bureaucracy with feudalism: its administration was bureaucratic throughout' (W.H. Moreland, *The Agrarian System of Moslem India*, pp. 218–19).

79 Habib, *Agrarian System*, p. 319.
80 'In the middle ages the citizens in each town were compelled to unite against the landed nobility to save their skins. The extension of trade, the establishment of communications, led the separate towns to get to know other towns, which had asserted the same interests in the struggle against the same antagonist. Out of the many local corporations of burghers there arose only gradually the burgher class. The conditions of

life of the individual burghers became, on account of their antagonism to the existing relationships and of the mode of labour determined by these, conditions which were common to them all and independent of each individual. The burghers had created the conditions in so far as they had torn themselves free from feudal ties, and were created by them in so far as they were determined by their antagonism to the feudal system which they found in existence' (K. Marx, *Pre-Capitalist Economic Formations*, p. 131).

81 In fact, there was a great demand for Indian products in Europe even before the discovery of the sea route to India from Europe by Vasco da Gama. Most of this trade was carried over the land route through Turkey, Iran and the Arab peninsula. However, the discovery of the sea route (1498) via the Cape of Good Hope gave a tremendous boost to the Indian industries which found a ready market in Europe. The purchasing power of Europe increased many times in the sixteenth century with the arrival of silver from Latin America. 'A systematic drain on precious metals from the whole world continued, primarily to the profit of the Great Mogul and his states [i.e., India]. The reader must take into consideration that all the gold and silver which circulates in the world ultimately goes to the Great Mogul as if to its centre. It is known that the metals that leave America go partly to Turkey and partly to Persia, via Smyrna, for silk after having roamed over several European kingdoms. But the Turks cannot do without coffee from Yemen or Arabia Felix. No more can the Arabs, Persians and Turks do without commodities from the Indies. This means that they send large sums of money by the Red Sea to Moka near Bab el Mandeb, to Bassorah at the bottom of the Persian Gulf, to Bandar Abessi and to Gommeron, and from there take it to the Indies on the ships.' The Dutch, English and Portuguese also made all their purchases in the Indies against gold and silver because 'we can only get from the Indians the merchandise we want to transport to Europe with hard cash.... But, as nothing is free, India had to pay dearly for its precious metals. *This was one of the reasons for its austere life* and also for the rise of its compensation industries, notably the textiles of Gujerat, a real driving force of the Indian economy even before the arrival of Vasco da Gama.... From the sixteenth century on, an enormous burst of industrialisation began there and spread towards the Ganges. In the eighteenth century, cotton prints flooded into Europe. They were imported by British merchants in large quantities until the moment came when England preferred to manufacture them itself and competed with them' (Fernand Braudel, *Capitalism and Material Life, 1400–1800*, pp. 338–9).

82 Mukerjee, *The Economic History of India*, p. 29.
83 Ibid., pp. 161–2.
84 Ibid., pp. 158–9.
85 Ibid., pp. xvii–xviii.
86 N.C. Sinha, *Studies in Indo-British Economy Hundred Years Ago*, p. 17.
87 Mukerjee, *The Economic History of India*, p. 76.
    Two factors were responsible for the political influence the merchants

were attaining. First, the weakening of the Moghul centralized state led to the consolidation of power by the *jagirdars* or revenue assignees. These revenue farmers became dependent on the *seths* to maintain their independence from the control of the central state and also to wage internecine warfare among themselves. Second, the European companies took active part in these struggles, at first to protect their own interests, and later on to curb the interests of other European companies. To do so, they had to make forts and build their own army. The native merchants who traded with them could seek their protection in need. However, the fate of two '*jagat seths*' (world bankers) of Murshidabad clearly indicates that their political power had no institutional base. Their conspiratorial careers were ended by Mir Kasim, the last 'independent Nawab' of Bengal.

88 Sinha, *Studies*, p. 32.
89 Gadgil, *The Industrial Evolution of India*, pp. 33–5.
90 Maine, *Village Communities*, p. 119.
91 Gadgil, *The Industrial Evolution of India*, p. 34.
92 Ibid.
93 Ibid.
94 Ibid.
95 Cited in M.N. Roy, *India in Transition*, pp. 98–9.
96 Anonymous, 'On the Formation of the Hindusthani Nationality and the Problems of its National Language', p. 9, cited in Mukherjee, *Rise and Fall*, p. 154.
97 However, in most parts of India, the unity between agriculture and industry remained unchanged. Moreover, the dissolving effect of commerce was more pronounced in the case of weaving than in other artisan industries (see chapter 5). It should also be kept in mind that the urban industry which catered to the court was, by nature, different from the village industry. 'It will be seen that a twofold division has thus been made in the old Indian industry. On one side are the village industries, which included the village servant class of artisans and also such classes as the country weaver, goldsmith, etc. The characteristic of this class was that they were spread throughout India. This class of industry was also confined, more or less, to the primary needs of man and the organization of the industry was of the crudest. The second class is that of urban industry, better organized and confined to the higher class of products. The division is obviously of a rough nature. In the village, a luxury industry was a very rare phenomenon, but in the town there were always some industries, which were akin in the nature of their products to the village industry group, for example, a certain amount of coarse weaving, ordinary pottery works, etc., were always to be found in the towns' (D.R. Gadgil, *The Industrial Evolution of India*, p. 45).
98 Roy, *India in Transition*, p. 97.
99 Marx, *Grundrisse*, p. 469.
100 S. Chowdhury, *Trade and Commercial Organisation in Bengal, 1650–1720, with Special Reference to the English East India Company*, p. 154; M.N. Roy, *India in Transition*, pp. 97–8.

101 Roy, *India in Transition*, pp. 97–8.
102 Cited in R. Some, *Jagrata Janata*, p. 12.
103 Weber, *Essays in Sociology*, p. 207.
104 Mukerjee, *The Economic History of India*, p. 67.
   Mir Jumla was governor of Bengal. He held this office during the reign of the last great Moghul emperor, Aurongzeb, in the early eighteenth century. 'In the 12th century A.D., Balasena who was ruling Bengal during those days was involved in debt due to his wars with the king of Manipur, and took a loan of rupees one crore (ten million) from Vallabhananda Adhya, and when he felt the necessity of further money, he again approached the same banker. The banker realizing foul play refused the grant of loan and thus became the victim of the wrath of the king' (B. Bhargava, *Indigenous Banking in Ancient and Medieval India*, pp. 223–4). This is the reason, Bernier states, the rich men, merchants, revenue collectors, etc., in India always feigned that they were poor.
105 See Percival Spear, *A History of India*.
   Immanuel Wallerstein made a mistake in claiming that feudalism had an ideological superiority over prebendal organization in forming absolute national monarchies or nation states in Europe. He says, 'a prebendal land-controlling class can better resist the growth of a truly centralized monarchy than a feudal land owning class, because the feudal value system can be used by the king insofar as he can make himself the apex of a single hierarchical system of feudal relations (it took the Capetians several centuries to accomplish this), to build a system of loyalty to himself, which, once constructed, can simply shed this personal element and become loyalty to a nation, of which the king is the incarnation' (*The Modern World System*, p. 58). In fact, the prebendal land-controlling class, as has been made very clear by Weber, was totally dependent on the state. The military violence by the state in the East (i.e., the relative weakness of the horsemen compared with the infantry) – the very factor mentioned by Wallerstein – was responsible for the weakness of the prebendal land-controlling class *vis-à-vis* the state. Moreover, contrary to Wallerstein's contention, the Capetians had to depend on the bourgeoisie to curtail the power of the feudal lords, and to create an absolute monarchy and a nation state (see note 78). Feudalism's contribution in creating the nation states in Europe did not lie in providing an ideology, but in creating a countervailing force against the state that provided an opportunity for the consolidation of power by the bourgeoisie. The nation states in Europe were the creations of the bourgeoisie.
106 Marx, *Pre-Capitalist Economic Formations*; see 'Introduction' by E.J. Hobsbawm, p. 46.

3 The victory of the British and its impact on the evolution of social classes in India

1 'Memorandum of the Nawab of Bengal to the English Governor, May, 1762', cited in R.P. Dutt, *India Today*, p. 101.
2 W. Bolts, 'Consideration on Indian Affairs', cited in R.K. Mukherjee, *The Rise and Fall of the East India Company*, pp. 302–3.
3 Mukherjee, *Rise and Fall*, p. 312.
4 B. Adams, *The Law of Civilization and Decay*, pp. 295–6.
5 Ibid., pp. 263–4.
6 A.G. Frank, *Latin America: Underdevelopment or Revolution*, p. 13.
7 C. Hill, *Reformation to Industrial Revolution*, p. 245.
8 Marx, *Capital*, I, p. 823.
9 The East India Company was given its first charter in 1600 by Queen Elizabeth I. The company era in India continued until 1858, when the crown took direct control of the administration of India. In fact, the company's domination of India was during the second half of the eighteenth century. Although trading depots were established in Surat, Madras, and Bombay in the seventeenth century, the new East India Company, which subsequently conquered India, received its first charter in 1698 and did not reach its final form until the beginning of the eighteenth century. 'The true commencement of the East India Company cannot be dated from a more remote epoch than the year 1702, when the different societies claiming the monopoly of the East India trade, united together in one single company. Until then, the very existence of the original East India Company was repeatedly endangered, once suspended for years under the protectorate of Cromwell, and once threatened with utter dissolution by parliamentary interference under the reign of William III.

'It was under the ascendancy of that Dutch Prince, when the whigs became the farmers of the revenues of the British Empire, when the Bank of England sprang into life, when the protective system was formally established in England, and the balance of power in Europe was definitely settled, that the existence of an East India Company was recognised by Parliament. That era of apparent liberty was in reality the era of monopolies, not created by Royal Grants, as in the times of Elizabeth and Charles I, but authorised and nationalised by the sanction of parliament. This epoch in the history of England bears, in fact, an extreme likeness to the epoch of Louis Philippe in France, the old landed aristocracy having been defeated and the bourgeoisie not being able to take its place except under the banner of moneyocracy or the "haute finance". The East India Company excluded the common people from the commerce with India [the East India Company was a monopoly company], at the same time that the House of Commons excluded them from Parliamentary representation. In this as well as in other instances we find the first decisive victory of the bourgeoisie over the feudal aristocracy coinciding with the most pronounced reaction against the people' (Karl Marx, *New York Herald Tribune*, 11 July 1858).

10 'The whole difficulty of trading with the East lay in the fact that Europe had so little to send out that the East wanted – a few luxury articles for the courts, lead, copper, quicksilver and tin, coral, gold and ivory were the only commodities except silver that India would absorb. Therefore it was mainly silver that was taken out' (L.C.A. Knowles, *The Economic Development of the British Overseas Empire*, p. 73).

11 Ibid., p. 74.

12 Ibid.

13 'At the commencement of the East India Company's operations, under the reign of Elizabeth, the Company was permitted, for the purpose of profitably carrying on its trade with India to export an annual value of 30,000 pounds in silver, gold and foreign coin. This was an infraction against all the prejudices of the age and Thomas Mun was forced to lay down in *A Discourse of Trade, from England unto the East Indies*, the foundation of the "mercantile system", admitting that the precious metals were the only wealth a country could possess, but contending at the same time that their exportation might be safely allowed, provided the balance of payments was in favour of the exporting nation. In this sense, he contended that the commodities imported from East India were chiefly reexported to the countries, from which a much greater quantity of bullion was obtained than had been required to pay for them in India' (Karl Marx, 'The East India Company – Its History and Results', *New York Daily Tribune*, 11 July 1853).

14 Lord Macaulay, *History of England*, vol. V, p. 2094.

15 Adams, *The Law of Civilization and Decay*, p. 305.

16 R.P. Dutt, *India Today*, p. 101.

17 L. Scrafton, 'Reflections on the Government of Indostan, 1763', cited in R.P. Dutt, *India Today*, p. 105.

18 Ibid.

19 Parliamentary Papers, House of Commons, *Select Committee's Ninth Report, 1783*, pp. 54–5.

20 Ibid., p. 47.

21 The extraction of revenue for capital accumulation was not restricted to Bengal alone. James Harrington, who has been called by R.H. Tawney 'the first English thinker to find the course of political upheaval in antecedent social change', wanted to extract as much revenue as possible from Ireland if necessary, even by settling the Jews in place of the slothful Irish and the English. He 'approved of its subjugation, regretted that it was not producing nearly as much revenue for England as it could do, and would have liked to see it repopulated with a more industrious and enterprising people, the Jews, whom he thought capable of improving Ireland's agriculture and increasing its trade to levels which produce 4 million pounds a year "dry rents", i.e., the net surplus product over and above the average wages of labour and the profits of enterprise. Of this surplus, he modestly proposed that only 2 million pounds a year (plus customs duties sufficient to maintain an army in Ireland) should be paid as tribute to England' (C.B. MacPherson, *The Political Theory of Possessive Individualism*, p. 180).

22 Besides these regular channels, the accumulated capital of India was also drained to England in another way. Enormous fortunes, as we have already noted, were made by individual officers of the company. Clive himself, who started as a writer or clerk in the service of the company, returned home with a fortune estimated at a quarter of a million pounds. In his own words, he accumulated fortunes of £100,000 in two years. The other servants of the company were not lagging far behind Clive in this noble occupation of making wealth. Sir John Shore reported in his minutes of 1787, in reference to Bengal: 'The exports of specie (bullion) from the country for the last twenty-five years have been great, and particularly during the last ten of that period. It is well understood, although the remittances to China are by the government (Indian bullion was used to pay for Chinese opium and other products) provided by bills, that specie to a large amount has been exported to answer them.... Silver bullion is also remitted by individuals to Europe; the amount cannot be calculated, but must, since the Company's accession to the Dewany, have been very considerable' (cited in Dadabhai Naoroji, *Poverty and Un-British Rule in India*, p. 79).

Marx also noted: 'During the whole course of the eighteenth century the treasures transported from India to England were gained much less by comparatively insignificant [compared to the direct looting but not in absolute terms] commerce, than by the direct exploitation of that country, and by the colossal fortunes there extorted and transmitted to England' (Karl Marx, *New York Daily Tribune*, 11 July 1853).

23 R.C. Dutt, *The Economic History of India*, II, p. 218.

24 The Royal Commission on Indian Expenditures, 1896, vol II, p. 305.

The following table appears in this report, and shows how India had to carry the expenses of the wars fought for the expansion of the British Empire:

	Foreign Wars whose cost was charged to India			
	Ordinary charges paid by		*Extraordinary charges paid by*	
Expedition	*India*	*England*	*India*	*England*
1st Afghan War	all	none	all	none
1st China War	all	none	none	all
Persian War	all	none	half	half
Abyssinian War	all	none	all	none
2nd Afghan War	all	none	all	except £5,000,000
Egyptian War	all	none	all	except £5,000,000
Soudan War	all	none	—	—

According to B.R. Thomilson, 'The greatest, because the only irreplaceable advantage the British derived from India was the use of the Indian army. In 1880 the Indian taxpayer supported 130,000 Indian troops and 66,000 British troops. During the First World War, the government of India recruited over 800,000 combatants and over 400,000 non-combatants. At the end of the War in 1918–19, the government of India's national debt stood at 370 million pounds. The strain on India's economy during the Second World War was equally severe. She raised an army of 2.25 million and at the end of the war her defense expenditure was a staggering sum of 38,130 million rupees. The last finance member of the government of India described the impact of the war of India in the following words in his budget speech of February 1946: 'While India has been spared the material destruction that has befallen many other countries, she has suffered in full measure, and in some direction, in greater measure than others, the economic consequences of the war' (B.R. Thomilson, *Economic and Social History Review*, July–Sept. 1976). The consequence was one of the worst famines in the history of mankind – the Great Bengal famine of 1942 in which about six million people died of hunger.

25 W. Digby, *'Prosperous' British India*, p. 224.
26 Ibid., p. 225.
    The importance and magnitude of this sum could be understood if we take into account the purchasing power of a pound at that period. The accumulated capital of the richest textile industrialist of England, Sir Robert Peel, at his death in 1830, was only one and a half million pounds. The initial capital of the industry which his father started in 1760 was not more than a few thousand pounds. 'The greatest of the early cotton industrialists was Sir Robert Peel (1750–1830), a man who at his death left almost one and a half million pounds – a vast sum for those days – and a son just about to become Prime Minister of Britain. The Peels were a family of yeoman peasants of middling status who, like others in the Lancashire hills, combined farming and domestic textile production, at any rate from the mid seventeenth century. Sir Robert's father (1723–95) still hawked his goods about the countryside, moved into the town of Blackburn only in 1750, and even then had not yet quite abandoned farming. He had ... perhaps £2,000–£4,000 worth in land, which he mortgaged in the early 1760s when he formed a calico-printing firm with his brother-in-law Haworth and one Yates, who brought into it the accumulated savings of his family's innkeeping business at the Black Bull. ... Three years later – in the middle of 1760s – its demand for cotton to print was such that the firm went into the manufacture of cloth itself' (E.J. Hobsbawm, *Industry and Empire*, p. 62).
27 What economic and extra-economic pressures were adopted by the metropolitan bourgeoisie to eliminate the nascent Indian bourgeoisie have been vividly described by various Indian scholars. See R.C. Dutt, *The Economic History of India* (2 vols); R.P. Dutt, *India Today*; and R.K. Mukherjee, *The Rise and Fall of the East India Company*.
28 E.J. Hobsbawm, *Industry and Empire*, p.86.
29 R.P. Dutt, *India Today*, p. 109.
30 Hobsbawm, *Industry and Empire*, p. 53
31 R.P. Dutt, *India Today*, p. 112.
32 Hobsbawm, *Industry and Empire*, p. 56.

33 In the silk industry, too, the Indian products were far superior to the British products. In 1673, complaints were made that the imports of Indian silk, chintz, etc., were ruining the home manufacturers in Britain.

34 Hobsbawm, *Industry and Empire*, p. 57.

'Cotton thus acquired its characteristic link with the underdeveloped world, which it retained and strengthened through all the various fluctuations of fortune. The slave plantations in the West Indies provided its raw material until in the 1790s it acquired a new and virtually unlimited source in the slave plantations in the southern U.S.A., which therefore became in the main a dependent economy of Lancashire' (ibid., p. 58).

35 'Parliamentary intervention, with regard to the East India Company, was again claimed, not by the commercial, but by the industrial class, at the latter end of the 17th century, and during the greater part of the 18th, when the importation of East Indian cotton and silk stuffs was declared to ruin the poor British manufacturers, an opinion put forward in John Pollexfen's *England and East India Inconsistent in Their Manufacturers*, London, 1697, a title strongly verified a century and a half later, but in a very different sense. Parliament did then interfere. By the Act 11 and 12 William III, Cap. 10, it was enacted that the wearing of wrought silks and of printed or dyed calicoes from India, Persia or China should be prohibited and a penalty of £200 imposed on all persons having or selling the same. Similar laws were enacted under George I, II and III, in consequence of the repeated lamentations of the afterwards so 'enlightened' [quotation marks are Marx's] British manufacturers. And thus during the greater part of the 18th century, Indian manufactures were generally imported into England in order to be sold on the continent, and to remain excluded from the English market itself' (Karl Marx, 'The East India Company', *New York Daily Tribune*, 11 July 1853).

36 It is interesting to note that even Napoleon was not successful in securing the complete prohibition of the illegal import of Indian textiles and silks into France until British industrial capitalism totally destroyed the Indian industries. We get a glimpse of the attraction European ladies felt for Indian muslin and silk from the autobiography of Queen Hortense, the step-daughter of Napoleon. 'Meanwhile France was prosperous. The government was being organized. Public works were undertaken on a vast scale. The luxury which is necessary to the life of every great nation reappeared (which disappeared after the French Revolution). The First Consul (Napoleon), in order to free us from paying tribute to England, forbade the wearing of muslin materials.... When my mother and I would come into the room wearing an elegant dress, his first question was, 'Is that gown made of muslin?' We often replied that it was lawn from Saint Quentin, but if a smile betrayed us he would instantly tear the guilty garment in two.... Fashion completed what the Consul had begun, and what he might not have achieved without her; for Cashmir shawls (Indian), in spite of being frequently threatened with

the fire, survived his taboo' (*The Memoirs of Queen Hortense*, p. 56).

37 Engels wrote: 'The conquest of India by the Portuguese, Dutch and English between 1500 and 1800 had imports from India as its object – nobody dreamt of exporting anything there and yet what a colossal reaction these discoveries and conquests, solely conditioned by the interests of trade, had upon industry; they first created the need for export to these countries and developed large-scale industry' (Marx/ Engels, *Correspondence*, p. 420).

38 James Mill, *The History of British India*, vol. III, p. 337, cited in Mukherjee, *The Rise and Fall*, p. 400.

39 Parliamentary Papers, *Ninth Report*, p. 64.

40 A. Smith, *The Wealth of Nations*, p. 593.

41 *Minutes of Evidence on the Affairs of the East India Company,* 1813, p. 3.

42 R.C. Dutt, *Economic History of India*, I, p. 256.

43 Ibid., p. 268.

Until 1813, 'the interests of moneyocracy which had converted India into its landed estates, of the oligarchy who had conquered it by their armies, and of the milliocracy who had inundated it with their fabrics, had gone hand in hand. But the more the industrial interest became dependent on the Indian market, the more it felt the necessity of creating fresh productive powers in India, after having ruined her native industry.... Besides, they found that in all attempts to apply capital to India they met with impediment and chicanery on the part of Indian authorities [i.e., the East India Company representing the merchant capitalists]. Thus India became the battlefield in the contest of the industrial interest on the one side, and of the moneyocracy and oligarchy on the other. The manufacturers, conscious of their ascendency in England, ask now for the annihilation of these antagonistic powers in India ... and for the final eclipse of the East India Company' (Karl Marx, *New York Herald Tribune*, 11 July 1853).

44 Mill, *The History of British India*, I, p. 385.

45 St G. Tucker, *Memorials of the Indian Government*, p. 494, cited in R.C. Dutt, *Economic History*, vol. II, p. 262.

46 Marx, 'The East India Company', *New York Daily Tribune*, 11 July 1853.

47 F. List, 'The National System of Political Economy', cited in R.C. Dutt, *Economic History of India*, I, p. 300.

48 Hobsbawm, *Industry and Empire*, p. 148.

49 Marx, 'The British Rule in India', *New York Daily Tribune*, 25 June 1853.

50 R.C. Dutt, *Economic History of India*, II, p. 112.

51 Marx, 'The British Rule in India', *New York Daily Tribune*, 25 June 1853.

52 Marx, *Capital* I, p. 471.

53 And also from India's excess exports over imports.

54 'A significant part of the surpluses needed for the general expansion of British industry was born from export profits. Exports, *particularly in cotton goods,* reached phenomenal proportions. Between 1870 and 1913, Britain's exports amounted to about one third of her total

industrial production' (S. Hetzler, *Technological Growth and Social Change*, p. 135).

55 In this period (1880–1913) Britain's exports to her traditional markets in Europe and North America were being hit by indigenous industrial development and tariff barriers, while her imports from these countries continued at the same level.

56 B. Ward, *India and the West*, p. 126.

57 F. Braudel, *Capitalism and Material Life, 1400–1800*, p. 64.

58 Marx, *Capital*, III, pp. 723–4.

59 Only on plantations – tea, coffee, and rubber – was the capitalist method introduced. It constituted less than one per cent of Indian agriculture.

60 P.A. Wadia and K.T. Merchant, *Our Economic Problem*, pp. 280–1.

61 See *Report of the Taxation Enquiry Commission, 1953–54*.

62 Marx, 'India', *New York Daily Tribune*, 5 August 1853.

63 Ibid.

64 Ibid.

Daniel Thorner, it seems, agrees with Marx that the private property in land introduced by the British in India was not the absolute private property we find in the West. 'If we reexamine the record a bit more closely, I think we will agree that this [introduction of absolute or unfettered private ownership] was precisely what Cornwallis and his successors did not do. Like the Moghuls before them, and the Guptas and the Mauryas before the Moghuls, the British insisted on the right of the imperial power to the first share of the fruits of the soil. But this type of a claim was already centuries out of date in England itself and belongs properly to a stage of economic development where there is, in effect, no other principal source of state revenue. The key fact about all of the British land settlements . . . was the new rights in the land were invariably sub-ordinate to the rights of the State. To no holder was granted the exclusive right to occupy, enjoy, and dispose of land which in practice, is the hallmark of western private ownership. Without this quality of exclusiveness, real property cannot be said to exist. Some of the rights normally associated with private property in land (e.g., mortgageability, transfer, hereditability) were indeed accorded to the new owners. But their privileges were restricted by the simultaneous recognition of rights both superior and inferior to their own in the same land. The State, as a superior landlord, claimed a share of rents; while the actual tillers exercised a traditional claim to occupancy [the zamindar's rights to evict ryots or tillers were restricted by later legislations]. . . . The early British officials assumed that since the State collected what appeared to them as a rent, the State must be the owner of all the land. Accordingly, as they took over territorial power from the various rulers, they established the right of the British Raj as the supreme or ultimate landowner; and with this justification they continued to collect revenues at the former, or more commonly, enhanced levels. What the British established in India might be described, in fact, as an imperfect or kaccha kind of private ownership of land. To this date [i.e. even after independence], there has not emerged in India a fully developed or pakka private property in land. It was the British insistence upon the State's prerogative as ultimate owners, which has given India's land tenures their distinctive character... in the new setting land had been made more of a commodity than ever before in Indian history. What we have here in India, today, then, is an unique agrarian structure. It represents a blending of remnants from the pre-British economic order (including, above all, the claim of the State to a share of the produce of the land), together with modern Western concepts of private property. The result has been a layering of rights from those of the State as super-landlord (or ultimate owner) down through those of the sub-landlords (penultimate owners) to those of several tiers of tenants. Both the State and the superior holders exercise the right to draw income from the soil in the form of rents wherever possible, the tenants also try to subsist by collecting rents from the working cultivators with rights inferior to their own' (Daniel Thorner, *The Agrarian Prospect in India*, pp. 7–11).

65 In *Ryotwari* areas, too, landlordism spread through the process of subletting and through the dispossession of the original cultivators by moneylenders.

Regular payment of rent, irrespective of the quality of the harvest, led to the peasants' increasing indebtedness.

66 Gadgil, *The Industrial Evolution of India*, pp. 161–2.

67 P. Baran, *The Political Economy of Growth*, p. 144.

68 Ibid., p. 150.

69 Lord Dalhousie, 'Minute on Railways, 1853', cited in R.P. Dutt, *India Today*, p. 132.

70 'Global metropolitanism is embedded in the circulation patterns of a global economy, out of which surplus value is being extracted. Different city forms are contained within that economy. Castells (1970), for example, differentiates between the metropolitan forms of North America and Western Europe and the dependent urban forms of much of the rest of the world. Dependent urbanism arises in situations where the urban form exists as a channel for the extraction of quantities of surplus from a rural and resource hinterland for purposes of shipment to the major metropolitan centres. This colonial form of urbanism is currently characteristic, for example in much of Latin America (Frank, 1969) but in the early nineteenth century it was, as Pred (1966) notes, dominant in the United States' (David Harvey, *Social Justice and the City*, p. 232). The U.S.A., until the early nineteenth century, was a hinterland of the metropolitan centre of the U.K. and other West European countries. The urban population in the U.S.A. at the beginning of the century was only 3.8 per cent.

71 Gadgil, *The Industrial Evolution of India*, pp. 144–5.

72 Marx, 'The Future Results of British Rule in India', *New York Daily Tribune*, 8 August 1853.

73 Throughout the negotiations commencing in 1828 for the East India Company's Charter Acts of 1833, the growing desire of the English

manufacturing classes to engage more actively in the Indian trade, and so harness with invested capital the raw materials available in India, had been actively brought to bear upon the British Parliament. The import of Indian cotton interested Manchester and was considered to be 'possible only through the introduction of European skill and capital'. The Liverpool East India Committee asked for better communication in India to 'facilitate movement of raw materials. The introduction of a uniform currency and substantial banking houses was demanded.' Most interesting of all, Mr Wallich tried to rouse the Board of Trade to the possibility of cultivation of tea in the foothills of the Himalayas (J.N. Bhagwati and Padma Desai, *India: Planning for Industrialisation*, p. 19).

74 R.P. Dutt, *India Today*, p. 133.
75 Gadgil, *The Industrial Evolution of India*, pp. 54–61.
76 A.R. Tripathi, *Trade and Finance in the Bengal Presidency*, p. 11.
77 Bhagwati/Desai, *India: Planning for Industrialisation*, p. 18.
78 Tripathi, *Trade and Finance*, p. 240.
79 M. Kidron, *Foreign Investments in India*, pp. 6–7.
80 Indian Industrial Commission, 1919, cited in D.H. Buchanan, *The Development of Capitalist Enterprise in India*, p. 157.
81 Buchanan, *Development of Capitalist Enterprise*, p. 157.
82 British capital reigned supreme until the beginning of the First World War.
83 Cited in V.B. Singh, *The Economic History of India*, pp. 507–8.
84 Ibid, p. 508.
85 Commenting on the import tariff history of India, Buchanan says, 'The effect of this policy on the minds of Indians has been complicated by the fact that before the factory system was developed in Europe, Indian manufacturers were excluded from England by high tariffs. At the end of the seventeenth century, English woollen and silk weavers found their home market being taken by cotton and silk goods from India. Acts passed, especially in 1700 and 1720 and remaining in force over a century, until 1825, prohibited the wearing of certain Indian goods and laid heavy taxes on others. Even in 1802, duties on Indian cotton cloths were from 20 per cent to 50 per cent of their value.... When cotton textiles manufactured from American cotton by power machinery started to flow in great quantity from England to India, the British industrial and mercantile classes pressed for completely free access to the market' (D.H. Buchanan, *The Development of Capitalist Enterprise in India*, p. 465).
86 Ibid.
87 Ibid.
88 Ibid., p. 468.
89 Ibid.
90 Ibid.
91 Ibid.
92 *Census of India, 1931*, vol. I, part 1, p. 285.
93 I.L.O. Report, 1938, 'Industrial Labour in India', p. 30.
94 B.B. Misra, *The Indian Middle Classes*, p. 63.

95 Ibid., p. 11.
96 See Weber, *General Economic History*.
97 Misra, *The Indian Middle Classes*, p. 11.
98 F. Bernier, *Travels in the Moghul Empire*, p. 252.
99 Tara Chand, *History of the Freedom Movement in India*, pp. 301–2.
100 W.H. Moreland, *India at the Death of Akbar*, pp. 24–5.
101 R. Some, *Jagrata Janata*, p. 37.
102 See R. Das, *Raja Rammohan*, pp. 140–3.
103 G. Ramanathan, 'Educational planning and national integration', cited in G. Myrdal, *Asian Drama*, III, p. 1639.
104 Cited in A.R. Desai, *Social Background of Indian Nationalism*, p. 130.
105 H. Sharp, 'Selections from the Educational Records'. Pt 1, p. 125 cited in A.K.N. Karim, 'The Modern Muslim Political Elite in Bengal', doctoral thesis, London University, 1964, p. 173.
106 W. Adam, *Adam's Reports on Vernacular Education in Bengal and Behar*, p. 77.
107 Cited in B.B. Misra, *The Indian Middle Classes*, p. 154.
108 Education Despatch dated 19th July 1854 to the Government of India, Para. 4.
109 C.E. Trevelyan, 'On the education of people in India' in Misra, *The Indian Middle Classes*, pp. 151–2.

4 Socialism in India: an ideology of state hegemony

1 *First Report of the National Income Committee, 1951*, p. 24.
2 Ibid.
3 *Report of the Taxation Enquiry Commission, 1953–54*, I, pp. 63–4.
4 *Report of the Committee on Distribution of Income and Levels of Living*, table 3.12.
5 Ibid., p. 15.
6 Ibid., table 3.19.
7 *Census of India, 1951*, vol. I, part 1B, 1955, p. 207.
8 P.A. Wadia and K.T. Merchant, *Our Economic Problem*, p. 85.
9 G. Blyn, *Agricultural Trends in India, 1891–1947*, p. 117.
10 Ibid.
11 R.P. Dutt, *India Today*, p. 205.
12 *The Royal Commission on Agriculture, 1928*, p. 433.
13 See A. Shonfield, *Modern Capitalism*.
14 'A Plan of Economic Development for India' (known as the Bombay Plan), p. 5. Signatories to the plan were: J.R.D. Tata, G. Birla, Shri Ram Purshottomdas Thakurdas, Sir Ardeshir Dalal, John Mathai, A.D. Shraff, and Kasturbhai Lalbhai.
15 Ibid., p. 27.
16 Ibid., p. 28.
17 Ibid., p. 29.
18 Ibid., pp. 9–10.
19 Ibid.

20 Planning in India, unlike planning in many other developing countries as well as some developed countries, covers almost all sectors of the national economy. In many European countries, planning had been adopted after the Second World War to accelerate the rate of economic growth and remove certain imbalances in the capitalist structure; but in almost none of these countries did planning include any provision whereby the state would own the basic industries.

21 Cited in H. Venkatasubbiah, *Indian Economy Since Independence*, p. 292.

22 J. Nehru, *The Discovery of India*, pp. 399–400.

23 An election was held in 1937 under the Act of 1935. In this election the Indian National Congress was elected in all provinces except Bengal, Punjab, and Sind.

24 Nehru, *The Discovery of India*, pp. 399–400.

25 Ibid., p. 400.

26 See *Report of the National Planning Committee*, p. 36.

27 Ibid., pp. 139–69.

28 Quoted in 'Modes of class struggle . . .' by G. Epsing-Anderson *et al.*

29 'The authors of the plan [Bombay Plan] are evidently orthodox believers in the creed of capitalism and laissez-faire and whilst they are reluctantly led to pay homage to a compromise formula, a via-media between state and private enterprise, they look upon state control as a temporary measure during the planning period' (P.A. Wadia and K.T. Merchant, *The Bombay Plan, A Criticism*, p. 18).

30 'Modes of class struggle and the capitalist state'.

31 See J. O'Connor, *The Fiscal Crisis of the State*; also A. Shonfield, *Modern Capitalism*.

32 Cited in P.R. Bramhanand, 'Industrial Development and Planning' in C.N. Vakil (ed.), *Economic Consequences of Divided India*, pp. 369–71.

33 See below, discussion on the Industrial Policy Resolution, 1956.

34 Industrial Policy Resolution, April, 1956.

35 See *Second Five Year Plan*, p. 12.

36 One of the reasons that led the Government of India to exclude the mention of the 'socialist pattern of society' in the First Industrial Policy Resolution might have been prompted by the desire not to offend the advanced capitalist societies, as they were at that time the only source of capital goods. By 1956, however, the U.S.S.R. had emerged as another viable source.

37 *Second Five Year Plan*, p. 12.

38 The continuing low standard of living (and its deterioration in the absence of industrialization) is a danger to the stability of any state.

39 'The State has been following a policy of supporting cottage and village and small-scale industries by restricting the volume of production in the large-scale sector, by differential taxation, or by direct subsidies. . . . The State will, therefore, concentrate on measures designed to improve the competitive strength of the small-scale producers' (*Industrial Policy Resolution, 1956*).

40 'Industrial undertakings in the private sector have necessarily to fit into

the framework of the social and economic policy of the State and will be subject to control and regulation in terms of the Industries (Development and Regulation) Act and other relevant legislation' (*Industrial Policy Resolution 1956*).

41 J. Nehru, *Recent Essays and Writings*, pp. 4–6.

42 Ibid., p. 21.

43 J. Nehru, *Speeches, 1946–49*, p. 92.
   'Now it is well known and we have often stressed this that production is perhaps one of the most important things before us today, that is adding to the wealth of the country. We cannot overlook other things. Nevertheless production comes first, and I am prepared to say that everything that we do should be judged from the point of view of production first of all' (J. Nehru, *Speeches*, vol. I, 1946–49, p. 110).

44 See A.R.. Desai, *Social Background of Indian Nationalism*, pp. 295–350.

45 Ibid., p. 349.

46 Rajendra Some, *Jagrata Janata*, pp. 107–8; see also Baldev Raj Nayar, *The Modernization Imperative and Indian Planning*, pp. 127–8.

47 Some, *Jagrata Janata*, p. 132.

48 Commenting on the issue of cooperative and collective farming, Nehru described the Indian peasants' apathy to part with their smallholdings in the following words: 'it is obvious that before you can think of them, you have to put an end to the present land system which prevails in the greater part of India... and that is not such an easy matter. It is not a matter of few, whom you might call capitalists, disliking it, but possibly a very large number of peasant proprietors disliking it. Obviously, whatever decision we may make must have the consent of a large number of people. We cannot force it down the throats of the vast majority of our peasants' (J. Nehru, *Speeches*, vol. I, 1946–49, p. 116).

49 The poor performance of the Communist party in the general election which was held in 1950 indicates that the situation was not propitious for a social revolution.

50 'Communism charges the capitalist structure of society with being based on violence and class conflict. I think this is essentially correct, though the capitalist structure itself has undergone and is continually undergoing a change because of democratic and other struggles. The question is how to get rid of inequality and have a classless society with equal opportunities for all. Can this be achieved through methods of violence, or can it be possible to bring about the changes through peaceful methods? Communism has definitely allied itself to the approach of violence .... If the society which we aim at cannot be brought about by big-scale violence, will small-scale violence help? Surely not, partly because that itself may lead to a big-scale violence and partly because it produces an atmosphere of conflict and and of disruption. *It is absurd to imagine that in a conflict the socially progressive forces are bound to win*' (J. Nehru, *Speeches*, 1957–63, pp. 116–18).

51 J. Nehru, *Speeches*, 1957–63, p. 139.

52 *Lok Sabha Debates*, Third Series, vol. II, p. 2062.

53 Lenin stressed the need for political domination or for state power to

execute the transition to socialism. 'If we are not anarchists, we must admit that the state, that is, compulsion, is needed for the transition from capitalism to socialism' (V.I. Lenin, *Questions of the Socialist Organisation of the Economy*, p. 126).

54 Nor could the state in India be called a socialist one in the sense of scientific socialism, because it had no organic relationship with either the workers or the peasants. It did not emerge from any social revolution, whether bourgeois or proletarian. In his letter to Kugelmann (dated 12 April 1871) Marx wrote: 'If you look at the last chapter of Eighteenth Brumaire, you will find that I declare the next attempt of the French Revolution to be: not merely to hand over, from one to another, the bureaucratic and military machinery – as has hitherto been but to *shatter* it [Marx's emphasis]; and this is the preliminary condition of any real people's revolution on the continent.'

5 The artisan and small-scale industries in India's social economy and their relationship with the state

1 *Census of India, 1951*.
2 According to the 1971 census the percentage of workers employed in household industry is 3.5% of the total working population. But the criteria of estimation of the 1971 census is different from that of the 1961 census, 'According to Census of India, 1971, the working population formed 32.9 per cent of the total population as against 42.9 per cent of the total population recorded as workers in 1961 Census. The decrease in the working population in 1971 as compared with 1961 is mainly due to the adoption of amended definition of "workers" in 1971 wherein the persons have been categorised as "workers" and "non-workers" according to their main activity. The secondary work is not taken into consideration' (*The Indian Labour Year Book, 1972*). The 10 per cent decrease in the number of workers has been achieved mainly at the expense of rural artisan workers, most of whom are engaged in secondary work. The point is discussed in detail later in this chapter.
3 V.K.R.V. Rao, 'Introduction', *Papers on National Income and Allied Topics*, II, p. 2.
4 Recent studies conclusively prove that taxes used to be paid to the state in both cash and kind. This does not, however, repudiate the basic thesis of Marx, that the Indian villages, based on an organic unity between agriculture and industry, remained self-reproductive.
5 K. Marx, *Capital*, I, pp. 392–4.
6 *Study of Village Artisans*, Planning Commission, Programme Evaluation Organisation, pp. 2–4.
7 Ibid., Appendix, Table II.
8 Ibid., p. 8.
9 Ibid., p. 12.
10 Ibid.
11 'Most of the families in a typical village belong to some peasant caste, but the village also contains one or more families from each of a number

of castes whose speciality is other than agriculture, though they may do some field work too. These include Brahmans, astrologers, soothsayers, barbers, goldsmiths, shepherds, oil pressers, potters, weavers, carpenters, and other artisans. Unlike Western farmers, who usually do many kinds of work besides tilling their fields and who may pride themselves on their versatility, the Indian peasant relies on the specialised services of these other castes. *Although the castes remain separate socially they are close knit together economically.* Traditionally, each peasant family had a permanent hereditary relationship with some family in each non-peasant caste in the village. In return for an annual share in the harvest of grain, these other families would undertake to supply the peasant family year after year with all its annual needs in specified kinds of goods or services. Barbers would give unlimited shaves, and potters would make as many pottery vessels as were required. In the exchange of goods and services, *each village caste was both a patron and a client of other village castes.* They were bound together in a permanent and relatively stable, unequal relationship, in which those who were the richest and most powerful were in a position to secure the better bargain in the exchange. There was a certain security in this arrangement known as the *jajmani* system. Though the peasant might have a bad harvest, his responsibility toward the artisans who served him continued. They would eat less well if he had ill-fortune, so did he' (B.P. Lamb, *India: A World in Transition*, p. 257, emphasis added).

12 This, however, seems more customary and circumstantial than legal. There are instances, throughout Indian history, as well as in its legends and myths, of castes pursuing occupations other than their own.

13 Marx, *Capital*, III, p. 386.

14 It is significant that Marx does not refer to the feudal class as the consuming class in the orient but to the state and by implication makes the state the most powerful social entity (separate from other classes), which appropriated to itself the major portion of the surplus product. This quotation from *Capital*, vol. III, clearly demonstrates that Marx did not abandon the concept of the 'Asiatic mode of Production' in his later life as many modern Marxists have argued.

15 Marx, *Capital*, III, p. 389.

16 See chapter 2.

17 Tara Chand, *History of the Freedom Movement in India*, vol. I, pp. 151–2.
       'Historically, money is often transformed into capital in quite simple and obvious ways. Thus, the merchant sets to work a number of spinners and weavers who formerly engaged in these activities as subsidiary occupations to their agricultural work, and turns a subsidiary occupation into a principal one, after which he has them under his control and sway as wage labourers. The next step is to remove them from their homes and to assemble them in a single house of labour.... Originally he [the merchant] has bought their labour merely by the purchase of their products. As soon as they confine themselves to the production of this exchange value, and are therefore obliged to produce immediate exchange values, and to exchange their labour entirely for money in

order to go on living, they come under his domination. Finally, even the illusion of selling him their products disappears. He purchases their labour and takes away their property in the product, soon also their ownership of the instrument.... The original historical forms in which capital appears at first sporadically or locally, side by side with the old modes of production, but gradually bursting them asunder, make up manufacture in the proper sense of the word' (Karl Marx, *Pre-Capitalist Economic Formations*, pp. 115–16).

18 Tara Chand, *History of the Freedom Movement in India*, vol. I, pp. 151–2.
19 P. Spear, *A History of India*, pp. 40–6; Tara Chand, *History of the Freedom Movement*, pp. 122–3.

Compare: 'For instance, when the great English landowners dismissed their retainers, who had consumed a share of their surplus produce of their land; when their farmers drove out the small cottagers, etc., then a doubly free mass of living labour power was thrown on to the labour market – free from the old relation of clientship, villeinage or service, but also free from all goods and chattels, from every real and objective form of existence, free from all property. Such a mass would be reduced either to the sale of its labour power or to beggary, vagabondage or robbery as its only source of income. History records the fact that it first tried beggary, vagabondage and crime, but was herded off this road on to the narrow path which led to the labour market by means of gallows, pillory and whip...' (Karl Marx, *Pre-Capitalist Economic Formations*, pp. 110–11).

The significant factor for the development of capitalism in India was that the paupers in urban centres were free labourers, unencumbered by any socio-economic ties. In this respect they had close resemblance with the free wage labourers of English manufacture. 'Before machines were introduced in England, at least the transition had been completed: *the transition from feudally tied labour to free capitalist labour*, from work measured primarily by the amount done to work based on a time unit, from work which chained a man in one specific locality and according to his accomplishments to work forced on him primarily by economic pressure – in other words, without work he could not live. The working classes in the England of 1760, like their forefathers before them, had already had an introduction to capitalist dependence and work discipline. This is the fundamental difference between the modern workers in England and those of all other countries: the same difference exists between the capitalists of England, with all their experience of capitalist development without machines and the capitalists of all other nations' (J. Kuczynski, *The Rise of the Working Class*, p. 145, emphasis added). See also Karl Marx, *Capital*, vol. I, pp. 394–404.

20 Marx, *Capital*, III, p. 389.
21 Ibid.
22 Ibid., pp. 392–3.
23 Marx, 'The Future Results of the British Rule in India', *New York Daily Tribune*, 8 August 1853.

24 It should be borne in mind that the capitalist penetration of the metropolitan bourgeoisie remained restricted only to the levels of exchange. Through the creation of private property in land, in the form of rentier classes and its appendage moneylenders, the surplus from agriculture (i.e. the only productive sector in the country in the absence of industrialization) was siphoned off to pay for consumer products imported from metropolitan centres. The commercialization of Indian agriculture did not result in a higher capitalist mode of production. Exploitation was carried on through the circulation of money and commodities between two unequal spheres of production, one pre-capitalist, and the other capitalist. Intense surplus extraction through the mechanism of the market led to the gradual impoverishment and ruination of Indian agriculture and its corollary, the village artisans. That is one of the reasons why, when the artisans were asked to enumerate the difficulties they had faced in selling their commodities, the most frequent answer (36 per cent of the total) was the low demand for products, not the competition of factory goods (see *Study of Village Artisans*, p. 13).

25 *Study of Village Artisans*, p. 11.

26 The study on village artisans mentions a few other consumer goods, such as bamboo and cane work, tailoring and masonry in which the customary payment system is gradually eroding.

27 *Study of Village Artisans*, p. 12.

28 According to the *All India Report on Agricultural Census*, published in 1975, out of 70 million agricultural holdings in the country, 64 million holdings or 92 per cent are wholly owned or self-operated. This makes evident that whatever capitalist development has taken place in Indian agriculture is insignificant compared to the predominant peasant economy.

29 In this connection it should also be noted that the growing monetization of the Indian rural economy does not necessarily mean that the old Asiatic mode is being replaced by a developing capitalist mode. The circulation of money and commodities between the two spheres of rural and urban economies and consequently between the two spheres of production can be independently carried on until institutional factors are removed to make possible for the circulation to seize hold of production in rural areas or production to develop to such an extent as to absorb circulation as a part of it.

30 *India: A Reference Annual*, 1975, p. 248.

31 The Industrial Policy Resolution, 6 April 1956.

32 *Karve Committee Report, 1955*.

33 Ibid.

34 Ibid.

35 Ibid.

36 *Reserve Bank of India's Review of the Karve Committee's Report*.

37 *Karve Committee Report, 1955*.

38 See H.G. Lakhani, *Problems of Economic Development of India*, p. 231.

39 Ibid.
40 *India: A Reference Annual*, 1975, p. 248.
41 *Third Five Year Plan, A Draft Outline* (Planning Commission), p. 196.
42 A. Hanson, *The Process of Planning*, p. 504.
43 *Economic Times*, Calcutta, 21 February 1977.
44 Ibid.
45 Ibid.
46 Ibid.
47 Ibid.
48 The central government has kept reserved 177 items for exclusive production in the "small-scale sector" (inclusive rural artisan industries) of which the majority are produced by the small-scale industry (*India, 1975, A Reference Annual*, compiled by the Research and Reference Division, p. 249).
49 As has been elaborately discussed by James O'Connor, in *The Fiscal Crisis of the State*, even in the most advanced capitalist country, the U.S.A., small-scale enterprises have been able to survive, but only in those areas in which large-scale industry had no interest or technical advantage. In advanced capitalist countries, small industries are normally ancillary to large-scale industries.
50 The Small Industries Development Organisation operates through 16 service institutes, 16 branch institutes, 55 extension production and training centres. These agencies 'will not merely provide technical advice in response to enquiries from small units regarding improved types of machines, equipment and processes, use of raw materials and methods of reducing costs, but their technical staff will contact small units and advise on their problems, thus providing a useful extension service. The institutes will also arrange to give demonstrations in the use of improved technical services and machines through their own workshops as well as through model workshops set up in centres outside the institute.... They will also provide marketing services by giving advice and information to small industries on existing and potential markets and on adaptation of their production to suit such markets' (*Second Five Year Plan*, p. 451).
51 *India: A Reference Annual*, 1975, p. 250.
52 Ibid.
53 Ibid.
54 Ibid.
55 *Economic Times*, Calcutta, 21 February 1977.
56 Ibid.
57 P.N. Dhar and H.F. Lydall, *The Role of Small Enterprises*, p. 84.
58 Ibid., p. 11.
59 Ibid., p. 25.
60 The author knows two small industrialists who quite often make their workers work more than ten hours a day.
61 Dhar and Lydall, *The Role of Small Enterprises*, p. 34.

6 The state and the growth of the public and private sectors

1 *The Industries (Development and Regulations) Act, 1951* (amended later); see also G.K. Shirokov, *Industrialization of India*, pp. 66–88.
2 *Report on the Working and Administration of the Companies Act, 1956.*
3 A.H. Hanson, *The Process of Planning*, p. 486.
4 See *Report of the Managing Agency Enquiry Committee, 1966; The Monopolies Enquiry Commission, 1964*; R.K. Hazari, 'Ownership and control: a study of intercorporate investment'.
5 The ministries which are normally represented in the Licensing Committee are: Finance, Industry, Railways, Labour, Steel, Mines, Fuel, and the Planning Commission.
6 *Lok Sabha, Ninth Report of the Estimate Committee*, pp. 200–1.
7 In 1966 the Administrative Reforms Commission made the following suggestions to make the D.G.T.D. more efficient in dealing with industrial applications: '319 (a) The work of the Director General of Technical Development (D.G.T.D.) should be divided among a number of directorates, each directorate being responsible for advisory service to a group of related industries. Above the level of directors, there should be three or four deputy-directors-general, each of them having under him a few directors dealing with broadly related subjects. (2) In ministries which have to deal with sizeable areas of industrial development or one or more major industries, there should be a complement of technical officers at senior levels drawn from the field, i.e., from the public undertakings and other organisations throwing up technical talents. (3) The advisory service provided by the D.G.T.D. should extend to sugar and vanaspati.

'321. The Director-General of Technical Development should be specifically charged with responsibility for promoting modernisation.

'322. The D.G.T.D. though placed in the Ministry of Commerce and Industry, should be viewed as a common service agency to the entire government of India. Ministries dealing with individual or sectoral industries or public undertakings should be able to draw upon this service directly.'
8 The control of capital issues has been considerably liberalized since 1966.
9 *Report of the Administrative Reforms Commission, 1966.*
10 Ibid.
11 Price controls could also be imposed under the Industries Development and Regulation Act. The price, sale and distribution of motor cars were controlled under this act from May 1959.
12 *Report of the Administrative Reforms Commission, 1966.*
13 'It is the executive in India which plays a dominant role, not only in initiating new policies but also in administering the vast powers delegated to it by the legislature in the planned and highly regulated Indian economy' (S.A. Kochanek, *Business and Politics in India*, p. 265).
14 Ibid.
15 Ibid.

16 Percival Spear, *India: A Modern History*, p. 238.
17 It is interesting to note that the term 'civil service' originated in India and was later exported to Europe. As Tyagi says, 'The term civil service, itself, owes its origin to the Company's [East India Company] rule. The term was first used to designate those servants of the Company who were engaged in mercantile work. This was done in order to distinguish them from those servants of the Company who were engaged in military or naval duties.... But when the Company changed from a trading corporation to a territorial government and its mercantile servants were engaged in civil administration, the term, civil service, got automatically widened in scope and came to connote not only a non-combatant status but also a status of civil administration. The term, having thus originated in India, was imported to the 'home' country from where it quickly spread to Prussia and later on to other European countries' (A.R. Tyagi, *The Civil Service in a Developing Society*, p. 7).
18 See L.S.S. O'Malley, *The Indian Civil Service*; H.F. Goodnow, *The Civil Service of Pakistan*; A.R. Tyagi, *The Civil Service in a Developing Society*; B.B. Misra, *The Administrative History of India*.
19 R.P. Taub, *Bureaucrats Under Stress*, p. 8.
20 L.S.S. O'Malley, *The Indian Civil Service*, p. 158.
21 Ibid.
22 Ibid.
23 H.F. Goodnow, *The Civil Service of Pakistan*, p. 35.
    'The present administrative structure of the Indian Union and the states is taken for granted by most politicians and administrators and its fairly recent historical roots are usually forgotten. It is necessary to understand these roots as much for practical as for academic reasons. To put it briefly, the British built up over the years a centralised administration together with enormous freedom and initiative for the man on the spot – the district collector' (V. Subramaniam, 'Administrators and Politicians: Emerging Relations').
24 L.S.S. O'Malley, *The Indian Civil Service*, p. 161.
    Here O'Malley makes a distinction between the private rent concept under the system of feudalism in Europe and that portion of the produce of the land which was appropriated by the state as land revenue in the Asiatic states (see chapter 2).
25 'The district collectorate system as originally evolved by Mogul and British practice was skillfully designed to provide the basic framework for imperial occupation and stable rule. After subdividing a region or an empire into provinces, the land was further subdivided into units, the districts. Upon this bedrock, the governance of the area rested. A corps of specially trained officials, loyal to the central power and usually not from the area, was placed in charge of a district. Each officer was given nearly absolute authority. Within the guidelines of the center, the district was ruled by a plenipotentiary, an agent of the center expressing the sovereign's will throughout the periphery. Frequent transfers, a well organized central bureaucracy, and well trained district officers could maintain large areas with minimum staff. The duties of revenue

collection and maintenance of law and order, the historic function of the district official, required intimate knowledge of local affairs, and when well-established and running smoothly, this system facilitates an intensive amount of information and collection at the bottom and relatively easy control from the top. The mediator and the linchpin was the district officer...' (Elliot L. Tepper, 'The Administration and Rural Reform', an essay included in *Rural Development in Bangladesh*, edited by Robert D. Stevens, Hamza Alavi, and Peter J. Bertocci, p. 37).

26　In Europe, the state's right to impose taxes was dependent on the consent of the estates, particularly the nobility, whose growing power led to the development of parliament and of the slogan, 'no taxation without representation'.

27　B.B. Misra, *The Indian Middle Classes*, p. 307.

From a sample survey conducted by Taub in Orissa, it is found that the predominance of upper castes in professions has not changed in India even after two decades of independence. 'Brahmins, the highest group, traditionally were priests, teachers and advisors to Kings. As priests, they have had the sole right to perform rituals. Ksatriyas were traditionally the warrior and ruling classes. Some scribe castes also claim Ksatriya status.... The Vaisyas are the business castes; and the Sudras who represent the bulk of the population are the agriculturists and other forms of labourers (the reader should note, however, that these divisions represent the prescription of a theological system. It is not clear that in practice the divisions were ever adhered to strictly. Historically, there have been exceptions, such as Brahmin and Vaisya kings).... with this brief description completed, we turn to the sample. Among the Hindus in the Indian Administrative Service, 15 of 23 (65%) are Brahmins. Six of the 10 Hindu engineers (60%) are Brahmins, and 5 out of 9 Hindu educators (56%) are Brahmins.... A further breakdown is interesting. Among the Indian Administrative Service, 15 members are Brahmins, 7 are Ksatriyas, and 1 is Vaisya. There are no Sudras among this group.... By comparison, the engineers include 1 Sudra among their ranks ... and educators contribute 2 each' (Richard P. Taub, *Bureaucrats Under Stress*, pp. 63–5).

28　V. Subramaniam, 'Administrators and politicians'.

29　Ibid.

30　S. Kochanek, *Business and Politics in India*, p. 270.

Subramaniam refers to this commitment to institutional mission as 'the professional consciousness of the middle class.... The Indian middle class had built up a strong professional consciousness and a commitment to non-interference by non-professionals in the professions' ('Administrators and politicians').

31　R.P. Taub, *Bureaucrats Under Stress*, p. 167.

32　Bhagwati has given an example of how the controls benefit the state functionaries (politicians and civil servants). 'For example, the distribution and sale of motor-cars was controlled from May, 1959 under the Industries (Development and Regulations) Act and an informal but effective price control was exercised. An important part of the distributive system was the allocation of a quota for official allotment to civil servants and politicians in government on a priority basis.' He adds the following as a footnote to the above statement: 'From a sociological point of view, it is interesting that controls (such as on cars), which redounded to the benefit of the groups recommending and implementing the controls, were more readily implemented than the controls (on food grains distribution, for example) which would have far greater, and ethically more acceptable, impact on income distribution' (J.N. Bhagwati and P. Desai, *India: Planning for Industrialisation*, pp. 276–7).

33 R.P. Taub, *Bureaucrats Under Stress*, p. 170.
34 *Report of the Committee on Distribution of Income and Levels of Living*, p. 30.
35 R.K. Hazari, *Structure of the Corporate Private Sector*.
36 *Industrial Planning and Licensing Policy, Final Report, 1967*.
37 Ibid.
38 *Industrial Licensing Policy Inquiry Committee Report*, 1969, p. 95.
39 *Report of the Committee on Distribution of Income and Levels of Living*, pp. 30–1.
40 Some of the important features of the joint sector are: (i) The joint sector will not be allowed in the Schedule A of the 1956 I.P.R. or in the areas reserved for small-scale industry. (ii) If any of the participants in the joint sector belongs to a large industrial house or a foreign majority concern, authorization from the Central Government will be needed. (iii) No private concern or person should be allowed to own more than 25% of the paid-up capital without prior approval from the Central Government.
41 Tata Memorandum to Prime Minister Indira Gandhi, 17 May 1972.
42 *Report of the Committee on Distribution of Income and Levels of Living*, p. 33.
43 G.D.H. Cole, *What Everybody Wants to Know About Money*, p. 511.
44 S. Kochanek, *Business and Politics in India*, p. 267.
45 Ibid., p. 269.
46 'In the last two years there has been very little investment activity in the private sector, particularly the organised sector. In fact, additional investment in the organised sector has almost come to a stand-still. At the same time the public sector has proceeded ahead with its Plan outlay and has allocated to itself for purpose of Plan expenditure Rs 4026 crores in the first two years of the Fourth Plan ('A Critique of the Fourth Five Year Plan by the Indian Institute of Public Opinion', vol. XI, no. 10, reprinted in *Some Problems of India's Economic Policy*, ed. C.D. Wadhva, p. 147). The *Economic Times* (Calcutta, 14 February 1977) agrees with the above assertion and states that the large 'industrial houses were not allowed to expand for several years except under certain circumstances.'
47 If we take into consideration the galloping rate of inflation since 1966–7, it is very likely that the increments in the total assets are not as significant as the figures indicate.

48 *Economic Times* (Calcutta, 14 February 1977).
49 *Annual Report of the Working of Industrial and Commercial Undertakings of the Central Government, 1974–5*, p.3.
50 Ibid.
51 Ibid.
52 Ibid., p.6.
53 The data on turnover, gross profit and net profit of the running concerns in the Public Sector Undertakings for the year 1970–1 have been taken from the *Annual Report on the Working of Industrial and Commercial Undertakings of the Central Government, 1971–2.*
54 *Annual Report on the Working of Industrial and Commercial Undertakings of the Central Government, 1974–5*, p. 88.
55 Ibid., p. 126.
56 *Industrial Policy Resolution, 1956.*
57 Despite the fact that the state can tap capital from sources other than banks – which, along with the state financial institutions are the only source of capital for the private corporate sector (except, of course, for the ploughing back of profits and dividends) – a growing proportion of bank loans in recent years has been diverted towards public sector enterprises. 'There has been a distinct shift in the deployment of commercial bank credit in favour of the public sector *vis-à-vis* the private sector in recent years. One out of every four rupees lent by commercial banks today is accounted for by the public sector compared with one out of every twelve rupees seven or eight years ago. Actual borrowing by the public sector outstanding as at the end of June 1976 amounted to Rs 3,342 crores, whereas they stood at just Rs 267 crores in June 1968 (i.e., on the eve of nationalisation of the large commercial banks), representing a rise of 1150 per cent.... Since the extent in the rise in borrowings in the public sector has been much more marked than in the private sector, the share of the public sector in the aggregate bank credit has gone up from 8.6 per cent in June 1968 to 29.0 per cent in June 1976, while that of the private sector has dwindled from 91.4 per cent to 71.0 per cent.... The growing share of the public sector in the deployment of commercial bank credit is also well illustrated by the sharp increase in the amount of credit authorised in respect of this sector under the Reserve Bank's Credit Authorisation Scheme since March 1973 when the public sector's undertakings including State Electricity Boards were brought under the purview of the scheme. The total credit limits in respect of these undertakings in force as at the end of June 1972 amounted to barely Rs 742 crores, representing 17.2 per cent of the aggregate credit limits of Rs 4,306 crores. By the end of June 1976, they had gone up to as much as Rs 4,440 crores, representing no less than 52.4 per cent of the aggregate credit limits of Rs 8,476 crores' (*Economic Times*, Calcutta, 28 March 1977). See also the table on p. 257.
58 In India public sector enterprises have definite status in law. As described in the *Annual Report on the Working of Industrial Undertakings of the Central Government (1974–75)*, they are 'statutory Corporations or Companies registered under the India's Companies' Act' (p. 1).

(Table to Note 57)

	(Rs crores) as at the end of June				
	1972	*1973*	*1974*	*1975*	*1976*
Working capital†	683	1,870	2,254	2,390	4,157
Sale of machinery on deferred payment basis	13	14	21	21	34
Term finance	46	131	208	233	249
Total – public sector units	742	2,015	2,483	2,644	4,440
Total credit limits – all units	4,306	5,857	6,699	7,253	8,476
Share of public sector units in total credit limits (%)	17.2	34.4	37.1	36.4	52.4

† Includes cash credit/overdrafts, bills purchased/discounted, and export finance.
Source: *Economic Times* (Calcutta, 28 March 1977).

59 'the depression of the 1930s had had disastrous effects on French industry – alone among the industries of the advanced Western countries, it had not managed to get back to the level of output reached in 1929, the high point of the prosperity of the 1920s. The First Plan of Modernization, launched by Monnet in 1946, formulated its production targets in relation to the 1929 figures. This was the summit of French economic achievement which now had to be recaptured' (Andrew Shonfield, *Modern Capitalism*, p. 125). Thus, French planning was, to a great extent, a response to a crisis in capitalism. Speaking on the nature of planning Shonfield says: 'One of the senior officials of the Commissariat du Plan once described the actual process of planning during the 1950s as "a rather clandestine affair". It relied essentially on the close contacts established between a number of like-minded men in the civil service and big business. Organized labour, small business and, most of the time, the ministers of the government of the day were passed by' (p. 131). Moreover, Shonfield clearly states that the aim of economic planning in France as well as in other capitalist countries was to generate confidence in the business community so that they would make further investment (p. 134).
60 In India the situation is reversed. Here the chairman or managers of public enterprises enjoy the status of a joint secretary or a secretary of the Indian Administrative service. In India, the stranglehold of the state over public enterprises through these bureaucrats is so complete that even a leftist journal *EPW*, in a post editorial, bemoans the lack of autonomy of public enterprises. The journal contends that the very bestowal of the status of secretary or joint secretary on a manager of a public enterprise means that 'the professional leader of an industry was not worthy of recognition in his own right but acquired authority and status only by virtue of his designation in the administrative hierarchy.

The secretary and the secretariat remained supreme and in command in the arrangement [emphasis added]. . . . There were occasions when discussion in the SAIL board [a public sector enterprise] and at other levels in the undetaking, were choked by Wadud Khan [the chairman of the enterprise] by contending that his ruling would prevail, however strong the reservation of others, because he was putting to them the directive of the government from his position as Secretary to the government' (*EPW*, 16 October 1976, p. 1649).

61 J. O'Connor, *The Fiscal Crisis of the State*, pp. 180–8.

7 The social economy of Indian agriculture and its effect on industrialization and the state

1 'Large landholders can raise loans, due to approved security, at rates varying from 9 to 12 per cent in most provinces. But in the case of small cultivators who constitute the bulk of the cultivators, rates charged . . . may be up to 300 per cent. The rate of interest charged per annum on grain loans is generally 50 per cent, but rises up to 100 per cent in several cases' ('Economic Background of Social Policy', *I.L.O. Report*, 1947, p. 46).

2 K. Marx, *Capital*, III, p. 925.

3 The growing impoverishment of many colonies, and as a result their declining buying power (i.e., the relative diminishing surplus extraction), forced the colonizing countries in recent years to seek their markets elsewhere. Despite the availability of low-priced agricultural products, particularly food, from the commonwealth countries or her erstwhile colonies, England had to forgo this privilege to be eligible to enter the E.E.C. where her industrial products could find a market in the face of a relative decline of the colonial market. The erstwhile colonial markets have shrunk (for the metropolitan centres) not only as a result of increasing tariff barriers for foreign products, but also due to their declining buying power.

4 *Report of the Indian Statutory (Simon) Commission 1930*, vol. I, p. 340.

5 *Report of the Land Revenue (Floud) Commission of Bengal, 1940.*

6 M.B. Nanavati and J.J. Anjaria, *The Indian Rural Problem*, pp. 91–2.

7 *Report of the Indian Famine Commission, 1880.*

8 Congress Economic and Political Studies, No. 2, 1936, cited in R.P. Dutt, *India Today*, p. 256.

9 Ibid.
   The Simon Commission reported in 1930 that the self-sufficiency of the Indian villages limited the scope of internal excess to a few articles such as salt, kerosine oil, and alcoholic liquors, for which the rural areas are dependent on extraneous supply.

10 *Report on the Improvement of Indian Agriculture (Voelcker), 1891*, p. 10.

11 Cited in P.A. Wadia and K.T. Merchant, *Our Economic Problem*, p. 177.

12 H.H. Mann, *Land and Labour in a Deccan Village*, vol. I, p. 46.

13 *Report of the Royal Commission on Agriculture, 1928*, p. 292.
14 B. Sen, *Evolution of Agrarian Relations in India*, p. 141.
15 See *National Sample Surveys on Agriculture*, 8th, 16th, 17th, and 26th Rounds.
16 The Indian peasant's situation is comparable with that of the Irish peasants in the nineteenth century who were probably not as thoroughly exploited as those in India. 'We are not now speaking of conditions, in which ground-rent, the form of landed property adapted to the capitalist mode of production, formally exists without the capitalist mode of production itself, so that the tenant is not an industrial capitalist, nor the mode of his management a capitalist one. Such is the case in Ireland. The tenant is here generally a small farmer. What he pays to the landlord in the shape of rent absorbs frequently not merely a part of his profit, that is, of his own surplus-labour, to which he is entitled as the possessor of his own instruments of production, but also a part of his normal wages, which he would receive under different conditions for the same amount of labour' (Marx, *Capital*, III, p. 733).

In other words, what the peasant gets from his labour on the land is less than what he can get by selling his labour power to a capitalist. But the problem is that where there are no industrial opportunities, as in India, there is no buyer for his labour power. Hence, he has no other alternative but to depress his consumption and surrender major portions of the product of his labour on the land (as absolute rent) to the landlord just to have access to the means of production (land). It has been observed in studies in the economics of farm management in India (1953–8) that when values are imputed to the family labour on smallholdings at the current wage rate, income generated from these holdings is less than their cost of production inclusive of imputed wages. On the basis of imputed wages farms below ten acres constituting about 80 per cent of total farms in India are operating at a constant loss. Why, then, are they being operated? It is because family labour cannot get employment outside agriculture.
17 Marx, *Capital*, III, pp. 925–6.
18 'Landed property is conditioned on the monopolisation of certain portions of the globe by private persons, for the purpose of making these portions the exclusive spheres of their private will and keeping all others away from it. With this in mind, the problem is to ascertain the economic value, that is, the employment of this monopoly on the basis of capitalist production. *With the legal power of these persons to use or misuse certain portions of the globe nothing is settled. The use of this power depends wholly upon economic conditions*, which are independent of their will. The legal conception itself signifies nothing else but that the landowner may do with the soil what the owner of commodities may do with them. And this conception, this legal conception of free property in land, arises in the ancient world only with the dissolution of the organic order of society, and in the modern world only with the development of capitalist production. Into Asia it has been imported by Europeans in but a few places. In that part of our work, which deals with primitive accumulation. . . . we have seen that this mode of production [capitalist

mode] presupposes on the one hand the separation of the direct producers from their position as mere attachments to the soil (in their capacity of bondsmen, serfs, slaves, etc.), on the other hand the expropriation of the mass of the people from the land. *To this extent the monopoly of landed property is a historical premise, and remains the basis of the capitalist mode of production,* just as it does of all other modes of production, which rests on the exploitation of the masses in one form or another. *But that form of landed property, which the capitalist mode of production meets in its first stages, does not suit its requirements.* It creates for itself that form of property in land, which is adapted to its requirements, by subordinating agriculture to the dominion of capital. It transforms feudal landed property, tribal property, small peasants' property in mark communes, whatever may be their legal form, into the economic form corresponding to the requirements of capitalism. It is one of the great outcomes of the capitalist mode of production, that it transforms agriculture from a merely empirical and mechanically perpetuated process of the least developed part of society into a consciously scientific application of agronomics. . . . that it detaches property in land on the one side from the relations between master and servant, and on the other hand totally separates land as an instrument of production from property in land and landowners, for whom it represents merely a tribute of money, which he collects by force of his monopoly from the industrial capitalist, the capitalist farmer...' (Marx, *Capital*, III, pp. 722–4, emphasis added).

   In India, what the landowners extract from the tenants (peasants, sharecroppers, etc.) is not capitalist ground rent (i.e., the surplus over the average rate of profit on capital), but pre-capitalist forced surplus labour. In this sense, the property in land in India has failed to generate capitalist property relations.

19 Ibid., p. 383–5.
20 Ibid., p. 391.
21 See H. Alavi, 'India and the colonial mode of production' and Geoffrey Kay's illuminating discussion about the subordination of merchant capital to industrial capital in *Development and Underdevelopment: A Marxist Analysis*, pp. 95–107.

   In this connection it may be pointed out that it was the merchant capital in Europe which first emerged as capital (in money form) by tapping its own rentier classes' consumption. The consumption requirements of rentier classes rose with the increasing commodity circulation which resulted from the opening of long-distance trade in Europe in the twelfth and thirteenth centuries. As we noted in the second chapter, the growth of trade not only augmented the coffers of the merchants, it also increased the exploitation of the peasants by the feudal lords whose needs for surplus continued to increase with the availability of more consumer goods resulting from expanding commerce. Thus, capital in Europe first appeared in the form of merchant capital long before it could bring production under its sway. However, this accumulation took place on the basis of an internal colonization of agriculture.

22 See List II of the seventh schedule of the Constitution of India.
23 *All India Report on Agricultural Census, 1970–71*, pp. 1–2.
24 *Review of the First Five Year Plan*, p. 315.
25 *A Study on Tenurial Conditions in Package Districts*, pp. 9–10.
26 *Review of the First Five Year Plan*, p. 320; for tenancy reforms, see *Agricultural Legislation in India*, vol. VI, 1955.
27 *Fourth Five Year Plan, A Draft Outline*, p. 130.
28 *Third Five Year Plan*, p. 223.
29 *Farm Management in India*, 1966, p. 102.
30 *Studies in the Economics of Farm Management in Muzaffarnagar District (U.P.)*, pp. 37–45.
31 Ibid.
32 Ibid.
   In 1960, Rs 15 per person per month was considered as just above subsistence expenditure. According to the F.M.S. (1954–5) the annual living expenses per member belonging to this size group (5 to 10 acres) covered the minimum required subsistence expense of Rs 15. The marginal and small households' expenditure per month was below this level.
33 Ibid.
34 See *Farm Management in India*, 1966; *Studies in the Economics of Farm Management in Muzaffarnagar District (U.P.)*; *Studies in the Economics of Farm Management in U.P.*; *Studies in the Economics of Farm Management in Madhya Pradesh*.
35 Ibid.
36 Ibid.
37 'The size of holdings in Punjab are comparatively bigger. It is estimated that 35% of the holdings in Punjab are of 6 hectares or above and cover about 65% of the area, and as such they can justify the use of small agricultural machinery. The gross irrigated area in Punjab in 1970–71 was about 65 per cent. The fertiliser consumption in Punjab in 1968–69 was 35 kg of nutrient per hectare as compared to 1.1 kg in the country. As a result of all this food grains production in Punjab has been more than doubled in the last six years' (Twenty-first National Conference of the All-India Kisan Sabha, Bhatinda, p. 16).
38 'The average size of an operational holding of 2.66 hectares was made up of 5.74 fragments (parcels of land) on the average' (*Progress of Agriculture in India*, p. 6).
39 In many parts of India, attached farm servants are recruited from the lower and 'scheduled' castes. The nature of the exploitation of these weaker sections of Indian society and the character of their growing resistance have been vividly brought out by Kathleen Gough in her article on 'Harijans of Tanjavur' (K. Gough and H.P. Sharma (eds.), *Imperialism and Revolution in South Asia*, pp. 222–45).
40 *Economic and Political Weekly*, August 1974, p. 1307.
41 Bijan Sen, *Agrarian Relations in Andhra*, Ganamukti Studies, no. 4.
42 See chapter 4, note 3 and chapter 5, note 1.
43 *India: A Reference Annual, 1975*, p. 248. This figure includes people employed in small industries.

44 A. Rudra, *Relative Rates of Growth of Agriculture and Industry*, p. 15.
45 'The implements and tools used by the cultivators in India are old-fashioned and out-of-date and have hardly undergone any change towards improvement during all these centuries. A majority of the implements and tools used by the cultivators are manufactured and repaired by the local workmen.... The total number of agricultural implements in the country in 1961 was as follows:

Wooden ploughs	38,372,000
Improved ploughs (iron)	2,298,000
Tractors	31,016

The wooden plough and small implements are owned practically by all the farmers in the country, but improved implements have not become much popular with the cultivators.... One of the most important reasons of our low productivity is that ... our cultivators have been using the same wooden implements and there has been no change in them at all. The wooden plough is an old implement, the furrows of which are only four to five inches in depth and the soil which it moves is at the same depth. It means that only four to five inches deep layer is being used for production of crops' (S.C. Jain, *Agricultural Policy in India*, pp. 40–41).
46 See *Studies in the Economics of Farm Management*.
47 Ibid.
48 'The two methods of "solving" the agrarian question in developing bourgeois Russia correspond to two paths of development of capitalism in agriculture. I call these two paths the Prussian path and the American path. The first is characterised by the fact that medieval relationships in landownership are not liquidated at one stroke; they gradually adapt themselves to capitalism and for this reason capitalism for a long time retains semi-feudal features. Prussian landlordism was not crushed by the bourgeois revolution; it survived and became the basis of Junker economy, which is capitalist at bottom, but which still keeps the rural population in a certain degree of dependence, as for example the Gesindeordnung, etc. As a consequence, the social and political domination of the Junker was strengthened for many decades after 1848 and the development of the productive forces of German agriculture proceeded very much more slowly than in America. On the contrary, in America, it was not the slave economy of the big landlords that served as the basis of capitalist agriculture (the Civil War crushed the slave estates) but the free economy of the free farmer working on free land, land free from all medieval fetters, free from serfdom and feudalism, on the one hand, and free from the fetters of private property in land, on the other. Land was given away in America out of an enormous land fund, at a nominal price, and it is only on a new, capitalist base that private property in land has now developed there' (V.I. Lenin, *Selected Works*, vol. I, pp. 210–11).
49 See E.J. Hobsbawm and G. Rude, *Captain Swing*, pp. 3–4; Marx, *Capital*, I, pp. 744–5.
50 In the U.S., the clearing of land was not necessary for the introduction of the capitalist method of farming.
51 Marx, *Capital*, I, pp. 744–5.

52 Lenin, *Selected Works*, I, p. 346.
53 In fact, as the number of workers increases in agriculture, whatever growth (average annual growth rate in agriculture was 2.9 per cent for the period 1949–50 to 1970–71 — *Progress of Agriculture in India*, p. 13) is registered in agriculture is consumed by the increasing population in agriculture. The average annual rate of increase in population for the decades 1950–51 to 1970–71 was slightly less than the average annual growth rate in agriculture (*Census of India, 1971*, paper 1 of 1971, Supplement, p. 36).
54 'The principal difficulty of India's agriculture is the continued exposure of vast areas in different parts of the country to vagaries of weather reflected by erratic rainfall, droughts, floods which setback occurred in 1965–66 and again in 1966–67, when widespread droughts resulted in sharp declines in the production of foodgrains' (*Progress of Agriculture in India*, p. 9).
55 V.S. Vyas, 'Structural change in agriculture and the small farm sector', p. 30.
56 Japan, as it was not colonized or semi-colonized, could become a full-fledged industrial nation before the First World War when the birth rate began to far outstrip the death rate (due to new discoveries in medical science) in most Third World countries. As a result, the standard of living (including literacy) improved in Japan leading to a falling death rate (due to new discoveries in medical science). Moreover, by that time, Japan was able to transfer a sizeable section of her agricultural population to the industrial sector (see Table 7.16).
57 Marx, *Capital*, III, p. 807.
58 S. Roy, *Bharater Dainya*, p. 177.
59 See *Report of the Working Group on Agricultural Implements*, cited in ibid.
60 Marx, *Capital*, III, p. 807.
61 See A.M. Carr-Saunders, 'Past growth and present trends', cited in R.P. Dutt, *India Today*, p. 50n.
62 Ibid.
63 *Statistical Yearbook* (New York: United Nations, 1978).
64 'About 11 per cent of the land surface of the Earth is considered suitable for cultivation. The rest is either too mountainous, too cold, too dry or wet, or too infertile' (Funk and Wagnall's *New Encyclopedia*, vol. 1, 1973, p. 291). In respect of cultivable land, India is one of the most fortunate countries of the world.
65 L.J. Zimmerman, *Poor Lands, Rich Lands*, p. 68.
66 We note that India's inability to industrialize in the eighteenth and nineteenth centuries led to the overcrowding of agriculture. In the first three quarters of the nineteenth century the destruction of Indian industry took place, leading to the ruin of formerly populous industrial centres.
67 See Kingsley Davis in S. Kuznets *etal. Economic Growth Brazil, India, Japan*, pp. 292–30.
68 F.W. Notestein, *Problems of Policy in Relation to Areas of Heavy Pressure*, Demographic Studies of Selected Areas of Rapid Growth, pp. 152–3, cited in ibid., p. 289.

69 'Japan, in many ways a model of rapid development, between the years 1878 and 1937 increased the net income of her agriculture sevenfold; but during the same interval she increased the net income of her non-agricultural enterprises by about forty-seven times. During this period, government revenue realised through taxation of agriculture declined by one half while those coming from non-agricultural enterprises increased by eight - nine times. Obviously, support for Japan's development did not derive its main or long-term sustenance from the farmer' (Stanley A. Hetzler, *Technological Growth and Social Change*, p. 120).

70 M. Weiner, 'The Politics of South Asia', in G.A. Almond and G.J. Coleman, *The Politics of the Developing Areas*, p. 175.

71 'When civilisations clash, the consequences are dramatic. Today's world is still embroiled in them. One civilisation can get the better of another: this was the case with India following the British victory at Plassey which marked the beginning of a new era for Britian and the whole world' (Fernand Braudel, *Capitalism and Material Life, 1400–1800*, p. 64).

72 S. Hetzler, *Technological Growth and Social Change*, p. 138.

73 It is very often claimed that Japan could develop rapidly on western lines because Japanese feudalism had close resemblances with European feudalism. As Weber points out, Japanese feudalism, unlike European and like oriental feudalism, was an office. 'Japanese feudalism, too, does not represent a complete feudatory system. The Japanese daimyo was not a feudatory vassal, but a vassal committed to supply definite war contingents, to provide guard units and to pay a fixed tribute; within his own district he exercised administrative, judicial and military authority practically in his own name, in the manner of a territorial ruler. He could be transferred to another district for disciplinary reasons. That he was not a vassal as such is demonstrated by the fact that the Shogun's real vassals (fudai), if damiyas-districts had been granted to them, could suffer transfer, because of their personal dependence for reasons of political expediency without any default on their own part. This very fact also proves that the district granted was an office, not a fief' (Max Weber, *Economy and Society*, p. 1075). India *jagirdars* and *zamindars* had more autonomy than the Japanese *daimyos*. Moreover, as in India, land was held in common by the village community in Japan. However, the interdependence between cultivation and artisan industry in India provided a more stable basis for the existing mode of production in India than in Japan.

74 S.N. Eisenstadt, *The Protestant Ethic and Modernization*, p. 53.

75 M. Weber, *The Protestant Ethic and the Spirit of Capitalism*, p. 183.

76 Marx, 'The Future Results of British Rule in India', *New York Daily Tribune*, 5 August 1853.

77 Ibid.

78 M.D. Morris, in his excellent study of 'Values as an obstacle to economic growth in South Asia', pointed out that there was no shortage of entrepreneurs and labourers in India, but they had very little economic opportunities to realize their desires. He also argued that the values and institutions in India did not remain static; they tended to adapt

themselves to changing economic environments (*Journal of Economic History*, vol. 27).

79 Marx, 'Future Results of British Rule in India', *New York Daily Tribune*, 5 August 1853.

80 Ibid.

81 Ibid.

82 See A.G. Frank, *Capitalism and Underdevelopment in Latin America*.

83 Marx, *Capital*, I, p. 493.

84 See A. Emmanuel, *Unequal Exchange: A Study of the Imperialism of Trade*; R. Howard, 'Expatriate business and the African response in Ghana, 1886–1939', Ph. D. dissertation, McGill University, June 1976 – especially the conclusion.

85 'to the degree that large industry develops, the creation of real wealth comes to depend less on labour time and on the amount of labour employed than on the power of the agencies set in motion during labour time, whose "powerful effectiveness" is itself in turn out of all proportion to the direct labour time spent on their production, but depends rather on the general state of science and on the progress of technology, or the application of this science to production. (The development of this science, especially natural science, and all others with the latter, is itself in turn related to the development of material production.) Agriculture, e.g., becomes merely the application of the science of material metabolism, its regulation for the greatest advantage of the entire body of society. Real wealth manifests itself, rather – and large industry reveals this – in the monstrous disproportion between the labour time applied, and its product, as well as in the qualitative imbalance between labour, reduced to a pure abstraction, and the power of the production process it superintends. Labour no longer appears so much to be included within the production process; rather, the human being comes to relate more as watchman and regulator to the production process itself. (What holds for machinery holds likewise for the combination of human activities and the development of human intercourse.)' (Karl Marx, *Grundrisse*, pp. 704–5).

86 F. Engels, 'The Peasant Question in France and Germany', in Marx and Engels, *Selected Works*, p. 623.

87 Lenin, *Selected Works*, I, p. 300.

88 Marx, 'The Eighteenth Brumaire of Louis Bonaparte', in K. Marx and F. Engels, *Selected Works*, pp. 170–1.

89 Ibid.

90 Marx, *Pre-Capitalist Economic Formations*, p. 69.

91 The colonial government derived its power from the metropolitan bourgeoisie, and thus remained superior to all indigenous social classes. It did not have to pose as the representative of the small peasants to keep in check the political aspirations of the indigenous bourgeoisie.

92 See Mrs Gandhi's Twenty-point Programme.

93 Marx, 'The Eighteenth Brumaire', p. 176.

8   Conclusion

1　See: R. Miliband, 'Marx and the state' The Socialist Register;
　　S. Avineri, *The Social and Political Thought of Karl Marx*; H. Lefebvre,
　　The Sociology of Marx, ch. 5; H. Draper, *Karl Marx's Theory of
　　Revolution*, chs. 14, 15, 16 and 19.
2　'In a word, the whole aristocracy is convinced of the need to govern in the
　　interests of the bourgeoisie; but at the same time it is determined not to
　　allow the latter to take charge of the matter itself' (Marx, 'Perspec-
　　tives for the New Coalition Government', *New York Times*, 28 Jan. 1853).
3　However, once a mode of production becomes dominant in a social
　　formation, it, to a great extent, determines the extent of the activity
　　social classes exhibit, as exemplified in the relative passive role of the
　　peasantry in the Asiatic mode of production.
4　R. Miliband, 'Marx and the state'.
5　D. McLellan, *The Thought of Karl Marx*, pp. 182–3.
6　Ibid.
7　D. McLellan, *Marx*, p. 61.
8　K. Marx and F. Engels, *The German Ideology*, p. 80.
9　K. Marx, *Grundrisse*, p. 884.
10　Marx and Engels, 'The Communist Manifesto', in *Selected Works*, p. 37.
11　F. Engels, 'The Origin of Family, Private Property and the State',
　　Selected Works, p. 578.
12　K. Marx, 'Moralising Criticism and Critical Morality', in Marx and
　　Engels, *Collected Works*, VI, p. 326.
13　In its attempt to acquire independence from the hegemony of the feudal
　　class the absolutist state forced the feudal lords to disband their
　　retainers. The demobilized retainers formed a part of the free wage
　　workers. 'The prelude of the revolution that laid the foundation of the
　　capitalist mode of production, was played in the last third of the 15th,
　　and the first decade of the 16th century. A mass of free proletarians was
　　hurled on the labour-market by the breaking-up of the bands of feudal
　　retainers.... Although the royal power [absolute monarchy], itself a
　　product of bourgeois development, *in its strife after absolute sovereignty*
　　[i.e. absolute independence] *forcibly hastened on the dissolution of these
　　bands of retainers*, it was by no means the sole cause of it' (Marx, *Capital*,
　　I, p. 789, emphasis added).
14　K. Marx, 'Moralising Criticism and Critical Morality, in Marx and
　　Engels, *Collected Works*, VI, p. 328.
15　F. Engels, 'Preface to the Peasant War in Germany', in Marx and
　　Engels, *Selected Works*, p. 243.
16　K. Marx, 'Lassalle', in Marx and Engels, *Collected Works*, VIII, p. 464.
17　K. Marx, 'Moralising Criticism and Critical Morality', p. 333.
18　F. Engels, 'The Constitutional Question in Germany', in Marx and
　　Engels, *Collected Works*, VI, p. 88.
19　'Like the French and English nobility of the last century, the German
　　nobility employed the rising level of civilisation only to squander its
　　fortune magnificently on pleasures in big cities. Between the nobility

and the bourgeoisie began that competition in social and intellectual education, in wealth and display which everywhere precedes the political dominance of the bourgeoisie and ends, like every other form of competition, with the victory of the richer side. The provincial nobility turned into a court nobility, only thereby to be ruined all the more quickly and surely. The three per cent revenues of the nobility went down before the fifteen per cent profit of the bourgeoisie, the three-per-centers resorted to mortgages, to credit banks for the nobility and so on, in order to be able to spend in accordance with their station, and only ruined themselves so much the quicker. The few landed gentry wise enough not to ruin themselves formed with the newly emerging bourgeois landowners a new class of industrial landowners. This class carries on agriculture without feudal illusions and without the nobleman's nonchalance, as a business, an industry with the bourgeois appliances of capital, expert knowledge and work' (ibid., p. 81).

20 Ibid., p. 78.
21 Ibid., p. 79.
22 Ibid., p. 89.
23 Ibid.
24 Ibid.
25 Ibid., p. 90.
26 Their exposition of the autonomy of the state is more comprehensive than Poulantzas's exposition.
27 Marx and Engels, *Selected Correspondence*, p. 368.
28 H. Lefebvre, *The Sociology of Marx*, p. 126.
29 Marx and Engels, *Selected Works*, II, p. 543.
30 The following commentary and note by the editor of 'the *Correspondence of Marx and Engels (1846–1895)*, V. Adoratsky, shows how Lassalle and Bismarck conspired to use the proletariat against the dominant classes including the bourgeoisie.'When the questions of universal suffrage and of the Schleswig-Holstein war came up, Lassalle was prepared to support Bismarck, who was proposing to utilise universal suffrage for his reactionary ends – against the bourgeoisie – and pointed out to him that the introduction of universal adult suffrage, which would in fact have meant a *coup d'état* against the bourgeois progressive majority of the Prussian Parliament, must, whatever happened, take place before the war. "Why can you do anything you like in peace time," Lassalle asks Bismarck in a letter written at the end of January or the beginning of February, 1864. "Why did I admit to you as long ago as last May that, so long as no external conflict arose, our country would quietly acquiesce even in the most severe absolutism?... In peace time the interests of private life completely predominate and reduce the mood of the people to one of indifference, whatever conditions may be." At the same time Lassalle placed all his literary activities at Bismarck's disposal. He sent Bismarck, for instance, the proof-sheets of his Bastiat-Schulze before it appeared and asked Bismarck to protect him from judicial confiscation of a book which "will lead ... to the most thorough destruction of the progressive party and of the whole liberal

bourgeoisie" (letter of 5 February 1864; this and the preceding quotations from letters are taken from Gustav Mayer's pamphlet, 'Bismarck and Lassalle', Berlin, 1928). The mistrust felt by Marx and Engels for Lassalle, their constant struggle against his false theory of the state, derived from Hegel are brilliantly justified by their correspondence [Engels's letter to Marx on 27 January 1865]' (*The Correspondence of Marx and Engels, 1846–1895*, pp. 178–9). Both Bismarck and Bonaparte took resort to universal adult franchise to maintain the state's independence from the encroachment of the bourgeoisie, the former by matching the proletariat against the bourgeoisie, the latter by drawing the support of the peasants. The latter phenomenon has been described by Marx in detail, in 'The Eighteenth Brumaire' and 'The Class Struggle in France'.

31 'And if the political power, that is, Bismarck, is attempting to organize its own bodyguard proletariat to keep the political activity of the bourgeoisie in check, what else is that if not a necessary and quite familiar Bonapartist recipe which pledges the state to nothing more, as far as the workers are concerned, than a few benevolent phrases and at the utmost to a minimum of state assistance for building societies *à la* Louis Bonaparte? The best proof of what the workers have to expect from the Prussian state lies in the utilization of the French milliards [refers to five thousand million franc indemnity imposed on France at the end of the Franco-Prussian War in 1871] which have given a new, short reprieve to the independence of the Prussian state machine in regard to society. Has even a single taler of all these milliards been used to provide shelter for those Berlin working class families which have been thrown on to the streets? On the contrary. As autumn approached, the state caused to be pulled down even those few miserable hovels which had given them a temporary roof over their heads during the summer' (F. Engels, *The Housing Question*, p. 68).

32 The number of unemployed in India stood at 18.7 million; of these 16.1 million were in rural areas.

33 *American Economic Review,* May 1975.

Bibliography

(a) Government and public documents

Adam's Reports on Vernacular Education in Bengal and Behar 1838, ed. Rev. Long (Calcutta: 1868).

Agricultural Legislation in India, vol. II (1950).

Agricultural Legislation in India, vol. VI (1955).

All India Report on Agricultural Census, 1970–71.

Annual Report on the Working of Industrial and Commercial Undertakings of the Central Government, 1971–72.

Annual Report on the Working of Industrial and Commercial Undertakings of the Central Government, 1974–75.

Banking Commission Report, 1972.

Census of India, 1931, vol. I, part 1.

Census of India, 1951, vol. I, part 1B.

Communist Reply to Tata Memorandum, by H.K. Byas (New Delhi: Communist Party Publication, 1972).

Companies Act Amendment Committee, 1957.

Company Law Committee Report, 1950–51.

The Constitution of India, as modified up to October 1969.

The Director, Foreign Area Studies, *Area Handbook For India* (Washington, D.C.: American University, 1975).

Documents of the History of the Communist Party of India, vol. I, 1917–1922, ed. G. Adhikari (New Delhi: People's Publishing House, 1971).

Famine Enquiry Commission Report, 1945.

Farm Management in India: a study based on recent investigations (New Delhi: 1966).

First Five Year Plan (1950–55).

First Report of the National Income Committeee, 1951.

The Flight of Technical Personnel in Public Undertakings, 1964.

Fourth Five Year Plan, A Draft Outline.

I.L.O. Report 1938, 'Industrial Labour in India'.

India: A Reference Annual, 1975.

Indian Industrial Commission Minutes of Evidence, 1916–18.

The Indian Labour Year Book, 1972, Government of India, Ministry of Labour.

Industrial Licensing Policy Inquiry Committee Report, 1969.
Industrial Planning and Licensing Policy, Final Report, 1967.
Industrial Planning and Licensing Policy (Hazari Report), 1967.
Industrial Policy Resolution, 1956.
The Industries (Development and Regulations) Act, 1951 (Amended) (Delhi: 1966).
Karve Committee Report, 1955.
Khadi and Village Industries Commission, Patterns of Assistance for Khadi and village industries, 1971.
Land Reforms in India, 1955.
Lok Sabha Debates, Third Series, vol. II.
Lok Sabha, Ninth Report of the Estimate Committee.
Minutes of Evidence on the Affairs of the East India Company, 1813.
The Monopolies Enquiry Commission, 1964.
National Council of Applied Economic Research, All India Rural Household Survey, vol. II (Income, Investment and Saving) (1965).
Notes on Perspective Development: 1960–61 to 1975–76.
Parliamentary Papers, *The Fifth Report from the Select Committee on the Affairs of the East India Company* (House of Commons, 28 July 1812).
Parliamentary Papers, *The Fifth Report of the Committee of Secrecy Appointed by the House of Commons on the State of the East India Company* (London: 1773).
Parliamentary Papers, *The Fourth Report of the Committee of Secrecy Appointed by the House of Commons on the State of the East India Company* (London: 1773).
Parliamentary Papers, *The Ninth Report of the Committee of Secrecy Appointed by the House of Commons on the State of the East India Company* (London: 1783).
A Plan of Economic Development for India (Bombay Plan), 1945.
Pocket Book of Labour Statistics, 1977.
Progress of Agriculture in India (Directorate of Economics and Statistics, Ministry of Agriculture, October 1972).
Re-Examination of India's Administrative System with Special Reference to Administration of Government's Industrial and Commercial Enterprises (Paul Appleby's Report), 1956.
Report, Congress Select Committee on the Financial Obligation between Great Britain and India, 1931.
Report of Administrative Reforms Commission, 1966.
Report of the Central Banking Enquiry Committee, 1929.
Report of the Committee on Distribution of Income and Levels of Living, Part I, 1964.
Report of the Famine Commission, 1901.
Report of the Indian Famine Commission, 1880.
Report of the Indian Statutory (Simon) Commission, 1930 (vol. I).
Report of the Land Revenue (Floud) Commission of Bengal, 1940.
Report of the Managing Agency Enquiry Committee, 1966.
Report of the National Planning Committee, ed. K.T. Shah.
Report of the Royal Commission on Agriculture, 1928.

Report of the Taxation Enquiry Commission, 1953–54, vol I.
Report on the Improvement of Indian Agriculture, 1891.
Report on the Working and Administration of the Companies Act, 1956.
Reserve Bank of India's Review of the Karve Committee's Report.
Review of the First Five Year Plan.
The Royal Commission on Agriculture, 1928.
The Royal Commission on Indian Expenditures, 1896, vol. II.
Rural Banking Enquiry Committee, 1953.
Second Five Year Plan.
Studies in the Economics of Farm Management; Bangalore District (Mysore), 1959–60.
Studies in the Economics of Farm Management in Madhya Pradesh, Combined Report for the years 1955–6 and 1956–7.
Studies in the Economics of Farm Management in Muzaffarnagar District (U.P.), Report for the Year 1967–68.
Studies in the Economics of Farm Management in the Punjab, Combined Report, 1963.
Studies in the Economics of Farm Management in U.P., 1954–55.
Studies in the Economics of Farm Management in West Godavari District (Andhra Pradesh), Combined Report for the Period 1957–58 to 1959–60.
Study of Village Artisans (Planning Commission, Programme Evaluation Organisation, 1956).
A Study on Tenurial Conditions in Package Districts (Report by Wolf Ladejinsky), Planning Commission, 1965.
Tata Memorandum to Prime Minister Indira Gandhi, 17 May 1972.
Third Five Year Plan.
Third Five Year Plan, A Draft Outline.
Twenty-first National Conference of the All-India Kisan Sabha, Bhatinda (Punjab), 19th to 23rd September, 1973 (New Delhi: Alks Publication, 1974).
White Paper on National Accounts Statistics, 1960–61 to 1974–75 (Central Statistical Organisation, 1977).

(B) Books and articles

Adams, Brooks, *The Law of Civilization and Decay: An Essay on History* (New York, 1896: reprinted 1943).
Alavi, Hamza, 'Bangladesh and the crisis of Pakistan', in R. Miliband and J. Saville (eds), *The Socialist Register* (New York: Monthly Review Press, 1971).
Alavi, Hamza, 'The state in post-colonial societies: Pakistan and Bangladesh', in K. Gough and H.P. Sharma (eds), *Imperialism and Revolution in South Asia* (New York: Monthly Review Press, 1973).
Alavi, Hamza, 'India and the colonial mode of production', in R. Miliband and J. Saville (eds), *The Socialist Register* (New York: Monthly Review Press, 1975).

Almond, G.A., and Coleman, G.J., *The Politics of the Developing Areas* (Stanford University Press, 1973).

Avineri, Shlomo, *The Social and Political Thought of Karl Marx* (Cambridge University Press, 1971).

Avineri, Shlomo, *Marx's Socialism* (New York: Lieber-Atherton, 1973).

Balkrishna, *Commercial Relations Between India and England*, (London: George Routledge, 1924).

Bamat, Thomas, 'Relative state autonomy and capitalism in Brazil and Peru', *Insurgent Sociologist* (Spring, 1977).

Bandopadhya, R.D., *Banglar Itihas*, vol. 1 (Calcutta: Nababharat, 1974).

Baran, Paul A., *The Political Economy of Growth* (New York: Monthly Review Press, 1968).

Bernier, François, *Travels in the Moghul Empire* (New Delhi: S. Chand & Co, 1941, reprinted 1972).

Bettelheim, Charles, *India Independent* (New York: Monthly Review Press, 1971).

Bhagwati, J.N., and Desai, Padma, *India: Planning for Industrialisation* (London: Oxford University Press, 1970).

Bhalla, S., 'New relations of production in Haryana agriculture', *Political and Economic Weekly* (27 March 1976).

Bhargava, Brijkrishna, *Indigenous Banking in Ancient and Medieval India* (Bombay: Taraporevala, n.d.).

Birdwood, G.C.M., *The Industrial Arts of India* (London: Chapman & Hall, n.d.).

Bloch, Marc, *Feudal Society*, vols I and II (Chicago: University of Chicago Press, 1974).

Blyn, George, *Agricultural Trends in India, 1891–1947* (Philadelphia: University of Pennsylvania Press, 1966).

Braudel, Fernand, *Capitalism and Material Life, 1400–1800* (New York: Harper & Row, 1975).

Buchanan, Daniel Houston, *The Development of Capitalist Enterprise in India* (London: Frank Cass, 1966).

Chambers, J,D., 'Enclosure and labour supply in the industrial revolution', *Economic History Review*, 2nd series, vol. V, no. 3 (1953).

Chowdhury, S., *Trade and Commercial Organisation in Bengal, 1650–1720, with Special Reference to the English East India Company* (Calcuttaa: K.L. Mukhopadyay, 1975).

Cobban, Alfred, *A History of Modern France*, vol. 1: 1715–1799 (Harmondsworth: Penguin Books, 1977).

Cobban, Alfred, *A History of Modern France*, vol. 2: 1799–1871 (Harmondsworth: Penguin Books, 1977).

Cole, G.D.H., *What Everybody Wants to Know About Money* (London: Victor Gollancz, 1933).

Coulborn, R. (ed.), *Feudalism in History* (Hamden, Conn.: Archon Books, 1965).

Das, R., *Raja Rammohan* (Calcutta: Ashoke Pustakalya, 1973).

Desai, A.R., *Social Background of Indian Nationalism* (Bombay: Popular Book Depot, 1959).

Dhar, P.N. and Lydall, H.F., *The Role of Small Enterprises* (Bombay: Asia Publishing House, 1961).

Digby, William, *'Prosperous' British India* (New Delhi: Sagar Publications, 1969).

Dobb, Maurice, *Studies in the Development of Capitalism* (New York: International Publishers, 1975).

Draper, Hal, *Karl Marx's Theory of Revolution* (New York: Monthly Review Press, 1977).

Duby, Georges, *Rural Economy and Country Life in the Medieval West* (Columbia: University of South Carolina Press, 1968).

Dutt, B.B., *Town Planning in Ancient India* (Calcutta: Thecker, 1925).

Dutt, Rajani Palme, *India Today* (Calcutta: Manisha, 1970).

Dutt, Romesh C., *The Economic History of India*, 2 vols. (London: Routledge & Kegan Paul, 1906/1956).

Dutta, K.K., *History of Bengal Subah, 1740–1770* (Calcutta, 1936).

Eisenstadt, S.N., *The Protestant Ethic and Modernization* (New York: Basic Books, 1967).

Emmanuel, Arghiri, *Unequal Exchange: A Study of the Imperialism of Trade* (New York: Monthly Review Press, 1972).

Engels, F., *The Peasants' War in Germany*, (1850) (Moscow: Progress Publishers, 1969).

Engels, F., *The Housing Question* (1872–3) (Moscow: Progress Publishers, 1970).

Engels, F., 'The constitutional question in Germany', in K. Marx and F. Engels, *Collected Works*, vol. 6 (New York: International Publishers, 1976).

Engels, F., 'The Prussian Constitution', in K. Marx and F. Engels, *Collected Works*, vol. 6 (New York: International Publishers, 1976).

Epsing–Anderson, G., Friedland, R., and Wright, E.O., 'Modes of class struggle and the capitalist state', *Kapitalistate*, 4–5 (1966).

Frank, André Gunder, *Capitalism and Underdevelopment in Latin America* (New York: Monthly Review Press, 1967/1969).

Frank, André Gunder, *Latin America: Underdevelopment or Revolution* (New York: Monthly Review Press, 1969).

Gadgil, D.R., *The Industrial Evolution of India in Recent Times, 1860–1939* (Bombay: Oxford University Press, 1971).

Ganguli, B.N., *Readings in Indian Economic History* (London: Asia Publishing House, 1964).

Ghosal, U.N., *The Agrarian System of Ancient India* (Calcutta: University of Calcutta Press, 1930).

Goodnow, H.F., *The Civil Service of Pakistan* (New Haven, Conn: Yale University Press, 1964).

Gough, Kathleen, 'Harijans in Tanjavur', in K. Gough and H.P. Sharma (eds), *Imperialism and Revolution in South Asia* (New York: Monthly Review Press, 1973).

Gough, Kathleen, and H.P. Sharma (eds), *Imperialism and Revolution in South Asia* (New York: Monthly Review Press, 1973).

Habakkuk, H.J., 'English landownership, 1680–1740', *Economic History Review*, vol. X, no. 1 (1940).

274   *Bibliography*

Habib, Irfan, *The Agrarian System of Mughal India* (London: Asia Publishing House, 1963).

Hanson, A.H., *The Process of Planning* (London: Oxford University Press, 1966).

Harvey, David, *Social Justice and the City* (London: Edward Arnold, 1975).

Hayami, Yujiro, and Ruttan, V.W., *Agricultural Development: An International Perspective* (Baltimore: Johns Hopkins Press, 1971).

Hazari, R.K., 'Ownership and control: a study of intercorporate investment', *Economic Weekly* (2 February, 25 April and 3 December 1960).

Hazari, R.K., *Structure of the Corporate Private Sector* (Bombay: Asia Publishing House, 1966).

Hetzler, Stanley A., *Technological Growth and Social Change* (New York: Praeger, 1969).

Hibbert, A.B. 'The origins of the medieval town patriciate', *Past and Present* (February 1953).

Hill, Christopher, *Reformation to Industrial Revolution* (Harmondsworth: Penguin Books, 1975).

Hilton, Rodney (ed.), *The Transition from Feudalism to Capitalism* (London: New Left Books, 1976).

Hindess, Barry and Hirst, Paul Q., *Pre-Capitalist Modes of Production* (London/Boston: Routledge & Kegan Paul, 1975).

Hobsbawm, E.J., *Industry and Empire* (Harmondsworth: Penguin Books, 1969).

Hobsbawm, E.J., *The Age of Revolution* (London: Cardinal, 1973).

Hobsbawm, E.J., and Rude, George, *Captain Swing* (London: Lawrence and Wishart, 1969).

Hortense, Queen, *The Memoirs of Queen Hortense*, vol. I, (London: Thornton Butterworth, 1928).

Huberman, Leo, *Man's Worldly Goods* (New York/London: Monthly Review Press, 1968).

Huque, Azizul, *The Man Behind the Plough* (Calcutta: Book Company, 1939).

Jain, S.C., *Agricultural Policy in India* (Bombay: Allied Publishers, 1967).

Joshi, M.S., *The National Balance Sheet of India* (Bombay: University of Bombay, 1966).

Karim, N., *The Changing Society of India and Pakistan* (Dacca: Ideal Publications, 1961).

Kay, Geoffrey, *Development and Underdevelopment: A Marxist Analysis* (New York: St Martin's Press, 1975).

Kidron, M., *Foreign Investments in India* (London: Oxford University Press, 1965).

Knowles, L.C.A., *The Economic Development of the British Overseas Empire*, vol. I (London: George Routledge, 1928).

Kochanek, S.A., *Business and Politics in India* (Berkeley: University of California Press, 1974).

Kosambi, D.D., *An Introduction to the Study of Indian History* (Bombay: Popular Prakashan, 1975).

Krader, L., *The Asiatic Mode of Production* (Netherlands: Van Gorcum, 1976).

Kuczynski, Jurgen, *The Rise of the Working Class* (New York: McGraw-Hill, 1975).

Kuznets, S., Moore E.E., and Spengler, J.J. (eds), *Economic Growth: Brazil, India, Japan*, (Durham, N.C.: Duke University Press, 1955).

Lakhani, H.G., *Problems of Economic Development of India* (Bombay: New Literature Publishing Company, 1967).

Lamb, B.P., *India: A World in Transition* (New York: Praeger, 1966).

Lefebvre, George, *The Coming of the French Revolution* (Princeton, N.J.: Princeton University Press, 1973).

Lefebvre Henri, *The Sociology of Marx* (New York: Random House, 1969).

Lenin, V.I., *Capitalism and Agriculture* (New York: International Publishers, 1946).

Lenin, V.I., *National Liberation, Socialism and Imperialism* (New York: International Publishers, 1968).

Lenin, V.I., *Questions of the Socialist Organisation of the Economy* (Moscow: Progress Publishers, n.d.).

Lenin, V.I., *Selected Works*, vol. I (New York: International Publishers, n.d.).

Lichtheim, George, 'Marx and the Asiatic mode of production' in *Marx's Socialism*, ed. Shlomo Avineri (New York: Lieber-Atherton, 1973).

Macaulay, Lord, *The History of England from the Accession of James the Second*, vol. V (London: Macmillan, 1914).

MacIver, R.M., *The Modern State* (Oxford: Clarendon Press, 1926).

McLellan, David C., *The Achieving Society* (Princeton, N.J.: Princeton University Press, 1961).

McLellan, David, *The Thought of Karl Marx*, (London: Macmillan, 1972).

McLellan, David, *Marx* (Glasgow: Fontana-Collins, 1976).

Macpherson, C.B., *The Political Theory of Possessive Individualism* (London: Oxford Univesity Press, 1972).

Mahalanobis, P.C., *Talks on Planning* (Calcutta: Statistical Publishing Society, 1961).

Maine, Sir Henry, *Village Communities in the East and West* (London: John Murray, 1872).

Majumdar, R.C., and Pusalkar, A.D., *The Classical Age* (Bombay: Bharatiya Vidya Bhavan, 1955).

Mandel, E., *The Formation of the Economic Thought of Karl Marx, 1843 to Capital* (London: New Left Books, 1971).

Mandel, E., *From Class Society to Communism* (London: Ink Links, 1977).

Mann, H.H., *Land and Labour in a Deccan Village* (Bombay: Oxford University Press, 1917).

Mantoux, P.J., *The Industrial Revolution in the Eighteenth Century* (London: Jonathan Cape, 1928).

Marx, Karl, *Selected Works*, vol. 2, ed. Adoratsky (New York: International Publishers, n.d.).

Marx, Karl, *Capital*, vol. I (1867) (Chicago: Charles H. Kerr, 1906).

Marx, Karl, *Capital*, vol. III (1894) (Chicago: Charles H. Kerr Company, 1909).

Marx, Karl, *Economic and Philosophical Manuscripts of 1844* (Moscow: Foreign Languages Publishing House, 1961).

Marx, Karl, *Critique of Political Economy* (1844) (Cambridge: Cambridge University Press, 1970).

Marx, Karl, 'The Civil War in France', in K. Marx and F. Engels, *Selected Works*, (Moscow: Progress Publishers, 1970).

Marx, Karl, 'The Eighteenth Brumaire of Louis Bonaparte', in K. Marx and F. Engels, *Selected Works*, (Moscow: Progress Publishers, 1970).

Marx, Karl, *Critique of Hegel's Philosophy of Right* (1843–4), ed. J. O'Malley (Cambridge University Press, 1971).

Marx, Karl, *Pre-Capitalist Economic Formations*, edited with an introduction by E.J. Hobsbawm (New York: International Publishers, 1971).

Marx, Karl, *Grundrisse* (1857–8) (Harmondsworth: Penguin Books, 1973).

Marx, Karl, 'The Class Struggle in France', in K. Marx and F. Engels, *Selected Works*, (Moscow: Progress Publishers, 1973).

Marx, K., 'Moralising Criticism and Critical Morality', in K. Marx and F. Engels, *Collected Works*, vol. 6 (New York: International Publishers, 1976).

Marx, Karl, and Engels, Frederick, *On Colonialism* (Moscow: Progress Publishers, 1968); includes Marx's contributions to the *New York Daily Tribune*.

Marx, Karl, and Engels, Frederick, *Selected Works* (Moscow: Progress Publishers, 1970).

Marx, Karl, and Engels, Frederick, *The German Ideology* (1845–6) ed. C.J. Arther (New York: International Publishers, 1976).

Marx, Karl, and Engels, Frederick, *Collected Works*, vol. VI (New York: International Publishers, 1977).

Marx, Karl, and Engels, Frederick, *Collected Works*, vol. VIII (New York: International Publishers, 1977).

Marx, Karl, and Engels, Frederick, *Correspondence, 1846–1945, A Selection with Commentary and Notes*, ed. V. Adoratsky (New York: International Publishers, n.d.).

Meillassoux, Claude, 'A class analysis of the bureaucratic process in Mali', *Journal of Development Studies* (January 1970).

Merrington, John, 'The theory and practice in Gramsci's Marxism', in R. Miliband and J. Saville, *The Socialist Register* (New York: Monthly Review Press, 1968).

Miliband, Ralph, 'Marx and the state', in R. Miliband and J. Saville, *The Socialist Register* (New York: Monthly Review Press, 1965).

Miliband, Ralph, 'The capitalist state: a reply to Nicos Poulantzas', *New Left Review*, no. 59 (1970).

Miliband, Ralph, *The State in Capitalist Society* (London: Quartet, 1976).

Miliband, Ralph, and Saville, J., *The Socialist Register* (New York: Monthly Review Press, 1965).

Mill, James, The History of British India, vol. I (London: James Madden, 1858).

Misra, B.B., *The Indian Middle Classes* (London: Oxford University Press, 1961).

Misra, B.B., *The Administrative History of India, 1834–1947*, 2 vols. (Bombay: Oxford University Press, 1970).

Moore, Barrington, *Social Origins of Dictatorship and Democracy* (Boston: Beacon Press, 1972).

Moreland, W.H., *The Agrarian System of Moslem India* (Cambridge: Heffer, 1929).

Moreland, W.H., *India at the Death of Akbar* (Delhi: Atma Ram, 1962).

Morris, M.D., 'Values as an obstacle to economic growth in South Asia', *Journal of Economic History*, vol. 27.

Mukerjee, Radhakamal, *Democracies of the East* (London: King, 1923).

Mukerjee, Radhakamal, *The Economic History of India, 1600–1800* (London: Longmans Green, n.d.).

Mukherjee, Ramakrishna, *The Rise and Fall of the East India Company* (Berlin: Deutscher Verlag der Wissenschaften, 1958).

Myrdal, Gunnar, *Asian Drama*, 3 vols (New York: Random House, 1968).

Nanavati, M.B., and Anjaria, J.J., *The Indian Rural Problem* (Bombay: Indian Society of Agricultural Economics, 1960).

Naoroji, Dadabhai, *Poverty and Un-British Rule in India* (Government of India: Publications Division, 1901/1962).

Nayar, Baldev Raj, *The Modernization Imperative and Indian Planning* (Delhi: Vikas Publications, 1972).

Nehru, Jawaharlal, *Recent Essays and Writings on the Future of India* (Allahabad: Kitabistan, 1934).

Nehru, Jawaharlal, *The Discovery of India* (New York: John Day, 1946).

Nehru, Jawaharlal, *Speeches*, vol. 1, 1946–49.

Nehru, Jawaharlal, *Speeches*, vol. 2, 1957–63.

O'Connor, James, *The Fiscal Crisis of the State* (New York: St Martin's Press, 1973).

O'Malley, L.S.S., *The Indian Civil Service, 1600–1930* (London: Frank Cass, 1965).

Oxaal, Ivar, (ed.), *Beyond the Sociology of Development: Economy and Society in Latin America and Africa* (London: Routledge and Kegan Paul, 1975).

Patel, Surendra J., *Essays on Economic Transition* (Bombay: Asia Publishing House, 1964).

Pirenne, Henri, *Economic and Social History of Medieval Europe* (New York: Harvest Book, n.d.).

Pirenne, Henri, *Medieval Cities* (Princeton, N.J.: Princeton University Press, 1925).

Pirenne, Henri, *Early Democracies in the Low Countries* (New York: W.W. Norton, 1971).

Poulantzas, Nicos, *Classes in Contemporary Capitalism* (London: New Left Books, 1975).

Poulantzas, Nicos, *Political Power and Social Classes* (London: New Left Books, 1975).

Poulantzas, Nicos, 'The capitalist state: a reply to Miliband and Laclau', *New Left Review*, no. 95, (1976).

Prakash, Om, 'The Dutch East India Company in Bengal: trade privileges and problems, 1633–1712', *Indian Economic and Social History Review* (1972).

Rao, V.K.R.V., 'Introduction', *Papers on National Income and Allied Topics*, 2 vols (Bombay: Asia Publishing House, 1962).

Ray, Indrani, 'The French Company and the merchants of Bengal (1680–1730)', *Indian Economic and Social History Review* (March 1971).

Raychowdhuri, Tapan, *Bengal Under Akbar and Jahangir* (Delhi: Munshiram Manoharlal, 1969).

Roy, M.N., *India in Transition* (Bomaby: Nachiketa Publications, 1971).

Roy, Subrata, *Bharater Dainya* (Calcutta: Udayan Press, n.d.).

Rudra, Ashoke, *Relative Rates of Growth of Agriculture and Industry* (Bombay: University of Bombay, 1967).

Sarkar, Jadunath, *Economics of British India* (Calcutta: M.C. Sarkar, 1917).

Sarkar, Jadunath, *Shivaji and His Times* (London: Longmans Green, 1929).

Sastri, Nalinikanta, *A History of South India* (London: Oxford University Press, 1955).

See, Henri, *Modern Capitalism* (New York: Adelphi, 1928).

Sen, Bhowani, *Evolution of Agrarian Relations in India* (New Delhi: People's Publishing House, 1962).

Sharma, Ram Sharan, *Indian Feudalism: c. 300–1200* (Calcutta: University of Calcutta, 1965).

Shelvankar, K.S., *The Problem of India* (Harmondsworth: Penguin Books, 1943).

Shirokov, G.K., *Industrialisation of India* (Moscow: Progress Publishers, 1973).

Shonfield, Andrew, *Modern Capitalism* (New York: Oxford University Press, 1974).

Singh, V.B. (ed.) *The Economic History of India, 1857–1956* (Bombay: Allied Publishers, 1965).

Sinha, N.C., *Studies in Indo-British Economy Hundred Years Ago* (Calcutta: A. Mukherjee, n.d.).

Smith, Adam, *An Inquiry into the Nature and Causes of the Wealth of Nations*, 2 vols, (London: Methuen, 1950).

Smith, Vincent A., *The Early History of India* (Oxford: Clarendon Press, 1957).

Some, Rajendra, *Jagrata Janata* (Dacca: Prativa Pustakalaya, 1957).

Spear, Percival, *India: A Modern History* (Ann Arbor: University of Michigan Press, 1961).

Spear, Percival, *A History of India*, vol. 2 (Harmondsworth: Penguin Books, 1965).

Srinivasan, T.N., and Bardhan, P.K., *Poverty and Income Distribution in India* (Calcutta: Statistical Publishing Society, 1974).

Stevens, R.D., Alavi, H., and Bertocci, P.J., *Rural Development in Bangladesh and Pakistan* (Honolulu: University Press of Hawaii, 1976).

Streeten, Paul, and Lipton, Michael, *The Crisis of Indian Planning* (London/New York/Toronto/Bombay: Oxford University Press, 1968).

Storry, Richard, *A History of Modern Japan* (Harmondsworth: Penguin Books, 1973).

Subramaniam, V., 'Administrators and politicians: Emerging Relations', *Economic and Political Weekly* (26 November 1977).

Tara Chand, *History of the Freedom Movement in India*, vol. 1 (New Delhi: Government of India Publication Division, 1961).

Taub, R.P., *Bureaucrats Under Stress* (Berkeley/Los Angeles: University of California Press, 1969).

Tawney, R.H., *The Agrarian Problem in the Sixteenth Century* (New York: Longman, 1912).

Tawney, R.H., *Harrington's Interpretation of His Age, Proceedings of the British Academy*, 1941.

Thompson, F.M.L., 'The social distribution of landed property in England since the sixteenth century', *Economic History Review* (December 1966).

Thorner, Daniel, *The Agrarian Prospects in India* (Delhi: University Press, 1956).

Thorner, Daniel, 'Marx on India and the Asiatic mode of production', *Contributions to Indian Sociology*, vol. IX (1966).

Toynbee, Arnold, *Lectures on the Industrial Revolution of the 18th Century in England* (London: Longmans Green, 1913).

Tripathi, A.R., *Trade and Finance in the Bengal Presidency* (Calcutta: Orient Longmans, 1956).

Tyagi, A.R., *The Civil Service in a Developing Society* (Delhi: Sterling Publishers, 1969).

Vakil, C.N., (ed.), *Economic Consequences of Divided India: A Study in the Economy of India and Pakistan* (Bombay: Vora, 1950).

Venkatasubbiah, H., *Indian Economy Since Independence* (New York: Asia Publishing House, 1961).

Viet, L.A., *India's Social Revolution* (New York: McGraw-Hill, 1976).

Vyas, V.S., 'Structural change in agriculture and the small farm sector', *Economic and Political Weekly* (10 January 1976).

Wadia, P.A. and Merchant, K.T., *Our Economic Problem* (Bombay: Vora, 1959).

Wadia, P.A., and Merchant K.T., 'The Bombay Plan: A Criticism' (Mimeo).

Wadva, C.D. (ed.), *Some Problems of India's Economic Policy* (New Delhi: Tata McGraw-Hill, 1973).

Wallerstein, Immanual, *The Modern World System* (New York: Academic Press, 1974).

Ward, Barbara, *India and the West* (London: Hamish Hamilton, 1961).

Weber, Max, *The City* (Glencoe, Ill.: Free Press, 1958).

Weber, Max, *Essays in Sociology* (London: Routledge & Kegan Paul, 1967).

Weber, Max, *The Protestant Ethic and the Spirit of Capitalism* (New York: Scribner's, 1958).

Weber, Max, *General Economic History* (Toronto: Collier-Macmillan Canada, 1966).

Weber, Max, *The Religion of India* (New York: Free Press, 1967).

Weber, Max, *Economy and Society* (New York: Bedminster Press, 1968).
Weber, Max, *The Religion of China* (New York: Free Press, 1968).
Weber, Max, *The Agrarian Sociology of Ancient Civilizations* (London: New Left Books, 1976).
Zagorin, Perez, 'The English revolution, 1640-1660', *Journal of World History*, vol. II, no. 3 (1955).
Zimmerman, L.J., *Poor Lands, Rich Lands* (New York: Random House, 1965).

Index

Note: Index headings refer to India except where another country is specifically mentioned.

For Product Safety Concerns and Information please contact our EU
representative GPSR@taylorandfrancis.com
Taylor & Francis Verlag GmbH, Kaufingerstraße 24, 80331 München, Germany

www.ingramcontent.com/pod-product-compliance
Lightning Source LLC
Chambersburg PA
CBHW060449290526
45791CB00001B/33

CHAPTER SIX

THE PROMOTIONS, KEY CLUBS, AND BREAK AND ENTER

OVER THE NEXT year I was promoted twice and became the chief instructor of the school. New teachers came and went. I became friends with one of the parents, and we would travel on the weekends to different places across Japan. Momo Matsumoto was one of the most talented ladies I had ever met. She had lived in Paris, France, and learned how to decorate cakes and was excellent at teaching my daughter and me about Japanese culture, even with her broken English. She had as much energy as her three children combined.

Kyoto, Japan

Things were going well at the school. In a year it had grown from forty students to over one hundred. Many new teachers were hired, and it became difficult to work in such a small, enclosed space with so many students and teachers.

It was now July of 2004. Time had flown by and I hadn't had much interaction with the owner of the school or her husband because I was always too busy. Some of the teachers started to express their concerns about the owner and her husband. There were minor complaints about the teachers' salaries being docked if they were one minute late clocking in.

One day all of the teachers were sitting and chatting in the tiny teachers' lounge. We discussed our future plans, and one announced that she would be leaving the school early. What was said next changed my perception of the school and the owner's husband. There had been some chatter amongst teachers about him, but I took it as idle gossip. Stanley Webber came trotting out of his classroom and into the teachers' lounge. His face was red and he was gushing with excitement. "You aren't going to believe what happened! Meme had her legs up on the table. She didn't have any underwear on and I could see her vagina. Now I know what her mother's looks like!"

There was silence...we sat there dumbfounded. The teachers looked at each other and didn't know what to say. Was this guy for real? Did he not know that all women's vaginas are different? Cathy's face turned red in embarrassment and she tried to change the topic.

"Stan," she began, trying not to laugh, "How did you start the school?"

He hesitated for a moment. "Well...Haruka and I used to own a key club."

"What's a key club?" she inquired.

"There are key clubs all over Japan. We used to host parties. Foreign men pay ten thousand yen and are given a key and one drink. Japanese women are invited for free and can drink for free. They, too, are given a key and have to find the man with a matching key. They talk and if they like each other, they go back to a hotel room." Again...silence. We looked around at each other. "That is how we got the money to start this school."

"Oh," said Cathy. No one said anything else for a minute or two. So they were sort of like pimps, I thought.

"Please don't tell any of the parents. It's not something we want people to know," said Stan.

Cathy changed the subject once more. "Where in the US are you from?"

"I'm from Alaska," Stan answered.

"Alaska? What was it like there," one of the male teachers asked.

"All I remember were the earthquakes and jumping over the rolling mounds of earth. My brothers and I used to break into people's homes," he bragged.

That ended our conversation and we went back to work. Although I had a bad feeling about Stan when I first arrived, I now felt sick to my stomach. Why would he feel the need to mention a three-year-old's vagina? The other teachers seemed to sense something was just a little off. Then I remembered what Steve had told us about his house being broken into twice and all of his electronics stolen. Did he suspect Stanley Webber? I didn't know what I was dealing with at that time. The true nature of Stan's character would be revealed as time passed.

CHAPTER SEVEN
THE MAN OUTSIDE OF THE BANK

FINALLY! I HAD been sitting in the bank for the last two hours. There was so much paperwork to be done in order to send money back home. I no sooner had taken a few steps out the door when I heard a male voice. "Hello," a man's voice said happily. I whirled around to see a tall, slender, middle-age Japanese gentleman with salt-and-pepper hair. I was surprised that he spoke English. I'd been in Japan for over a year, and he was the second person I met who spoke English well. I could barely see his eyes as he squinted in the sunlight. "My name is Sora Suzuki. I saw you in the bank and I wanted to meet you. I have many foreign friends here in Japan."

"Hello... Colleen," I replied and shook his hand.

"Where are you from?"

"Canada."

"What are you doing here in Japan?" I pointed to the name on my school uniform. "Ah, you are a teacher!"

"Yes."

"Would you like to have dinner with me sometime?" he asked.

"Would it be okay if I brought a few of my coworkers with me? I don't usually hand out my phone number to people I don't know," I replied.

"Yes, of course. What time do you finish work tomorrow?"

"Around six o'clock."

"There is a restaurant right over there." He pointed. "It is just around the corner. Let's meet at seven o'clock."

"Okay, I will see you then." I hurried back to the school to finish my notes and told my coworkers about the man and invited several of them to have dinner the next evening.

The day whizzed by and school was over. We all punched out on the clock and left together to go to the restaurant. "Are you sure you want to go to dinner with this man?" asked Tomiko.

"Sure, why not? He seemed like a very nice person. I will pay for everyone's dinner because I invited you."

"No, no, that's okay; we all wanted to go out anyway," Cathy replied.

We arrived after a short walk, and Sora was there waiting at a table for five. He extended his hand to everyone, and they introduced themselves. "Thank you for coming." We talked about his life and the lives of the other people at the table, mainly small talk. "It's my garden," Sora said.

"What does that mean?" I asked. Everyone looked puzzled.

Tomiko spoke up. "It means he will pay for everyone's meal." All refused but he was insistent. We thanked him and went on our way.

SORA SUZUKI AND NATALIE COLE

THE PHONE WAS ringing and ringing and I wasn't about to hop out of the tub to answer it. My muscles were aching from climbing Fuji San (mountain). Earlier in the morning my daughter had pulled me out of bed. The nine-hour hike up the mountain and the four-hour run down the mountain had taken a toll on my legs. Diana was out with one of her Australian friends. I crawled out of the tub in agony and reached for the phone.

"Hello?"

"Hello, Colleen. How are you?"

"Not bad, Sora. A little sore because I climbed Fuji over the weekend, but okay."

"How would you like to go to a Natalie Cole concert with me and two of my friends? I have tickets and would like to invite you. The concert is this Saturday."

"Sure, I think that sounds great!"

"My friends are doctors and will join us." He gave me the name of the bar where the jazz singer would perform.

Saturday rolled around and I met Sora and the Japanese ladies at the bar. They were very pleasant and had a lot of questions. Natalie Cole was raising money for Whitney Houston's drug rehabilitation. Natalie Cole's voice was perfect and the concert very entertaining. At the end of the evening, I thanked Sora and the ladies for a great evening and said goodbye. This was the last time I saw Sora Suzuki. He called several times, but I was mostly busy. I spoke to him close to the end of my contract to tell him I was leaving Japan. Little did I know that Sora Suziki would show up in my life again and the final time in a most unusual way.

CHAPTER EIGHT
IS THIS REAL?

I T WAS SEPTEMBER 2004, and Kelly Wright and I were upstairs completing our daily notes. Six-year-old Jennifer Webber was sitting with us at the table. Her father was cleaning the floors a few feet away in the next room. Jennifer was completing her Kumon homework and talking. Suddenly she had a pouty look on her face. "What's the matter, Jennifer," Kelly asked.

Her eyes were cast downward and she looked as though she was about to cry. "Sometimes my daddy touches me," she said quietly. Neither Kelly nor I could question her any further because her father was within earshot. I shot a glance over at Kelly, and she changed the subject and asked Jennifer what she was working on. We kept her talking until she was smiling again.

When it was time for us to go home, I put my daily notes on the counter in the kitchen. "I hope you know Jennifer is a pathological liar," a male voice said from behind me. I didn't know what to say and actually couldn't even make eye contact with him. There was enough tension in the air that you could cut it with a knife.

"Oh." *Do six-year-old pathological liars exist?* I wondered.

"We have had a lot of trouble with Jennifer since she was a little baby," he continued.

"I see. I am sorry to hear that. Have a good evening, Stan." I grabbed my backpack and headed home, happy to leave the day behind me.

At home I contacted a woman I used to volunteer with at a sexual assault crisis center. All of the interactions I had were with adults, and I hadn't given much thought about the signs of sexually abused children. I'd read about it in the past but wanted a second opinion. Stella had volunteered longer than I had, so I explained the child's behavior and she agreed that it merited an investigation. The next day I found a time to talk to the mother to tell her what Jennifer had told Kelly Wright and me. Perhaps the mother could talk to her and find out the exact meaning of her words. Instead, Haruka Yamada said she'd also received phone calls from Jennifer and Maria's day care about it, and she believed they had learned the behavior from other children at the day care. At that time, I was not aware that the three-year-old had the same behavior because I hadn't taught her. Anything is possible and I didn't want to broach the topic with a six-year-old again. I didn't want to make it out to be a big problem but would continue to observe and document in my notebook until I felt I had enough evidence to go to police if I felt it was warranted.

Over the next few months, Jennifer's issues became increasingly worse. I only taught her in one class, but teachers would complain to me about both girls. Jennifer and Maria were constantly masturbating. Cathy in particular didn't want to teach the youngest one because she felt sick. In my class the middle child was displaying the behaviors of a sexually abused child. "Why is Jennifer always doing that, Ms. Colleen?" a student inquired.

"Well, I haven't really been watching her. I was talking to another student." I decided to take corrective action and spoke to her after class and told her what she was doing in the class should be done in private. Other teachers were asked to tell her to keep her hands on the top of the desk. I told her ten times each class and after a few weeks it seemed to work but not completely.

Both girls continued with their behavior, and the teachers decided to have a meeting with the father. "Stan, could we please talk about Jennifer and Maria masturbating in class all the time?" His face turned crimson red. "Stan," said Cathy, "I need to say this, but I don't know how. I feel sick and I am tired of telling Maria to keep her hands on the desk."

Angrily, Stan stood up. "I will talk to them. That concludes the meeting." All the teachers looked at each other and thought that his reaction was out of the ordinary.

"Well, that went over real well," said Kelly.

"No kidding," Cathy replied.

"We brought up what was going on and notated it," I said. "Let's conclude the meeting."

I started to feel very uncomfortable in the school and tired, so I gave Stanley and Haruka three months' notice. My contract would end seven months early. In my opinion, the owners treated me very well at first and promoted me to chief instructor, bought a camera as a gift, and were never critical. But other teachers left because of the way they felt they were treated. There were cameras in all of the classes, and parents could go into the computer room and watch their children. One came up the stairs and told a male teacher how to interact with his students. He was open to suggestions but didn't like being yelled at in front of his students. He left soon after. Teachers felt they were under constant scrutiny and were being micromanaged.

A few days after I had given my notice, I went downstairs and Stan called me into the main office. "Look," he said, handing me a résumé. "You are applying for your old position."

I looked at the résumé: the name on it was Colleen Norman. She was ten years younger, and from the US. I laughed and said, "Hire her."

CHAPTER NINE

CHRISTMAS 2004

I WAS CLOSE to the end of my contract. Two other children had complained about Stan and a third one to a Japanese teacher. She seemed to be in shock by what the child told her about Stan. Again, I want to be fair and say that I don't know what was said in detail but I got the gist. The other two complaints were more about privacy issues.

There was a Christmas party coming up, and all teachers had to work for a few hours on Christmas Eve day. We were there for eight hours and hosted two children's Christmas parties. At the end of the day, we cleaned up and Webber handed us an envelope. One of the teachers opened it up and quietly asked me how much I had been paid. I opened the envelope and there was only 2,000 yen, or twenty dollars, in it. It was the same for all of the teachers. We were paid $2.50 per hour. Webber's excuse... "That's because all of you have a bad attitude." Actually we were tired of being overworked and needed a holiday. Labor infractions started at this point but earlier for others.

I thought back to a conversation three teachers had in July of 2004. Kelly Webber felt that someone had invaded her privacy in her home because the school owner seemed to know that she and her husband had had an argument. Dave, another teacher, felt the same way too. Parts of conversations he had with his girlfriend came up at the school. At that time, I never really thought about it much, but later a few coincidental things came up. There was an earthquake and the table we had in the kitchen was too small for Diana and I to take cover. "We need a larger table," said Diana. The next morning, our doorbell rang and there was a larger table and chairs outside our door. It had been put there by Webber. How did he know we needed a larger table? The following day, after work, I put my key into the lock, entered, and Diana and I looked at each other. "Someone has been in here," we said in unison. Diana looked at me and said, "I am going back to Canada. This is screwed." One week later, she left Japan and stayed with a friend of mine while I finished up my contract.

My contract was coming to an end, and I had gone on several outings with one of the parents from the school. We climbed Fuji Mountain and had gone to Kyoto and Hida Takayama. She asked me to come and stay at her home for three months and then she would come to Canada with me for three months. I agreed and when my contract was finished, she picked me up and I went to her home. I'd already met her father-in-law, mother-in-law, and parents. Momo Matsumoto had already decided to leave the school because her third child had been born and it would be too expensive to send all three to the school.

I was given a large room overlooking the street at the front of the house. She had bought a new comforter and fixed up the room for me. The children would come in late at night, and I would read them a bedtime story. I spent a lot of time traveling and going places with them. Time flew by and we had a lot of fun together until Stanley Webber started to get involved.

CAR DRIVES THROUGH THE WALL

IN EARLY JANUARY 2005, Chika, a parent from the school, and I went to celebrate the New Year; the end of my contract and life in general. She drove to a restaurant where we would eat lunch. The front section was pretty crowded, but there was a table for two in front of the window. "How about here?" I asked.

"Too many people. Let's go to the back where it is quieter."

"Okay," I said, and off we went to the back of the restaurant.

The waitress brought us a menu, and we had coffee and tea to start. It was very relaxing to be able to sit quietly with a really great person, talk, and not have to worry about anything. The waitress brought our food and we began to eat. Five minutes later, we heard a loud bang, people screaming and dishes breaking on the floor. Chika and I looked at each other. "What was that?" we said together. It sounded like someone had dropped a tray of food. "Let's go see!" I got up and everyone was standing around staring. When we got to the main entrance, a table was overturned and two women were sitting there screaming. A car had driven through the wall and window. The window was cracked and bent inward. As the car hit the wall and window, it also hit the table and knocked the women onto the floor. The table had toppled over. Both women appeared to be okay but were in a state of shock.

I couldn't speak Japanese at that time, and no one seemed to be helping them. Finally, a member of the staff went over to help them and asked if they needed an ambulance. Chika and I looked at each other and went to the back room and finished our lunch. "Good thing you suggested that we sit back here."

"I had a bad feeling about sitting there," she said. I looked over at her and at that very second had a bad feeling in the pit of my stomach. Something told me to leave Japan. It was probably Chika transferring her own energy to me, which is not uncommon. We talked about that feeling of an impending sense of doom. I shook it off and we went outside to survey the damage after we'd paid our bill. It was pretty bad. An older man stepped on the accelerator instead of backing up. It would cost a lot of money to repair the car, wall, and window.

When I look back at this incident, it was sort of like a bad omen. It seemed to set the tone for things to come. I don't know if it is just me, but weird things happened all the time.

CHAPTER TEN
REPORTING WEBBER TO THE POLICE

I T WAS JANUARY 2005, and Momo and I went to Aichi Prefectural Police Headquarters with our suspicions about the father abusing his children. I felt that I had an obligation to report because I had been the chief instructor, and the behaviors of the children had become worse instead of better. It was important for me to get help for them.

The front desk officer asked if she could help us. Momo spoke Japanese to her and explained why she was there. A plainclothes officer came down the stairs. "I want to make a report," Momo said in Japanese.

"What has been going on?" asked the detective.

She explained the situation to him, and he looked at both of us for a moment before replying, "I have had three other people come in and file a similar complaint about the same man. Were you aware of that?"

"No, we didn't know," said Momo.

"In Japan," the detective continued, "the child has to come into the police station and file a complaint. It is not easy for police to catch the perpetrator in the act."

Momo and I looked at each other. "The laws here are crazy," I said.

The officer took our names and did little else.

"So, there are other people who have reported him," I said as we went outside.

"Yes, yes. I think the police are stupid in Japan. Everyone knows that they don't help anybody," said Momo. That was the first and last time we went to the police station to get help for these children.

I was not satisfied with the answer Japanese police gave me, so I wrote an email message to the American Embassy. Two days later, the Federal Bureau of Investigation called and asked what was going on. "I reported the abuse of two half-American/Japanese children to police and told the agent, the police would not do anything about it. Could you contact police and push to have them investigate?"

"It has been the experience of the FBI that it is difficult to get the Japanese police to do anything if they don't want to. Even on the most serious of cases," stated the agent. The FBI agent seemed to be irritated that I had reported the abuse and wanted to know why it was so important. The children were American and Japanese. Why not ask Aichi Prefectural Police to investigate? Has our society become so desensitized that we don't care about little kids?

I didn't hear back from the FBI, so I called the agent several weeks later to see if anything had been done. He put me through to the Regional Director of Security for Asia Pacific, Keating. "Keating speaking. What's going on?" I told him about the response the Japanese police had to our report. "All I can do is place him on a list of suspected pedophiles. If the police don't want to investigate, my hands are tied," replied Keating. I don't know whether or not Stanley Webber's name was ever placed on a list, but I did my job. There was a record of the report should anything else come up. I thought this was the end; little did I know what was in store for me, my daughter, Momo, parents, and teachers.

LABOR OFFICE AND TEACHERS

JANUARY 18TH, 2005, Momo and I sat talking at the kitchen table when the phone rang. Cathy, an American teacher, called and asked if we could meet with her and three others. Things had gone from bad to worse at the school. The complaints were about being fined, threats to fire teachers, teachers not receiving their full pay and being docked money for things that they hadn't done. We agreed to meet them for lunch. They said they were worried that if Stan caught them meeting with me, they would be fired. I thought this was a strange statement because I left the school on good terms.

The teachers talked about the problems they were having at the school, and Momo and I agreed to take them to the labor office, which we did several days later. There were four teachers who went together to complain. An older Japanese man who seemed to be in a foul mood stepped out into the waiting area. "Why are so many of you here?" Momo told him in Japanese about the complaints. "I cannot take four reports at the same time. Make an appointment and come back one at a time." None of the teachers could come back because they were working. I never did find out whether or not the labor disputes were resolved. I would only have contact with one of the teachers two more times.

EXTORTION ATTEMPT

I HAD LEFT the school early because the atmosphere had changed and I felt extremely stressed and tired. In mid-January, a letter arrived addressed to Momo Matsumoto from the school. The owners were accusing me and her of pilfering students. How could that be when I slept the entire first month due to extreme exhaustion? He was trying to collect $500,000 American for something we'd not done. At that time I didn't even speak Japanese, and this lady had three small children. Where were we supposed to find the time to allegedly pilfer students? There were three children who came over to her house but only because their mothers said the children missed their teacher. One had quit the school long before I'd left. This is where things got a little weird.

Matsumoto said she would pay $5,000 to see a lawyer. Why? We'd not done anything. And the writing on this alleged paper was all in Japanese so I couldn't read it. Now I can but not then. Something was not believable about this whole thing. Most initial appointments with lawyers offer a free consultation. Why would anyone have to pay $5,000? I started to look at Matsumoto at that point and wonder if this was some kind of a scam.

Sean, an acquaintance of mine, had gone to Shanghai, China, twice, and both times was subjected to a scam. An English-speaking woman walked up to him and struck up a conversation. She asked him to go to a coffee shop with her. He agreed, they sat down, and the next thing he knew, platters of food were brought to the table and drinks. "Wait a minute," he said. "I never ordered this and I'm not paying for it." Two big Chinese men came out of a back room and shook him down. He ended up paying over $200 by force. You would have thought that he would have learned his lesson the first time, but it happened a second time, and $500 was lifted from him. He went to police and they got most of his money back. Perhaps as foreigners in a foreign country, we are simply sitting ducks. We are friendly, outgoing, and engaging people and are targets for fraudsters. Now, add a suspected psychopath into the mix who is now trying to extort money, and you are able to see how his mind operates. Sadistic psychopaths try to control your life financially. Nothing ever came of the extortion attempt. Wait until you read about what the school owners did next!

CHAPTER ELEVEN
THE CHASE

I T WAS LATE February 2005, and two of my friends were off to the doctor to have their babies immunized. I was going to take the four older children to the park to play soccer. Momo went downstairs to the van ahead of me. When I reached the van full of kids, Momo yelled at me to get into the van.

"Why? What's wrong?" I asked.

"Oh...look, Mr. Stan is videotaping."

So what? I thought. Why the sense of urgency?

"Mr. Stan is looking very angry!"

"Okay," I said as I climbed into the van. What happened next was the single most irresponsible thing I have ever seen a grown man do.

Momo's husband took off and looked in the rearview mirror. "Mr. Stan is behind us!"

I turned around and he was tailgating two feet behind us. Our van picked up speed to get away from Stan. Stan in turn sped up faster. "Does this man realize there are five young children in this vehicle?!" I exclaimed. Momo was holding her nine-month-old son in her arms.

"He is crazy," Hiro said. "Look at his face!"

Stan appeared to be trying to ram the van full of children. We rounded the corner at a high speed. Stan was still two feet behind us. The chase continued for about five minutes.

"There is a police station around the corner. Let's go there," I said.

Hiro pulled up to the police box (station) and went inside to talk to the police. Stanley Webber drove by very quickly and kept right on going. A police report was made and we returned to Momo's home. "Ms. Colleen, please stay inside with the children," she said.

"Mr. Stan is a bad man," said one of the children.

Momo started laughing and said, "Why chasing? Ms. Colleen, and Momo is nothing wrong doing!"

I can't imagine what went through Stanley Webber's mind. The mothers took their children to be immunized, and I popped a movie into the DVD player for the kids.

The phone rang. It was Cathy, who was still working at the school. "Colleen, Stan has a video of you getting into a van full of kids, and he says he is going to sue you."

"Um...okay, sue me for what? Momo and her friend took their kids to be immunized. There is no problem. I was going to play soccer with the children at the park."

"Oh," she said.

Why was everyone in a panic? I understand that Stanley (Otaku-geek) Webber had chased a van full of kids and endangered their lives, but we hadn't broken any laws. Why would this man and his wife believe that they had the right to control the lives of their former teachers and former students? This was insane and gave me a true glimpse at their thought processes, which were seriously skewed. At no time did Momo or I break any laws. Were Haruka Yamada and Stanley Webber mobsters? They owned a key club. They certainly acted like it. I reflected back to the seventeen months I'd spent at the school and all the teachers who had been victimized in one way or another. One teacher was not given her bonus or part of it because she wanted to leave her contract two days early. She forfeited a $2,000 bonus. I, on the other hand, forfeited a $7,500 bonus, which I believe would never have been paid. The company did give me a $500 bonus for seventeen months of hard work. How far would this couple carry things?

OTAKU'S VICTORY POWWOW

IT WAS EARLY March 2005, and Momo and I were having a birthday party for her middle child. We decorated the house and waited for the guests to arrive. The kids were going to make food, play games, eat, and have some cake. One by one the guests arrived. When all of the children were there, we started the party. Some of the parents had decided to stay and watch when suddenly I heard a woman say, "Oh my god! Ms. Colleen, Momo, come here. I can't believe my eyes!" Two of the parents spotted Haruka Yamada videotaping the guests arriving at the party. This is the same lady married to Stanley Webber. We put on a video for the kids to watch and looked out the window. Directly across the street on the second floor of an apartment building was a woman crouched down, videotaping. *What an idiot*, I thought.

One of the parents called police. Momo and I went over to the back door of the apartment building, walked up the stairs, and waited for police to arrive. Her husband had one month earlier irresponsibly chased a car full of children for no reason. I actually wanted to go in the room before police got there and hit this idiot over the head with a frying pan. I'm not violent but this lady ruined a child's birthday party! The guests felt uncomfortable and took care of the children while we talked to police. Police arrived within ten minutes, and a uniformed officer opened the door and spoke with Haruka. Haruka claimed that Momo and I were pilfering students from the school and interfering in her business. I believe she said this to cover up her husband's actions. Remember, four different people had reported him as a suspected pedophile. The first time we caught him videotaping, he chased a van full of kids, endangering their lives. How were we doing anything wrong when we were going to the park to play while the younger children were being immunized?

Police listened to what Momo said. He explained to Haruka that nothing was going on and it was just a birthday party; everything else she had invented in her mind. In Japanese he asked both parties to go to the police station. Momo and I went back to the house, and the two parents who stayed behind took care of the children and played games with them. I received a phone call from one of the teachers still working at the school. "Colleen, Stanley just got a call. Haruka has been arrested. He is on his way to the police station," she added shakily.

"Cathy, we were having a birthday party for Sakura. This is ridiculous!"

"Be careful, Colleen."

Momo and I arrived at the police station and climbed the staircase to the second floor. Haruka was in another room, and Momo and I sat on a bench and waited. Ten minutes later Webber arrived in a panic and asked for his wife. Having heard his voice, Haruka walked out of a room to let him know where she was. Webber looked over at Matsumoto and me, and he did a victory dance, sort of like an Indian powwow. There he was, six-foot-three Stanley Webber doing his thing in the middle of the police station, police watching. A true otaku. The detective whom I had spoken to before watched the dance with a disapproving look on his face. Momo and I looked at each other and laughed. When he went into a separate room with his wife and the detective, Momo said: "Mr. Stan is crazy...why dancing?" Japan seemed to be weirder than fiction.

"I don't know, Momo. Maybe he thinks he's won something." Then I thought for a second. "So far he has accused us of pilfering students because two kids needed to be immunized, and then this. Do you think maybe he is paranoid? We are going to Canada next year in March, so why do this?"

"Haruka and Stanley Webber may have thought they could extort money from us," Momo said. I remembered Haruka telling me that Momo's family was very wealthy.

The police spoke to Momo and me briefly. The detective told us Haruka and Stanley Webber had been given a warning and that they were the problem. Next time they could face charges of criminal harassment. We left the police station and went back to Momo's house. The parents had kept the party going and the kids ate. We sang happy birthday and had some cake. I felt really bad for Sakura because this was supposed to be a fun party. We apologized for the unprofessional behavior of Haruka Yamada and Stanley Webber. The parents were livid about their irresponsible actions.

CHAPTER TWELVE
THE BEST SCHOOL

A T THE BEGINNING of March 2005, I was hired to work at an international school on the outskirts of Nagoya. The owner was Japanese and her husband was from Pakistan. I worked with two other foreigners and two Japanese teachers. The students were from all over the world: Myanmar, Turkey, Pakistan, Malaysia, Sri Lanka, and Japan. Most of the students were bilingual or trilingual because their parents were from different races and the children were of mixed race.

Each month one parent would host a party to celebrate their culture. They brought traditional items, wore traditional clothing, and made their culture's food. The students received a rich and diverse education at this school. The Australian teacher and I both represented our countries and taught them about our own culture. This was the best school I had worked at, and I learned a lot from the owner and the students.

The school was not without incident. I completely trusted all of my coworkers. One day we were all in our classes, and no one was in the office. I went to get something out of my backpack and noticed my wallet was not in its usual compartment in my bag. Someone had taken 60,000 yen, or $750 Canadian, and left 20,000 yen in my wallet. Had a student taken it? Did someone walk in and take it? If this person was a real thief, why would they leave 20,000 yen? The same pattern of behavior would recur in Paris, France, seven years later. The owner told me they had money go missing in the past. Again, none of the staff would take it because we all worked very hard to earn our money.

JUDO GUY

SPRING WAS HERE and it was an unusually warm day. This was my second day of work, and I was on my way to the new school on the outskirts of

Nagoya. The train was crowded and I stood for the entire half-hour journey to my destination. The brightness of the sun hurt my eyes, so I kept them cast down toward the floor. Once in a while I would look up at the other passengers as they got on and off the train. Out of the corner of my eye, I caught a glimpse of a tall, muscular young man looking in my direction. His long black hair was tied back in a braid. He approached me and seemed nervous. "Hi, I noticed you when I got on the train. You look like you work out. My name is Kato Yamaguchi by the way."

"Colleen."

"What are you doing in Japan?"

"I am a teacher here. Excuse me, please, my stop is coming up," I said as I tried to get to the door.

"Yeah, I am late for my appointment too. Let's work out sometime," he said quickly. "Let me get your number and I will put it in my phone." I hesitated and then gave my number as the train screeched to a halt. He got off the train and continued to talk. He finished entering my phone number and said he would call me.

I arrived at work less than twenty minutes later. I'd no sooner told my coworker about him when the phone rang. It was Kato Yamaguchi calling to tell me how happy he was to have met me and that he was looking forward to working out with me. After I'd hung up the phone, it struck me as odd that he would contact me immediately. Over the next fifteen years, he would insert himself in my life both in person and online. Was Webber behind all of these incidents? Was Kato Yamaguchi his friend?

THE ASSAULT

YAMAGUCHI CALLED ME the next day and asked if we could go to a gym on my next day off. I had a membership at a gym near my home and I could bring him in as a guest. We agreed to meet at the main subway station in Nagoya. I waited about fifteen minutes, and he didn't show up. As I turned to leave, he called out my name. We took the next subway to Iwatuska-cho. He mainly talked about his life and told me he had three black belts, was a mixed martial arts fighter and a grappler. He seemed to tower over me at six feet and 230 pounds. He said he taught English, was a part-time bouncer, and had lived in the United States. We arrived at our destination and walked to the gym.

He said he had to go to the store and he would meet me at the door in a few minutes. I got a guest pass and waited for him. Ten minutes later we set off to different changing rooms to get dressed and ready to work out. He was already on the floor when I got there, stretching. I got down on another mat and stretched. He was eyeballing someone closer to his own age, so I exited the mats and went to run on the treadmill. I ran for thirty minutes and then cooled down and told Kato I was going to hit the shower. When I came out of the women's shower, he was waiting on a bench. I didn't even notice if he had worked out or not.

"I am pretty tired because I had a grappling match last night and I have been training really hard. I am sorry if I don't seem to be in a good mood today. It is so hot and I drank one and a half liters of green tea today. Let's go to the main station in Nagoya and have a coffee."

"Okay, let's go. I'm not even tired," I replied.

"Did you have a good run?"

"It was only thirty minutes. I will run for ninety minutes when I get back from the subway station."

"You have a lot of energy, don't you?"

"Yes, I love to run."

We continued to chat and were approaching a new and empty subway station when without provocation, Yamaguchi spun around on his left leg and tried to kick me in the face with his right foot. He was quick but I was quicker. I turned to the right and blocked the shot with my left arm. He held his leg up for what seemed like five seconds, and I had a clear shot at his testicles. I almost took that shot but then I remembered Momo and Chika telling me that if a foreigner hurts a Japanese national, the foreigner goes to jail. I'd never been in trouble with the law in my life, so I didn't hurt him. He put his leg down.

"Do you have a black belt? You're pretty quick!"

I told him I'd never studied martial arts.

"Then how did you do that?"

"Maybe I just have lightning-fast reflexes." Hindsight bias, I should have nailed him as hard as I could in that not so special place because there were no witnesses around the new subway station.

His kick for all intents and purposes was to inflict injury. I hate to think what my face would have looked like had his foot made contact.

My wrist was already throbbing and when I looked down I noticed it was quickly turning black and blue. "I think I will just head home now," I said.

He grabbed me by the arm. "No, no. You didn't think I was going to hurt you, did you," he said, laughing.

I went to the subway station, took him back to the main terminal, and left. "I'll be seeing you," he said in an ominous tone of voice. *Um...I don't think so*, I thought.

When I returned to Momo's house, I told her what had happened and that he had tried to kick me in the face and showed her the bruise that ran four inches down my wrist. "Uh...Ms. Colleen, Kato's Stan's friend maybe?" she said.

"I don't think so, but I am going to email him and tell him to get lost."

"Momo is thinking... Mr. Stan and Kato friends and try to hurt Ms. Colleen," she said in her broken English.

"Maybe but I don't know that. I haven't done anything wrong."

"Mr. Stan is maybe angry. He is knowing Momo and Ms. Colleen are police going about Jennifer. Ah...I talking to father-in-law about this situation and see his thinking," she added.

Everyone in the house felt that Stanley Webber was behind the assault. I didn't have enough proof at that time.

KATO

THE NEXT DAY I decided to go for a run. I ran about one kilometer when a black truck drove by me and Yamaguchi's head stuck out of the left-side passenger window. He had a smug look on his face. He actually looked quite stupid. It was at that very moment I envisioned a transport truck hitting him in the head to wipe that smug look off his face. I continued to run a few more kilometers, showered, and went to sleep early.

It was after three in the morning and my cell phone rang. I got up to answer it, but each time I did, the person hung up. I turned the phone off and went back to sleep. Was this the same person who drove by me with his head stuck out the window of a black truck earlier? First, this enormous, three-time black belt, grappler, judo guy tried to kick me in the face, followed me, and now three phone calls in the early morning. More psychopathic behaviors were yet to come! The stalking intensified.

THE STALKER

YAMAGUCHI WROTE TO me two weeks after he'd tried to kick me in the face. He said he wanted to apologize for his behavior and stated that he was allergic to caffeine and drank a lot of tea that day. "I want to work out with you and I promise that I will never try to hurt you again. It was a mistake I made and I wanted to make sure that you understood what happened. The caffeine causes some type of psychosis. So I really do want to say I'm sorry again." I didn't know what to think. If you have a caffeine allergy, why would you drink green tea and why did it take him two weeks to come up with this excuse?

I told Momo what he said. "Is he crazy? Kato is speaking liar things only. I want to see his face. Tell him coming to gym again and I watching him." So, I emailed dear Kato and invited him to work out with me once more at the same gym. Gym day arrived and Momo drove me to the gym. "Kato is touching Ms. Colleen, I hitting him with the car," she said laughingly. Kato arrived three minutes later.

"There he is."

"Where?"

"Right there."

"Ms. Momo is no liking his face. Ms. Colleen is no going. Kato dangerous. If there a problem I asking manager to watching Kato. After Momo is get Ms. Colleen, okay? Ms. Colleen is no go anywhere Kato! See you in one hour."

"Okay, I will see you then," I said.

When I walked out of the change room, I went to the warm-up mats. There was Kato, doing his thing. He was wearing a florescent orange muscle shirt and skin-tight black spandex shorts. All eyes were on him as he did the splits. Kato and I worked out for an hour and didn't speak much to one another except during the warm-up where I made up an excuse to go to the bikes. I think he knew I didn't want to be around him. "I'm hungry, do you want to go and get some food?" he asked. There was a Nepali restaurant right across from the gym. I called Momo to tell her that I was going to investigate to see if he was Stan's friend. Besides, one of the fitness instructors worked at the restaurant, which was owned by her father. We went to the restaurant and ordered naan bread and other Nepali food.

He apologized again and he said he needed to tell me the truth. "My dad is this big, fat slob who used to beat me when I was a kid. So, I have some problems because of him, and a doctor said I suffer from psychosis because of it. My mom is a really nice lady and used to be a model. My grandfather was a kamikaze in the second world war." He seemed to be making up stories on the fly and was trying to convince himself that they were real.

I just sat there and nodded or said, "Oh really?" Dinner ended, thank god. "Well, my friend Momo is here to pick me up."

"Okay, see you. Is it okay if I phone you?"

"Well, I am very busy. Bye for now."

Yamaguchi seemed to be suffering from psychotic episodes, even at dinner. The stories were not believable because of the way he told them.

HACKING

I GOT HOME and checked my email. The email was gone and I was not able to retrieve it. I tried the next email. It was gone too. I was able to retrieve the third email but only because I had used my credit card. When I entered the number, I got my account back from MSN.

I decided to go for a ten-kilometer fun run, and just as I was heading out the door, the phone rang. It was Yamaguchi. "Where are you going?"

"Excuse me? How did you know I was going somewhere?"

"It was a lucky guess."

"I am going running."

"Watch you don't get hit by a car!"

"What's that supposed to mean?"

"I was just telling you to stay safe."

"Yeah, right...not with that tone of voice."

Something was not right in this guy's mind. This is another example of psychopathic behavior. He lets the victim think that he is monitoring her every move and utters indirect threats. This type of behavior is geared to make the victim question her own judgment. Well, was that a threat or wasn't it? Gut instinct. It was! I would later catch him at his own "hacking" game.

CHAPTER THIRTEEN
AICHI PREFECTURAL POLICE HEADQUARTERS

LAWS VARY IN different countries, and back in 2005, Japanese stalking laws were prehistoric. Given that there are many xenophobic people in Japan, I believe laws are different for foreigners than for Japanese nationals. It is simply a part of both cultural and police bias. It is a priority for police to protect their own citizens, not the troublemaking foreigners. If you are a woman and a man is stalking you, it is your problem. He is just being a guy.

On May 17, 2005, I headed to Aichi Prefectural Police Headquarters. It had been two months since I'd met Yamaguchi and he had tried to assault me, followed me, and threatened me. Someone kept calling me, and emails had disappeared. He would know what I was doing, and despite many politely worded emails, he would not leave me alone. It was clear that there was an element of mental illness at play with Yamaguchi. I would later identify the illness as a personality disorder. While residing in Nagoya, I found that there was a large population of people who were mentally disordered walking the streets, and no one to care for them. I was informed by Japanese nationals that this was not out of the ordinary. It seemed commonplace in every country I'd lived.

My objective was to have police speak to Yamaguchi and ask him to leave me alone. "How may I help you," a woman at the front desk inquired.

"I would like to file a stalking complaint."

"One moment please." The front desk clerk picked up the phone and spoke Japanese. "Please go up the stairs to the second floor."

Detective Hatsumoto waited at the top of the stairs. "Follow me," he ordered. He pointed toward a seat and gestured for me to sit down. After shuffling some papers on his desk, he turned toward me. "Why are you here today?"

"I wanted to complain about a young man I had met on a train and would like someone to go and speak to him. He has been stalking me and I would like to be left alone. Despite telling him on the phone, by email, and in person, he is still bothering me."

"Why do you think he is stalking you?"

"Well, he knew I was going running one day, he tried to kick me in the face, he drove past me and stuck his head out of a window of a vehicle, and many of my emails have been hacked and are now gone."

"Why would he try to kick you in the face?"

"I don't know what his motivation would be except he's alluded to the fact that he was diagnosed with a mental illness."

"Did you have sex with him?" the officer blurted out.

"No, why?"

"In Japan, our laws only allow police to investigate stalking if you have been in an intimate relationship with that person. If we investigated all reports of stalking in this country, we would never solve any other crimes," the detective stated. "If you think that someone is going to hurt you, then we can send police to your home. Other than that there is nothing we can do for you." The detective sat there looking at me, and I just stared back at him for a second. What could I say? Laws needed to be changed. Had I been insistent that the detective investigate, he would only have become more defensive. Was he not aware of the different typologies of stalkers?

In 2005, you could go onto YouTube and find videos made by men on "How to Stalk Women in Japan." Stalking was part of the culture and seemed to be a national sport that men prided themselves on. The video would show men at a subway station or a shopping center, following a beautiful woman. He would ask the woman if she'd dropped 1,000 yen and hand it to her and make it look like he was a nice guy to be returning it to her. Then he could make his move and get her number and sometimes go so far as to steal her cell phone out of her bag. One of my coworkers had experienced a similar problem, and stalking behaviors were not out of the ordinary at that time. In fact it was promoted. Japanese movies had a common theme—men in their forties abducting teenage girls and holding them hostage, starving them until they submitted to having sex with them.

I have reflected back on the laws in Japan. Had police investigated back then, there would have been a greater possibility that these two stalkers would not have bothered me for sixteen years. Better laws need to be put in place to deal with stalking and cyberstalking. The crimes listed at the end of the book are only a partial glimpse into the minds of these two mentally delusional and sadistic individuals. Words cannot explain how twisted these two really are. I can only describe it as being a mouse under the control of two cats. You can't breathe because you know they are right around the corner. That is the type of stress I was kept under for years. Had I not been a psychology professional, and as knowledgeable as I am, I might not be here today.

CHAPTER FOURTEEN

MOMO AND AUTISM

I WAS WALKING to my apartment when a man in his late thirties, with a protruding belly, stepped in front of me and waved. "Hi." It was clear that he had a form of autism.

"Hello," I said.

"I know your friend." I was surprised by his English skills. "Momo."

"Oh, you know her."

"Bye." He hadn't made direct eye contact with me and headed in a different direction. I walked home laughing about the encounter.

I'd reached home when the phone rang. "Colleen, could you look after Daichi and Himari for a few hours? The baby is very sick and I have to take him to see the doctor. I think maybe he caught a cold." Ten minutes later the children arrived. No sooner had their mom, Ichika, left when the doorbell rang.

"Who is that?"

"I don't know." I opened the door and the man with autism was standing there with a bewildered look on his face.

"You live here?"

"Yes, I do." I turned around and the children looked frightened. "Don't worry, he is a very nice person."

"Nose," he said. He used his right index finger to point at his nose.

"Ah, yes, very good."

"Okay, bye." He was gone in a flash.

I closed and locked the door. "Do you know that man?" Daichi said with concern.

"No, he is a friend of Momo's." I never knew the autistic man's name, but he later proved to be a useful ally.

Ichika arrived several hours later and picked up the children. It turned out that my ally lived a few houses up the street from me. He was my great protector! Every time he would walk by, he greeted me and then moved on with his day.

YAMAGUCHI AND THE GREAT PROTECTOR

THE THIRD TIME I had met with Yamaguchi, before going to police to ask for help, we were walking near my home. Out of nowhere came a man I will call The Great Protector. He walked up to Yamaguchi and poked him in the chest several times. "English teacher my friend. No hurt English teacher. I hurt you." The man meant business! It has been my experience that children and autistic persons have a natural instinct about people. He knew from the beginning that Yamaguchi was not of sound character and felt that he was trying to harm me.

Yamaguchi looked surprised by the encounter. "I am not going to hurt her."

The Great Protector said "bye" and left. I could have hugged him for his chivalry. He would reappear in my life several more times, and he was indeed my favorite person in Japan. He was humorous and highly intelligent.

CUT GLASS IN PROTEIN SHAKE

YAMAGUCHI AND I walked to a restaurant near my home. He was fine the second time I had worked out with him. I was bored so I agreed to have dinner with him. We talked about his family again, and he seemed distracted and talked on his phone for about ten minutes.

"How's your running going?" he finally asked.

"Great. I am running five kilometers in the morning and five in the evening, most days. How about you?"

"I have a big grappling match coming up."

"I sent you a picture. Did you get it?" he asked.

"Is that the one of you kicking? Yes, I got it."

"I have a question for you. Do you buy protein powder?"

"Yeah, I drink it all the time. Why?"

"Well, I bought some protein powder, and twice I have had a physiological reaction to it." I explained how it affected me.

"Sounds like there's cut glass in it. If I were you I wouldn't drink it anymore."

Cut glass, I thought. How did he come up with that answer? We finished dinner and he forgot his debit card and I paid. When I got home I started looking at the physiological symptoms of ingesting cut class. The symptoms were identical to what I had experienced. Yamaguchi's theme seemed to be murder. Everything he'd talked about alluded to someone getting hurt or killed. He forgot his debit card. Did he also lead a parasitic lifestyle?

CHAPTER FIFTEEN
THE PILOTS

I T WAS EARLY March 2005, and I decided to take my friend's two little girls out for a walk. It was a cool day but the sunshine warmed us up. I brought a ball for the three-year-olds to kick around. After I'd dressed them warmly, we headed down the street, past a school. The girls kicked the ball and laughed. By the time we'd rounded the corner, it was too warm and they handed me their scarves and I undid their jackets for them. We only got a few blocks past the school when Ayano needed to use the bathroom. Funny thing about kids. They go before you leave and then need to go a few minutes later. "Can you hold it until we get to the house?" I asked.

"Yeah, I'm okay."

We turned around and headed back to Momo's house. Ten minutes later, we'd arrived.

"Excuse me," said a voice. I turned in his direction. There stood a Japanese man of average height and weight in his early thirties, wearing an American baseball cap.

"Yes?"

"I saw you walking with the two Japanese girls and was curious about who you are. It is unusual to see a foreigner walking down the street with two little Japanese girls."

"These are my friend's children. I finished my teaching contract back in December. We are going to go to Canada in March of 2006, and they will stay with me for six months. Originally we were going to go in 2005, but the timing wasn't right."

"My boss sent me to invite you over for a coffee. My name is Hiroshi Sato and my boss's name is Takahashi Ito. We are both helicopter pilots."

"Oh really? I used to fly as well. My ex was a pilot and he taught me how to fly helicopters. We flew fixed wing as well. I've only flown for about nine hours rotary wing, and it was years ago."

"I will pick you up at ten tomorrow morning, and we will walk around the corner and down the road to the office."

"Okay, that sounds great."

The girls were listening and playing while I'd had a short conversation with Hiroshi Sato. "Ms. Colleen, who is that man?" asked Ayano.

"He saw you and Sakura walking down the street with me and wanted to know who we were."

"Oh," she said, laughing.

"We'd better go in so you can use the bathroom."

"I don't have to go anymore," she said, laughing again.

Their mothers, Chika and Momo, stuck their heads out the door. "Did you have fun Ayano?"

"Yeah!"

We walked up the stairs and I told them about the pilot who followed me to Momo's house and told them that his employer wanted to meet me.

The next morning at ten o'clock, Mr. Sato was at the gate. I walked down the stairs, and we went to a large manufacturing company. "Mr. Ito, Colleen is here," Hiroshi called out. Ito looked up and waved. He finished his conversation on the phone and began to walk in our direction. "Mr. Ito owns a window manufacturing company, and he has most of the contracts for office buildings in Nagoya. He lived in France and is creating a website for his business. Do you speak French?"

"Yes, I do, but my grammar is not the best. It has been years since I have spoken French."

"Perhaps you can help him with the website."

"I can, and I will have a friend check the grammar."

Ito held out his hand as he approached. "We saw you walking by yesterday, and I wanted to meet you. Hiroshi tells me you fly."

"Yes, I have flown both fixed wing and rotary wing."

"I own a Eurocopter," he said. "Have you ever flown one?"

"No, I only have nine hours in a Bell and I haven't flown in nine years."

"Why don't you come flying with us next Saturday? My wife will join us."

"That sounds very nice. Thank you."

"Let's go upstairs and talk in my office."

Hiroshi and I followed Mr. Ito to his office, and we talked for a few minutes. Shortly after, Ito excused himself because he had a meeting.

Hiroshi and I talked about his job in the United States and about Ito's company.

I reached Momo's house an hour later and told her that I was going flying with the two pilots on Saturday. "What...Ms. Colleen is pilot?" she asked sarcastically. I had never told her that I used to fly when I was in university. Unfortunately, the school was shut down by the RCMP. "Oh...Ms. Colleen, many men following. Why talking? Mr. Stan's friends?"

"It is normal to meet and talk to many people in different cultures. In fact, foreigners from other countries go out and meet dozens of people. Mr. Ito's wife will be there too."

Saturday at 8:30 Hiroshi and Ito pulled up in their car. I hopped in the back, and we were off to Ito's trailer near the Nagoya airport. "It will take us forty-five minutes to get to my property, and my wife will meet us there." We chatted about Ito's and Hiro's life along the way. The scenery was beautiful because the cherry blossoms were in full bloom. Some of the streets were lined with blossoms, and a light breeze blew them gently off the trees.

We arrived at a large trailer, and off in the distance I could see a hangar. "My wife will be here in about ten minutes. Come on, let's go inside and have a coffee." We exited the car and went inside the trailer. There were maps on the wall, a small kitchen, and pictures. "Sit down. Would you like a coffee?" The phone rang again. Ito said: "My wife will be about another half hour." We looked at the pictures in the trailer and talked about them. Thirty minutes later, I heard a car door slam shut. "My wife is here. I will be right back." Hiroshi and I waited for his return.

Five minutes later a tall, thin, attractive lady twenty years Ito's junior stepped through the door. "*Konnichiwa*," she said. Her husband introduced her as Aye. "Hello, Colleen." Her husband translated for her for the first few minutes and then he and Hiroshi went to pull the Eurocopter out of the hangar. Half an hour later they were back. "Helicopter is fueled, and we are ready to go, ladies."

There were a few expensive cars in the hangar, a Porsche and a Lamborghini. "Nice cars," I said.

Ito smiled. "Let's go this way," he motioned. We walked out to the helicopter on the trailer and got in. The owner had told me to sit in the front and handed me a headset. The rotors whirled and the helicopter began to shake. Ito called the tower to let them know he was airborne. Four meters off the ground and he said, "You've got control."

"I've got control," I replied. Hiroshi was behind me, and Ito beside me giving me instructions.

I flew toward Gifu Prefecture, and ten minutes before landing, Ito said, "Okay, now I am going to have you hover. Keep it steady." The first hover was not too bad. "That was a bit wobbly. Try it again and hold it for a minute."

My second hover was perfect. I looked over to Ito and asked, "How's that?"

Ito smiled. "That was perfect." I began to descend and Ito said, "I will take control from here."

"You've got control," I said into the microphone. Ito landed the helicopter on the helipad at his friend's restaurant.

I unfastened my seat belt, and we walked to the restaurant. A large wooden structure stood in front of me. It was equally beautiful inside as outside. Mr. Ito greeted the owner, and a waitress brought us to a private room and gave us menus. "What would you like?" he asked. At that time, I couldn't speak or read Japanese, so I asked what was on the menu. I ordered tofu. Mr. Ito asked if I had ever tried bees cooked in ginger and honey. Neither Hiroshi nor I had, so Ito ordered a bowl. Japanese believe it is healthy for you. The bowl was set on the table, and Hiroshi tried one first and then told me to try. "Just use your fingers to pick one up." I did and popped it into my mouth. It tasted a little fuzzy, mushy, and sweet all at the same time. "How is it?" Ito and Hiroshi asked.

"It's okay!"

Hiroshi ate the rest of the bowl. It was very expensive at 5,000 yen. "Let's go. I have a meeting at five."

I sat in the back of the helicopter with Aye as we readied for departure. The helicopter blades started up, and two carloads of people got out of their vehicles and made their way toward the helicopter. As we took off, they stood there clapping their hands. I felt rather silly watching them, but to some flying would have been something fantastic. I thoroughly enjoyed the flight. "Let's go out to Nagoya Harbor and show Colleen the scenery." Hiroshi flew out over the harbor, and we could see sailboats and Little Italy! Half an hour later we landed back at the hangar.

"Can I pay for half of the fuel?" I asked.

"No, it is okay, we were going flying anyway. On weekends I often fly to my friend's restaurant." The day was over, and I was dropped off at my apartment. "Stop by anytime you want to talk."

"Thank you for everything. I really enjoyed the day."

I went to Momo's and showed her the pictures that Hiroshi had taken. "Oh, Ms. Colleen is helicopter flying," she said, laughing.

"Yes, it was a lot of fun." I motioned with my hand to tell her we landed at a restaurant in Gifu Prefecture.

She snorted, walked away, and said, "Ms. Colleen is man?" She seemed to disapprove of it. I decided to go home, and that was the beginning of the end of our friendship. It felt as though she was trying to control my life, and if I didn't do what she wanted, I was "stupid." If it didn't involve her or her children, then I shouldn't be going places with other people. Perhaps it was just part of Japanese culture, which I would never get used to. Even if one lives in a culture for three years, one cannot even scratch the surface of understanding. Momo was very liberal-minded and had lived in Paris, France, so I didn't quite get the attitude.

I stopped by and spoke to Hiroshi once for a few minutes. I never saw either him or Ito again after March 2005, and there was never any mention about the website they needed help with. The owner had lived in France and wanted to develop a French website. Hmm...another French connection and another mystery!

CHAPTER SIXTEEN
THE WANKER AND OTAKU

IT WAS JULY 2005, and Momo and I had done a lot of walking late into the evening because temperatures would soar to about 40 C in the sunlight during the summer. We went walking one night, and we rounded a corner and saw a very tall man in an empty field. He was staring between the boards of a fence that separated a house from an empty lot. It was dark out and he was five meters away from us. "What is he doing?" A young woman could be seen cooking in the kitchen. He was spying on her. As we walked up the road and turned left, he spotted us and started to walk toward us. He got closer and closer when I noticed something was not quite right. I looked at Momo and said, "What happened to his pants?" He was wearing a business shirt, but part of his attire was missing. He wasn't wearing any pants and was holding his thing in his hand. He was a wanker! "Quick, run, Momo. He is walking toward us." Momo took off running, laughing, and choking on her water. I was close behind. When we got back to her house, we couldn't stop laughing. There was a businessman who looked like Clark Kent doing his thing.

The next evening, we walked in a different direction in order to avoid the wanker, and it was later than the night before. Momo wanted to lose a few pounds, so we walked for two hours. It was 11:35 p.m. and Momo pointed and whispered, "Miss Colleen, look." I looked up and Stanley Webber was reading a book under a streetlight. "What Stan doing? Oh, strange, Ms. Colleen." He looked up, tucked his book under his arm, and ran with Momo in hot pursuit. His final destination was a hotel at the end of the street. We never followed him inside and went to our own homes. Why would he be standing under a street lamp at 11:35 p.m. reading a book? There is only one answer. He is an otaku. This whole Japan situation was getting weirder by the day. I, too, lived on the ground floor and didn't want to encounter otakus or wankers. This was getting annoying!

AICHI POLICE HOT ON THE TRAIL OF OTAKU

JULY SEEMED TO be a busy month for Stan "the man" Otaku. His school van could often be seen parked at a car dealership near my home. This meant one thing...he was on the prowl. One July day, he walked by my house and yelled something at me. My window was open and I was cooking a late lunch. I looked out the window and there he was, Stanley Webber again! I called Momo and she called Aichi Prefectural Police, who searched for him. I never did learn of the outcome of his silliness because I went to a lady's house to learn Japanese. His unwanted harassment continued. I would later find out through the Teacher's Union in Japan that a large population of school owners were mentally ill.

CHAPTER SEVENTEEN

SUMO PARTY, THE UNDERWORLD, AND YAKUZA

I N 2005, A coworker was given free tickets to a fundraising dinner for sumo wrestlers and invited us to attend with her. Sumo wrestling has long been Japan's favorite sport and a huge tourist attraction. Sumo wrestlers are known for their strength and are referred to as *rikishi* in Japanese or 力士 in Kanji, meaning "strength" and "warrior." The primary objective of sumo wrestling is to force one's opponent out of a ringed platform or have him touch the surface with any part of his body except the soles of his feet. In recent years, the sport of sumo has been infiltrated by the Yakuza—Japan's organized crime gangs. Allegations of match fixing, dope smoking, orgies, and betting have recently been at the forefront of the media, seriously damaging the image of the sport. The supporters of sumo are called *tanimachi*. I was told that some of the wealthier supporters take the sumo to restaurants, buy expensive gifts, provide free medical care, and often give them money. My Australian coworker Brooke and I decided it would be a very interesting time and went to the dinner.

When we walked into the dimly lit room, I looked around and saw a Japanese man with slicked back Elvis hair, red tinted sunglasses, and a red shirt with black dragons on it. Women were dressed in elaborate clothing, some in long dresses others in sparkling sequin blouses and skirts. It was like a scene from Martin Scorsese's mafia film *Good Fellas*. Seated at the tables were larger-than-life sumo, dressed in their summer *yukata* with different-colored *obi*, symbolizing rank. Different ranks also had different hairstyles. There are six divisions in the sport of sumo: the top is Makinouchi, followed by Ozeki, Sekiwake, Komusubi, and Maegashira. I was told that the top sumo wore their hair in a topknot (mage) and used wax to hold it in place. Their topknot is long and waxed forward on their head, and the lower-ranking sumo have a smaller topknot.

We were brought to our tables by a man named Riki and had dinner together. After dinner we mingled with the sumo wrestlers. A few spoke English well. I'd met the most famous sumo in Japan, turned sportscaster, Mainoumi Shūhei, seen in the top photo. He became famous because he was able to take down opponents who were twice his size. We talked for about fifteen minutes, and he told a funny story about perming his hair to meet the minimum height requirement of 173 centimeters to compete as a sumo in his weight class. I moved to another part of the hall and stood next to a Sherman tank. I was dwarfed by that sumo who was over six feet, four inches tall and 350 to 400 pounds. He seemed even taller because he was wearing *geta* (gaita) shoes, which have a one-inch lift.

Brooke and I were unsure of what we had walked into when we entered the dinner party, but in the end, it turned out to be a great time, and I learned a lot about the sport of sumo and had great conversations with some of the wrestlers. It didn't matter to me if there were Yakuza at the dinner or not. We thanked all involved and departed from the Japanese version of the Good Fellas.

CHAPTER EIGHTEEN
THE VISITOR

I N OCTOBER OF 2005, my friend Sean was to take up a teaching position in Tokyo. He needed a place to stay, so I offered him my spare room to the left of the kitchen. We had met and become friends in South Korea. He was younger than I was by a few years, and I was happy to help him out. Sean arrived from Korea and took a train to the station and then took a taxi to my residence. Momo, he and I, as well as her children, went out for dinner that evening. The next day we went to Little Italy by the waterfront and did some shopping. Little Italy is a tiny area packed with things to do: shopping, gondola rides, and lots of restaurants.

Momo drove us there and brought her children. She was always willing to help everyone. I think that is why we initially got along so well. We had a lot of fun climbing Mt. Fuji and traveling to Kyoto and other cities. Our friendship had shifted dynamics, and I needed some space because she'd become too controlling. At Little Italy we walked through the shops, went on a gondola ride, ate, and enjoyed the day. We drove back to my apartment and thanked Momo.

Sean decided to have a shower after a long day. When he was finished, he sat down at the kitchen table. He looked down and said, "What is this?" He was holding up a four-inch-long, thick hair from what was evidently an Asian man's pubic region.

"Oh gross!" I exclaimed. We had been gone all day, and I had cleaned the table this morning after breakfast. This added more evidence to the fact that someone had been entering my home.

"You should ask the owner who has keys to the apartment. That was not here this morning," Sean said.

"It could have been transferred there on someone's clothes," I said. He just looked at me for a second and said nothing.

He asked if he could use my computer to check his email. "Sure, let me turn the computer on." I let him check his email and then I tried to check mine. It was gone once more. I used my credit card again to retrieve my account. Then the phone rang and Yamaguchi started yelling at me, saying, "You blocked my email on MSN!"

I did but denied it. "Not that I am aware of. As you know I have a hacker, so perhaps he or she blocked you. How would you know it was blocked?"

"I just knew."

"So what you are saying is that you are the one hacking me?"

"No, honestly I didn't do it." He calmed down a bit. "What did you do today? I went to Little Italy with friends."

"Sounds romantic," he declared and hung up. These were the very words my friend Sean had just stated. "If you were with your girlfriend, Little Italy would be very romantic." Something wasn't right.

Sean looked at me. He had heard Kato. "This guy sounds like a creep. Why don't you leave Japan?"

"Why should I leave Japan because of some stupid guy? Besides, I am leaving in March when my contract is finished."

The next day, we went to a pottery shop to paint plates. The pottery house bakes the plate and sends it to you when it's finished. I didn't want our plate, so it was sent to Sean's house in Tokyo. Japanese are some of the most talented artisans. People all around us were painting Fuji and other Japanese images and I was impressed with their painting skills. The painting on the plate we'd painted looked like something a three-year-old was capable of. We only stayed a few hours and then Sean left to start his teaching position in Tokyo.

CHAPTER NINETEEN
THE PROJECTILE

NOVEMBER AND DECEMBER seemed to be busy months for criminality. It was a cool day mid-November and I was washing the dishes when Matsumoto knocked on the door. She seemed in a hurry and her three kids were not with her. "Where are the kids today?" I asked.

"They are visiting my mother."

Matsumoto had decided to leave for Canada early because school started in March. I would not be able to go because my contract didn't end until the beginning of March. Our friendship began to deteriorate after I went flying with Ito and Sato. It was as though this lady was trying to control every aspect of my life, which didn't fly with me. I continued to wash the dishes and stepped away from the sink for one second when there was a strange noise. It sounded like a loud bang. A projectile flew through the window and landed with a thud against a wall. I looked out the window and saw a truck carrying construction equipment. Hmm... I thought it must have been a piece of metal that got under the tire and flew through the window.

Matsumoto had a horrified look on her face. "What thing?!"

"Maybe a rock or something from under the tire of the truck," I said. I walked into the living room and searched for the projectile for about five minutes but didn't find anything. I was glad I wasn't in front of the window, because that shrapnel or projectile might have hit me in the head and killed me. It was embedded in the wall somewhere, but where? I couldn't find it. I never thought of it again after that. At least not until a sweeper was brought in. It wasn't worth mentioning to anyone at that time. I only listened to the sounds of an air pistol years later on YouTube, and that was exactly what it sounded like before the projectile flew in. Many things could mimic that same sound. Matsumoto left soon after and went to pick up her kids. She seemed to think it was more. She didn't say so much in words, but it was written all over her face.

MAN ON THE BALCONY

ONE EVENING I was busy working out and went for a run. When I came home I decided to read a good book after showering. It was about 9:30 when I heard a sound on my balcony. I pushed my chair away from the kitchen table and crept into the bedroom to the right of the kitchen. Both bedrooms had double patio doors. I couldn't see anything at first, so I went into the kitchen and turned the light off. Then I went into the bedroom to the left of the kitchen and could see a massive person standing on the balcony with a white construction worker towel on his head. He hopped off the balcony and disappeared.

My balcony was on the side of my apartment, on the ground floor, and stretched the length of two double patio doors. Across from the balcony was a business with a light that would shine from outside of the company, lighting up the driveway and my balcony. This allowed me to get a pretty good visual of the man. He had long hair like Kato and a similar build. I'd not heard from Kato since he had hacked and threatened me back in October while my friend Sean was visiting. I picked up the phone and called Kato Yamaguchi. "Hello," he answered.

"It's been a while." I got straight to the point. "Were you just on my balcony? There was a man who looked similar to you who was on it and jumped off my balcony."

All he said was "Sounds ominous! It wasn't me" and hung up. What an idiot! Psychopaths try to instill fear.

CHAPTER TWENTY

PHONE NUMBER OR POSTAL CODE?

I HEARD THE sound of the mailman at my door as he dropped a piece of mail on the floor through the mail slot. I walked over and picked it up; it was my Internet bill. Tearing it open, I read through it and saw something different at the bottom. It was a phone number. I picked up the phone and called it. "Fukuyama Travel Agency."

"Hello, do you have a representative by the name of Sora Suzuki?"

To my surprise she said, "One moment please and I will transfer you." She transferred my call to Suzuki, the man I met in front of the bank who took the staff for dinner and took two doctors and me to a Natalie Cole concert. Why was his phone number on my Internet bill? Could life get any stranger than this? Only staff at my old workplace knew about Sora Suzuki because they had joined us for dinner.

"Hello," answered Suzuki.

"Sora, this is Colleen. Do you remember me?"

"Oh Colleen, yes, I thought you went back to Canada."

"No, after I talked to you, I decided to stay and live outside of Nagoya now."

"How can I help you? It is good to hear from you."

"Sora, this is going to sound very weird but I got your phone number off of my Internet bill." I remembered he had called me before I had left, but I had not spoken to him in over a year. I had misplaced his phone number.

"What do you mean my phone number is on your bill?"

"That is how I got this number."

"Well, I certainly didn't put our company phone number on your bill."

"I didn't think that, but I will send you an image and you can see it." I told him about the two hackers' tag teaming me and stealing my emails.

"You know what? I just read about this in the paper." He told me about what he'd read about hackers and gave me several suggestions on how to protect myself on the Internet.

"Thank you, that information may be helpful," I said.

"I have to go now because I have an appointment. Good luck!"

Hmm...he sounded a little angry and a little defensive.

I decided to go over and ask Momo's husband about this number. I put on my warm winter jacket and headed over to their home. I knocked on the door and it took a few minutes for it to open. "Ah, Ms. Colleen, come in, come in."

"I came here to show you this bill. Do you see this phone number? It goes to a travel agency. I called and a Japanese man I went to a concert with answered. His name is Sora Suzuki."

"No, Ms. Colleen, it is not phone number; it is mmm..." He looked the word up on his phone dictionary. "It is a postal code."

"A postal code?"

"Yes, see?" He showed me the translation on his phone.

"But I talked to this man when I called that number."

"This is strange!" He looked at me and told me, "Don't worry; it is okay. It is nothing." I think he might have thought I was crazy.

I walked down the street back toward my house thinking, *How can a postal code be the same as a business phone number? Something doesn't add up.* Another strange coincidence. Every great detective knows that there is no such thing as a coincidence. Was Suzuki a hacker too, I wondered? Another unknown element. I also thought back to him letting the phone ring thirty-two times in a row. Why would anyone let a phone ring thirty-two times? Someone had to be behind this whole thing. Momo was in Canada, so I couldn't talk to her about it, and her husband's English was very limited. A psychopath will try to play with your mind and lead you to believe that there is something wrong with you and you are losing your mind.

TURNING UP THE PRESSURE
THE HOLE IN THE WALL

I CAME HOME after having a coffee with Chika in early December. As soon as I opened the door, I noticed something was a little off. There was dust from gyprock on the computer. I looked up and a hole had been drilled about one centimeter from the top of the ceiling. It had been drilled from the utility closet into my apartment. What was the purpose of the hole? I thought no more of it, but after Stanley Webber's wife's videotaping back in March, his powwow dance at the police station, chasing a van full of kids, walking past my apartment making stupid comments, talking about a little girl's vagina and a key club, I was getting a different picture of what was going on. He had bragged about breaking and entering as a teenager, and I thought about the other teacher's home being broken into twice. Was he the perpetrator? He seemed to have a love of electronics. I was not the only victim, and there were more to come...subjected to the same insanity of an otaku and an alleged three-time black belt.

I looked online to see what the purpose of the hole in the wall might be. I found a snake wire camera that could be inserted into that hole and someone from the utility closet could look into my apartment. Again let me emphasize that this is NOT out of the ordinary in Japan. I tried to cover all possibilities to protect myself. On December 31, 2005, one of the psychopath's motives became transparent.

CHAPTER TWENTY-ONE
THE BREAK-IN

S INCE I HAD left the school at the end of 2004, Haruka Yamada and Stanley Webber had unleashed a number of attacks on Momo Matsumoto and me for no reason. Threats by Kato, perhaps Stanley Webber's sidekick; missing emails, break-ins, threats, a hole drilled through the wall, videotaping, stalking, chasing, and a man on the balcony; all of it seemed bizarre. I sat there in disbelief. I'd never experienced anything quite so strange and had never had problems with anyone in my life. It had been quiet for about a week now. Was this idiocy finally over? Psychopaths take a short break or hiatus from stalking and then resurface.

I worked out a bit and decided to go to sleep around ten. I went around to every room to make sure it was secure and then closed the sliding shoji door between the kitchen and bedroom to the left of the kitchen and then turned on the heater. A sound woke me out of a deep sleep that night. Was that man on my balcony again? I knew someone had been in my house but who? I closed my eyes and then heard the shoji door sliding open very slowly, as if not to wake me. It was a soft, slow, muffled sound. I turned around and my heart started pounding because when I opened my eyes, there was someone, a giant-size someone standing in the doorway between the kitchen and the bedroom. Holy crap! I was in for the fight of my life! I could hear my blood rushing in my ears, my heart pounded, and I could barely catch my breath. Both fight and flight mode kicked in. Was this the man from my balcony or Kato Yamaguchi? It was difficult to see because the usual light that was on at the company next door was off.

I didn't say anything to him because no sound would come out of my mouth. I was petrified. Instinct kicked in again and I kicked him as hard as I could, missed that special place, and tried to run and jump past him. If I could get past him, I could get outside and get some help. Then I remembered being told that Japanese culture is such that even if someone was stabbing you to death, no one would help. I ended up kicking him around the right region of his hip. He blocked the doorway and there was a wretched smell of alcohol. I wanted to vomit! All I remember was this giant grabbing at me, and I kept on kicking him until I finally hurt him and got partially past him into the kitchen.

His left hand grabbed my right arm, and I was spun around and thrown against the wall close to the bathroom. My left arm was jammed into a space between a little countertop and the wall. He held my right arm with his left hand. I yelled and he reached for my throat with his right hand and shoved his body up against me. I recall bringing my knee up to nail him in that special place, but he had me pinned tightly against the wall and I couldn't move. This man was far larger than I, and all the martial arts training in the world would not have allowed me to defend myself when I was pinned between a countertop and a human wall. The guy smelled like he had serious body odor too! The perpetrator squeezed my throat with one hand and still held my arm with the other. I couldn't breathe. When someone squeezes your throat, it feels like your face is going to explode. Whatever he'd said to me in Japanese, I didn't understand.

He let go of my right arm and moved his hand upward. Bang, with lightning speed I nailed the bastard as hard as I could right on the bridge of the nose with an open palm. His grip tightened around my throat for a second and then he let go as he stumbled a bit. I must have passed out for a few seconds only because my next memory was the sound of a door closing and the key turning in the lock. I was lying partially in the doorway of the bedroom and three-quarters of my body in the kitchen.

A car door slammed and an engine started. My gut instinct told me to get up and get a look at the car that was pulling out of the driveway. I stood up, slipped in something, and caught my balance. Quickly and quietly I pulled open the kitchen window where I could get a view of the street. A dark blue Volvo was backing up out of my driveway. I could not see the driver because of the frost on the back window, and the driver sits on the right-hand side of the vehicle. Daylight was barely visible on the horizon. I ran to turn on the kitchen light. When I looked down, there was blood all over the floor near the bathroom and droplets on the countertop and down my legs. A trail of tiny toe prints and partial footprints could be seen going to the window. My right toenail was cracked and bleeding, and the left was turning black. The nails on my fingers hurt because they had been bent back but seemed okay. There was slight reddish-black bruising under the tip of the nails, and one was ripped a quarter of the way down.

I got a towel and wiped up the blood on the floor. Cleaned everything up and later called a friend and asked her if she could make a doctor's appointment for me. If I called police, I would need to first find a translator, and I didn't want to go through the humiliation. My body was covered from neck to toe in bruises, but I had to go to work. I'd missed a few days already due to stress. I put gauze and bandages around my big toenails and on one finger after I had a shower. I taped my big toe to the toe beside it so it wouldn't hurt as much when I walked. A turtleneck covered the large bruises on my neck but not my arms, so I put a sweater over the turtleneck.

In my living room there was a closet with huge sliding doors. For the next two weeks, I threw my futon into the bottom of the closet and slept with a large butcher knife beside me. The toenail on my right foot came off the next day and the one on my left foot three days later. Was this man associated with Stanley Webber or was I an easy target because I was on the ground floor? I thought back to the wanker looking at the woman in the kitchen. This is not unusual in any country, and the big guy on my balcony in November could have been a dry run before he chose to attack.

I'd checked my door and it was locked. Was it a former tenant or a friend of a former tenant who had a key? While I was at work the day of the attack, my Australian coworker asked where I had gotten all of the bruises from. I had taken my sweater off as the day warmed up, and my bruises were visible. I told her I went to a karate class. I didn't want to go over what had happened to me because I am a very private person. Interestingly, three days later, near my home Kato Yamaguchi was driving the same car that I saw pulling out of my driveway. Was he visiting someone in the building or was he the rejected attacker? He, too, would be in Paris, France, at the same time as Stanley Webber, in 2011. Another unwanted French connection in my life.

CHAPTER TWENTY-TWO
ATTEMPTED BREAK-IN BY AN OTAKU (GEEK)

N O ONE HAD been on my balcony for the last two weeks, so I felt okay to sleep in my usual spot in the bedroom to the left of the kitchen. I still kept a knife beside me but not today because I went to take a nap. My workday was shorter than usual because it was New Year's Eve, so I headed home to relax and enjoy the holiday. Just when I started to feel semi-comfortable in my home again, something out of the ordinary occurred.

What a day! What a year! It was the last day of the year, December 31, 2005, and I decided to go to sleep for a few hours because my head was pounding. A migraine had set in. I took my Japanese futon out of the closet and laid it on the tatami mats and threw two pillows on top. It was cold outside and older Japanese homes do not have central heating, so I closed the shoji door and put the heater beside the futon to stay warm. My head hit the pillows and it was lights out.

I was awoke by a crunching sound outside. It sounded like someone was walking on the snow. It was dark now and all the lights in my ground-floor apartment were off. Was I dreaming? Was this the same big Japanese guy? I had a hard time breathing. Another sound came from the balcony, and I turned to look at the time; 7:31. I'd been asleep for three hours. I rolled over to face the white sheer curtains and could see the silhouette of a man on my balcony. "Hey, I know you," I said. It was the silhouette of Stanley Webber. I panicked for about ten seconds because of his body language, which told me he was enraged. He was quickly and aggressively trying to pick the lock. Why? I hadn't done anything to him. A million thoughts raced through my head. Should I grab a knife from the kitchen? It was early in the evening, and this was the one day I hadn't slept with a knife beside me. Statistically, in 90 percent of all cases, if the victim has a knife and attacks the intruder, the victim dies. *Do I open the door, sneak around the back, and scare him? How about a frying pan?* If I called Japanese police, I would have needed a translator. All of my friends might be away because it was New Year's Eve.

I thought for a second. There, standing on my balcony stood six-foot-three-inch, 200-pound Stanley Webber, otaku (geek)—tools in hand, backpack on the ground beside him—vigorously picking the door lock on the balcony to my apartment. What was he after? Here I was, five foot four, a 118-pound lightweight. And there stood the second person on my balcony since November. I no longer felt panicked as I watched him. I was calm and I had control of the situation. Ah, the element of surprise! I did the next logical thing. Quietly, I tiptoed up to the sliding glass doors, took hold of the sheer white curtains with my right hand, whipped them open, and yelled "Boo" at the top of my lungs. In a split second, Otaku grabbed his bag, hopped over the balcony, and ran as fast as his daddy long legs could carry him. I stood there in disbelief. Was this guy for real?

I picked up my phone and called Ichika, who had not left yet for the New Year's celebration. I explained to her what had just happened and I was laughing because I felt I'd caught him at his own game. I laughed at the thought of him having to wash out his knickers after being scared off. She told me to call police. I explained about the translator issue and that my chances of finding a translator on New Year's Eve would be next to impossible. Ichika asked if I was okay, and I said I was fine.

"Maybe I'd better write to my daughter and wish her a Happy New Year." I turned on the computer and opened up my browser. Someone started to type across my browser, "Getting Paranoid?" I deleted it and wrote "What's the matter? Did your mommy want you home by nine o'clock?" Webber's wife was a decade older than he was. Who breaks into someone's house at 7:31 p.m., on New Year's Eve? An otaku. He never wrote after that, so I messaged my daughter. Then I recalled a comment made by Otaku in front of all the teachers. "My brothers and I used to break into people's houses when we were teenagers." Webber didn't know that he had been caught on camera by my investigator. I'd met him at an Izakaya across the street from my residence. Stanley Webber's motive became transparent. The words "getting paranoid" told me everything I needed to know about him. All of his and Kato's threats and actions now made sense, albeit his motivation for these attacks made no sense. This was one of their ways to manipulate the object of their unwanted attention. Psychopaths do not think like you and I and are extremely dangerous. I wonder how far he would have taken things had he been able to break into my residence.

POLICE AND LAWS

I REMEMBERED I had Detective Hatsumoto's contact card in my wallet. I called the police on January 2, 2006 and spoke to Hatsumoto. "Hello, Detective Hatsumoto. I visited you back in May and reported a stalker. Do you remember me?"

"Did someone try to hurt you?"

That was an odd question. I didn't tell him about the person on my balcony or the person who had broken in. "Yes, but I caught someone on tape trying to break into my home." I told him what I did to Stanley Webber. "It was my former employer. Shall I bring in the videotape?"

"No, the courts do not accept videotapes. You need to have pictures. They need to be eight-by-ten black-and-white photos for the courts to accept them."

Wow, I thought, *this is stupid*. I phoned Ichika and told her what the police said about the photos.

"Agh...they are so stupid here" was her response.

I did tell her it was videotaped but I didn't say who did the videotaping. Now I had three answers. Webber and Yamaguchi both hackers, and Japanese police had objections to every piece of evidence I'd offered them, including videotaped evidence. All foreigners are viewed as troublemakers according to one Aichi Prefectural police officer. The fact is we are the ones usually trying to communicate and resolve the issues.

INTERPOL

IT WAS JANUARY 2006, a new year and new things to look forward to. After my former employer had tried to break into my house the night before, I decided I was going to get a spy camera. A friend and I went to a market to buy a few things, and I found a spy camera in a coffee can, but I would also need a DVD player to record. What was great was the older man we bought it from added a service after my friend told him about the break-in. He offered to come over and sweep my apartment. We set up a time and in a few days he arrived with a long, rectangular baton.

He went into the kitchen and checked, waving his baton over different areas. Then I remembered the projectile that had flown through my window back in November. If it was metallic, then he might find it. The man went into the living room when suddenly there was a beeping noise. He'd found something in the living room! What? "What is it?" I asked Chika."

"I don't know." She spoke Japanese to him and he came out of the living room. He seemed to be confused about something.

"Does he know what it is?"

She ignored the question. Interestingly, I don't recall him checking the other rooms. I never did find out what he'd found. A story told to me by the Japanese was that even when a loved one is in the hospital dying of cancer, the doctors leave it up to the family to tell them. In some instances they never tell their loved ones why they are ill. Perhaps not telling me was her way of either protecting me or alternatively, covering something up.

In my opinion, the projectile was just a piece of metal that got under a tire of a truck and flew through the window. After she left, I decided to contact Interpol. I could not get Japanese police to investigate, and I was under attack, and it is my belief that Stanley Webber was at the root of all the problems. I'd never been in any kind of trouble anywhere as previously stated!

I picked up the phone and called Interpol.

"Interpol," said a voice on the other end of the phone.

So far, the police had refused to investigate, and a man had been on my balcony in November, one tried to kick me in the face, another broke in, and now my former employer had tried to break and enter.

"Yes," I said, "I would like to ask you a question."

"Are you a police officer?"

"No, I am not."

"We do not usually speak to civilians. What's going on?"

"Well, I reported my former employer as a suspected pedophile and I have been attacked by two people, and on New Year's Eve, my former employer tried to break into my residence. When the Japanese police did not investigate, I wrote the American Embassy, and the FBI called me. My main concern is for the safety of the children who complained to myself and other teachers."

"It sounds like you are in danger. I would recommend that you pack up and leave Japan immediately."

"Okay, thank you." I hung up and knew that it would be best to leave.

I felt angry and sad. Angry that the laws in this country were not better and sad because no one helped these kids. As an adult, I dealt with what happened to me, but why would they attack? What did they have to hide? Was it because children had exposed Webber as a suspected pedophile? My daughter's email accounts had been hacked at the school before I had even left. Later Webber would try to brag that he had taken nude photos of my daughter when she was fifteen. Does the word creep apply? Seven years later there would be a reappearance in France by two or more of these culprits. Remember, sadistic psychopaths take a hiatus and then return to their usual patterns of stalking behavior. Their themes were death and nudity.

I spoke with a detective from the Toronto Sex Crimes Unit in 2006. The detective asked me why I thought Webber and company would get so aggressive with me. I told him about the allegations of child sexual abuse, and he said, "These guys will do anything to hold onto their own." An American I'd met online thought I had run into a ring of suspected pedophiles. Anything is possible. I can't imagine what he did to the other teachers once I'd left Japan. I had no further contact with any of them and tried to move on with my life.

CHAPTER TWENTY-THREE

HACKER CAUGHT RED-HANDED

O N JANUARY 21, 2006, I opened up a new email and tried to catch one hacker. I used an assumed name, hid my IP, and sent a message to Kato Yamaguchi. He wrote back, "Who is this?"

"This is the person whose emails you have been hacking." Within minutes, he contacted me from a payphone at 13:06, 13:25, and 14:54. How did he know to contact me? He'd also set up a different account to write to me. He was indeed one of the hackers as suspected! I told him to get lost and leave me alone for the fourteenth time.

Two days later he called and said he felt as though someone was setting him up and he was worried that he could be charged. Police would have to catch him in the act, I told him. He seemed relieved. In his ominous tone of voice, he said, "Keep in touch. See you in the future." It was seventeen months later when he wrote via email to ask if I was in Canada or Japan. There was one final phone call from him in January 2006.

I started to pack toward the end of January 2006, and was going to visit my family for a few weeks. I paid my bills, packed everything up, and then my phone rang. "Hello...I hear you are leaving Japan. Hurry up and leave and never come back."

"I'll get right on that" was my sarcastic reply. It was Kato on the phone. I'd not heard from Kato Yamaguchi in a few days, and now he was calling to threaten me and knew that I was leaving. Only Chika and Momo knew I was leaving Japan. The phone went dead. "What a loser!" How did he know I was leaving? He was hacked into my computer perhaps and saw my ticket. Did he know Chika? What were the chances of me meeting two people with personality disorders?

On February 6, 2006, Chika drove me to the airport. "I cannot wait with you. I have to get back to my son," she said.

"That's okay. Thank you for driving me here."

"It's not a problem." She left with her daughter, and we never saw each other again. I was going through customs and I had to empty my suitcase because my daughter had left a tiny keychain lighter in it. Before I boarded the plane, I was pulled out of the line-up and met a lady who asked, "Are you from Homeland Security? I am with Homeland Security, and I thought customs was pulling all of us out of the line to check us."

"No, I am from Canada." I waited for her to get her boots on.

"They make you take your belt and boots off, and search you. Good luck," she said.

I was searched and then boarded the plane.

CHAPTER TWENTY-FOUR
OTAKU STRIKES MIDAIR

I WAS EXHAUSTED and slept on the flight home, but little did I know someone was back up to his usual tricks. When I arrived in Oshawa at my daughter's place, I checked my emails. Someone had graciously sent $4,200 worth of fitness equipment to my mother's house, and another $750 was removed from my bank account without my authorization. I contacted the sellers and stopped them from sending the fitness equipment and got my money back a week later. Then I traced the IP. Japan! No one in Japan knew my mother's address except for Stanley Webber. The IP of the perp was 58.92.65.102 and showed full documentation of the nice gifts sent an hour and a half into my flight. How nice of them to think of me!

I called Oshawa Police and an officer was dispatched out and I made a report. It was like the Spanish Inquisition: "What happened? Why were you in Japan? Who has it in for you? Why?" Three days later, Detective John Van Seters called from Major Fraud. He could not get to my case because a caregiver for a disabled man had run off with his life savings, and the disabled man was about to be evicted from his home. The disabled man absolutely took precedence. I had taken care of the fitness equipment being sent, and all was well. I only wanted to see the person charged because it was fraud. Over the next decade more fraud and more interference in my life occurred.

I was not satisfied with the answers from Oshawa Police, and because eBay is in the USA, I filed a complaint with the FBI-IC3 Unit or cyber unit. At this point I had been hacked and had forty-two emails taken and now fraud. Seventy-two emails would completely disappear over a fifteen-year period. Could they catch this person? Could they prove who did it? There were never any answers from either police force. The crime spree would intensify over time. At this point I'd been in contact with Interpol, the FBI, Aichi Prefectural Police, FBI-IC3, Oshawa Police and Major

Fraud, Toronto Police Sex Crimes Unit, and the Regional Director of Security for Asia Pacific. No answers. It was about at this point I realized what I was dealing with. Not one but two suspected psychopaths.

CHAPTER TWENTY-FIVE

ANOTHER VICTIM AND THE AUSTRALIAN CONSULATE

I N 2006, I left Canada to teach in Nowon-gu, South Korea. I taught at a great school and had no problems there. There were only two Japanese elements during my time at the school. First, the Teacher's Union in Japan contacted me to ask if another teacher, James Michaels, could contact me. The union representative reported that another teacher claimed to be a victim of the school owners in Nagoya, Japan, and wanted to talk to me. I agreed, and the man wrote to me and told me that he had worked for Stanley Webber. He was being threatened, followed, and the owner had sent out dozens of emails to prospective employers saying "Don't hire me, I am too stupid" in the cover letter. He wanted to sue Stanley Webber for defamation of character. The owner was telling him he was going to have him thrown out of the country and at one point was in a shouting match with him. He, too, went to police to report suspected child sexual abuse.

Everything that happened to this man was what the owner had done to me. I was very concerned and contacted the Australian Consulate in Nagoya because police did not do anything to help me. I didn't want this man to get hurt, because he had beaten cancer. I only had contact with the consular twice, and James Michaels did tell me they contacted him to ensure he was okay. The behavior was a repeat pattern of exactly what had happened to me and other teachers. Later, I would find out that something also happened to two American teachers, which included breaking and entering, extortion, and threats.

A week after having contact with James Michaels, I received a mysterious phone call from a Japanese man.

"Norman, Colleen Sama?"

"Hai," I replied. Sama is an honorific term to show respect when addressing someone by name. Click, he hung up, and there were no other issues in 2007 except hacking and a few messages from Yamaguchi.

VANCOUVER POLICE DEPARTMENT

IN 2007, I contacted Vancouver Police Detective Tina Fuchs. What happened to me in Japan had finally hit me, and I was worried that these people would keep up their harassment. She advised me to cut off all contact with all Japanese people, including closing all emails. I did exactly that but it didn't stop the idiots from hacking and stealing more emails. Vancouver seemed like an ideal place to set up a company, and I went so far as to think about changing my last name to get away from Otaku and Kato. Unfortunately, Detective Tina Fuchs told me she did not have enough evidence to warrant changing my last name and social insurance number. How much evidence does one need? I had a green garbage bag full of evidence at that point.

I did explain what had happened and that I was not the only victim and I did have a mountain of evidence. Then I was told crimes would have to have occurred in Canada. Yet another failure in the system. If this was happening to me, then how many others have gone through this but have actually died due to police inaction? Near death was not too far off in the distant future.

CANADA 2007-2008

SIX MONTHS OF my life were spent in Canada. I thought about opening a homestay business but decided against it after the manager of the housing community committed a crime. I was in contact with RCMP Corporal Jeff Coles and his partner. The manager was known to police and had quit his job after the incident. This was not a crime committed against me but someone known to me. I got my rental money back from the company without issue and chose not to open the business. I spent six months in Canada training for a marathon. As previously noted, hacking occurred and fraud on one of my credit cards. Although I'd moved, I was still being bothered by these idiots.

YONGIN 2008-2009

YONGIN WAS AN interesting town to live in. There I met a good friend, Park Kyung Mi, and the director, John Duck Bach (Park). It was an international music school, and I taught kindergarten and middle school as well as developed the curriculum. The students were from various background, and some were troubled students who didn't fit into the mainstream Korean educational system. The first apartment I looked at was not for me. The owner opened the door and there were a thousand flies buzzing around. Someone had left the window open. The second one we found was okay. There was a Japanese element here as well. My coworker Kate Jung arrived at my apartment. We often spoke after work until late in the evening. I told her something strange was going on in my building, and someone was playing recordings to me. All I did was open my door, and it was so loud I could record it.

Kate listened to the recordings. "Oh my god. It sounds like someone having sex." Then someone was speaking Japanese. "This is strange. Why don't you move to the school?"

I did. After I moved to the school, there were no more issues other than continued hacking. The worst was yet to come!

CHAPTER TWENTY-SIX

VANCOUVER 2008-2011

I WORKED FOR a number of companies in Vancouver and opened my own. I contacted Detective Tina Fuchs at the end of 2008 because both my daughter and I were being hacked again and threatened. Yamaguchi had reappeared in 2008 and so had Webber.

Fuchs referred me to the Burnaby Detachment of the Royal Canadian Mounted Police because the area where I resided was within their jurisdiction. I went in and made a report with Constables Foster and Ibbotson. They went to talk to their supervisor to see if they could investigate and they came back and said they would. I felt relieved because I just wanted my life back. Three months later, there was no word from either constable, so I contacted Ibbotson. She was curt and said, "There is nothing to investigate" and hung up. I picked up the phone and called her supervisor, who was at that time supervising SWAT. I told him there was no investigation, and he said that the RCMP lacked leadership and funding. Hacking in Canada and an assault in another country was not high on their priority list. I never heard from either officer again, and nothing was ever done. Fraud and more hacking, but it was my problem.

An email arrived from Stanley Webber, who tried stating again that he had naked pictures of my daughter from when she was fifteen years old and in Nagoya. I didn't believe him. When my daughter and I went to print the email off, it had been deleted. There were dozens if not hundreds of instances of this kind of email stupidity. At one point someone had tried to put nude photos of women and children on my computer, and someone else took them down.

I contacted a private investigator in Vancouver to ask about catching the hacker, and he said that even if you catch them in the act, it is very difficult to prosecute from overseas. The game continued.

CHAPTER TWENTY-SEVEN

PARIS, FRANCE: ALL HELL BREAKS LOOSE: TERRORISM

I MADE THE decision to move to Paris, France. After all, I had my own online teaching business, I was European, and I wanted to learn proper French. If the police in Canada wouldn't help me, I would leave. I went online and found a tiny *chamber de bonne* to rent for a year and then I would move to a larger place. I wanted to see all of Paris.

When I arrived, I took a taxi from Charles de Gaulle Airport and met the owner of the apartment. I entered a tiny elevator for two and went to the seventh floor. The owner was a Canadian married to a Frenchman. "Now I have to tell you about this lock..." Lynne said. "It is very tricky. You need to check it because sometimes it doesn't lock properly. The double bolt should be okay."

The apartment was very small and had a shower, but the bathroom was outside the room, around the corner. I was so happy! Paris! Off I went to look around the neighborhood and got lost a few times in the first week. I had Internet and could teach online.

HIRED

SOON AFTER ARRIVING I applied for other jobs and was hired to work at some of the largest companies in Paris to teach heads of security, human resources professionals, lawyers, account executives, publishing agents, and artisans. On the 7th of July, I met with my friend Park, Kyung Mi and went to have a picnic on the grass near the Eiffel Tower. As we walked around the tower, we heard footsteps quickly approaching to the left of us. A man was running, holding something that bulged out from under his jacket. Undercover police leapt through the air and tackled him. He was a purse snatcher. There's always something exciting going on in Paris.

BREAKING AND ENTERING

I LIVED IN the 17th arrondissement, a twenty-minute walk from the tower. Kyung Mi and I had a great lunch and walked over to Le Louvre and took some pictures. When we arrived back at my tiny apartment, we exited the elevator, and my apartment door stood wide open. We had both checked it before we'd left. "What happened? Huh! The door was locked when we left!" Kyung Mi exclaimed. "How can they get in? There are three doors to go through. Oh my god! You are lucky your computer is still here! I hope they are not the Japanese again!"

I called the landlady to tell her what happened and asked her if she had been in there. She said she was at work. This meant a former tenant or the building manager had keys. My heart sank because I could hear Japanese speaking on the fifth floor. That spelled trouble to me. And I was right. I was wishing at this point that something a little less exciting would be going on in Paris.

MAN IN BUILDING AND THREATS!

I WAS AWOKEN by a man in my building shouting my name. I didn't know anyone in Paris other than Kyung Mi, and the voice was that of Kato Yamaguchi. My memory flashed back to Japan and the two people on my balcony and of the one who broke in. I retrieved a knife from the drawer just in case he broke through the door, and I remained silent and waited. A few minutes later, I heard someone take the elevator to another floor. How did Yamaguchi know where I lived? How did he get into the building? He had been hacked into my computer in Vancouver, because I had never given him my Skype address and yet he had contacted me via Skype. It was possible that he saw my address online. It seemed pretty odd that someone would travel all the way to France to harass me. Why would someone spend a lot of money to fly from Japan to Paris, unless they were being paid? Was Webber behind the whole thing?

The next day, I could hear what sounded like an arrest outside of my building. I hopped up on the kitchen counter with my camera and began recording.

"Get in the car!" a man shouted.

"I didn't do anything!" a voice returned.

"Get in the car now!"

I filmed an angry man who looked like Yamaguchi sitting in a vehicle. He turned around and shouted, "I am NOT going to jail for something I didn't do!" I hopped off the counter and when I looked again the vehicle was gone. I never saw who the second person was because my visual field was obscured by a ledge.

Once I was sure the coast was clear, I brought the emails to the police on the Champs-Élysées near my home and reported the stalking incident. After leaving the police station at the Champs-Élysées, I walked next door to the Palais, a building designed by Gustave Eiffel. The front door was locked, closed for renovations. I thought perhaps I would get better pictures if I went around to the back of the building. There I saw a group of workmen. "Hello, the Palais is closed for construction," one of them said.

"Yes, I am aware. I just thought I could get a clear shot through the glass of the inside."

A man stepped forward to introduce himself. "I'm Pasquali," a short, rotund, balding man said. "This is my work crew." A group of hardworking men were carrying tools and loading them into the back of a truck. "We are just finishing up for the day. I may be able to sneak you inside as a member of my work crew. I can tell the security you are here to take photos of the progress."

Two minutes later, in I went and took photos. The architecture was incredible.

It turned out that Pasquali was a very nice man, a very nice married man, who had invited me to dinner. I left the Palais with his phone number in hand, which landed in a trash can on my way home. I think he knew I would not call him because he said, "You can't blame a guy for trying. After all, it is Paris." There's always something interesting going on in Paris. It seemed as though every day was an adventure.

CHAPTER TWENTY-EIGHT

OTAKU AND THE ARC DU TRIOMPHE

I T WAS A hot July day and I had finished work, so I took a stroll down to the Arc du Triomphe, and no sooner had I arrived than I saw a familiar face. "Hey, that looks like Colleen." Guess who? Stanley Webber was standing there. I can't say that Otaku did anything wrong in France, but my apartment door was open and he bragged to his staff about breaking into people's homes as a teen. Also, many teachers had their homes broken into, even after I'd left Japan. Revenge for scaring him away from my balcony window back in Nagoya in 2005? I said nothing to Webber and left. Great, so Webber was in Paris and so was Yamaguchi. I ignored both of them and moved on with my life until...weird things started to happen.

I hopped on the elevator and went downstairs and put my trash in the bin. I taught a few classes online and then went to go back downstairs when I noticed a trash bag like the one I had already brought downstairs sitting next to my door. What the heck? I contacted a friend and told her about it. Japanese on the fifth floor? There was a second instance when I returned home and the door was left ajar. Both times nothing was missing. Hmm...the plot thickens. My neighbor heard the man yelling at me earlier in the month, and saw my door ajar. I didn't report this to the police because I didn't catch the person who had broken in, and Webber didn't threaten me at the Arc du Triomphe. The man I'd videotaped was off in a distance, so it was hard to tell if it was Yamaguchi. All I could do was tell police I had a stalker or two.

A MELTDOWN AND SIX HOT FIREMEN IN MY CHAMBER DE BONNE

IT WAS A hot day in August; the entire month was a national holiday in Paris, France. I went for a walk around Park Monceau in between the Russian and American Embassies, and when I returned, I could smell something burning. There had been a problem with the ceiling fan, and I'd called the landlady beforehand but she was away. The fan sounded like a helicopter. I looked up in the shower and the whole fan was melting downward. I shut the fan off and got a screwdriver and pulled it down to make sure there was no fire. Had I been gone a little longer, I think the building might have burned to the ground because it was so old.

I went down the street to the flower shop. I'd not yet bought a phone but had an active phone from Canada and asked to use their phone. A man spoke English and I requested he call the fire department. I didn't see a fire, but maybe to be on the safe side I should call them, I thought.

"Why didn't you call from your house? Are you stupid?" he asked. Ignoring him I went back to wait for the firefighters.

Five minutes later six firemen were in my tiny chamber de bonne. Two in the shower and four in the living quarters searching for any signs of fire. One in the shower took the fan right off the ceiling and cut the wires. "It looks like faulty wiring. Good thing you caught it in time." They checked the floor above me and there was no fire. *Stupid me for pulling the fan down*, I thought. After six hot firemen left on that hot August day, I took pictures of the ceiling as well as the fan and sent them to my banker and landlady. My insurance sold by the bank would cover the costs. In Paris, all tenants must have building insurance. Whew! Was this an accidental meltdown? Why would a shower ceiling fan suddenly melt? Remember, Webber wrote "getting paranoid?" in my browser after I scared him away from my patio door. Now, two break-ins before the meltdown. The plot thickens again! The projectile flying through my window and a ceiling fan melting. Just two accidents in my opinion until an incident in Liverpool, England, that was potentially explosive.

CHAPTER TWENTY-NINE
SNCF AND THE WAR ROOM

THE NEXT DAY in Paris, I headed to SNCF to teach one of the persons in charge of the National Railway System. There were no rooms for me to teach in, so my client had to get permission to allow me into the "war room." If there is war or a terror attack, they are able to monitor the trains in Paris from this room. I didn't get to see it while it was operating but had a few minutes alone to stand in the doorway and stare into the center of operations. It was not all that interesting but an important room nonetheless. Had the monitors been turned on then, there would have been much more to see. Through teaching heads of security, I was able to learn more about France's National Security, which later helped me in my terrorism studies.

GAS MASKS

THE SECOND COMPANY I went to that day showed me things in their company that I was not supposed to know about. I felt like a spy in the Cold War. Otaku and Yamaguchi were in Paris; there were threats, a ceiling fan meltdown, two break-ins, and I'd only been there for two months. There were no rooms for me to teach in, so I taught in a room that housed gas masks, hazmat suits, and a shower. It was very disconcerting to learn that the French government required companies to have this equipment in case of the release of a chemical nerve agent.

There is only one problem. Years later I researched chemical nerve agents and wrote an article about them. The masks the government had provided French citizens with would not have protected them well, because it only covered their faces. VX gas and Sarin gas are absorbed through the skin and inhaled. Wearing the mask might slow down the effects of the gas and may give the workers time to be injected with the antidotes, atropine and pralidoxime, but the masks would not fully protect them. My clients were very interesting and informative. Again the information provided drove my research into chemical nerve agents, public knowledge about them and emergency preparedness.

PUBLICIS AND A GUNMAN

I HAD WORKED at a company that was just down the road from Charlie Hebdo, site of the 2015 terror attack. It was 2011, and I taught three account executives that day. One told me that six months earlier, a gunman had been walking down the road. One recollected that a van was driving by, stopped, grabbed him, and threw him in. Three women from the company had witnessed it and were afraid. They felt that Paris was no longer a safe city and advised me to be careful. Was this a trial run for an attack on Hebdo? In November of 2011, a different location of Charlie Hebdo was firebombed. This piqued my curiosity, which would two years later lead me to earn a master's in forensic psychology and to complete my dissertation on terrorism. Something very sinister went on as I neared the end of my degree. There is always a French connection and a French element!

STICKY FINGERS IN PARIS

AFTER TEACHING THE account executives, I went to a bank machine along the way to my apartment and withdrew a large sum of money from my Canadian account and one other account. It was payday so I was going to my bank, LCL, to make a deposit. My briefcase has a side pocket in the briefcase itself, and a zipper closes it. Then there is a second zipper that closes my entire briefcase. When I reached my bank, I noticed that the zipper was partially open. It had been zipped shut and the second pocket was open. The envelope I'd put the money in had disappeared. The banker came out and asked if everything was okay. "No, I put an envelope full of money in my briefcase and it is gone."

"Did you lose it?"

"No."

"Some people in Paris have very sticky fingers. Sometimes they can follow you from the bank machine and will steal. I doubt you will get the money back," he said.

"Welcome to Paris!" another customer said.

Wow! A meltdown, theft, two break-ins, gunmen, and gas masks. This was insane!

GARE DU NORD POLICE AND PASSPORT THEFT!

I WAS EXHAUSTED because I had visited almost every museum in Paris, and the 17TH arrondissement, where I lived, was close to the Champs-Élysées. All night I could hear motorcycles driving up the narrow street, beeping their horns, and people living it up. I stayed at a hotel across from the Gare du Nord railway station because I needed sleep! In the morning I walked out of the hotel and headed home. The night before I had my passports, but now they were gone.

I walked up to the hotel clerk, thinking that maybe he hadn't given them back to me. Hmm...I then asked where the closest police station was to report the theft. First, thousands of dollars went missing and now both passports. My friend was supposed to meet me for breakfast, but I didn't see him. Maybe I had time to run to the police station to report them missing and could then run back here before he arrived. I called his phone and could not reach him.

Off I went to the police station and I made a report. The officer and I went through every pocket of my briefcase. Had someone had a key card for my hotel room? My next step was to contact both embassies to advise them they'd been stolen. I arrived back at the hotel an hour later, and my friend Max was there waiting for me, holding something in his left hand. "Where did you get those?" I asked.

"I caught someone taking them from the side of your briefcase and followed him," he said.

I noticed that Max's middle knuckle had a small cut and it was bleeding. Why hadn't he said he was going after the thief? I didn't have to call the embassies and called police to advise them my passports had been found. He couldn't stay for breakfast and we went our separate ways, only to meet again in January of 2012. This would be the last time I saw him because he died in March 2012, of a sudden heart attack.

THE EMBASSY OF IRELAND
AND THE BRITISH AMBASSADOR

MY HOUSE HAD been broken into twice while my friends had been with me. I had been to police twice, and there wasn't much they could do. So, I went to the Irish Embassy early in the morning in July 2011. The Irish Embassy is just on the other side of the Arc du Triomphe. I woke up early and walked over to where it was located. When I arrived the large door was still locked. I checked my watch and I was a bit early. I waited.

A man drove up in an expensive, white, antique Rolls-Royce. Maybe this was the ambassador, I thought. It was not the right one. "Hello, is the door not open yet," said a gentleman in his British accent.

"No, it is 9:15 and it opens at 9:30."

"I am the British ambassador to Ireland."

"I am Colleen."

Out of the corner of my eye, I spotted two men dressed in suits, poking their heads around the corner of the building. "Are those two men your security guards?" I asked.

"No, ambassadors do not have personal security." We talked a bit more and then he looked past me at the two men ducking in and out of an alcove. "They are acting rather oddly, aren't they?"

"Yes, that was why I thought they were your security. Maybe they thought I was a threat to you."

Soon after, the embassy doors were opened and I said good-bye. A lady met me at the counter, and we talked about what had happened to me in France. She took a report and then I left the embassy and headed to work. I wanted to ensure that if anything happened to me, my family would be notified. Who were those two men? Why were they acting so oddly? When I looked up the image of the regional director of security for Asia Pacific, one of the men bore a similar resemblance. Then again, many people look alike.

CHAPTER THIRTY

FRENCH NATIONAL POLICE HEADQUARTERS AND A TERRORIST?

WHY THE THREATS from Yamaguchi in Paris? Why had he traveled all the way from Japan, along with Webber? So, I moved on with my life once again, changed apartments, and set up my business as an auto entrepreneur. In order to do that I had to go to the French National Police Headquarters. I moved from the 17TH arrondissement after the ceiling fan meltdown, two break-ins, passport theft, theft of thousands of euros, running into Otaku, and threats by Yamaguchi. What a world!

I entered the French National Police Headquarters in Paris. An armed officer asked me to put my bag down to be x-rayed before I was allowed to go up the stairs. The officer gave me instructions on where to go. Of course I went in the wrong direction, and another officer caught up to me and showed me to the registration office. I filled in the forms, took out my Irish passport, and waited in line. A clerk took my forms, copied my passport, and told me to come back in twenty minutes. I went outside the doors and took a seat on the bench. As I did I noticed a young man fling his papers at one of the clerks. "There is nothing on the form," she exclaimed.

"Hold on to it and I will be right back," he replied. He looked as though he was of Middle Eastern descent, had short hair, stood five foot eight, and was slender, clean-shaven, and neatly dressed.

He walked toward me and sat down. "Hello, where are you from?" he asked.

"Canada and Ireland. How about you?"

"I just moved here in July of 2010, with my older brother from Belgium. I am from Morocco. Why are you in Paris?"

"I wanted to do something different and opened my own business. Where did you learn to speak English so well?" I asked.

"I worked in construction in the Middle East and in oil. My brother and I are going to open a construction company. How long will you be in Paris? Do you plan on spending a long time here? Do you have any family here? What are your long-term plans?" He asked too many questions and I gave little information to him.

After a while, I told him I had to go back in five minutes to pick up my registration form. He stood up and said he was going to go do that as well. I watched him go downstairs instead of back to the registration office. Maybe he changed his mind about opening up a company.

Four years later I awoke to the media image of Salah Abdel Salam and the attacks at the Bataclan. The image was identical to the man I'd met four years earlier at the French National Police Headquarters, where I was registering my business. When I saw his face on my computer, the first thing out of my mouth was "Hey, I know you." Both Salah Abdel Salam and the mystery man from the French National Police Headquarters had moved to Paris at about the same time, and had an older brother, but they had different birth places. Abdel Salam was born in Belgium and the mystery man in Morocco. Later images of the terrorist captured in Belgium proved it was definitely NOT the man I'd met in Paris. The terrorist was taller and thinner, but his facial features in the picture were very similar to the man I'd met four years earlier. My terrorism research in 2015 would once again connect me to France in more ways than one.

MOVED!

THE NEXT THREE months would be relatively quiet for me. I continued to teach online, and at this time neither culprit from Japan knew where I was residing. The move was done covertly, and no one knew my address. My daughter's friend lived in the apartment downstairs from me. She and her boyfriend were from Iran. Over the next few months, we would spend hours and hours walking and talking while visiting sites on the outskirts of Paris.

All was well until I entered my place and found the shutters and the windows opened from the outside to the inside. I thought the wind had blown them open. But the next morning when I had spoken with my friend's boyfriend, I went upstairs to get my wallet, and there were 390 euros missing. My door was locked. The strange thing about it was they left sixty euros in my wallet. Just like Japan, where someone took 60,000 yen and left 20,000 yen in my wallet at work. A similar pattern of behavior had been established. One final note on this paragraph: When I was at my second residence, I could hear someone mention the word "firebomb" on TV. Charlie Hebdo was threatened and then firebombed four days later. The word "firebomb" would also play an important role in Liverpool in 2017, while I was searching for the Manchester bomber's target.

Otaku or Yamaguchi I moved for the third time—this time to the Kremlin Bicêtre and more weirdness. Weird things don't just happen to me all the time, and someone had to be responsible for it all. I shared rent with a lady who was from Iraq. She seemed to be very quiet and somewhat depressed. The story I had been told was that her husband had abducted her daughter and taken her back to Northern Iraq. He was a paraplegic. But when I looked down at the floor, there were no markings from a wheelchair. I saw a picture hanging on the wall of her daughter and her husband. She and I would communicate through Google translate because I only spoke French to an intermediate level.

AN ACCIDENT

IT WAS EARLY December and I was in a rush to get to ADP to teach one of the executives. I got lost in the subway and hopped on the elevator to go downstairs. There a large man, whom I later identified as someone with a Georgian accent, slipped on something in the elevator. His elbow came up, and I got hit by accident. My head sort of rotated, and I could hear a cracking or crunching sound. The man had reached to grab onto something to catch his balance and accidentally hit me. At first I felt fine and went to work as usual.

My friend downstairs asked me to go grocery shopping with her. I declined and told her what had happened. Later that evening, I started to vomit and spent the next few weeks sleeping a lot. I visited the doctor and he said that I had a head injury and I should be okay in a few weeks. No bones in my neck were broken, but when I turned my head from side to side, there was a crackling sound. I went about my business and did a lot of teaching from home. Only later did the injury resurface and cause breathing and heart problems.

CHAPTER THIRTY-ONE
PARTIES AND PARAMEDICS

ONE EVENING IN late January 2012, there were three parties going on in the building where I'd just moved to. On that day, there was an unusual visitor. She was thinking about renting one of the bedrooms in the apartment. Something wasn't right. The young, raven-haired, heavyset Portuguese lady didn't walk down the hall to look at the room; instead she made a beeline to me, sat down next to me, and asked if I was okay. She thought I looked rather stressed. "I'm fine," I replied. She started to talk and looked as though she wanted to tell me something but didn't. The owner of the apartment took her down the hall to look at the room. She said she would get back to her. And then things got stranger.

All night, I could hear loud music and people chatting. One man could be heard shouting that he wanted someone out of Europe before this whole thing went down. What thing and who? All night I tried to sleep but couldn't. At one point I could hear Japanese people speaking and recorded them with my cell phone. Early in the morning, one contractor called me to see if I was going to work. I advised him I would be absent. It is strange that he would call and ask. Then, I looked out the window and said to him, "Bob, I want you to remember me telling you this. There is a little red firetruck outside of my building. Someone has kept me awake all night, threatening either me or another woman close by. Something isn't right! If anything happens to me, please remember me telling you this." I said good-bye and something stranger happened.

Five minutes later, paramedics from that little red fire engine showed up at our apartment door. They said that they'd been looking for the place for over half an hour and that someone in the apartment had committed suicide. Suicide? I saw this as an opportunity to get out of the situation I was in, so I went with paramedics to a hospital. They dropped me off, put me in a wheelchair, and said good-bye. There was nothing wrong with me. I waited ninety minutes to see what was going to happen next and who was behind all of the silliness. I was not registered and no doctor treated me for an alleged suicide. How would anyone know that someone had attempted suicide unless there was a spy camera in the room? I have no scars, liver damage, or any other form of damage, so why were paramedics dispatched to that apartment? Wrong apartment? Japanese? Need I say more?

I got up and ninety minutes later walked out of the hospital unnoticed. I called my investigator/friend and explained what had happened, and he told me to go to a hotel. My phone started to ring, and Leila from the second place where I'd rented was calling me. She wanted to know where I was and if I was okay. She had arrived when the paramedics did. At this point I told her not to worry, I was fine, and went to sleep. The next morning, I once again changed hotels and made the decision to leave France because of what had been occurring. I bid Paris a fond adieu and left the crazy Japanese behind. I left Paris, France, five days later with no answers, no charges, and a whole host of crimes committed by others.

I passed out on the flight to Canada and recall nothing except the plane was almost empty, and I remembered the plane touching down in Toronto. It appeared that the head injury was worse than I'd expected and in Canada would affect my heart and lungs. It felt like my heart was in a vise grip, and it would frequently skip a beat, which led to me to gasp for air. It was my autonomic system trying to keep me alive. The injury was so bad that it took thirty-two months for me to be able to breathe properly and to not have to sleep seated upright with four pillows behind me. Otaku and Yamaguchi became like a bad rash, appearing everywhere. Years later these incidents would repeat themselves in Liverpool, England. The unexpected was about to occur.

CHAPTER THIRTY-TWO

UIJEONGBU, KOREAN AND US MILITARY, AND COUNTERTERRORISM

IT WAS A hot September day in 2012, and after the disasters in Paris, France, and Canada, I moved to Uijeongbu, South Korea. These were the best and the worst four years of my life. Does that make sense? Well, not really. Apartments are provided for teachers in Korea, and, wow, did I get a nice one. Note the sarcasm. I arrived and entered my apartment and just about died. The balcony was full of junk covered in two inches of thick dust; there were 100 or more toenail clippings under the bed, used clothing hanging in the closet, too much furniture, and the wallpaper was torn or bubbling in places. The bathroom door had expanded from water hitting it and would not close properly. It was a proper dump!

Exhaustion had set in and I still didn't feel well from the head injury I'd sustained in France, and this apartment was over the top. I cried for an hour and slept with four pillows propped up. The housing in Paris was bad enough, but this was horrendous. It was so dirty it took an entire month to clean it properly. The clutter was cleared away and put in the trash, and by the time I was done, it looked better. How do people live this way?

When we travel we meet all kinds of people, at airports, on planes, buses, trains, boats, and then there are the people who already live in the apartments around us. I've met hundreds of thousands in my travels but remember a fraction of them. We have no control over the people around us and what they do, especially when they are unknown. A Korean soldier created problems for everyone in the building and was super noisy. At one point one of my neighbors knocked on his door and threatened him because it was 3 a.m. and he was having some type of meltdown. The military came in and took him away for a week at one point. Although everyone in my building was sleep deprived, we did our best to ignore the crazed soldier.

Six weeks after my arrival, someone had been in my apartment. If I told you what they did, you would throw up. I advised my employer and asked him to have a locksmith come over and change the locks. The locksmith came over and replaced the old one with a digital lock. "Code," he said in his limited English. I entered my code and could hear the six beeps. The soldier upstairs yelled out the exact code I'd entered. The locksmith had a surprised look on his face, but I didn't know how to tell him to change it to silent mode. Once again I told my employers about it. They kept telling me to call police. What could they do?

BRAIN RETRAINING

I HAD SUFFERED a serious head injury in Paris in an accident, and I noticed there were deficits in my spelling, so I went online to Live Mocha Café and learned twenty-five different languages to retrain my brain. Beginner level Hindi, Farsi, and Norwegian were my favorite languages to learn. I couldn't speak them well but I could read. For fourteen months I worked full time and studied languages and counterterrorism at Leiden University.

My head injury finally started to heal after twenty months. Although it had left me gasping for air sometimes and feeling like my heart was in a vise grip, it was getting better. I went for an echocardiogram and treadmill test, and it looked like there was only a slight valve issue. The video of the echocardiogram was sent to a cardiologist for further examination. At thirty-two months post-injury, the gasping and heart issues had improved by 99 percent. But when I was sleep deprived, the gasping for air would recur.

The stress from the harassment by the soldier above me in Uijeongbu became so bad that I would vomit daily and had to struggle with my physiological health. A combination of fatigue and stress became unbearable at several points. To counteract the stress, I would walk for two to three hours after work to get out of the environment I was in. Everyone was affected by this Korean soldier, not just me.

HACKING

THERE WERE MANY incidents of hacking again, and someone added 800 military to my Skype. There were generals and other high-ranking officials, including a fake George Bush. I contacted three and asked who added them. "You did," they replied. Ugh... Ten percent had Japanese names. Otaku or Yamaguchi? Skype said the last IP was traced to Japan, but they are not supposed to tell me that, and I didn't hear it from them.

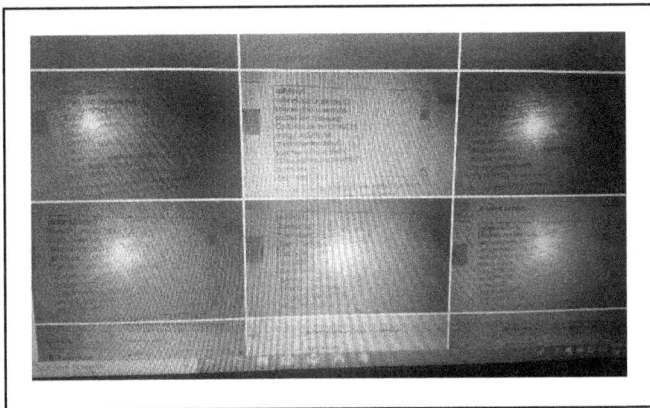

Finally, a three-day holiday. I got to go on a tour of the DMZ. I hopped on a bus and off I went. I did a lot of studying and traveling from 2012 to 2016. Much of the travel was to get away from the noise in my building. I'd applied to get into the University of Liverpool's Master of Science in Forensic Psychology and Criminal Investigation. I waited for their reply.

CHAPTER THIRTY-THREE

NORTH KOREAN SNIPERS, ROK SOLDIERS, AND THE THIRD TUNNEL

MY FIRST TOUR in Korea was spent at the DMZ, or demilitarized zone, which borders North and South Korea. It is the most heavily fortified border in the world with 160 North Korean guard posts and sixty in South Korea. Our bus wound up the mountains toward the DMZ, with our guide talking about the North and South Korean border and the American military. All buses are boarded by US military because of the danger in the region, and they made good tour guides.

I sat in the back of the bus, which was boarded by three other male teachers, one Korean-American, one Australian, and a Canadian. In front of us sat a greasy-haired man who was trying to obscure his face. He was slouched down and said something rude, and the three male teachers said, "That's not her." I am not quite sure who they were talking about, but the grease ball was not on the tour with us when we got out of the bus. He just disappeared and was not on the tour or the bus on the way back either. Another strange occurrence. Maybe the North Koreans got him!

We walked through a building and then out to the United Nations Command Military Armistice Commission Staff Conference Building. This was the only building that borders with North Korea that our tour was allowed in. Before we went out, we were told not to make any sudden movements because North Korean snipers might shoot. I momentarily hid behind a bald man wearing sunglasses. He didn't know it, but he was on the front lines. There were cameras everywhere, and we were advised not to take pictures of any of the building with cameras. A North Korean soldier with giant binoculars stared us down. I thought binoculars like those were only in cartoons. In the windows above him were soldiers watching us.

We were then escorted into the command building and told half the building is in North Korea and the other half in South Korea. As I walked into the building, to my left was a South Korean ROK soldier whose hands were enormous. His job was to stand there all day, hands clenched. It is an intimidation tactic. Right in front of me was a North Korean ROK soldier, much thinner and less intimidating. This building is used to host meetings between presidents, diplomats, and other officials. Our military tour guide advised us that the North Koreans didn't know the difference between the South Korean flag and toilet paper.

South Korea ROK Soldier

North Korean ROK Soldier

We got back on the tour bus after taking pictures and learning about the history and went to the third tunnel. We took a monorail deep under the ground for ten minutes. It was kind of creepy because all we could see in front of us were the silhouettes of the people and one bright light. It was a slow ride that seemed as if it was never going to end. It was like traveling into the abyss. Finally, we got to the bottom of the rail line. I got off of the monorail, then walked to the opening of the tunnel.

Our wonderful tour guide said we could not take pictures because

North Koreans had dug the tunnel. If we got caught taking pictures, we'd be fined $3,000 American and could face up to six months' jail time. We entered the tunnel and walked on boards; water dripped down and there really wasn't much to see to the untrained eye. Sure enough some idiot tourist took a picture and was escorted from the tunnel by soldiers. The tunnel was historically significant because the North Koreans had attempted to infiltrate the South undetected, but the tunnel was discovered before they could do so. Tunnels are dug through the mountains from the North, and spies come into the South. The border remains a danger to South Koreans to this day, but it was by far the best tour I've ever been on.

THE BLUE HOUSE AND THE BACKSIDE

MY SECOND TOUR in Korea was to go to the presidential palace, also known as the Blue House. It is guarded by the presidential security service or "Men in Black." They all wear black suits and black sunglasses, even on a cloudy day. We walked through the gardens of the presidential palace and then went to a restaurant for lunch. Wherever you go in Asia, there are errors in grammar and sentence structure, which is to be expected because it is a second language. To be honest, I am surprised at how well most Koreans speak English and the improvements made over an eleven-year period.

When we first got to the restaurant, we went to the restroom. I closed the door and saw an interesting phrase on the back of the door. "Your toilet button is on your back side." I pulled out my cell phone and took a picture of it. I could hear my friend two stalls away asking me why I was taking a picture. When she came out of the bathroom, I explained to her what the phrase meant. It is one of those things you can't go without mentioning.

THE PHOTOGRAPHER

The soldier upstairs from me had created issues for everyone in my building for months. It was December of 2013, and it got dark by 5 p.m. At this point, I'd become tired of the idiocy of my former employer, Yamaguchi, and now the soldier above me. I came home and ate dinner, went to brush my teeth, and there were camera flashes in my bathroom. My entire bathroom lit up. Ugh...the soldier upstairs again. I waited until I could hear him walking in the bathroom upstairs, took out my camera, turned the flash on, and pointed it outside of my window and took three pictures. I don't know if the soldier could hear me or not, but I told him how small it was and if he didn't stop bothering me, I'd put the pictures on the Internet. He was quiet after that, at least for a little while. I reversed everything he'd done to me, except break into his house, and in 2014, I moved to a new place. He continued to bother everyone until I was able to move.

CHAPTER THIRTY-FOUR
FORENSIC PSYCHOLOGY AND THE UNIVERSITY OF LIVERPOOL

AN EMAIL POPPED into my inbox from Liverpool. The university had accepted me to their online Master's in Forensic Psychology course, which surprised me because only seventy-five people were admitted into the program. It was a tough program and they don't hand out grades in the UK. Every week I had to hand in two assignments and write at least five responses to one assignment, properly cited. Additionally, there were two major assignments worth 10 percent of our grade, 5,000 words each.

My first course started and the Korean soldier upstairs was becoming more annoying by the day. It was difficult to sleep, work full time, and complete a master's degree. Twenty-four hours a day, this guy would turn up the volume on his computer or play music loudly and wake me up. I would fall back asleep, and he would do it again.

I started to study behavioral patterns amongst terrorist organizations. ISIS was being framed in the media as *the* organization to join. Tens of thousands of people were being recruited and sold a utopian dream. I looked at military models, the US war on Iraq (high-value targets), and applied them to modern-day terrorist groups. Al Qaeda generally warned when they were going to attack a target. It was a game of "catch me if you can." The 9/11 terror attacks were screaming with key indicators that an attack was imminent. Key indicators can be behavioral patterns, global news accounts, frequency of media accounts, political climate, threats, manifestos, Internet posts, and a host of other clues. ISIS was a completely different organization and went after civilian targets, usually in large gatherings. They didn't warn before terror attacks, and people were caught off guard. Studying the behavioral patterns of these groups and observing key indicators and assigning a value to them led me to be able to predict some of the places ISIS would attack in advance.

THE MOVE AND YEARS 3 AND 4 IN UIJEONGBU

BEFORE I SIGNED a new contract, I requested a new apartment. I told the owners I would pay to move the furniture, but they didn't hire a van for me. Instead, I ended up in a nice, new apartment with Eiffel Tower wallpaper in my living room, and it was empty. No furniture. I bought a table, slept on a pile of comforters, and bought a treadmill to train. I am not the only teacher who has been in this kind of situation. It seems to be more of a norm these days. When I first went to Korea, it was great. People were polite and fun to be around. Now, times have changed and owners are rude toward teachers. Some stories told by other teachers about treatment by Korean school owners were horrendous. It is unfortunate that some Koreans had no honor or respect.

I started on my dissertation, my survey was approved, and I sent it out through various social media sites and even recruited a member of ISIS to answer my survey. The day after the online ISIS member answered my survey, a person yelled out, "The military shut down all of the ISIS websites!" I checked and the website had been blocked by military. How did this person know I had asked someone from ISIS to answer my survey? Military hacker? Why the great interest?

I did not expect the reaction I got to the survey, but it was exciting to interact with some of the people I'd met. A Hamas supporter hoped that I would fail, an Arab sent an image of his crotch rocket, an eco-activist group contacted me to advise me of their organization's views, professors were ripping the survey questions apart, some sheik felt my survey was biased, but overall, people were very supportive of my research. Military analysts were all over my LinkedIn, and a person hacked into my computer and I could see Arabic/Farsi all over it. And the US military was hacked in too! My greatest supporters were Europeans, who were very liberal and open-minded as were Canadians. Women from developing countries were too intimidated by the content of the survey to answer it. It was almost as if the topic was taboo. Through my research I met an amazing young Iraqi man, Aso Anwar, who helped me to recruit respondents for a number of research projects. Today I am still in contact with many really great people from Iraq and other countries.

PSYCHOLOGICAL TORTURE?

MY SURVEY WAS complete, and I had three weeks to hand in my dissertation. I'd caught a cold, had a swollen pancreas, gallbladder, and duodenum, and spent a week running to the hospital, where I had a CAT scan and other tests, was prescribed medicine, and to top it all off, had an anaphylactic reaction to the meds. I had my own theory about the cause of the swelling of my internal organs. I was being sleep deprived in my environment and harassed constantly. Three times a week I would inform my employers and they told me to call police.

While completing my dissertation, I'd read about psychological torture tactics used on terrorists in Guantanamo Bay. Psychological torture must meet four criteria: a lack of direct physical violence, suffering, infliction, and a sensory assault: degradation, threats, loud music, or shouting. What the CIA did to Guantanamo detainees was not much different than what someone had done to me and possibly those around me. I can only say that whoever was harassing me was very cruel and liked degrading people. It was as though the persons were using a form of psychological torture. The CIA used Pavlovian conditioning to induce fear and anxiety in terrorists; it makes the captive feel as though they are helpless and under the control of others. I didn't feel helpless, but the constant threat was present. Ten times a day, this person would tell me that he had ruined my life and he was going to continue to do so.

Fear, threat, and powerlessness lead to fear pathology such as PTSD. Very strong memories are developed and fail to extinguish, thereby becoming debilitating for the victim. Coercion in itself implies threat, fear, and powerlessness, which in turn have a direct impact on the spinal cord and organ integrity. Psychological torture or environmental manipulation inflicts pain experienced in the brain and extends to different organs and physiological processes.

The organs in the human body begin to break down with sleep deprivation. There are long-term physiological effects: impaired perception, increased aggression, difficulty in speech, inability to concentrate, and risk of obesity and diabetes as well as other comorbidities. Impairment of performance is prevalent after twenty to twenty-five hours of sleeplessness and can be compared to ethanol intoxication at the level of .10 blood alcohol concentration.

Studies into the long-term physiological effects of sleep deprivation have shown rats will die within two to four weeks of being sleep deprived. Similar results have been shown across all species, including cockroaches and humans. My tests results showed there were no organic causes for a swollen pancreas, gallbladder, and duodenum. For example, there was no presence of gallstones. Was this another subtle attempt by two psychopaths to damage my life further? The harassment was almost twenty-four hours a day! And I believe it was computer generated. In 2019, a man was recorded next door to me in Huddersfield, England, telling me this was being done by computer.

I'd finally fallen asleep after an anaphylactic reaction and had slept only a few hours when I could hear a lady in a nearby building yell out, "Hey, stupid! Where have you been the last two days? There is a huge terror attack in Paris. You didn't get that one, did ya?!" Hackers were in my computer and knew via emails that I had successfully predicted terror attack sites. I had communicated this with two of my professors. When I opened up my computer to look at the news, the picture of the man I saw staring back at me looked identical to the Moroccan-born man I'd met at the French National Police Headquarters in 2011, when I was registering my business.

DISSERTATION HACKED AND DESTROYED

THREE DAYS AFTER returning to work, I came home and turned on my computer. A red box framed my computer screen, as though I was sharing Skype. I had my dissertation on the screen, and a malware program or hacker ripped it apart in a matter of seconds and ruined it. Pages disappeared and other pages came out in triplicate. I screamed for the hacker to "get out of my computer" and shut it down. I turned the computer back on and surveyed the damage. This was going to take two days to fix. I knew there was a hacker in my system, but I was smart about it. I had hidden parts of my dissertation all over my computer, in One Drive, emails as drafts, and other places. I'd worked so hard to get all of my work done and I was NOT going to let some jerk destroy it. I pieced it back together within seven hours, checked it, although I was sick and exhausted, and handed in a 100-page dissertation draft and final dissertation four minutes apart. Why? The hacker was close by. He was in the building behind me, which was several meters away, telling me he was going to break in and delete my final project.

I contacted one of my classmates and told her what had happened and kept my fingers crossed that I had passed it. A *$42,000 investment* and this person was still trying to destroy my life. Concerned, I contacted the DA who oversaw the project, and she said that she believed I did enough to pass. The hacker was deleting my respondents, so I failed to get the numbers I needed for the survey, and my dissertation was not perfect. I'd like to have graduated with distinction, but I knew this was not going to happen due to my external environment.

THE RESULTS

I WAS DEVASTATED when I got the results. I'd worked so hard to graduate with distinction, only to have stupid men with egos trying to fail me. The good news was I'd passed and so did all of the others I'd connected with during our online studies. If I could have found that hacker, I would have kicked him in that not-so-special place really hard and watched him writhe in excruciating pain. The conditions where I lived and studied were horrendous; the harassment childish and immature, the hacking juvenile, and the hacking of my data irresponsible. When I found out I passed, I yelled, "IN YOUR FACE" to the hacker in the next building over. My window was open and he would talk to me all the time and I didn't know him. I ended up with a "B" Canadian overall and graduated in Liverpool in July of 2016. It was perfect! My gift was a trip to Rome.

Several years after I had left this teaching position, I received a bill for almost $4,000 Canadian in taxes from the Korean government. Their letter stated I had been self-employed in Korea and that I owed them taxes. The fact is I had an E-2 visa, and taxes had been deducted from my paychecks. More fraud or human error? The fraud totaled $14,268 at this point, and there was more to come.

KOREAN POLICE CYBER UNIT

UPON MY RETURN from Rome, my contract was nearing an end. I went to the cyber unit on my day off. I was free and I could finally ask for help. An officer from their traffic unit drove me over to the cyber unit. The officer asked what happened and put me on the phone with a translator. I explained to her, and she spoke to him. "Come back next week with an English-speaking friend," he said.

I was gone the next week and didn't say anything. I never went back to the police station. The usual response I get is "Change your password" or "I don't see how hacking and papers disappearing from your computer is our responsibility!" Wow! Another hole in the system and it's getting bigger. This would later become a problem because twenty-two people would end up dead, and they didn't have to die.

Between 2012 and 2016, I was able to travel throughout Korea, Ireland, Austria, Venice, Milan, and Rome, Italy, Germany, United Arab Emirates, United Kingdom, Czech Republic, and Switzerland. I worked hard for four years amid extremely stressful conditions and beat the hackers-psychopaths at their own game. They would later try to fail me again in every course I took, some courses costing as much as $8,000 Canadian. I would pass all psychometric courses above the 90th percentile. Psychopaths hide behind their computer, committing crimes where they remain anonymous and are offered more protection than those they victimize.

CHAPTER THIRTY-FIVE
LIVERPOOL, FIREBOMB, TRACKING A TERRORIST TARGET, AND MERSEYSIDE POLICE

IN SEPTEMBER OF 2016, I moved to Liverpool, United Kingdom, to further my training and become a member of the British Psychological Society. There was so much to learn about the UK and how their society worked. It was very different from any country I'd lived. Opening a bank account took several weeks. I went to Reeds Rains letting agency and found a two-story brick home. It was an old war home at 8 Kedleston, Merseyside.

I spent the first four days running around Liverpool looking at all the great architecture along the waterfront, went on a bus tour, rode in big black taxis, and bought things for my new place. I arrived home on day four and there was a letter from the City Council stating I would be fined a thousand pounds if I didn't stop with all the noise. What noise? I wasn't even living there yet. I called the council office and all the man said was "He is up to his games again, eh?"

I asked, "What games?"

"Don't worry about it. I will take care of it" was his reply.

The fifth day there was a note in my door. "I hate to be the bearer of bad news, but there are mice between the walls. Council has set up traps to catch them. Seriously? Between the walls? Signed Zoe and Matthew." I threw the note out. On day six I had received a water bill addressed to "Ms. Colleen Reeds Rains." In Japan, I was Ms. Colleen. Was I becoming paranoid because of all of the crimes being committed over the last eleven years? Why had someone changed my water bill into my name when there was a note telling me it had been paid six months in advance? I'd have changed it over myself.

TRACKING A TERRORIST TARGET AND PSYCHOLOGICAL TORTURE

I BEGAN TO teach online; worked as a teaching supervisor in Liverpool schools; and conducted research for my doctoral proposal, which disappeared from my computer for the second time. I was working on a model designed to predict terror attacks in advance. There was a slight problem with the model. I could predict the attack site and the date, but not the exact time, date, and place together. For example, Paris was locked down for months after the attacks on the Bataclan and other soft targets. Would terrorists strike in Paris? No, because their chances of being captured, shot, and killed increased with a military presence; therefore, it would be logical to move south to Nice or other cities. One of the signatures or recognizable patterns of behavior with ISIS was attacking crowded places to increase the number of casualties. When and where do large crowds of people gather? There are large crowds on Bastille Day. The issue with the model is you can narrow the focus to a city but where in the city? My prediction was five kilometers from the actual targeted site in Nice. The second challenge was assigning a subjective value to each of the key indicators that would total up to 100 percent, indicating an attack was imminent. I would find indicators through local and international media reports.

Media reports saturated the news about Charlie Hebdo's characterization of the Prophet Muhammed. How the media frames events, the number of news agencies reporting, and frequency of reports influence public perception. As Margaret Thatcher said, "Publicity is oxygen for terrorists." The media reports garner support and may inflame people to commit attacks of terrorism. Charlie Hebdo was on every news channel, and it was imminent that they would be attacked. The media innocently provided the indicators which led to that attack on Hebdo on January 7, 2015.

The sarin gas attacks on the Tokyo subway in 1995 could have been a lesson learned for the media. The cult Aum Shinrikyo received seventy-nine days of media attention on television and 114 days of front-page news reports. The media coverage sensationalized the cult and influenced the public, which in turn motivated viewers to become supporters of the cult. Tens of thousands of people flocked to support the cult due to the positive framing of the media reports and the length of time they were reported.

Stockholm syndrome occurs when people form a psychological connection with abusers or captors. Could repeated media accounts not be viewed as a form of psychological torture albeit unintentional? Had Japanese media unknowingly psychologically tortured the public via an unprecedented amount of media coverage, causing thousands of members of the public to eventually identify with the cult Aum Shinrikyo? One might go so far to say that the media held its audience captive.

In 2016, while replicating my master's study, I happened to cross paths with the news reporter Igor Sahiri, BFMTV or Channel 24, who fielded a call from one of the terrorists who attacked Charlie Hebdo, Said Kouachi. I had not listened to the phone call previously, and Said Kouachi felt the need to justify Al Qaeda's acts of terrorism. This was very interesting because my research used a five-point Likert scale to measure which terrorist acts the public felt were justifiable. This research gave insight into the cognitive processes and system of beliefs of members of the public. It also provided insight into those with extremist views and values. Interestingly, the sole terrorist who answered my survey did not give the answers I'd expected. The terrorist did not condone extreme violence. It does not mean he or she answered the survey truthfully either.

I applaud the media for all of their hard work and for keeping the public informed. Their insightful reporting allowed me to successfully predict attacks on Hebdo, the Belgian airport, Parsons Green, and other attack sites, including tracking the Manchester bomber's target in May of 2017. I tried to determine where the target would be via geo-profiling and by forming a fifty-mile concentric circle between Liverpool and Manchester. I stayed up all night Sunday, May 21, 2017, and could not determine where the attack site would be. There were dozens of venues at this time, and it was very difficult to narrow the focus. Monday, May 22, 2017, twenty-two people died because of a terror attack, including an eight-year-old. I failed to achieve my objective in this instance. Although I failed to predict the attack on the Manchester arena, this model proved to be useful in predicting numerous other attacks. Using key indicators to predict attack sites is not an exact science but is a tool that can be used in conjunction with intelligence information gathering to counter terrorism.

CHAPTER THIRTY-SIX

POLICE, POLICE, AND MORE POLICE. AND THEN...AN AMBULANCE!

THERE WAS A knock on my door in early October 2016. I was busy teaching online but could see outside of my window. The row houses were so close together that when someone knocked on your neighbor's door, it sounded like your own. Police were at their door and then moved to mine. The first three times police arrived, I couldn't answer the door because of my job. The fourth time they showed up, I was able to answer the door because one of my classes was cancelled. "Hello, can I help you?" I said.

"Do you know where your neighbor is? We have received a noise complaint."

"I just moved in, work a lot, and have not met my neighbors. But I do see many different people coming and going. Can you hear all of the noise now?"

"Yes, I can hear it," the female officer stated as she did a funny trot across my front parlor. I also heard someone in the neighborhood threatening to firebomb someone's house.

"Why don't you move," inquired the young male officer, "if there is so much noise."

"I just moved in. Why should I have to move?" Satisfied that I was not the one creating the noise, they left. Only one other officer showed up in front of my house. She arrived sirens blaring, lights flashing, and screeched to a halt.

The lady next door to me opened up the door. "There is nothing going on here!"

The officer said "okay" and sped away.

Later that evening I fell fast asleep on my sofa when there was a knock on my door and I could see flashing lights. Oh no! Not police again! It was 11:00 p.m. and I'd been asleep for three hours. I inserted my keys in the door to unlock it, and there stood a tall, smiling, redheaded ambulance attendant. A ginger they call them in the UK. "Yes, can I help you?" I asked sleepily.

"You called?"

"No, I've been asleep on my sofa for over three hours. Would you like to see my cell phone?"

"No, I believe you," he answered.

"Is there perhaps an 18 Kedleston?"

"No, it was eight," he replied.

"Do you have the number of the person who called it in?"

"No. Okay, I will go then."

"Have a nice night," I replied, my curiosity piqued. I closed the door and thought, *That was weird.* Then I remembered the paramedics showing up in France. I contacted police and then the ambulatory service and could not get answers as to who called an ambulance, not even under the Freedom of Information Act. So...someone sent paramedics in France and an ambulance in the UK. Was this a French connection or a coincidence? Was Otaku back up to his games?

DECEMBER FIREBOMB

A MONTH AFTER I had arrived in Liverpool, a new double decker bus caught on fire at Liverpool Lime Street Station, which may have been a firebomb. On the same day, October 2, 2016, another bus caught fire at Liverpool Street Station in London. These firebombs were indicators that terrorists were getting ready for a larger attack. My daughter was visiting in October, and we went out to shop. Upon our return, we found the door unlocked and the lock had been broken. Nothing was taken, and a similar pattern of behavior had been established once again. Break-ins in France, but nothing stolen from the first apartment. Someone could be heard on the street around this time stating, "I am going to firebomb her house. Where does she live?" I wasn't sure who this man was talking about. This phrase was repeated on several occasions. My daughter left for Paris and then went on to Germany to visit friends.

Late December rolled around, and I went down the stairs one morning. A very strong odor of gas was being emitted from the kitchen. I called the gas company and asked them to send someone out to check. The gas was turned off at its source, and I waited a few hours for the repairman to come out. The windows were opened to let fresh air in. Two hours later, there was a knock on the door. In walked a man with his gadgets to check the gas. He pulled out the oven and looked at the hob and asked, "Who connected the gas to the stove?"

"I have no idea. I've only lived here a few months."

"Do you have a gas security certificate?"

"I might have one." I took some papers out of a drawer and found nothing there.

The gas man had both a puzzled and worried look on his face. "The reason I asked was this looks like a home hook-up job," he stated matter-of-factly. He declared the hob immediately dangerous and told me to call the landlady. Hmm...was this an attempt at a firebomb? Was this negligence on the part of the owner and the letting agency? In the UK a gas safety certificate must be issued prior to anyone moving in. The agency and the landlady were both negligent if a gas safety certificate had not been issued. Had I turned on the hob, I might possibly have taken out an entire block. I couldn't figure out why an older man from the letting agency came to my home and told me to move. He said there was a noise complaint when in fact there wasn't. Police knew the noise came from next door. Was this done to get me to move because the landlady and agency were both negligent and subject to a potential lawsuit or was it someone trying to firebomb my home?

GAS LEAK

IMPORTANT GAS SAFETY WARNING NOTICE
(Issued in accordance with the Gas Safety (Installation and Use) Regulations 1998)

TO THE USER OF GAS - This notice explains a situation has been identified which is, or could be, dangerous. This situation is in relation to the part of the gas installation that we have examined. The gas equipment MUST not be used. It is an offence to continue using an unsafe appliance. SEE IMPORTANT INFORMATION OVERLEAF

WHEN FILLING OUT THIS FORM - please tick and number in the appropriate boxes

Customer's Name: MISS NORMAN

Address: 3 KEDLESTON STREET LIVERPOOL

POST CODE: L8 9RP

Telephone Number:

Landlord's/Agent's Name:

Address:

POST CODE:

Telephone Number:

DEFECTS ON APPLIANCE / INSTALLATION / METER — SAFETY CATEGORY

Appliance Type	tick	Number	Location	tick	Nature of Problem	tick		tick
Cooker	✓		Kitchen	✓				
Fire			Lounge		Escape	✓	Ventilation	
C/htg Boiler			Dining Room					
Warm Air Unit			Bedroom					
Water Heater			Hall		Flue		Other	
Wall Heater			Landing					
Non Domestic			Utility					
Internal Pipework			Bathroom					
Meter								

CO Awareness leaflet left ☑ Yes ☐ No (tick)

Describe fault on appliance or installation

LEAK ON HOB GAS CONNECTION + FAULTY BURNER ON OVEN. HOB+ OVEN DISCONNECTED.

SAFETY ACTION TAKEN (Delete as appropriate)

The appliance/installation has been disconnected and labelled "Immediately Dangerous". ☑ ID

The appliance/installation has been turned off and labelled "At Risk". ☐ AR

RIDDOR

Reported to HSE under RIDDOR 11 (1) Gas Incident (e.g. CO) ☐

Reported to HSE under RIDDOR 11 (2) Dangerous Gas Fitting ☐

If you do not already know a suitable 'Gas Safe' registered installer, visit the Gas Safe Register website, www.GasSafeRegister.co.uk This will provide you with a choice of registered installers in your area. Alternatively, you can call our Helpline on 0800 371 782. I acknowledge receipt of this notice and understand that defects noted above were found or suspected when the National Grid representative visited.

Gas Supplier Details:

Temporary Heating/Cooking Supplied ☐ YES (tick)

Temporary Appliance Details:

The gas user was not present and this notice has been left on the premises

Customer's Signature X

Date 21|12|16

Position held if non-domestic customer

Engineer's Signature

Date Issued 21|12|16

Pay No. 50604127

Job Voucher No 3 0 0 2 6 1 5 5 0 5

nationalgrid DCI Team (Data Assurance), Brick Kiln Street, Hinckley, Leicester LE10 0NA Tel: 0845 835 1111

National Grid is a trading name for National Grid plc • Registered Office 1-3 Strand London WC2N 5EH Registered in England and Wales No. 2006000

CUSTOMER COPY

My landlady was actually quite nice and fixed every problem in the house immediately. First, break-ins in Japan, a projectile flying through my window, break-ins in Paris, France, and a ceiling fan meltdown, and a break-in in Liverpool, and a potential firebomb. The appliance was labeled immediately dangerous. A pattern of behavior had been established. Was it bad luck, coincidence, or Otaku and Yamaguchi? Remember, sadistic psychopaths subtly make attempts on victims' lives by cutting brake lines or by creating a gas explosion.

Other weird things that happened: my gas and electric were cancelled although I had a 215-pound credit; a double payment came out of my bank account, and a man kept knocking on my door trying to get my debit card and claimed to be raising money for a children's hospital life flight helicopter from Germany. One night he was banging on my door saying that he just wanted to explain what was going on.

POLICE INVESTIGATING

A WEEK BEFORE the Manchester bombing, I booked a flight back to Canada to visit my daughter and then went on to Pyeongtaek, South Korea. I left the UK because of the unusual occurrences and because I felt that it was unsafe to reside there. Once again, there was a Japanese connection. There were eighteen crimes committed, which were petty nuisances compared to Japan and France. Although I physically went into the police station in Liverpool, I was told they didn't have a cyber unit and to file a complaint on the Internet. I wrote to find out who was responsible for sending an ambulance through the Freedom of Information Act again. A wall had been put up and there were no answers. The holes in the policing system grew larger.

CHAPTER THIRTY-SEVEN

PYEONGTAEK, NATIONAL CYBERCRIME UNIT, SEVEN BREAK-INS, PROPERTY DAMAGE

PYEONGTAEK, SOUTH KOREA

AFTER THE DISASTER in Liverpool, and the potential explosion, I headed to Pyeongtaek, South Korea. At this point, I felt like a Ping-Pong ball going back and forth between South Korea and other countries around the world to avoid the crimes being committed against me. Pyeongtaek was a nice little town, not much to see. I worked all day and then went home and worked another four hours online in the evening. The money I earned online went toward all of the psychometric qualifications I would take in 2019–2020 and for my doctorate.

Strange things began to happen again, and hackers were back in my computer. Emails disappeared, a computer was broken, an Apple iPhone was broken, and the cord of a brand-new flat iron was yanked out of its base; pictures of my neighbor's apartment were on my computer, things that I had done in 2010 had been back-dated to 2006 in my Google drive, and images were uploaded from my Facebook account into my Google drive. There were seven break-ins, the heat turned up or off. I sent images of the hacks to one of the Korean teachers, and he contacted police fifteen times and they did not respond with a satisfactory answer to one of his complaints.

I was completing an online training course with a forensic psychiatrist and a psychologist, and was being harassed the whole time I was doing the training. Because of the time difference, I had to stay up all night and had a difficult time concentrating on what I was doing. Each qualification or certification costs between $1,500 to as much as $8,000 per course. The same persons were indeed responsible for what was going on. I went into the building next door to me in error after my first day of work. I went up to the fourth floor and tried to go in the wrong door. I could hear Japanese once more coming from the apartment beside the wrong door I had tried to enter.

I found a military computer hacked into my network and wrote to the Department of Defense twice to ask why there were 800 military added to my Skype and why military from Yongsan Garrison were on my network. My life and studies were being interfered with constantly. There was never a response but a military officer from the Department of Defense did look at my LinkedIn Account.

Two emails went missing and I tried to recuperate them and the initials of one of the people was KA....Kato Yamaguchi. Again you can see one or more of the psychopaths at work. Damaging property, hacking, and trying to send books from Amazon, invading my privacy, as if it was normal. It got worse from there and their mental illness became clearly evident. Police missed dozens of opportunities to thwart the effort of these two individuals, including two or more possible subtle murder attempts.

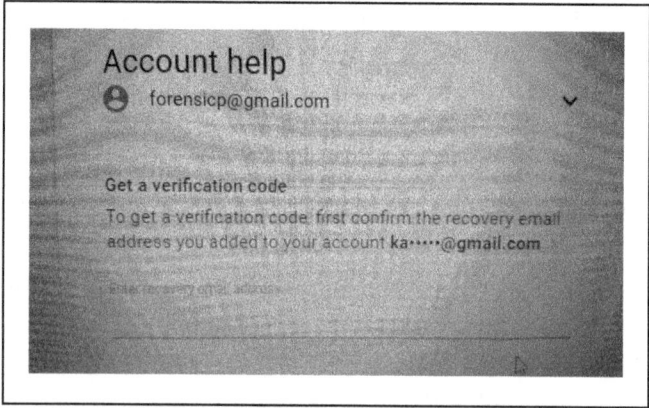

"Getting paranoid" typed across my browser gave me a clue about how this person was going to try to discredit me. So, rather than report all of the crimes to the police, I gathered evidence, hired private investigators, and documented as much information as I could. In fact, there were so many crimes committed in so many places, if I told police about every crime, they would question my sanity. Psychopaths will go to great lengths to discredit their victims, and it is part of their game. Things got out of control in Huddersfield, England, and I recorded these individuals playing their game and caught them on camera.

CHAPTER THIRTY-EIGHT

WEST YORKSHIRE POLICE, JAPANESE HACKERS, AND MI5

F INALLY ON MY way to Huddersfield, England. I loved the narrow streets and the old, majestic Victorian buildings, parks, monuments, and greenery of Huddersfield. I forfeited earning a master's level teaching degree at City of Liverpool College due to a lack of communication and chose to study a few psychometric qualification courses instead.

I moved into a small duplex on a quiet street on August 14, 2018. I stood there looking around; it looked empty with only three suitcases sitting on the living room floor. Fortunately, I found a furniture store that was going out of business, and I was able to furnish my entire house for about 5,000 pounds. I started to teach online again and supported myself while I studied and traveled back and forth to different places to complete various psychometric qualifications and try to write my PhD proposal once more.

On my first day in Huddersfield, I could hear someone say, "Time to move." There was an Asian lady next door to me whom I'd never met. The walls were very thin and I could hear everything being said. At first, I didn't think it was directed at me. At night it was very quiet and then it became increasingly noisy. Then hackers were back in my computer. On October 22ND, I called police, who came out to take a complaint. I hired Microsoft to go into my computer to check for any Trojans or other spyware, and there were two hijack hack programs found on my computer from Japan.

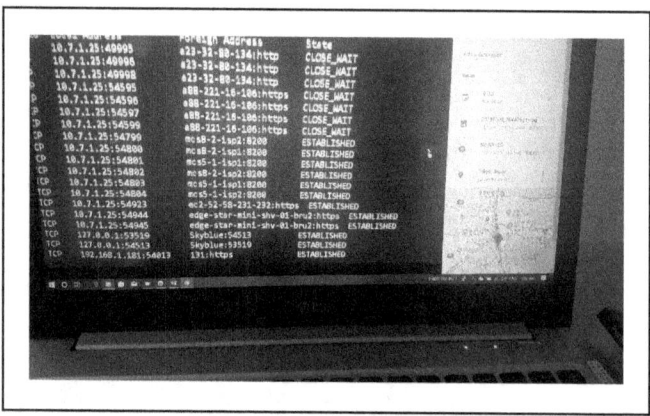

A man kept talking to me through the wall next door and would bother me every time I was teaching online or studying. I recorded him with my cell phone. Then I could hear two women talking to me. I recorded them too. One was telling me I was delusional and I didn't have a master's degree, and another one would hurl insults I'll not repeat. They must have been hired by someone because they were addressing me by name. I didn't say anything to the police because the recordings were not loud when I recorded them on my phone. So, I enhanced them by re-recording them at a louder volume but kept the originals. It is possible that they were speaking through a microphone because I had a squealing sound on my phone.

Here's a short list of things said: "Eventually, you are going to commit suicide, Colleen. (Yamaguchi) You did this all to yourself; I thought you were supposed to be retired by fifty-five, Colleen. What happened to all of your friends, Colleen? Yes, they are here. They are harassing you. They are police, Colleen. I think you are crazy. None of this is real; it is all in your own mind. You don't have a master's degree, Colleen. If it were up to mem I would have you institutionalized." They would swear, and at one point a man could be heard saying: "Feel like you're pinned down, Colleen? Like your every effort is being thwarted? Just when you get your leg up, someone is there to knock the stool out from under you? I am going to do this until I drive you right into the ground... Sorry if we ruined your businesses. Sorry if we ruined your life. So much for your fairy-tale princess life, Colleen! I can't wait to see your obituary."

Whenever these persons struck up a conversation, I would tell them I was not their therapist. Over one thousand hours of conversation from Huddersfield were recorded. By December they had become really annoying, so I decided to do to them what they did to me. Every time they bothered me, I would record them and play it back to them, unleashing a little therapy of my own on them. The noise continued to bother me because it was there almost twenty-four hours a day. One man was recorded telling me it was all being done online by computer. Another recording was a former coworker telling me Webber's wife was the root of the problem. These recordings can all be heard at the back of the book. Webber and company had started playing these recordings in Paris, France, and had continued it over the years. When I called a private investigator in Huddersfield, she asked me if they kept setting up next door to me. I asked her how she knew that. Her response was that it was not out of the ordinary.

FRAUD AGAIN!

I WENT TO Dublin, Ireland, on January 3, 2019, to complete more psychology training courses. Upon my return on January 4, I had to write an invigilated open-book test for part of a Master's of Education course that cost $6,000 Canadian, including the cost of psychometric manuals. The minute I opened the test online, two women came flying in next door, screaming I was not allowed to write the test. This proved they were hacked into my computer. How else would they have known that I was writing a test? They tried to fail me, and can be heard on tape stating that certain answers were wrong, when they weren't. I returned verbal fire on them as I worked through the test. Some of their comments were "We hope you fail." When I wrote the test, I could not concentrate because the harassment was so bad. I scored a 96/100 on the test and made one error. There are people recorded telling me, "The police are doing this. They are stupid here." I didn't believe for one second that police were harassing me, but I found evidence that they may have been in my computer. I traced the longitude and latitude of a hacker and it landed on the Bradford Cyber Unit. I sent the recording of the idiots next door to the company I was taking the course from to protect myself in case there were accusations of wrongdoing during the exam.

Whoever was online next door would keep me awake all night, interfering in everything I did, so I would have entire conversations with them in Japanese and English. I did this so I could identify who these persons were and I recorded them as I had in Uijeongbu, Liverpool, and Huddersfield. They spoke back to me in Japanese. I played the tapes for two of my neighbors who clearly heard the recordings. One man thought they were "bloody bonkers."

You could hear a man on different days tell me my house was clean, my pink comb was behind my headboard (and it was), I had a pink duvet on my bed, and my new lamp was broken. There were dozens of more things they (male and female) said and did which led me to believe they were in my house on numerous occasions. I was being told what was in my fridge and that there were coins in my closet and they could have stolen them. I could hear a woman once again saying, "There's nothing going on here, Colleen. You are paranoid." Microsoft had caught Japanese hacked into my computer and I videotaped it. Still, no police investigation. A man can be heard on one of the tapes bragging, "See, I told you I would ruin her life...lol." Was this person Korean military?

In February, I was back in Ireland to continue with the psychometric training required and upon my arrival at the Fitzpatrick Castle Hotel, I found that someone had canceled my booking. The website I had booked my hotel at was legitimate. The original cost was 240 pounds for three nights, and I had to pay another 259 pounds. When I returned to Huddersfield, I contacted the bank and a fraud investigation began. I received 240 pounds back. Again, psychopaths do their best to disrupt your life and cost you as much money as they can. This is their attempt to control you financially, as stated in Chapter One.

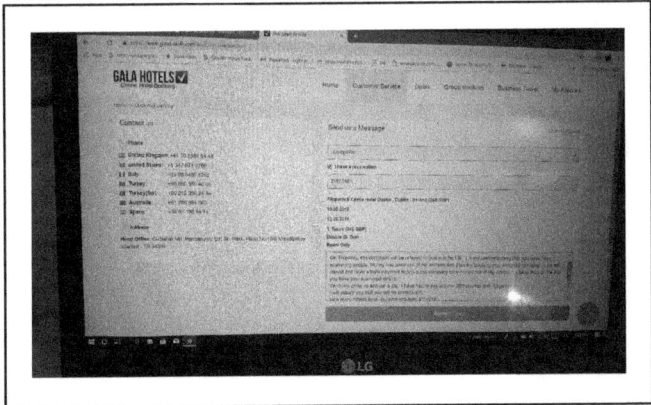

I called West Yorkshire Police at the beginning of March 2019. They stated they would send out a unit as soon as possible. Four days later, no police. I called and was told all calls were prioritized. Two weeks later, no police, three weeks later, no police. Twenty-eight days later and four phone calls, they finally showed up. At no point in my life did I ever contact police with the exception of reporting crimes that had or were being committed.

Two short female officers arrived at my residence. I had to suppress my laughter when they arrived at my door because they looked so serious. One was a petite blonde in her early forties and the other a brunette in her thirties. "Come on in and have a seat."

"Thank you," they said, looking around the living room. I told them what had occurred and I had them listen to the recordings on my cell phone. The brunette listened for about ten seconds. It is difficult to hear the persons speaking because I didn't have speakers to enhance the volume of their voices. It was loud in my home but when I recorded them it was not as loud. "Is that you on the phone?" questioned an officer.

"Why would it be me?" I asked. The voice was away from the microphone. If it was my voice it would be loud because I would be closer to the microphone. I told the officers about the stalkers, Liverpool, and the suspected break-ins in Huddersfield.

CHAPTER THIRTY-NINE
MI5 AND
SHEIK KHALID YASIN

WEST YORKSHIRE POLICE recommended that I contact MI5 because of the occurrences in Liverpool and the terrorist connection in Paris, France. Things got weird after police left my place in March of 2019. Five minutes after they'd departed my residence, a woman next door could be heard. "Did you check Internet Explorer? There is something there about you!" Rarely do I use Internet Explorer. I typed in my name and there was a website with a German URL and the title of my research. The website was owned by Sheik Khalid Yasin, an allegedly radicalized Muslim cleric living in Manchester. I didn't know him and had never heard of him, so I looked him up. Manchester? I thought it was ironic that an Amir (Muslim cleric) from Manchester would have a website up with my research on it. I had been tracking the Manchester bomber's target back in 2017. Coincidence? The website had the title of my research and only one page from my dissertation, Vladimir Putin in a meeting, articles about French terrorism history, images of ISIS, and writings about the PKP. (This website can be viewed via the link at the back of the book.)

I remembered the police telling me to contact MI5 and hesitated because I felt the hacking and stalking problem was not an issue of national security, albeit important for me to bring about a speedy resolution so I could get my life back. I actually wonder if I had not been harassed in Liverpool, would I have found the Manchester target in time to possibly thwart the terror attack. I would have called the antiterrorism hotline. The bigger question would have been: would MI5 listen to me? I did not have enough empirical evidence or intelligence information to justify calling them because the evidence had been hacked and removed from my computer. Several coworkers had sent emails telling me that I was correct with the target predictions. Only one had been left in my computer, and I didn't feel as though it was enough evidence of the accuracy of the model I'd used.

MI5 is in charge of counterterrorism, espionage, cybercrimes, and counter-proliferation. I sent the link of the website with my research on it and explained that I was a researcher and was being stalked and hacked. I expressed my concern about opening my business soon and I was worried it, too, would be hacked. The next day the website had been blocked, and I received a response from MI5 with a safe webhosting site. MI5 did nothing more, nothing less. I wrote to them and thanked them. MI5 was the ONLY organization that had assisted me in the fifteen years of being stalked and hacked! I question whether or not Sheik Khalid Yasin was the owner of the website. Yasin was probably NOT involved, but someone knew about him and used his name as they had used my research. One of the articles was about France and terrorism. Everything you've read to this point is an accurate account of what happened to me over a fifteen-year period. Once again, I have not included the worst crimes.

The ending of the book is a surprise. A Toronto police officer told me that my story sounded *"fantastical,"* despite all the evidence I have. If I had reported every crime to police, it would have been even more fantastical. Chapter 40 is dedicated to those officers who would not actively listen, were ill-trained and lacked expertise in stalking and cyberstalking. It is indeed fantastical.

CHAPTER FORTY
THE FANTASTICAL

BELFAST AND THE IRA PARAMILITARY!
KIDNAPPED!

M Y THIRD TRAINING course was finally finished in Dublin with the exception of one assignment. I rushed to my taxi and left the Fitzpatrick Castle Hotel for the train station. For the next month I would be renting a hotel room at the Jury's Inn. My PhD research brought me to the north, and I wasn't even sure if I would make all of the right connections for my study. My study was to examine the personality types and the cognitive processes of different members of terrorist groups and compare them to a random sample of the general public. The Real Irish Republican Army splinter group and other freedom fighters was a place to start my research since Ireland was closest to my home in Huddersfield, England. I was happy to be away from there because of the harassment from the Asians next door.

It was raining heavily outside just like the last time I'd been to Belfast in 2014. The streets had been flooded, and there was construction going on at city hall. I began to doze off when I suddenly felt the train jolt and then stop. Four people got on the train, three men and a woman. Two sat across from me and one next to me. The woman went to find a washroom. Their names were Liam Gallagher, Finn O'Sullivan, Blaine Kelly, and Fiona Byrne.

Liam was a quiet, soft-spoken man and I guessed his age to be about thirty-eight. He was the oldest among the group. It turned out he was forty-three. He looked slightly younger than his years and was very thin. Finn was the youngest of the group. His curly, strawberry blond hair fell just past his shoulders, and his blue eyes were full of life. I later learned he was only nineteen years old. Blaine had a shaved head and was heavier set than the rest of his companions and was in his early thirties. Fiona was Blaine's girlfriend and was in her late twenties. She was rough-looking and appeared to be a heavy drinker. Her thin, dirty blond hair was tied back in a ponytail, and it looked as though her hair hadn't been washed in days. Her clothes were out of fashion, and she was rather plain-looking. The only part of her that stood out were the dark circles under her eyes.

"Hello," Blaine Kelly said.

"Hi." I looked out the window, not in the mood for chatting with strangers.

Finn asked, "And where would you be from?"

"I live in the UK but I am both Canadian and Irish."

"Do you have family in Ireland?" he inquired.

"No, I don't. I am in Belfast to do research."

"What kind of research?"

"I am looking to interview freedom fighters."

"Freedom fighters?"

"Paramilitary."

All three men looked at each other. "Why in the devil would you want to interview paramilitary from the Nort of Ireland?" asked Liam.

"It is part of my research for my doctorate."

Finn looked as though he was about to say something when Liam kicked him in the shin. There was silence for a moment, and I could see their reflections in the train window. Each one glanced my way.

Fiona arrived and sat at the table across from us. "Would you like to sit with your friends?" I offered to give my seat to her and move.

"No, I'm okay." She ignored me and chatted with her friends. Nothing more was said during the trip. There was an awkward silence.

Belfast at last! Three suitcases to haul to my hotel. I walked to the front of the car and started to pull them out of the bin. Finn walked up and helped. "How long are you here for?" he asked.

"I will be here for at least a month."

He handed me a piece of paper. "Liam asked me to give this to you."

I didn't look at it and stuffed it into my coat pocket. "Thank you for your help, Finn."

"Always happy to help."

I got off the train and headed to a black cab. "Jury's Inn, please." It was only 0.1 miles away, but it would be difficult to drag my heavy suitcases that distance. I handed the driver ten pounds and we left the station. The driver helped me with my bags and I checked in. "Room 343, here is your keycard. The elevator is right around the corner to your left. Devin will help you with your bags." Up I went to my room to put my things away and freshen up.

It was close to dinner time, so I decided to head down to the restaurant. It was bustling with tourists and businessmen, and the only empty space was on a bar stool. "Can I order dinner from here?" I asked the bartender.

"Yes, you can. Here is a menu for you. Can I get you something to drink?"

"May I have a glass of red house wine, please?"

The couple beside me got up and left.

"What can I get for you?"

"I'll have the buffet."

"The plates and utensils are right next to the buffet. Please enjoy."

When I returned to my seat, there was a young man sitting next to my stool drinking a pint. I sat down. The man looked forward and said nothing. I could see his reflection in the mirror amongst the bottles of alcohol. He seemed to be lost in thought, so I didn't want to bother him by talking. I ate and ordered another glass of wine. "There is a table for two available next to the window. Would you like to move?" the bartender offered.

"Sure, that would be great," I said.

"Follow me."

I picked up my backpack while the bartender grabbed my glass of wine. I moved to the window and watched the people and traffic pass by. An hour later I went back to my room.

I remembered the piece of paper that Finn had handed to me on the train and took it out of my jacket pocket. There was a number on it and Liam's name. I would call him the next day to see what he wanted, but for now a hot bath and emails were my priority.

The next morning, I picked up the phone and called Liam Gallagher. "Hi, Liam. It's Colleen. I met you on the train yesterday."

"Colleen, I tink I can help you wit your research," he said with his thick accent. "Can you meet me at the Arts Ekta Car Park?"

"Yes! What time?"

"Now...I will wait for you. It is just down the road to the right of the Jury's Inn."

I thought for a moment. I never told him where I was staying. I was intrigued. "I will be there in five minutes."

I grabbed my coat and my backpack and headed out to the car park.

Seven minutes later, I could see Liam and Fiona waiting by a black van. They waved me over. "How did you know where I was staying?" I asked.

"We saw ya wit your bags when we drove by," Fiona said.

"Git in the van," said Liam.

"Listen, I don't know you well and I am not sure about this," I said.

"Do you want help with your research or not?"

Do I risk it? I thought. "Yes. Why not? Not much more could possibly happen."

I hopped in the black van and didn't expect what happened next. Finn and Blaine grabbed me and put a black hood over my head and tied my hands behind my back. "We are doing this for your own safety. You'll not be hurt."

"Great! Now what?" I could hear the zipper of my backpack being opened and bag searched. Thieves?

"I am taking your cell phone and will give it back afterwards," said Finn.

I couldn't breathe with this black hood over my face and didn't like the fact that my hands were tied up. Then I could feel Finn's hand searching my body. "Hey," I said.

"We are just making sure you are not wired. Colleen, have you figured out who we are yet?" asked Liam.

"Let me guess, freedom fighters?"

The van moved off the highway and onto a bumpy road. "Do you like hiking, Colleen?" asked Fiona. "We have a bit of a hike from the road."

After what seemed like an eternity, the van stopped. I tried to remember the route that the van had taken but it was futile. The doors opened and Blaine and Finn pulled my feet, then both grabbed my arms on either side. "A ten-minute hike and we can take the burlap bag off your head. Fiona, grab her backpack," said Liam. I still couldn't see clearly through the black sack on my head except for a bit of light and green grass. I stumbled and almost fell a few times. "We're here, Colleen," announced Finn.

I could hear the squeaking of hinges and was walked up three steps. Once I was inside, they took the black sack off of my head. Laughter could be heard and Finn said, "Your hair looks like mine now." I looked around at my surroundings. It looked like an abandoned home. The wallpaper was torn, there were holes in the ceiling, and it smelled musty. Why would they bring me to this place up in the hills?

"So, Colleen, tell us about your research. It seems very odd that a Canadian would come all the way to Northern Ireland to seek out freedom fighters, as you called us," Liam stated. I explained my research to him. "Do you tink of us as thick?"

"No."

"And tat is the right answer to give. Where was your family from?"

"Newtownstewart, County of Tyrone."

"What's the family surname?"

"Scott."

"Was your grandfather the only person from Ireland?"

"Yes."

"And his occupation?"

"Soldier."

All four of the freedom fighters started to laugh. "We are all soldiers here in the Nort, Colleen," Fiona said. I was starting to get worried at this point because no one knew where I was. Were they going to try to hurt me? Was I stupid for coming here to risk my life over PhD research?

"Was your grandfather Catholic or Protestant?" asked Liam.

"He never told me. He spoke little of Ireland." I knew that he had fought with the Royal Inniskilling Fusiliers, was an Orangeman, and a supporter of the crown. I dared not say that to any of the four in a room, in a cabin, in the hills, someplace. When I was young I only got to see him a few times. He was an older man who married my younger grandmother. He didn't speak of Ireland or the war often. He passed when I was quite young.

"I see. Have you done any other research?"

"Yes, I have for my master's degree."

"I know because I looked you up online. I like the way you tink, Colleen," Liam said. "We're busy today. Finn, hood her and take her back to the van." And he did. An hour later, I was back in the Arts Ekta Car Park. Finn hopped in the back and took the bag off my head and untied my hands. He held the door open and said, "See you soon." I grabbed my backpack and off I went back to my hotel. That was strange. When I got into my room, I ran to the bathroom and threw up. "Holy shit!" My heart was still pounding. I'd been in an IRA safe house in the hills.

I didn't dare take my eyes off Liam when I was there. I'd looked around a bit but didn't see any weapons. Why would these four identify themselves as para-military? There must have been something more they wanted. They usually disguised their faces even in front of the media, and only spoke on the condition that the media adhered to IRA protocols. Why would these four want to help me?

I opened my bag and they'd forgotten to give me my cell phone back. Oh man! My wallet was empty too. The hundred pounds had been taken. It was a good thing I'd left my debit cards, passports, and other important documents hidden in the ceiling. I'd lifted up one of the panels and put everything there before I'd left. My health card was in my wallet as my sole piece of identification. I guess I could go and buy a used phone and a new SIM card. I wondered if they were ever going to contact me again. Well, off to paramilitary bars this evening to see who else I could get to answer my survey for my study. It was at that moment that I looked in the mirror. Nice, I thought. I looked like something the cat had dragged in.

I got cleaned up and looked online for paramilitary hangouts. I wasn't much of a drinker but had budgeted to buy others drinks to entice them a little to answer my questionnaire. It was extensive and I needed to administer several psychometric tests. I had talked to the hotel manager and he agreed to rent a small office to me at an hourly rate. I'd handed him 200 pounds under the table.

BAR HOPPING AND THE HUNT FOR PARAMILITARY

It was seven o'clock and I headed to Kelly's Cellars, a bar I'd found on the Internet. I'd done a bit of research beforehand to find different bars with paramilitary, but it was understood that they don't always readily identify themselves. I walked into Kelly's Cellars, and loud Irish music was playing. Located at the front of the bar was a band. The music stopped and the band took a short break as I took a seat. It was only seven o'clock and everyone appeared to be having a great time.

Most of the people in the bar were older. There weren't many young people. A table of people left and I went over and sat down to watch the band. A man and his female companion asked if they could sit at my table. "Sure, please go ahead." They became known to me as Aodhan Flanagan and Siobhan (Shivon) Cole, MI5. I didn't know who they were until later. Aodhan (Aiden) was about twenty-four, and his companion was in her thirties. He was five-foot-ten and slender, with short brown hair. He must have been a mechanic because he had black dirt all over his hands. Siobhan on the other hand looked like a professional office worker. Her long curly brown hair fell halfway down her back; she was slender and wore a dark blue suit. They looked like an odd couple.

The music began to play again. I felt awkward and didn't want to mingle with the crowd. Most were already drunk and it was only nine o'clock. I ordered another Guinness and let it sit there. Shivon looked at me but said nothing. Aodhan struck up a conversation and asked where I was from, why I was here, and what my plans were in the future. This bar seemed to be a dead end. *Maybe I should talk to the manager back at the hotel. He might be able to help*, I thought. Next bar, Maddens. Off I went and left the Guinness on the table.

Maddens was hopping and lively. There seemed to be a lot of energy in the bar. Maybe I'd struck gold. I found a seat and ordered a glass of wine. Then I heard two familiar voices at a table behind me. Aodhan and Siobhan were seated behind me. I didn't say anything and enjoyed the music. After two hours, I'd spoken to no one and I decided to call it a night. As luck would have it, in walked Liam Gallagher and Finn. They walked past my table and then turned to look at me. I motioned for them to take a seat. "Aye, Colleen, good to see you." Just this morning this man had hooded and tied me up. "Can I get you something from the bar?" Finn held up his hand and motioned for the waiter. "I'll have two pints and a glass of red wine." I handed the waiter twenty pounds and told him to keep the change.

"Did we scare you today, Colleen?"

"Yes, a little."

"Good, my advice to you is don't underestimate who we are, Colleen. We are not nice people." Finn's eyes were cast downward as if he was embarrassed. "You don't know anything about the Irish, Colleen, or the paramilitary. I will help you, but if you don't do what I say then we'll have words. How many people do you need for you survey?"

"As many as possible. It will take two hours or more to answer the questionnaire, and to take the two tests. There are several tests to be administered and I will explain those when you give informed consent," I said.

"Finn, go grab us another beer." Liam roughly grabbed my arm and squeezed it. "What is said between us, stays between us."

"No problem for me. Just let go of my arm." He released his grip a second later. God, I hated talking to drunks. They made no sense.

Finn came back with two beers. "Where's Blaine, Finn?"

"He's at Fiona's moms for the night. It is her da's birthday or something."

"The music is too loud in here. I can't hear meself think," Liam said. "Let's go to a quieter bar."

"Why don't we go to the bar downstairs, at my hotel?" I offered. "It's very quiet."

"Okay, Finn, finish up your beer and let's go."

We walked to the Inn and sat in the bar downstairs. I'd forgotten about Aodhan and Siobhan. They walked in the bar behind us. Liam looked up. "Do you know them?"

"No, I just saw them at Maddens." They took a seat next to us.

"Buy you a beer?" asked Aodhan.

"Now why would I need YOU to buy me a beer?" Liam seemed a little defensive. "I don't bloody know you. Bugger off, you eejit."

"No offense intended, sir." The MI5 agents moved to a different table.

"I'll go first next Monday, then Finn, Blaine, and some others. I mean for your test."

"How about Monday at 11 a.m.?" I inquired.

"Okay."

"Finn? Monday at 3 p.m.?"

"Aye...sounds good."

"Thank you." We spent some more time talking about their families. Liam's grandfather was from the county of Tyrone as well. Finn's family was from Galway.

Finally I said, "Well, I am exhausted and need to sleep."

Liam extended his hand. "Have a good sleep, Colleen." I got up and went back to my room only to find the door open. Ugh...not this again. Had the maid been in my room and not closed the door? I put the key card into the card reader on the wall and the lights came on. My clothes were strewn all over the room and my computer was gone. I looked up to where I'd hidden my identification and the panel was still in place.

Whew! My backup computer and external drive were hidden in the ceiling, untouched.

"Front desk? Could you come up to my room? Someone has broken into it. The door was open when I got here, and my computer has been stolen."

The front desk sent a manager up who told me not to touch anything. "Is there anything else missing?"

"No, just a silver computer."

"The Gardai are on their way here and you can make a report."

I went into the bathroom, and the silver computer was sitting in the tub. "That's weird."

"What?"

"My computer is open and in the bathtub. I never left it there."

"Can you check it and see if it works."

I picked it up out of the tub and turned it on. It worked. Then I thought about the gardai and the paramilitary downstairs. "Cancel the gardai please. I don't want to waste their time as nothing seems to be missing."

"Very good, is there anything else I can do for you?"

"No, that will be all."

The manager left, closing the door behind him. Who broke in? Otaku? Kato? Blaine and Fiona?

I spent the next hour cleaning up when I heard my phone ring. What the heck? I began to search the room and found my phone under my pillow. "I forgot to return this to you, Colleen. Sorry about the mess." The caller hung up. It was Fiona! I looked at my computer again and the files seemed to be in place, nothing deleted. What was the purpose of the visit? So...she was not at her mother's after all. I had a very difficult time sleeping that night. First Webber and Kato had broken in in Japan and now Blaine and Fiona breaking into my hotel room. In the morning, I'd ask to change rooms.

It was six o'clock when I went downstairs. "Is the manager in?"

"Yes, one moment please. May I inquire as to what you'd like to talk about?"

"My room was broken into last night, and I would like to change rooms. I don't feel very comfortable staying in there now."

The manager came out and searched through the computer. "I do have a room for you on the second floor; room 2 3 3. Here is the key and please be sure to drop off the key card to your other room."

"Thank you." I went up to the third floor and closed the door behind me. I stood on the desk and reached into the ceiling, retrieving my identification and backup computer. One by one, I dragged the heavy suitcases down one flight of stairs to my new room, then went to the front desk and handed in the key card. I spent most of the day getting ready for the two men arriving tomorrow.

Monday and the testing began in the little office in the hotel. Over the next three weeks, I tested a large group of people who Liam and Finn had recruited for my study. I was very excited to test each person. Out of the fifty-four tested, only four refused to finish one of the tests. Everything had turned out perfectly. All I had to do was complete the data analysis and begin the 80,000-word write-up. It sounded like a daunting task, but so far the results of the test fit my hypothesis. I was done and returned to Huddersfield. I thanked Liam and Finn but never saw Fiona or Blaine again.

IRISH, WEBBER, AND KATO

TWO DAYS TO go and I would be at a conference in London. I'd completed my research and was halfway through the write-up. I looked online and purchased return train tickets to Huddersfield. Once that was done, I conducted a security check on my computer. It had been about three weeks since I'd last been hacked, so maybe Webber and Kato had moved on. I'd told Finn about them and what they'd done to me. "There are eejits everywhere, Colleen." Finn was my favorite paramilitary because he had confided in me. His dream was to travel the world and go back to school. I felt he didn't want to be part of the paramilitary.

THEY'RE HERE!

Stanley and Kato arrived in London on separate planes. They would stay at separate hotels too. This was the way they operated. Their rule was simple. They should never be seen traveling together unless they had a job to do. Stanley Webber was a detestable character who was not well liked because of his complete disregard for everyone's privacy. Kato Yamaguchi was no different. He was a grappler who liked to tag team people with Webber.

Kato's phone rang. "Meet me at Trafalgar Square in half an hour." The caller hung up. Kato called a taxi and was on his way.

Webber waited for thirty minutes. "Howdy."

"Hey," replied Kato.

"I found a nice Aston Martin parked by parliament. Follow me," said Webber.

They both set off for parliament. "The red one or the blue one?" inquired Kato.

"Blue one."

Seven minutes later they were driving away from the front of the British parliament. They turned and looked excitedly at each other. "Wee-hoo!" Webber cried. There was a sudden explosion. A giant plume of smoke shot up into the sky. Debris landed on cars, setting off alarms. People could be heard shouting and screaming and were seen running for cover. In the distance sirens were blaring. "What's going on?" asked a frightened woman, taking cover behind a car. "A car bomb," shouted a police officer.

SWAT and other police had arrived and secured the area while bomb experts searched nearby cars.

Firefighters moved in and put the Aston Martin fire out and then moved to the other vehicles that had caught on fire. "There are two unidentifiable bodies in the car, Commander; they are burned beyond recognition. A second bomb has been found on the other side of parliament strapped under a car. The bomb squad is about to detonate it."

"Very good, keep me posted," he commanded.

A man was standing ten feet from the car. "Excuse me...excuse me, sir," he yelled, trying to get the officer's attention. "I believe that to be my car. Mine was parked in front of the parliament building but it's gone."

The officer moved toward the man. "Might I know your surname, sir?" "Certainly, I am Sir Godfrey Reinhardt, member of parliament for Kensington and Chelsea."

"Sir, come with me. Officer Blake, take Sir Godfrey into protective custody. That bomb may very well have been meant for him. Today was your lucky day, sir, but not a lucky day for those two blokes."

Sir Godfrey Reinhardt glanced at the burnt car, then jumped into the back of the police cruiser and was driven away. As the investigation progressed, the second bomb was found to have been aimed at another parliamentary member.

LONDON

I CHECKED INTO the Marriot and was looking forward to the terrorism conference being held by the British Psychological Society. Experts from The Hague, London, and Pakistan were amongst the guest speakers. I wanted to get out and decided to go buy a new suit for the conference. Unbeknownst to me there were two people in the crowd that I was completely unaware of. I walked to Harrods and went through the big doors, read through the directory, and headed up the escalator to the designer clothing area.

I tried on a form-fitting blue jacket and skirt. It was a perfect fit. Then I heard the voice of the sales clerk. "Excuse me, sir... Can I be of assistance?" An older man stood in the doorway watching what I was doing. I didn't pay any attention to him and he spoke up. "Remember me, Colleen?!"

His voice was familiar, but who was he? I didn't like his menacing tone. I turned to face the man speaking to me. "My apologies... Do I know you?"

"Yes, you know me," he shouted angrily.

"I am sorry...but where have we met?"

"Toronto."

"Miss, is there a problem here?" inquired the clerk. "Shall I call security?" I nodded.

"I know you, but you don't remember me, eh?" He reached inside his jacket. I held my breath for a split second because in his hand was a shiny black nine-millimeter handgun. It wasn't pointed at me but toward the floor. A second later, a loud gunshot rang out and a bullet shattered the glass window in the shop. Dr. Eaton Bas fell to the floor. The shop clerks and I ducked down and I covered my face with my hands.

Seconds later, I put my hands down and out of the corner of my eye, I caught a glimpse of another man who looked familiar. He was holstering his weapon. Where did I know him from? I directed my attention back to the older man who had had a gun in his hand. He was now lying on the floor, and a pool of blood had begun to form around his head. Suddenly, it dawned on me who he was. Oh my god! He was the psychiatrist from the conference in Toronto! What was he doing here? I hadn't seen this man in twenty years! Our conversation had been brief, and I had never called him. It was then that I realized he'd been shot. I stood there in a pervasive state of shock when another shot rang out. People were scrambling for their lives while others stood in place screaming, looking at a second fallen body. None of this seemed real and it was as though it was taking place in slow motion.

When I looked toward the area where the second gunshot came from, there stood Aodhan and Siobhan. I'd seen them three times in Belfast, and both were holding guns in their hands. The man who'd shot the psychiatrist was lying on the floor. "What's going on?" a woman shouted. I backed away from the change rooms and headed out the back doors, left my clothes behind, and kept the suit. Down the escalator I went with my backpack in hand, running for my life! I ran as fast as my little legs could carry me and found a taxi. "Driver! The Marriot near parliament please! Hurry!" As we pulled away from Harrods, sirens were wailing in the background and cruisers were blazing past us. My heart was beating out of my chest. *That face, I know that other man's face. But where do I know him from?* We arrived at the Marriot amid heavy traffic half an hour later.

I looked down and the price tags were still on my suit. I tucked one into my waistband and the other down the back of the jacket. "Fifty quid, miss." I gave the driver a ten-quid tip and ran to the hotel, bolted through the doors and up to my room. I looked in the mirror and then down at my shoes. My shoes were blood-spattered. I changed, threw the shoes in a garbage bag, and went outside my room and threw them in a rubbish bin. My bags were then packed and I left the hotel quickly. The conference was a no-go. I headed for the train station and bought a ticket to Huddersfield. I would send the money to Harrods when I got home.

It cost 200 pounds to buy a last-minute ticket. I opened up my computer on the train and it showed a burnt-out car in the news. A car bomb had killed two. Police were searching for the terrorists. All I could think about was the shooter's face. Why would he shoot the psychiatrist? Was he a mental patient? Then I recalled where I had seen that face. Paris, France, at the French National Police Headquarters, when I was registering my business. Had I lost my mind? Could this be him? Why would he be in London? Why did Siobhan and Aodhan shoot him? The answers were in the news a few days later.

I awoke early in the morning two days after the shooting and turned on my computer. There were all the faces I knew. Liam Gallagher, Finn O'Sullivan. Blaine Kelly, and Fiona Byrne were charged with terrorism.

They had planned and plotted to kill two British parliamentary members. The two men who died in the stolen Aston Martin were none other than Stanley "Otaku" Webber and Kato Yamaguchi. Just as I started to read the article, there was a knock on the door. Oh no, I hadn't paid for the suit yet! I ran upstairs and looked downward. There was a police car in the driveway. West Yorkshire Police! I ran back downstairs and opened the door.

"Ms. Norman?"

"Yes?"

"May we come in?"

"Sure... What is this regarding?"

"We have a few questions for you."

"Am I in some kind of trouble?"

"Yes and no. You had reported a hacker in the past to our police. Well, the Bradford Cyber Unit were monitoring your computer and they found five different hackers in it."

"Five?!"

"You might want to sit down because this is going to take some time. There was a man who was shot and killed at Harrods department store two days ago. He was an alleged psychiatrist. The fact is he wasn't a psychiatrist, but a mental patient who liked to pose as different people."

"Why was he shot?"

"Well, in 2011, you'd met a man at the French Police National Headquarters. His name is Aabid al Baghdaddi and he was the second hacker. Al Baghdaddi claims that he was monitoring Dr. Eaton Bas in your computer and he said Bas was planning to hurt you, so he shot him."

"Is Al Baghdaddi dead?" I asked.

"No, he is in serious condition but has been charged with murder. He was also wanted in Morocco on two more murder charges. The third hacker was Yamaguchi and the fourth Webber. Both are dead. They were killed in an explosion outside of parliament, and it appears they'd stolen a vehicle belonging to parliamentary member Sir Godfrey Reinhardt. The fifth hacker was a military intelligence service from Yongsan Garrison-Casey. They were in your computer because a soldier found out that a terrorist was indeed hacking in during your studies in South Korea, whilst you were completing your online forensic psychology degree. We are unsure of how long or how many times military intelligence was in your computer."

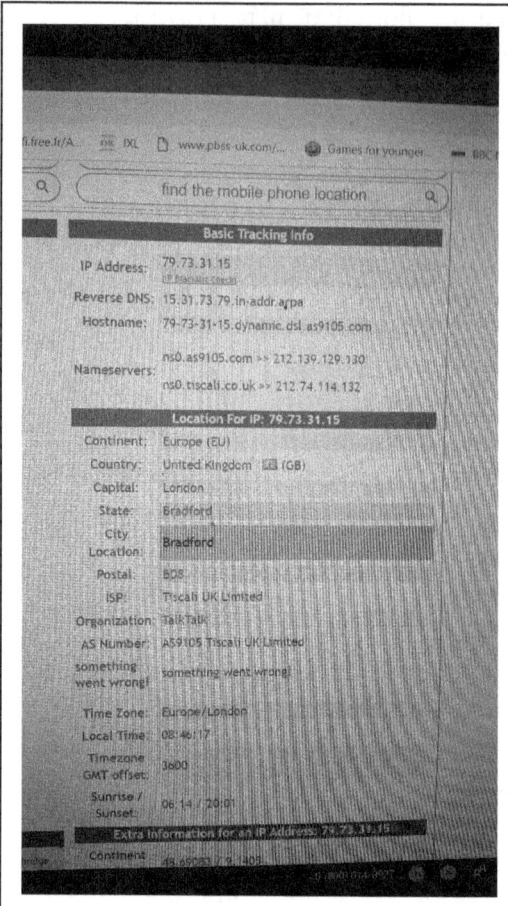

Bradford Police Cyber Unit Hacked into Computer

By entering the longitude and latitude in a search, it lands on the Bradford Cyber Unit. They were doing their job and tried to catch the hackers.

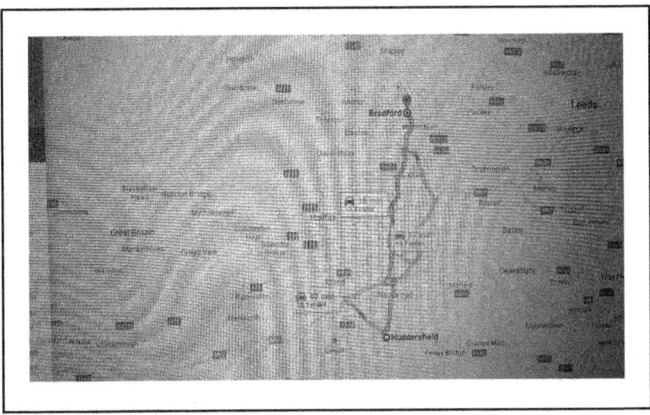

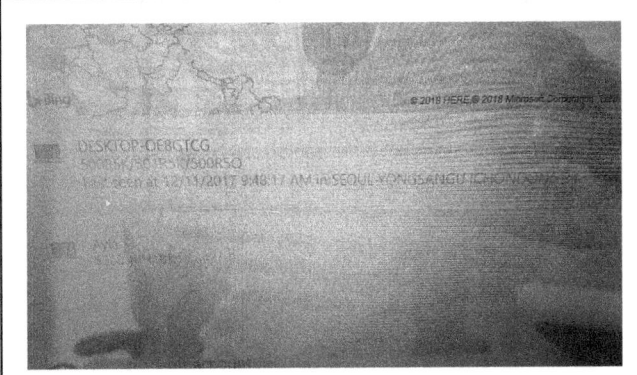

*Military Intelligence Hacked into Computer
from Yongsan Garrison-Casey*

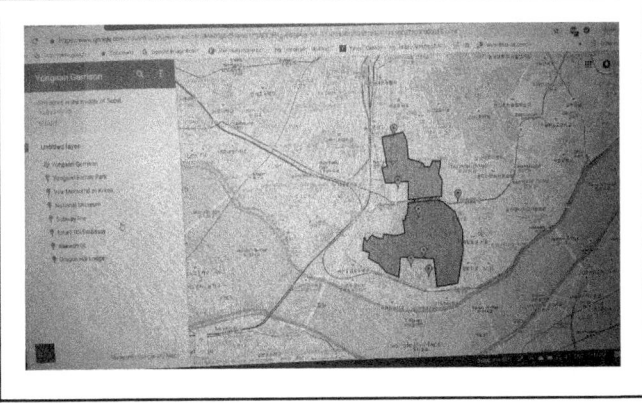

"There was a soldier living above you who was aware that you were predicting terror attacks all over the world. He notified his XO or second in command. You might have found a number of different defense analysts on your computer trying to figure out what type of model you were using to make these predictions. That said, we do need you to come in and make a statement and you will be questioned about your research. Is tomorrow at nine okay? I would bring you to the station to give a full statement today, but all this news must be shocking. Do you feel the need to see a doctor? We have the names of several professionals you can speak to."

"No, I am fine. I just need some time to think about this."

"We'll expect you tomorrow at nine."

I saw the officers out and locked the door behind them.

Had fifteen years of hacking and stalking actually come to an end? Were Otaku and Yamaguchi really dead? Part of me wanted to jump for joy and another part of me felt sickened. The next day at nine o'clock I went to the police station and gave my statement to the police, and they asked a few questions about my research. I forwarded payment to Harrods Department Store for the suit.

CHAPTER FORTY-ONE
REALITY AND IOPC

E VERYTHING THAT HAPPENED in each chapter was exactly accurate with the exception of Chapter Forty, which was written to make a point. What seems fantastical can be reality when suspected psychopaths are at play, as highlighted throughout the book. The reality is police have never charged anyone with any of the crimes in my case. The psychiatrist I had met in 1999 was real, but his name was changed as were most names in the book to protect their identities. No terrorists abducted me in Northern Ireland; however, the hackers in Chapter 40 are real. Stanley Webber and Kato Yamaguchi still walk the planet and did not get blown up in an Aston Martin. The young Moroccan-born man I'd met at the French Police National Headquarters was not shot by MI5. The stalking and hacking continues to date. What I have written about was what has happened over the last sixteen years. To many it may sound fantastical but to those being victimized, it is a reality and needs to be taken seriously. Most police were professional, but here are some of the comments police, lawyers, and administrators made:

"Your story does sound fantastical." (So I made Chapter 40 fantastical. Why? Because it showed what fantastical is, and what happened to me certainly was not. Officers should be trained to identify the behaviors of psychopathic stalkers.)

"We don't investigate police unless you have broken bones or you are dead."

"Do you feel paranoid because of all of the crimes that have been happening?"

"Our officers took twenty-eight days to respond to your report, but there is no wrongdoing on the officers' part." (It didn't matter about fraud, break-ins, invasion of privacy, or interference with my life, etc.)

"How are missing emails and someone hacking your computer a police matter?"

"Are you sure this was not all in your head?"

"Well, just because you show me evidence, it doesn't mean it is real." (I am a professional clinician; why would I fake evidence? All I asked was to get these two psychopaths out of my life.)

"None of this happened to you. It is all in your mind. No one has hacked you, and your stalkers were not in Paris. It is PTSD! That's all!" (One stalker was videotaped. So maybe my investigator is also paranoid and delusional. My neighbor too, because we talked at length about the man who was threatening outside of my door in Paris.)

"Why don't you just move on with your life?" (That was the point in my contacting police, investigators, and lawyers...to end this sixteen years ago.)

I wrote to the IOPC (Independent Office of Police Conduct) in the United Kingdom. It is my belief that if police had gone over to talk to the neighbor, none of the harassment would have continued and I would have graduated with my doctoral degree by now. My complaint: First, the police did not speak to my neighbor about the harassment; second, there was no attempt to catch the persons hacked into my computer despite a mountain of evidence, and third, it took twenty-eight days for police to respond to my complaint. The crimes that had been committed were hacking, breaking and entering, interference in my life, fraud, nonstop harassment, and threats as well as interference in my business.

The IOPC investigator wrote to me months later to say there was no wrongdoing on the part of police, and there was nothing more they could have done. Then several months later, I received a similar email from the IOPC with the same message. The IOPC stated that an officer reported that I appeared paranoid (are police clinicians?) and that I had spoken to a nurse at length while residing in Huddersfield. I have the police recordings, and at no time did any officer allude to mental illness. The officer asked if I felt paranoid at all because of all the crimes that had been committed. Hypervigilance is a symptom of PTSD, and persons may believe the stalkers or perpetrators are repeating the same actions because of strong memories that have not been extinguished. Trauma affects all persons differently. I had proof of the harassment; recorded, documented, and hired an investigator to catch the perps.

There were inaccuracies in the IOPC letter. First, it stated that I'd refused to see a doctor and I'd spoken to a nurse at length. I am not sure why this was even written because I hadn't spoken to a doctor or nurse in Huddersfield. Then, there is another part of the letter that says police knocked at my door and could hear a voice in my apartment but I wouldn't answer the door. I explained to the officer later that I teach online and couldn't disrupt my classes. The recordings at the back of the book are of the first officer I spoke to in October of 2019.

My other neighbor was indeed having a difficult time with her husband because she was the sole caregiver and he was extremely ill. She did have a nurse at her residence frequently to assist her. Perhaps there was a miscommunication and the incorrect house number was given. If I were paranoid, how could I get through five psychometric courses (two MEd courses and score over the 90TH percentile) on each and function on a daily basis amid constant harassment? I question the investigative integrity of the IOPC and their ability to be impartial. I looked up the IOPC and found an article online about the organization's cover-up of police misconduct in a homicide.

The emails from the IOPC disappeared from my computer, but I'd downloaded them, and two recordings of West Yorkshire Police also disappeared from my computer. Are there more suspects in this case other than Otaku and Yamaguchi? First, 800 military were added to Skype, military intelligence were in my computer, Bradford Police Cyber Unit, Yamaguchi, Otaku, Japanese, and others hacked in. Someone set up a website trying to connect me to an allegedly radicalized Muslim cleric in Manchester and to discredit me. Who are the main culprits?

One of the officers who was at my residence in March of 2019 advised me to write to a member of parliament and I did. Not just a member of the British Parliament but a Canadian member as well. I'd asked for an independent inquiry into the Manchester bombing and what had gone on in Liverpool. An inquiry began in 2020 but was unrelated to my request. Additionally, I once again sent evidence to the RCMP and asked why they didn't investigate and why they'd lied about investigating? There was never a response from anyone except the IOPC. It was not the answer I'd expected. The wrongdoing was there was NO investigation.

Despite my mountains of evidence, recordings, police reports, witnesses, and medical reports, there were no answers due to police failures and poorly defined laws governing stalking and cyberstalking. I recorded police in my home and on my phone to document their failures. I have listed the crimes below, and as recently as 2020, one stalker was trying to talk to me on Facebook. I blocked him. The image below shows the stalker's email, which has been blocked (the last email on the list), and the first name on the list is the stalker.

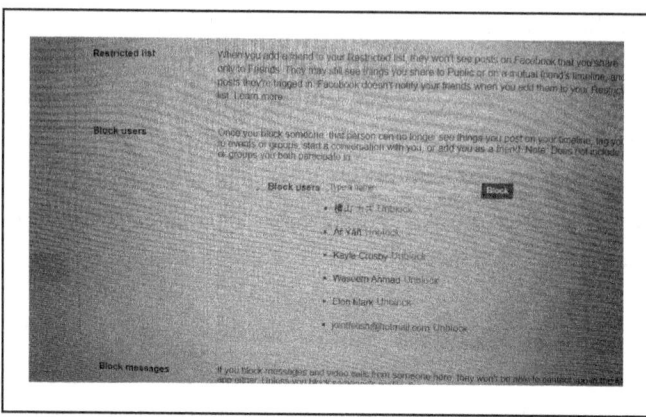

I was once again forced to move due to the harassment, interference in my life, and the lack of police investigation. Before I had left Huddersfield, I donated my furniture to a hospice and called police and told them not to bother coming to my residence again. I will *NEVER* report another incident to police. Instead, I will hire private investigators because they get the job done. I have *zero* confidence in police investigations and the laws. I moved to Songdo, South Korea, and recorded Japanese once more.

The email below dates to 2008, when I asked stalker #2 to get out of my life and leave me alone and advised him that his behaviors were that of a stalker. I've also included a photo of a hacked email dating back to 2017 with the initial KA in the book. One police officer eluded to me that I have a problem. What problem? Seriously? There are over 15,000 documents in my possession. I have not even typed up the 4,000 hours of recordings. This is utter police incompetence!

As a forensic psychology professional, I understand the mentally ill. These individuals' problems needed to be addressed over the years. Psychopathology is complex and these crimes are real and I have tried to get help for both individuals, by reporting them to police.

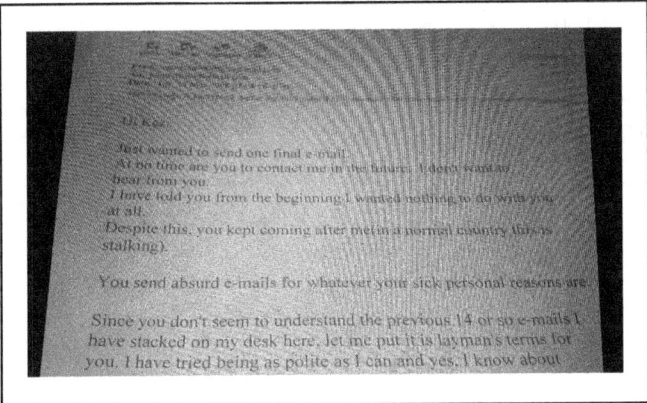

Upon my return to Canada in August of 2020, someone had been in my computer, hacked into my MSN. The CCET certificate I'd earned was sent from my own email to another email of mine. This was one of the signatures of the stalkers in Japan right before they defrauded my accounts. I traced the IP to Fort Worth, Texas, and forwarded it on to the FBI-IC3 Unit. Someone has gone to great lengths to disrupt my life, and fail me at every turn. I get the sense that these persons dislike women, particularly women in a position of power.

There are legal ramifications with my current business because these individuals continue to invade my privacy. Data protection is of paramount importance to any clinician and their client. I have halted training with a Canadian geoprofiler and other professionals because of the continued hacking. Police continue to ask: "How is any of this a police matter?"

"Why do I pay taxes?"

I've lost three businesses, moved twenty-five times, bought and rebought furniture, changed computers ten times, hired investigators, cyber experts, and lawyers, moved to five different countries, paid thousands of dollars for flights, replaced broken items, paid thousands in training while hackers tried to fail me on every level, had my PhD proposal stolen twice, cost me years of my career, cost me the ability to retire, damaged my reputation, and almost cost me my life on several occasions. In Songdo, South Korea, in May of 2020, I left a $5,500-a-month online teaching position due to the harassment but remained in Korea and completed a contract with my school (I'd worked seven days a week/ninety hours to accomplish my objectives). My financial losses total over 1.2 million dollars Canadian and counting. This is only a brief glimpse at the havoc wreaked by two suspected psychopaths. A country's security service should *NOT* have had to deal with the removal of a website aimed at discrediting someone and linking them to a suspected radicalized terrorist, whom I'd never heard of. Thank you to the one security service that did believe me and helped: MI5.

CHAPTER FORTY-TWO
INTERNATIONAL
STALKING LAWS

U NDER THE CRIMINAL Code of Canada (s.264), stalking qualifies as criminal harassment. It is defined as repeated and unwanted attention that causes the victim to fear for their personal safety or for the safety of someone they know. This is too broad a definition of stalking, and an international definition needs to be clearly defined as opposed to separate domestic definitions. If the definition is too broad, there is greater potential for avoidance and the abuse of existing laws. This was evident in my case. The perpetrators have gotten away with breaking and entering twenty-three or more times, hundreds of hacks, seven instances of Internet fraud (two of which were thwarted), hundreds of criminal code offenses, seven instances of theft, interference in online courses (MScFPCI, MEd., CPT3A, TESOL, PhD), assault, and assault causing bodily harm to name a few.

Cyberstalking is a complete void in policing. In fact the laissez-faire attitude of police is another way for them to not have to deal with the crimes being committed. Instead the blame is shifted to the victims, leaving them less likely to report further crimes and allowing the perpetrators to continue on with their stalking campaign, which is precisely what has occurred. The evidence speaks for itself.

When I think about stalking, I also think about terrorism because both need to be more clearly defined. Stalking is a form of terrorism and should fall under a sub-paradigm written into law in extreme cases. There would be benefits to labeling stalking as terroristic at both a national and international level. First, by labeling stalking as terroristic, it can lead to more serious penalties. Secondly, the suspicion of stalking can permit special means of investigation by police who possess the expertise in that particular field. Thirdly, international legal cooperation can be intensified to make it easier to catch and extradite stalkers and prosecute.

BIBLIOGRAPHY

Anderson, N., Kent, K. (2014). "Psychopathy: Developmental Perspectives and their Implications for Treatment." Restor Neurol Neurosc, 204 Jan. 1: 32 (1): 103-117.

Agsoglu, M. *Torture and Its Definition in International Law—An Interdisciplinary Approach*. Oxford University Press, 2017.

Boon, J., Sheridan, L. (2001). "Stalker Typologies: A Law Enforcement Perspective." *Journal of Threat Assessment*, 1, 75-97.

Chang, W. (2020). "Cyberstalking and Law Enforcement." ScienceDirect. Procedia Computer Science 176 (2020) 1188-1194.

Cloudberg, Admiral. Missing the Point: The Crash of Air China Flight 129. December 14, 2019. Retrieved December 18, 2020.

Cvetkovic, D., Cosic, I. (2011). *States of Consciousness: Experimental Insights into Meditation, Waking, Sleep and Dream*. Springer.

DreBing, H.; Gass, P.; Scheultz, K. Dtsch Arzteble Int. 2020; 117: 347-53 The Prevalence and Effects of Stalking—a replication study.

DreBing, H.; Bairler, J.; Anders, A.; Wagner, H.; Gallac, C. (2014). "Cyberstalking in a Large Sample of Social Network Users: Prevalence, Characteristics, and Impact upon Victims." *Cyberpsychology, Behavior, and Social Networking*. Volume 17, Number 2, 2014.

Ettinger, E. (1948). *Precognitive Dreams in Celtic Legend*. Folklore, 59 (3), 97-117.

Fields, R.M. (2008). "The neurobiological consequences of psychological torture." In A.E. Ojeda (Ed.). "Disaster and trauma psychology. The trauma psychological torture." (p. 139-162). Praeger Publishers/Greenwood Publishing Group.

Hare, R. (2008). Hare psychopathy checklist–revised (2nd edition) (pcl–r). In B. L. Cutler (Ed.), Encyclopedia of Psychology and Law (Vol. 1, pp. 349-350). SAGE Publications, Inc.

"Hostage-taker allegedly wanted to kill branch head." *The Japanese Times*. September 18, 2003. Retrieved December 9, 2020.

Japanistry, Sumo: The History and Rules. [https://www/japanistry.com/sumo/] Retrieved on January 8, 2021.

Johnson, L.; McGuire, J.; Lazarus, R.; Palmer, A. "Pavlovian fear memory circuits and phenotype model of PTSD." *Neuropharmacology* 62 (2012) 638-646.

McEwan, T.; Daffern, M.; MacKenzie, R.; Ogloff, J. (2017). "Risk factors for stalking violence, persistence, and recurrence." *The Journal of Forensic Psychology*, 2017 Vol. 28, 1, 38-56.

McGuire, B., Wraith, A. (2000). "Legal and psychological aspects of stalking: a review." *The Journal of Forensic Psychiatry*.

Michaelson Monaghan, E. (2020). "The allure of mysteries." *The Psychologist*. British Psychological Society.

National Commission on Terrorist Attacks upon the United States. (2004). The 911 Commission Report Executive Summary. Washington, DC: National Commission on Terrorist Attacks upon the United States.

Ojeda, A. What Is Psychological Torture? Center for the Study of Human Rights in the Americas. Workshop on Neurobiology of Psychological Torture Center for Mind and Brain. September 30, 2006.

Orzel-Grygleuska, J. (2010). "Consequences of sleep deprivation." *International Journal of Occupational Medicine and Environmental Health*, 23 (1), 95-114.

Papakitsu, V. (2020). "Cyberstalking, a new crime. The nature of cyberstalking victimization." *Dialogue in Clinical Neuroscience and Mental Health*, 2020, Volume 3 Issue 3, p. 197-202.

Polonska-Kimunguyi, E. Gillespie, M. (2016). "Terrorism discourse of French International Broadcasting. France 24 and the case of Charlie Hebdo attacks in Paris." *European Journal of Communication* 31 (5) pp. 568-583.

Sheridan, L., Lyndon, A. (2010). *The Influence of Prior Relationships, Gender, and Fear on the Consequences of Stalking Victimization*. Spring Science+Business Media, LLC.

Sheridan, L., James, D. (2015). "Complaints of group stalking (gang stalking): an exploratory study of their nature and the impact on complainants." *The Journal of Forensic Psychiatry*, Vol. 26, No. 5, 601-623.

Thatcher, M. (1985). Speech to the American Bar Association. Albert Hall, South Kensington, Central London: 1438c1515.

Vrij, A.; Meissner, C.; Fisher, R.; Kassin, S.; Morgan, A.; Kleinman, S. (2017). "Psychological Perspectives on Interrogation." *Perspective on Psychological Science*. 2017, 12(6): 927-955.

Wick, S. Elizabeth; Nguyen, Anh Phuong; West, Jaclyn T.; Nagoshi, Craig T.; Jordan, Catheleen; Lehmann, Peter (2020). "Cyber Harassment, Coping and Psychological Maladjustment in College Students." *College Student Journal*, Volume 54, N.1, 15 March 2020. pp.77-87.

Link to police recordings and evidence:
https://cforensic1.wixsite.com/website